DEVIANT BEHAVIOR

DEVIANT BEHAVIOR

ALEX THIO

OHIO UNIVERSITY

HOUGHTON MIFFLIN COMPANY   Boston
Dallas   Geneva, Ill.   Hopewell, N.J.   Palo Alto   London

PRINTED IN THE U.S.A.

Library of Congress Catalog Card Number: 77-90439

ISBN: 0-395-25323-3

This book is dedicated
to the memory of my father,
whose life and death taught me
a great deal about the human condition.

CONTENTS

PREFACE

This textbook is intended to make the instructor's teaching experience and the student's learning experience as interesting and rewarding as possible. With this objective in mind, I have tried to do the following.

First, I have tried to make the book very readable and interesting. Too often my students have complained about the various texts that I have adopted for classroom use as well as those that I have recommended for outside reading. They even complained about what I considered to be the better texts in the field. Their most common complaint is that those texts are too boring. This is a shame because deviant behavior is an inherently interesting subject. The problem is that too many texts apparently have been written for professional sociologists rather than for undergraduate students. They are overloaded with highly abstract and complicated discussions. Therefore, to make this text easily readable, I made sure that every sentence was written in a concrete and straightforward manner. In cases where this could not be done because of the highly abstract nature of the subject, I used concrete examples, which are often interesting and dramatic, to ensure comprehension by the average student reader.

Second, I have tried to be reasonably comprehensive in presenting the literature on deviant behavior. Many theories and many types of deviant behavior are covered here. Consequently, this book is more comprehensive than most other texts. In addition to covering all the standard topics found in other texts, this book also deals with profitable deviance and swinging as well as with the phenomenological theory of deviances. In striving to be comprehensive, I have minimized my own theoretical bias by presenting various theoretical views as fully and fairly as possible. As a result, the present work contrasts with many other texts and readers that are theoretically one-sided and thereby give short shrift to other theories.

Third, I have tried to present the deviance literature in a systematic and integrative way. Some texts discuss various theories and types of deviant behavior without showing how they are related to one another. By contrast, I have organized the disparate theories into two groups. One group consists of "scientific theories," which some sociologists prefer to call "positivist theories." The other group consists of "humanistic theories." Furthermore, I have attempted to integrate these two groups of theories by proposing a power theory. As for the specific forms of deviant behavior, they are presented in a systematic, coherent manner. What society considers to be the more serious forms of deviant behavior are discussed in the earlier chapters, while what society regards as the less serious forms are presented in the later chapters. So the discussion flows from the "most serious" forms of deviant behavior to the "least serious." This means, from the perspective of my integrated theory, that the deviants discussed in the earlier chapters are more likely to be "objects" acted upon by social forces, thereby reflecting the scientific perspective toward deviance. On the other hand, the deviants discussed in the later chapters tend more to be "subjects" acting out their free will against social forces, thereby reflecting the humanistic perspective toward deviance.

Fourth, I have offered my own theory of deviant behavior not only as a means of integrating the disparate theories, as has been suggested, but also as a device for putting the existing theories and data in proper perspective. While most of these theories and data focus only on the deviant behavior of relatively powerless people, my power theory shows how more powerful people may also be involved in deviant activities. In presenting my power theory, however, I have tried to avoid the trap that other authors of deviance texts have fallen into. These authors let their own theoretical perspectives determine which theories and types of deviance are to be discussed. Consequently, they discuss their own theories and their favorite types of deviance in great detail while paying very little attention to other theories and other types of deviance. In order to avoid this one-sided presentation, I have first discussed as fully as possible all the important theories and data. Only then have I put them in perspective, either by presenting my power theory in a separate chapter or by demonstrating its application to each type of deviant behavior in a separate section of a chapter. In this way, the instructor and his or her students are given the opportunity to judge for themselves which theory is better, which in turn will allow them to engage in lively class discussions and debates.

Because the way this book has been put together depended so much on my teaching experience, I am indebted to the many students I have had in my classes. I am also indebted to many sociologists and other scholars whose works are reviewed here. I particularly want to express my deep gratitude to the following four sociologists who carefully read the entire manuscript and offered many useful criticisms and suggestions: Professor James T. Carey, University of Illinois, Chicago Circle; Professor John R. Hepburn, University of Missouri, St. Louis; Professor Charles H. McCaghy, Bowling Green State University; and Professor Arthur L. Wood, University of Connecticut. Finally, I would like to thank Mrs. Carolyn J. Tolliver for her excellent typing of the manuscript.

A.T.

I GENERAL DEFINITIONS AND THEORIES OF DEVIANT BEHAVIOR

Before we can study deviant behavior, we have to define it. Various sociologists define it differently, however, each being influenced by certain philosophical assumptions about the nature of deviant reality. These assumptions and the resulting definitions will be the subject of Chapter 1.

Once we have dealt with the definition of what deviant behavior is, the next task will be to explain and interpret its occurrence—why deviant behavior occurs, as well as how and why people react to it. This will be the subject of Chapters 2, 3, and 4.

1 WHAT IS DEVIANT BEHAVIOR?

There is a great diversity among lay people as to what they consider deviant. In a study conducted by J. L. Simmons in 1965, when a sample of 180 ordinary people were asked what they thought was deviant, they listed 252 different acts and persons. Some of these were: homosexuals, prostitutes, alcoholics, drug addicts, perverts, beatniks, murderers, the mentally ill, communists, atheists, liars, Democrats, reckless drivers, self-pitiers, the retired, career women, divorcées, Christians, suburbanites, movie stars, perpetual bridge players, prudes, pacifists, psychiatrists, priests, liberals, conservatives, junior executives, girls who wear make-up, smart-aleck students, and know-it-all professors.[1] If you are surprised that some of these people are considered deviant, your surprise simply adds to the fact that there is a good deal of disagreement among the public as to their conception of deviant behavior.

There is a similar lack of consensus among sociologists. One could say that the study of deviant behavior is probably the most "deviant" of all the subjects in sociology. For sociologists disagree more over the definition of deviant behavior than they do on any other subject. Let us see how various sociologists define deviant behavior.

CONFLICTING DEFINITIONS

Talcott Parsons defines deviance as a departure from "the normative standards which have come to be set up as the common culture." [2] He further explains that "a tendency to deviance in this sense is a process of motivated

3

action, on the part of an actor who has unquestionably had a full opportunity to learn the requisite orientations, tending to deviate from the complementary expectations of conformity with common standards so far as these are relevant to the definition of his *role*." [3] (Emphasis added.) In other words, there is in society a widely shared expectation that we should behave in a certain way when performing a social role, and if we behave otherwise, our behavior is said to be deviant. Robert Merton, a prominent student of Parsons, defines deviance in about the same way: "Deviant behavior refers to conduct that departs significantly from the norms set for people in their social *statuses*. . . . When a man acts 'like a child' or a layman acts 'like a physician,' he engages in deviant behavior." [4] (Emphasis added.)

For Albert Cohen, deviant behavior does not only mean violation of expectations about our social statuses and roles; it refers to violation of any rule anywhere as long as the violation "excites some disapproval, anger, or indignation." Thus deviance refers to such behavior as "knavery, skulduggery, cheating, unfairness, crime, sneakiness, malingering, cutting corners, immorality, dishonesty, betrayal, graft, corruption, wickedness, and sin." [5]

Since such deviant behaviors as suicide and mental illness may not "excite disapproval, anger, or indignation," Cohen excludes them from his list. But John Lofland includes them in his. To Lofland, deviants are "persons toward whom there is experienced fear, hate, threat and defensiveness *and*, on occasion, compassion, concern and hope of redemption." [6] (Emphasis added.)

Edward Sagarin uses a broader definition than those mentioned above. While other sociologists restrict deviant behavior to the act of violating normative rules, Sagarin's definition includes both rule breakers and people who have committed no deviant acts. The latter group includes the crippled, the mentally retarded, the spastic, the badly scarred, the leprous, the blind, the deaf, and the mute. Although these people have not broken social rules, they are similar to physically normal people who have, in that they are held in low social esteem. Sagarin states: "As persons in a given status, whether or not they commit acts associated with their groups and imputed to them, they are disvalued and reacted to in a negative manner by large numbers of persons in the society." [7]

Although Sagarin's definition is so broad that it covers many diverse types of deviance, Norman Denzin broadens the definition still further. While Sagarin considers as deviant only those people and behaviors that are strongly disvalued by society, Denzin includes in his list of deviant acts those that are even mildly disapproved. In fact, he feels that sociologists should pay more attention to the "mundane, routine, ephemeral, or normal" forms of deviant behavior that surround us every day, such as the violation of rules of etiquette. [8] Mundane deviance may also include such acts as "violations of colleague standards and university rules among members of sociology department, . . . cheating among students, bad manners at the dinner table, acts of philandering on the part of married persons, masturbation, breaches of social etiquette by members of social fraternities, and belching." [9]

Although mundane deviance is basically not serious, society still considers it something negative. Indeed, most sociologists limit the use of the term *deviance* to what the public considers objectionable behavior. Thus they reject the use of the same term for referring to unobjectionable, though rare, behavior. For example, William Rushing considers it "rather ridiculous and fruitless" if such unobjectionable people as "all the noncoffee drinking adults in the United States are defined as deviants." [10] Nevertheless, there are some sociologists who disagree with Rushing. To Leslie Wilkins, for example, even such unobjectionable people as the genius, the reformer, and the religious leader are just as deviant as the criminal.[11] Frank Scarpitti and Paul McFarlane agree with Wilkins, and, in addition, list intellectuals and saints as deviants.[12]

There is yet another, and far better known, controversy over the definition of deviant behavior. Sociologists who are known as *labeling theorists* define deviance as a *label* imposed upon a given behavior. Howard Becker, for example, states that "deviance is *not* a quality of the act the person commits, but rather a consequence of the application by others of rules and sanctions to an 'offender.' The deviant is one to whom that label has successfully been applied; deviant behavior is behavior that people so label." [13] Kai Erikson also means about the same: "Deviance is not a property *inherent in* certain forms of behavior; it is a property *conferred upon* these forms by the audiences which directly or indirectly witness them." [14] The labeling theorists' definition has been widely accepted since it was presented in the early 1960s. But it has also been subjected to numerous criticisms.

While many sociologists agree with labeling theorists and regard their definition as significant and original, Merton considers it trivial and banal: "It is blatantly true and trivial: namely, the statement that behavior cannot be considered 'deviant' unless there are social norms from which that behavior departs. It seems banal and safe to stipulate: no rule, no rule-violating behavior." [15]

A number of sociologists point out that the labeling theorists' definition in emphasizing the deviant label as the determinant of deviant behavior is an overstatement and thus a misleading definition. Ronald Akers, for example, says, "The label does not create the behavior in the *first place*. People can and do commit deviant acts because of the particular contingencies and circumstances in their lives, quite apart from or in combination with the labels others apply to them." [16] Similarly, Jack Gibbs argues that people generally impose the deviant label on a person's behavior because the behavior is deviant rather than the reverse.[17] In essence, these critics contend that the labeling theorists' definition is misleading because, in overemphasizing the deviant *label*, it greatly ignores the importance of *behavior* as the determinant of deviance.

Some sociologists have criticized the definition of labeling theorists for its failure to specify exactly what kind of reaction should be used for identifying deviant acts. Suppose some people have discovered that a father has committed incest. Will that father's behavior be considered deviant if those people react mildly by simply calling him "that crazy old man"? What if they react strongly by getting the police to arrest him? How strong or mild should the reaction be before a given act is accepted by sociologists as deviant? Also, how many people should be involved in labeling a person deviant? Such questions, the critics point out, are not answered by the labeling theorists' definition.[18]

As suggested by the preceding paragraph, these critics—and many other sociologists—would prefer a precise definition to an ambiguous one. This is understandable in view of their rigidly trained obedience to the scientific canon of precision. But David Matza, for one, unabashedly opts for an ambiguous definition. Thus he defines deviance as "straying from a path or standard," without bothering to specify what that path or standard is. Matza believes that such an ambiguous definition is, in effect, superior to a precise one. He explains:

Students of society must tolerate such ambiguity. Finely drawn and strictly operational conceptions leaving no place for ambiguity may be a source of satisfaction for the analyst, but he will find that ordinary subjects of inquiry have the capacity to subvert such conceptions and render them useless. Whether the phenomenon personified, say, by a waitress in topless attire is deviant is a question that will yield a clear-cut answer if our conception of deviation is sufficiently rigorous and operational. But the clear-cut yes or no will be gained only by suppressing, and thus denying, the patent ambiguity of this novel phenomenon and the easily observable tentative, vacillating, and shifting responses to it.[19]

In other words, because deviant behavior is itself ambiguous, why not use an ambiguous definition to represent it rather than inventing a precise definition to misrepresent it?

Recently, all the foregoing definitions as well as their authors have been criticized for an implicit bias. Alexander Liazos, for example, points out that the people hitherto listed by sociologists as deviant have one thing in common. They all are oppressed, powerless individuals whose deviant behavior is of a dramatic nature—such as prostitution, homosexuality, juvenile delinquency, and the like. This means that sociologists have neglected to study the powerful persons "who break laws, fix laws, violate ethical and moral standards, harm individuals and groups, etc., but who either are able to hide their actions, or, when known, can deflect criticism, labeling, and punishment." [20] All this leads Liazos to charge that these sociologists and their definitions of deviance are imbued with "basic ideological biases," namely, of a conservative type.

This criticism, however, has generated some countercriticisms from traditional sociologists. Travis Hirschi, for example, criticizes Liazos and other sociologists who have implicitly or explicitly brought up the charges of conservative bias on two related grounds. He criticizes them for assuming that they themselves are blessed with moral superiority while traditional sociologists are cursed with moral inferiority. Second, he criticizes the assumption that moral superiority guarantees truth, while moral inferiority guarantees error, in disregard of what the facts may be. More positively, Hirschi suggests that we continue to go about our traditional business of seeking scientific truth, without paying attention to the charge of conservative bias. [21]

Despite their disagreement over the ideological issue of bias, most sociologists, whether charging others with bias, being charged by others with bias, or merely sitting on the fence, seem to agree on one thing. They seem to agree that sociologists have so far focused their attention largely on the deviance of lower-class people, thereby ignoring the deviant activities of more powerful members of society. [22]

The different definitions of deviant behavior and the sociologists who offer them can be classified into two large and conflicting groups. In one group we may place those sociologists who prefer a narrow definition, those who emphasize the importance of behavior as the determinant of deviance, those who would insist on a precise definition, and those who would continue the search for scientific truth about powerless deviants only. In the opposite group we may put those who prefer a broader definition, those who emphasize the importance of labeling, those who feel comfortable with an ambiguous definition, and those who would go beyond the traditional study of powerless deviants and investigate powerful deviants as well.

The ways in which these two groups of sociologists define deviant behavior seem to reflect the two major perspectives that have long influenced the works of sociologists—and of other social scientists. Since each perspective contains diverse elements, it has been referred to in diverse terms. One perspective has been referred to as positivist, deterministic, logico-empiristic, objectivistic, absolutist, behaviorist, environmentalist, mechanistic, tough-minded, operationistic, elementarist, realist, and priestly. The other perspective has been called idealist, voluntaristic, *Verstehen*, antideterministic, subjectivistic, relativistic, existentialist, dynamistic, tender-minded, intuitionist, holistic, nominalist, and prophetic. [23] But it seems best to use more general terms to refer to those two perspectives. Thus we may refer to the first perspective as *scientific* and the second as *humanistic*. At the same time, we may consider the first group of sociologists as *scientific sociologists* (also as *scientists*) and the second group as *humanistic sociologists* (or *humanists*). Let us now examine how each perspective has led each group of sociologists to view deviant behavior in certain ways.

THE SCIENTIFIC PERSPECTIVE

The scientific perspective consists of three related assumptions, beliefs, or attitudes, which are sometimes explicit and sometimes implicit in the sociological writings on deviant behavior. I shall discuss each of them in some detail.

DEVIANCE AS INTRINSICALLY REAL

The scientific perspective holds deviant behavior as intrinsically real, in that it possesses some characteristics that distinguish it from conforming behavior. Relatedly, the scientific perspective distinguishes deviant persons from conforming individuals. Thus sociologists who are influenced by such a perspective (referred to as *scientists* as well as *scientific sociologists*) tend to view deviant behavior as an attribute that is inherent in the individual.

This view was first strongly held by the early criminologists who were the progenitors of the modern sociology of deviance. Around the turn of this century, criminologists believed that criminals possess certain biological traits that are absent in noncriminals. The biological traits were believed to include defective genes, bumps on the head, long lower jaw, scanty beard, ugly face, and tough body build. Since all these traits are inherited, people were believed to be criminals simply because they were born criminals. If you were born a criminal, you would always be a criminal. It is like saying: "If you've had it, you've had it." So, no matter where you might go—you could go anywhere in the world—you would still be a criminal.

Then the criminologists shifted their attention from biological to psychological traits. Criminals were thus thought to have certain mental characteristics that noncriminals do not have. More specifically, criminals were thought to be feeble-minded, psychotic, neurotic, psychopathic, or otherwise mentally disturbed. Like biological traits, these mental characteristics were believed to be inherent in individual criminals. And like biological traits, mental characteristics would stay with the criminals, no matter what society or culture they might go to. So, wherever they went, criminals would always remain criminals.

There are several glaring weaknesses that have since been revealed in the early criminologists' view of criminals and criminality. First, numerous research studies have failed to uncover any significant biological or psychological traits that distinguish criminals from noncriminals. Second, early criminologists based their notion of criminality not on law violation per se but on the biological or psychological characteristics that they falsely presumed to be criminalistic in nature. Third, being extreme absolutists, early criminologists failed to see the relative, changing nature of criminal status and of biological and mental states. A person's criminal status does not remain the same across time and space; instead, it changes at different periods and with different societies. Jesus was nailed to the cross as a criminal in his time, but he is widely worshiped as God today; a polygamist is a criminal in our society but a law-abiding citizen in Moslem countries. Similarly, a person's biological and mental states are subject to different evaluations and treatments in different societies. An obese girl is socially undesirable in our society but may become a beauty queen among some African tribes; a person who sees things is a psychotic in our society but may become a spiritual leader among some American Indian tribes. But the early criminologists failed to see this relative nature of criminal status, biological state, and mental condition.

These weaknesses in the early criminologists' view of criminals and criminality have been corrected by modern scientific sociologists. Nowadays, the use of biological and psychological traits for differentiating criminals from noncriminals has been abandoned. Deviant behavior is no longer thought to be an absolutely unchanging part of the person. Instead, it is simply defined as a norm-violating act, and the person who commits the act is considered a deviant. This means that some recognition should be given to the notion of norm. As norms tend to vary from time to time and from place to place, modern scientific sociologists have softened the early criminologists' extreme absolutist stance toward the idea of deviance. Deviance and the deviant person are now defined relative to a given norm, time, or society.

But it should be noted that this principle of societal, cultural, temporal, or normative relativity is merely taken for granted rather than seriously and strongly emphasized. Such an attitude is well illustrated by Merton when he says that it is "blatantly true and trivial" to define deviance as a departure from some social norm.[24] Merton implies that since he and other scientific sociologists have considered this relativist definition of deviance as blatantly true and trivial, there is no point for them to pursue it any further. To pursue it would be the same as to raise pseudoquestions, for it is impossible to raise real questions about something that is already blatantly true. Consequently, scientific sociologists prefer to raise questions about something that is, in their view, not blatantly true and thus genuinely problematic. In other words, they prefer to study something that they do not fully know but are eager to find out—namely, the nature of deviant behavior per se. Such a preference reflects an absolutistic more than relativistic attitude.

Other scientists are more direct than Merton in expressing their absolutistic conception of deviance as intrinsically real. Countering the relativistic notion of deviance as basically a *label* of *deviant* imposed on an act, Hirschi argues: "The person may not have committed a 'deviant' act, but he did (in many cases) do *something*. And it is just possible that what he did was a result of things that had happened to him in the past; it is also possible that the past in some inscrutable way remains with him and that if he were left alone he would *do it again*." [25] Moreover, countering the relativistic notion of mental illness as a label imputed to some people's behavior, Gwynn Nettler explicitly voices his absolutist stance: "Some people *are* more crazy than others; we can tell the difference; and calling lunacy a name does not *cause* it." [26] These scientific sociologists seem to say that, just as a rose by any other name would smell as sweet, so deviance by any other label is just as real. All this suggests that although they are by no means extreme absolutists like their predecessors, modern scientific sociologists are nonetheless more absolutistic than relativistic and thus can be considered as *moderate absolutists*.

As moderate absolutists, scientists seem to identify the intrinsic characteristic of deviant behavior as the ability to injure, hurt, anger, or otherwise affect disagreeably some members of a society. This means that in order for an act to become deviant, it must possess the ability to affect people disagreeably. For example, murder, mugging, robbery, rape, and the like are deviant because of their ability to affect their victims disagreeably.

Therefore, scientific sociologists assume deviant behavior to be basically real in itself. As Nettler says, "It seems wiser to operate with the assumption that there is a 'real world out there' than to adopt the notion that it is 'all in our head'." [27] Nettler's phrase "out there" further implies another dimension of the scientifically assumed deviant reality, which is the subject of the following section.

DEVIANCE AS OBJECTIVE FACT

The second assumption of the scientific perspective has to do with the objective nature of deviant behavior. The nature of deviant behavior is objective in the same sense as the nature of, say, this book is objective. This book has an objective nature in that it is something out there and thus can become the *object* of your observation, perception, or thought but not the observing, perceiving, or thinking subject. You are the latter in relation to the former. You can therefore observe and study this book *objectively*, that is, without falling in love with it as you might with a woman or man, or without hating it as you would your sworn enemy. In assuming deviant behavior as something out there with an objective nature, and in treating the deviant person as if he or she were an object, scientists have attempted to observe and study deviant behavior and the deviant person objectively, just as you would your book.

Of course, scientific sociologists are sophisticated enough to know that deviant behavior and particularly the deviant person are not exactly like the material object in your hands. The difference is obvious. The material object does not have any feelings and other subjective experiences but the deviant person does; you as the observer are unlike the material object but you are like the deviant person in being human. Inescapably you will have personal feelings for or against the deviant person but not the material object. It is therefore much more difficult for you to be objective about the deviant and his or her behavior; your emotions will more likely distort your observation. All this may be extremely plain to you, as it is to present-day scientists, but it was not recognized by the earlier scientific sociologists.

Around the beginning of this century and during its first four decades, many sociologists were enthusiastically trying to establish their field as a scientific enterprise. One leading member among them declared sociology as "the last and highest of the sciences." [28] Another proclaimed that "to betray an emotional attitude with reference to human facts is as compromising as an exchange of mysticism for literalness would be in astronomy or physiology." [29] Given such unbounded enthusiasm and confidence in equating sociology with the natural sciences, it is little wonder that the early sociologists failed to appreciate the unique problem of personal bias in observing human behavior. Without appreciating the problem, they did not make a special, self-conscious effort to tackle it. And without making a special, self-conscious effort to tackle the problem, they easily fell victim to the problem. Thus their personal biases, which were further increased by their rural or puritanical backgrounds, overwhelmed the early sociologists, thereby distorting their observation of deviant behavior. The distortion can be illustrated by the following lines from a popular textbook of those days:

Sin, vice, crime, corruption, all consciously directed anti-social forces, offer a primrose path of pleasurable activity, albeit they eventually lead to destruction. Beguiled by clever leaders and the desires of the moment, man is continually selling his soul for a mess of pottage. . . . Those unhappy creatures who offer themselves for sex hire represent the most demoralized of all sex offenses.[30]

Such a moralistic condemnation of deviant behavior tells us more about the sociologists themselves than about the nature of deviant behavior. By projecting their own negative feelings onto certain behaviors, the sociologists misled themselves into believing that those were descriptions of deviant behavior. They did not realize that the natural scientists, whom they tried to emulate, would never have adopted the same moralistic and condemnatory view of animals, plants, molecules, and atoms. The natural scientists would never have made such statements as "this animal is the most demoralized, that plant continually sells its soul . . ."

Learning from the earlier sociologists' futile attempt to imitate natural scientists, more recent sociologists have come a long way in their scientific study of deviant behavior. While they firmly adhere to the scientific principle of objectivity, they are nonetheless acutely aware of the difference between scientific sociology and the natural sciences. They are aware that the observer's personal bias presents a far greater problem for sociology. Such an awareness has enabled modern sociologists to control their personal biases. Hence, they have forced themselves not to pass moral judgment on deviant behavior, but instead to study the subject matter as it is. Furthermore, these sociologists have tried hard to obey the scientific rule that all their ideas about deviant behavior shall be subject to public test. This means that other sociologists should be able to check out these ideas to see whether they are supported by facts and evidence.[31]

Such a drive to achieve scientific objectivity has made modern sociologists more objective than their predecessors. They have therefore produced works that can tell us much more about the nature of deviant behavior. No longer in vogue today are such value-loaded and subjective notions as maladjustment, moral failing, debauchery, demoralization, sickness, pathology, and abnormality. Replacing those outmoded notions are such value-free and objective concepts as innovation, retreatism, ritualism, rebellion, culture conflict, subcultural behavior, white-collar crime, norm violation, learned behavior, reinforced behavior, and so on.

To demonstrate the objective reality of these concepts, scientific sociologists have used the following: official reports and statistics, clinical reports, intensive case studies, surveys of self-reported behavior, and surveys of victimization. Scientific sociologists recognize the unfortunate fact that the deviants who are selected by these methods do not accurately represent the entire population of deviants. For example, the criminals and delinquents reported in the official statistics are a special group of deviants, because most crimes and delinquent acts are not discovered and, even if discovered, not reported in the official statistics. Nevertheless, scientists believe that the quality of information obtained by these methods can be improved and refined. In the meantime, they consider the information, though inadequate, useful for revealing at least some aspect of the totality of deviant behavior.[32] A major reason for using the information is to seek out the causes of deviant behavior. This brings us to the third assumption of the scientific perspective.

DEVIANCE AS DETERMINED BEHAVIOR

The third assumption of the scientific perspective is that deviant behavior is something that is determined or caused by some other things, events, occurrences, or phenomena in the environment. Implicit in this determinist or causal view is that a given thing cannot simply appear out of nothing or nowhere. Take this book as an example. Once you have established the reality of this book, you would find it hard to believe that this book has been produced by itself. Instead, you would reason in a deterministic manner: there must be somebody, either you or somebody else, who has caused the book to be where it is; the book has not produced itself but rather has been produced by an author, printer, printing machine, ink, and paper. Natural scientists hold the same deterministic view about various occurrences in nature. When sociologists follow natural scientists, they adopt the deterministic view and apply it to human behavior.

As we have seen, many early sociologists were overly enthusiastic about the prospect of turning their discipline into a science. They were so enthusiastic that they literally equated humans with animals, plants, and material objects. Consequently, just as natural scientists deny that there is free will in animals, plants, and material objects, so the early sociologists denied that there is free will in humans. In the early sociologists' view, the acknowledgment of human free will would contradict their scientific principle of determinism. If a person is thought to will or determine his or her own behavior, then it does not make sense to say that that behavior is caused by something else. If a murderer is thought to will or determine a murderous act, then it does not make sense to say that the murderous act is caused by such other things as the individual's physical or mental condition, family background, or various social experiences in the society. Therefore, in defending their scientific principle of determinism, the early sociologists stuck to their denial of free will. They argued that the notion of free will is a holdover from the prescientific age; that human beings create the fiction of free will so as to feel superior to other animals; and that scientists can still explain human behavior in causal terms by ignoring free will—which, after all, does not exist in the first place. Here is how an early sociologist expressed his opposition to the idea of free will:

The illusion of a free human will (the only miraculous factor in the
eternal ocean of cause and effect) leads to the assumption that one can
choose freely between virtue and vice. How can you still believe in the
existence of a free will, when modern psychology, armed with all the
instruments of positive modern research, denies that there is any free
will and demonstrates that every act of a human being is the result
of an interaction between the personality and the environment of man?
And how is it possible to cling to that obsolete idea of moral guilt, according to which every individual is supposed to have the free choice to
abandon virtue and give himself up to crime?[33]

This is indeed an extreme position against the idea of free will. Today,
scientists assume a more moderate position. Unlike their predecessors,
modern scientific sociologists believe that humans do differ from other animals, plants, and inanimate objects in that the former possess free will whereas
the latter do not. Furthermore, unlike their predecessors, modern scientists
do not believe that the assumption of free will destroys the scientific principle of determinism. No matter how much a person exercises free will by
making choices and decisions, the choices and decisions do not just happen
but are determined by some causes. If a man chooses to do his wife in rather
than make love to her, he certainly has free will or freedom of choice so
long as nobody forces him to do one or the other. Yet the man's choice of
one alternative over another, or the way he exercises his free will, is caused
rather than uncaused. Thus, according to modern scientific sociologists,
there is no inconsistency between freedom and causality.

Note that although scientific sociologists allow for human freedom of
choice, they do not use it to explain why people behave in a certain way.
They will not, for example, explain why the man kills his wife by saying
"because he chooses to kill his wife." This is no explanation at all, as the idea
of choice can also be used to explain why another man does not kill his
wife—by saying "because he chooses not to kill his wife." According to
scientific sociologists, murdering and loving one's wife or, more generally,
deviant and conforming behavior, being two contrary phenomena, cannot
be explained or caused by the same thing, such as choice. The idea of
choice simply cannot explain the difference between deviance and conformity; it cannot explain why one man chooses to kill his wife while the
other chooses not to kill his wife. Therefore, although scientists do believe
in human choice as much as they may believe in Satan, they will not attribute
deviance (or conformity) to human choice, just as they will not attribute it
to Satan. No matter how much emotional or spiritual satisfaction one may
get from attributing deviance to choice or to Satan, one still adds nothing to
our knowledge of deviance.

It is clear, then, that attributing deviant behavior to choice is a form of pseudoexplanation. But scientific sociologists, particularly those of the past, have produced their own pseudoexplanations for deviant behavior. They have attempted to explain criminal behavior as being caused by general human desire, such as the desire for happiness, for money, for social status, or for eliminating frustration. It is true that all these human desires can cause criminal behavior, but they can also cause noncriminal behavior. For example, the desire for money also causes many people to do honest work.[34] Thus the notion of human desire is just like the notion of choice; it cannot explain the difference between criminal and noncriminal behavior.

In order to increase our knowledge of deviance, most scientific sociologists today avoid pseudoexplanations. As the above discussion implies, one is likely to produce a pseudoexplanation if one asks why a deviant becomes a deviant, rather than why some people become deviant and others do not. Since they have asked themselves the latter question, many scientists have had better luck in generating real explanations of deviant behavior. The causal factors that they use as their explanations are generally located in the social environment. Examples of the causes of deviance are broken homes, unhappy homes, lower-class background, economic deprivation, social disorganization, rapid social change, differential association, differential reinforcement, and so on. Any one of these causes of deviance can be used to illustrate a real explanation of deviance; for example, broken homes are more likely to cause delinquency than nondelinquency. Before we go too far afield, we should keep in mind the initial reason why scientific sociologists search for explanations of deviant behavior. The initial reason is their deterministic assumption that deviant behavior is caused rather than uncaused.

In sum, the scientific perspective on deviant behavior consists of three related assumptions. First, deviant behavior is *intrinsically real*. Second, deviant behavior is *objective*, in that the deviant person is like an object and thus can be studied objectively. And third, deviant behavior is something that is *determined* by other things.

THE HUMANISTIC PERSPECTIVE

Since the 1960s, the humanistic perspective has emerged to challenge the scientific perspective, which had earlier been predominant in the sociology of deviance. Let us take a look at the three related assumptions, beliefs, or attitudes of the humanistic perspective, which challenge those of the scientific perspective.

DEVIANCE AS LABEL

The humanistic perspective holds that deviant behavior by itself does not have any intrinsic characteristics unless it is thought to have those characteristics. The so-called intrinsically deviant characteristics do not come from the behavior itself; they come instead from some people's minds. To put it very simply, an act appears deviant only because some people think it so. As Becker says, "deviant behavior is behavior that people so label." [35] So, no deviant label, no deviant behavior. The label is the *cause* and the behavior the *effect*.

Scientific sociologists disagree and argue along these lines.[36] How is it possible for a label to occur *before* what is labeled exists? How is it possible for the label to create deviant behavior? It should be the other way around, namely, that it is the behavior that makes people react, think, and then impose the label *deviant* on it. If the behavior does not exist in the first place, people cannot possibly pay attention to it, let alone put a label on it. Of course, it is possible that some people may hallucinate, see something that does not exist, and then label the nonexistent thing as *deviant behavior*. But most people are not that crazy. More realistically, it is possible that some people may mistakenly see an innocent act as deviant. Yet most people do not always make that mistake. It is obvious that the behavior is not by itself deviant; it must be defined as such. This does not, however, contradict the observation that the behavior has to occur first, before people can notice it and then define or label it for what it is. So, scientists conclude, no deviant behavior, no deviant label—the behavior is the cause and the label the effect.

Humanistic sociologists (or humanists) agree that the occurrence of behavior is prior to its being labeled. What humanists also believe, however, is that scientists have put too much importance on the intrinsic nature of the so-called deviant act. They have assumed that whenever a person violates a rule, other people will automatically label the person a deviant. Scientists, humanists think, do not stop and ask themselves whether those people will in fact automatically label a rule breaker as deviant. As Becker points out, "scientists do not ordinarily question the label 'deviant' when it is applied to particular acts or people but rather take it as given." [37] They believe that people in the society share the same rules and therefore are in common agreement on defining a given rule-breaking act as deviant. In essence, according to humanists, scientists overemphasize the reality of deviant behavior because they assume that there is widespread *value consensus* in the society, which makes it easy for them to objectively identify deviant or conforming behavior.[38]

Humanists reject the assumption of value consensus. They argue that this assumption is correct only if applied to a simple and traditional society whose population is homogeneous. But the assumption is false when applied to a complex industrial society such as the United States, where the population is heterogeneous. In our society, people belong to different groups on the basis of their social class, ethnic, occupational, and subcultural backgrounds. Consequently, they do not share the same set of rules for what is proper and what is deviant. Suppose you were an Italian immigrant who went on making wine for yourself and your friends during the Prohibition days. You would have been considered as acting properly in accordance with Italian immigrant standards, but you would have been treated as a criminal for breaking the law of your new country.[39] In short, humanists contend, it is not reasonable to assume that there is widespread consensus on values and norms in every society.

Since they reject the assumption of value consensus and therefore also reject the assumed reality of deviance, humanists are not interested, as scientists are, in the question of why people become deviant. Instead, humanists are more interested in the questions of whether and why a given act is defined by society as deviant. This means that, in contrast to scientists being concerned with deviants, humanists are preoccupied with those people who label others as deviants—such as the police and other law-enforcing agents.[40]

In studying law-enforcing agents, humanists have found a huge lack of consensus as to whether a certain person should be treated as a criminal. The police often disagree among themselves as to whether a suspect should be arrested, and judges often disagree among themselves as to whether those arrested should be convicted or acquitted. Furthermore, since laws vary from one state to the other, the same type of behavior may be defined as criminal in one state but not so in another. There is then a relativity principle in deviant behavior; behavior gets defined as deviant relative to a given norm, standard of behavior, or the way people react to it. Without relating a given behavior to the norm or to the reaction of other people, the behavior is in itself meaningless—it is impossible to say whether it is deviant or conforming. Humanists strongly emphasize this relativistic view. They often like to say that, like beauty, deviance is in the eye of the beholder.

DEVIANCE AS SUBJECTIVE EXPERIENCE

The second assumption of the humanistic view is that the supposedly deviant behavior is a subjective experience and the supposedly deviant person is a conscious, feeling, thinking, and reflective subject. Humanists insist that there is a world of difference between humans (as active subjects) and non-human beings and things (as passive objects). Humans can feel and reflect, but animals, plants, things, and forces in nature cannot. Furthermore, humans have sacred worth and dignity, but the others do not. It is proper and useful for natural scientists to assume and then study nature as an object, because this study can and does produce scientific or objective knowledge for controlling the natural world. It may also be useful for social scientists to assume and then study humans as objects, because it may produce scientific or objective knowledge for controlling humans. But this goes against the grain of humanist values and sensibilities.

Humanists are strongly opposed to the control of humans; instead, humanists emphasize the protection and expansion of human worth, dignity, and freedom. One result of this humanist ideology is the observation that so-called objective knowledge about human behavior is inevitably superficial whenever it is used for controlling people. For example, in order for a racist government to control blacks, it needs only the superficial knowledge of blacks as being identifiable and separable from whites and of their age, sex, occupation, and residence. Such superficial knowledge is in fact employed to support and perpetuate the white racist regime in South Africa. But in order to achieve the humanist goal of protecting and expanding blacks' human worth, dignity, and freedom, a deep understanding of blacks is needed. To acquire this understanding, you must appreciate and empathize with them; you must attempt to experience as much as possible what they experience as blacks; and you must see their own lives and the world around them from their, not your, standpoint. You must look at the black experience from the inside as a participant rather than from the outside as a spectator. In a word, you must adopt the internal, subjective view rather than the external, objective one.

The same principle, according to the humanists, should hold for the understanding of deviants and their deviant behavior. Humanists contrast this subjective approach with the scientists' objective one. Humanists argue that scientists treat deviance as if it were an immoral, unpleasant, and repulsive phenomenon that should be controlled, corrected, or eliminated. In consequence, scientists have used the objective approach by staying aloof from deviants, by studying the external aspects of deviant behavior, and by relying upon a set of preconceived scientific ideas for guiding their study. The result is a collection of *surface facts* about deviants, such as their poverty, lack of schooling, poor self-image, low aspirations, and so on. All this may be used for controlling and eliminating deviance, but it does not tell us "what a deviant does in his daily round of activity and what he thinks about himself, society, and his activities." [41] In order to understand the life of a deviant, humanists believe, we need to use the subjective approach, which requires our appreciation for and empathy with the deviant. The aim of this subjective approach, in Matza's words, "is to comprehend and to illuminate the subject's view and to interpret the world *as it appears to him*." [42]

But scientists would oppose the subjective approach by pointing out its pitfalls. Merton, for example, uses research evidence to show that subjective data are extremely unreliable, because people tend to glorify the group of which they are members.[43] Thus, in accepting these people's self-glorification as a true presentation of themselves, humanists actually romanticize them rather than discover the truth about them. In addition, Merton argues that authentic understanding can be achieved without using the subjective approach, and he quotes Weber saying "one need not be Caesar in order to understand Caesar." [44]

Humanists would respond to these criticisms in two ways. First, they would concede that one can understand Caesar without being Caesar himself. But they claim that such understanding is not deep understanding but, instead, superficial knowledge. As Matza says, "Without appreciation and empathy we may gather surface facts regarding a phenomenon and criticize the enterprise connected with it, but we will fail to understand in depth its meaning to the subjects involved and its place in the wider society." [45]

Secondly, humanists countercharge that scientists themselves often engage in romanticism and falsification. They do so by using conceptual abstraction or scientific euphemism, which tends to cover up the human reality of misery, suffering, and pain. As Matza argues, "Conceiving complicated families full of turmoil, distrust, and fighting as an instance of the well-known primitive system of 'serial monogamy with a female-based household' [an example of conceptual abstraction or scientific euphemism] is fundamentally to romanticize and falsify the lot of those living in that condition. . . . It comes close to making a silk purse out of a sow's ear." [46] After thus arguing that scientists often engage in this kind of romanticism and falsification of human reality, humanists claim that they are more able than scientists to discover the truth about deviants.

As a result of their subjective and empathetic approach, humanists often present an image of deviants as basically the same as conventional people. This implies that so-called deviant behavior, because it is like so-called conventional behavior, should not be controlled by society. Again, scientists may equate this humanist image of deviants with romanticism. Yet humanists consider it a much closer and truer picture of real-life deviants than the scientists' presentation of deviants as undesirable objects to be controlled. The idea of the basic similarity between deviance and conventionality is intimately connected with the humanists' next assumption.

DEVIANCE AS VOLUNTARY ACT

The third assumption of the humanistic perspective is voluntarism. It holds that the putatively deviant behavior is a voluntary act or an expression of human volition, will, or choice. Humanists take up such a stand, because they are disturbed by what they claim to be the dehumanizing implication of the scientific view, namely, that the human is like "a robot, a senseless and purposeless machine reacting to every fortuitous change in the external and internal environment." [47] Like most people, humanists do not want to believe that they are like passive, reactive, senseless, and purposeless machines, nor do they actually feel that they are. As a result, they criticize the scientific view as dehumanizing and then attempt to replace it with their humanistic view. For example:

The confusion began when primitive social scientists—many of whom are still vigorous—mistook the phenomenon under consideration—man— and conceived it as object instead of subject. That was a great mistake. . . . [According to the humanistic view] man participates in *meaningful activity*. He creates his reality, and that of the world around him, actively and strenuously.[48]

The fundamental point made by humanists is that human beings, because they possess free will and choice-making ability, determine or cause their own behavior. As has been discussed, scientists, while not denying free will in humans, consider it useless for *explaining* human behavior. But humanists respond to this in two related ways.

First, humanists believe that the scientists' attempts to explain deviant behavior have failed. Ever since they adopted the natural scientist's deterministic approach, they have first used biological factors, then psychological factors, and finally sociological factors as the determinants or explanations of deviant behavior. But, the humanists say, all these efforts have been futile. Matza contends: "A reliance on differentiation, whether constitutional, personal, or sociocultural, as the key explanation of delinquency has pushed the standard-bearers of diverse theories to posit what have almost always turned out to be empirically undemonstrable differences." [49] In other words, scientists cannot successfully explain deviant behavior because they hold a false assumption about what they attempt to explain—that there is a basic difference between deviant and conventional behavior.

Second, scientists, according to humanists, are so preoccupied with explaining the difference between deviance and conventionality that they fail to ask themselves whether the difference is real in the first place. Humanists challenge the scientific assumption of that difference. Humanists believe, instead, that in the real world the distinction between deviant and conventional phenomena is "blurred, complicated, and sometimes devious." [50] The following are two illustrations of how they view deviance as inseparable from conventionality; the first reveals the overlap between organized crime and conventional business, and the second shows the continuity between prostitution and conventional sexual behavior.

Crime, in many ways, is a Coney Island mirror, caricaturing the morals and manners of a society. The jungle quality of the American business community, particularly at the turn of the century, was reflected in the mode of "business" practiced by the coarse gangster elements, most of them from new immigrant families, who were "getting ahead" just as Horatio Alger had urged.[51]

There are elements of prostitution in the behavior of most women in our culture. This is perceived in the salesgirl who "charms" a male customer into purchasing goods, the sale of war bonds with kisses by actresses, and the sexual submission of a secretary to her boss in order to hold her job.[52]

Since they view deviance as behaviorally the same as conventionality, humanists generally avoid asking the etiological question that scientists have routinely asked. Humanists do not ask: Why are some people deviant and others are not? Or, why do some people engage in deviant behavior and others do not? Instead, humanists ask: How does society, through its social control agencies, define some people as deviant and carry out its sanction against them? These humanist studies, as Edwin Lemert correctly points out, are "preoccupied with the work of official agencies of social control, accenting the arbitrariness of official action, stereotyped decision-making in bureaucratic contexts, bias in the administration of law, and the general preemptive nature of society's controls over deviants." [53] Implicit in those studies is the related humanistic assumption of voluntarism. For those studies convey the strong impression that members of the control agencies, being in positions of power, exercise their free will by actively, intentionally, and purposefully controlling the "deviants."

The assumption of voluntarism also influences humanist studies of those people who have been labeled deviant. Even though they are comparatively powerless, the "deviants" are not presented as if they were robots, passively and senselessly becoming what labeling theorists call "secondary (full-fledged) deviants." Rather, they are seen as actively interpreting the actions of official labelers against them, as well as exerting some control over their own actions.[54]

In summary, the humanistic perspective consists of three related assumptions. First, deviant behavior is not real in and of itself, but basically a *label*. Second, the supposedly deviant behavior is a *subjective* experience rather than an objective entity; the supposedly deviant person is a conscious, feeling, thinking, and reflective *subject* rather than a nonconscious, unfeeling, unthinking, and unreflective object. And third, the putatively deviant behavior is a *voluntary, self-willed* act, rather than an act caused by forces in the internal and external environments.

TOWARD AN INTEGRATED PERSPECTIVE

To know what deviant behavior is, we need both the scientific and the humanistic perspective. The combination of both can give us a better picture than either one can by itself. The two perspectives may appear to be in sharp contradiction, but their differences are largely in emphasis. By emphasizing one side, we do not necessarily deny the reality of the other. Both scientists and humanists, in emphasizing their own view, do assume the other to be correct in its own way, but merely think of it as less important than their own.

Now that we know the two opposing perspectives, we can bring them together. As Chinese are fond of saying, "Things that oppose each other also complement each other." [55] Thus we may see deviant behavior as being both real and a label. One cannot exist without the other. If there is no real act, there is no deviant *behavior;* if there is no label, there is no *deviant* behavior. In order for us to use the label *deviant,* the behavior must occur. Similarly, in order for us to understand that behavior, the label *deviant* must be used.

But in complementing each other the two conflicting perspectives are not necessarily equally applicable to all types of deviant behavior. On the contrary, one perspective seems more relevant than the other to the study of the types of deviance that can more easily satisfy the assumptions, beliefs, and attitudes of the sociologists embracing that perspective.

Specifically, the scientific perspective is more relevant to the study of what society considers as relatively serious types of deviant behavior, such as murder, forcible rape, armed robbery, and the like. The study of such types responds well to the scientific perspective for three reasons. First, these forms of deviant behavior, which characteristically enter into the official statistics analyzed by scientists, can be clearly defined as really deviant in the sense that they are intrinsically more harmful than conforming behavior, more likely to elicit wide consensus from the public as to their deviant characteristics, and therefore precisely distinguishable from conforming behavior. Second, people who commit these serious crimes generally come from the lower classes, unlike the scientists who study them. That is to say, these are crimes that scientists themselves would not commit or could not conceive themselves capable of committing. Thus it is easy for scientists to be aloof from these criminals, analyzing their behavior objectively—without empathizing with them or romanticizing their behavior. Third, since the people who commit serious deviant acts can be easily separated from the scientists, it is natural for scientists to study these deviants as if they were passive objects "out there" rather than active subjects "in here" (like the scientists themselves), and thereby investigate their behavior in terms of being determined by social forces rather than by themselves.

On the other hand, the humanistic perspective is more pertinent to the *less serious* kinds of deviance, particularly those that do not gravely harm other people. This perspective, as Alvin Gouldner puts it, "finds itself at home in the world of hip, drug addicts, jazz musicians, cab drivers, prostitutes, night people, drifters, grifters, and skidders: the 'cool world.' " [56] The study of such people may conveniently fit the humanistic perspective also for three reasons. First, there is a relative lack of consensus in society as to whether these nonserious forms of deviant behavior are indeed deviant or not. Some members of society may label them deviant, while others may not. It is, therefore, logical for humanists to emphasize that deviant behavior is basically a matter of labeling. Second, those so-called deviants are considered by society as less dangerous than the criminals studied by scientists. They also engage in the so-called deviant activities that humanists themselves could enjoy, participate in, or at least feel themselves capable of engaging in—quite unlike the more dangerous acts committed by "common" criminals. The consequence is that humanists can more easily empathize with these supposed deviants and thereby rely on the latters' subjective experience for understanding deviance. Third, since they empathize with these nondangerous deviants, it is natural for humanists to consider them active subjects like themselves rather than passive objects, and therefore emphasize the voluntary, self-willed nature of the putative deviants' experience.

The foregoing discussion suggests that, at bottom, the types of deviant behavior—seen through the scientific and the humanistic perspective—differ in the *amount of public consensus* regarding their deviant nature. On the one side, a given deviant act is, from the scientific standpoint, "intrinsically real," largely because there is a relatively great public consensus that it is really deviant. On the other side, a given deviant act is, from the humanistic perspective, "not real in itself but basically a label," largely because there is a relative lack of public consensus supporting it as really deviant. We may integrate the two views in our definition of deviant behavior.

Thus, we may define deviant behavior in terms of public consensus. We may define it as *any behavior considered deviant by public consensus that may range from the maximum to the minimum.* Deviant behavior can be classified into two types: higher- and lower-consensus deviance. *Higher-consensus deviance* is the type that has been studied by scientists; *lower-consensus deviance* is the kind that has been studied by humanists.

In addition to covering those deviant acts that scientists and humanists have hitherto studied, the definition also refers to those that have been merely proposed as subjects to be studied. These are of two kinds. First, the mundane, ordinary acts, such as violating etiquette, lying, cheating, or otherwise sinning that occur in everybody's daily life, and, second, the deviant activities of powerful persons, such as corporate malfeasance, political skulduggery, governmental corruption, and war crime. These two types apparently belong in the category of lower-consensus deviance.

SUMMARY

In sociology there are many conflicting definitions of deviant behavior. They are of two major types, one being influenced by the scientific perspective and the other by the humanistic. These two perspectives differ in three ways. On the one side, the scientific perspective assumes that deviant behavior is intrinsically real, is observable as an object, and is something that is caused by other things in the environment. On the other side, the humanistic view assumes that the so-called deviance is largely a label, is in itself a subjective experience, and is a voluntary, self-willed act.

These two views are here integrated into a larger perspective that sees deviant behavior as an act that can be located at a point on a continuum of maximum to minimum public consensus regarding the deviant nature of the act. More concretely, according to this integrated view, deviant behavior is divided into two major types. One is referred to as *higher-consensus deviance*, which is generally serious enough to earn a comparatively great amount of public consensus that it is really deviant. This type is more fitting for scientific investigation. The other is called *lower-consensus deviance*, which is generally less serious and thus receives a lesser degree of public consensus on its deviant reality. This type is more appropriate for humanistic analysis.

SUGGESTED READINGS

Akers, Ronald L. "Problems in the Study of Deviance: Social Definitions and Behavior." *Social Forces* 46 (June 1968): 463–464.

Becker, Howard S., ed. *The Other Side: Perspectives on Deviance.* New York: Free Press, 1964.

Bierstedt, Robert. "Sociology and Humane Learning." *American Sociological Review* 25 (February 1960): 3–9.

Cressey, Donald R. "Epidemiology and Individual Conduct: A Case from Criminology." *Pacific Sociological Review* 3 (Fall 1960): 47–58.

Gibbs, Jack P. "Conceptions of Deviant Behavior: The Old and the New." *Pacific Sociological Review* 9 (Spring 1966): 9–14.

Glass, John F., and John R. Staude, eds. *Humanistic Society: Today's Challenge to Sociology.* Pacific Palisades, Cal.: Goodyear, 1972.

Hook, Sidney, ed. *Determinism and Freedom in the Age of Modern Science.* New York: Collier, 1961.

Liazos, Alexander, "The Poverty of the Sociology of Deviance: Nuts, Sluts, and Preverts." *Social Problems* 20 (Summer 1972): 103–120.

Merton, Robert K. "Social Problems and Sociological Theory." In Robert K. Merton and Robert Nisbet, eds. *Contemporary Social Problems,* 3rd ed. New York: Harcourt Brace Jovanovich, 1971, pp. 793–845.

Nettler, Gwynn. *Explanations.* New York: McGraw-Hill, 1970.

Thio, Alex. "Class Bias in the Sociology of Deviance." *The American Sociologist* 8 (February 1973): 1–12.

2 SCIENTIFIC THEORIES OF DEVIANCE

In general, we may consider a theory of deviant behavior as a coherent body of ideas which makes some sense out of the phenomenon. More specifically, though, scientists and humanists in sociology seem to differ as to what the theory is supposed to be. To scientists, the theory must explain deviant behavior; to humanists, it can be a way of understanding or interpreting the behavior. Thus scientific explanation usually points at the *etiology* of deviance, while humanistic interpretation tends to bring out the *meanings* of deviance.

But we should note that, by focusing on the meanings of deviance, humanists do not completely shy away from etiological matters. On the contrary, they do sometimes deal with etiology, but mostly in connection with the meanings of deviance. In other words, although they do not seek as scientists do the causes of primary deviance, humanists may search for the causes of societal reaction and secondary deviance.[1] Yet humanists tie such a search to their dominant interest in the meanings of deviance by showing how the people in question impute meanings to each other's behavior.

There is, then, a difference between scientific theories, which largely focus on the causes of deviance, and humanistic theories, which mostly deal with the meanings of deviance. This difference is actually derived from that between the scientific and humanistic perspectives discussed in the preceding chapter.

A simple illustration may be sufficient to clarify the difference between those two types of theory. Suppose a group of people are reported to be homosexuals. Scientists will zero in on the nature of homosexuality, because they presume this deviant behavior to be a real thing. So their scientific theory may point at, say, poor childhood experiences as the cause of homosexuality. On the other hand, humanists will not aim at homosexuality as such, for they view it as largely a label. They would instead explore the meanings of homosexuality. Thus their humanistic theory would set forth what homosexuality means to those who engage in it and to the social control agents who react to it, as well as how and why these people behave in accordance with those meanings.

In sociology today, there are six major theories of deviance. Three of them—anomie theory, differential association theory, and control theory—may be listed as primarily scientific. The other three—labeling theory, conflict theory, and phenomenological theory—may be classified as essentially humanistic. Let us discuss the first group of theories in this chapter and turn to the second group in the next chapter.

ANOMIE THEORY

Anomie theory was first developed by Robert Merton. Later, Albert Cohen formulated his theory of juvenile delinquency, which appears to be an extension of Merton's ideas. Finally, two other sociologists, Cloward and Ohlin, attempted to improve on Merton's theory. All this will be discussed in some detail in the following.

MERTON: GOAL–MEANS GAP

In 1938 Robert Merton was dissatisfied with Freud's psychoanalytic theory of deviant behavior. The psychoanalytic theory says that criminal, pathological, or socially dangerous behavior represents the free expression of the libido, biological impulses, or animal desires that the individual is born with. The defect of this theory, according to Merton, lies in its assumption that "the structure of society primarily restrains the free expression of man's fixed native impulses." [2] This means that society *dis*courages the individual from engaging in deviant activities. Merton called that a "fallacious premise." So he went for the opposite idea, namely, that society *encourages* the individual to engage in deviant activities. With such a premise, Merton developed his anomie theory.[3] Today the theory is still very influential in sociology.

In Merton's view, American society emphasizes heavily the cultural value of success. From kindergarten to college your teachers motivate you to achieve a high scholastic record and to have great ambition for your future. The books, magazines, and newspapers that you read often carry success stories that encourage you to become successful yourself. The games, sports, and athletic events that you watch in the stadium or on television impress you with the supreme importance of winning. If you participate in an athletic event, the coach will prod you to win. If you simply want to enjoy the simple pleasure of playing the game, and sarcastically argue that "winning is not everything," the coach may argue back even more sarcastically: "Right, winning is not everything—winning is the *only* thing!" This cultural value of success is so pervasive in this society that people of *all* classes are expected to have the desire to be a winner, to be somebody, to be ambitious, or to entertain high aspirations. Even poor people are told that their children have the chance of becoming president of the United States if they have as much ambition as the young, poverty-stricken Abraham Lincoln did. In this sense, the cultural *goal* of success is freely available to all people, regardless of their social class backgrounds.

In contrast, the institutionalized or legitimate *means* of achieving the high success goal, such as getting a good job, is not freely available to all classes of people. The society is structured in such a way that people of the lower social classes, when compared with those of the higher, have lesser opportunity to realize their success aspirations. Thus lower-class people find themselves trapped in a very difficult situation. They have been encouraged by the society to hold high success aspirations but they are not given the opportunity to realize those aspirations. To get themselves out of that predicament, many lower-class people resort to *il*legitimate means of achieving their success aspirations, such as stealing, robbing, and other similar forms of deviant activities. So lower-class people are more likely to engage in deviant activities. As Merton sums it up,

It is only when a system of cultural values extols, virtually above all else, certain *common* success-goals for *the population at large* while the social structure rigorously restricts or completely closes access to approved modes of reaching these goals *for a considerable part of the same population* [namely, the lower classes], that [their] deviant behavior ensues on a large scale.[4]

We have just seen that the *cause* of those lower-class deviant activities is the societal condition marked by the disjunction between society's *over*emphasis on the success goal and its *under*emphasis on the use of legitimate means for achieving that goal. Merton describes this goal-means disjunction —which he calls *anomie*—in this way: "Contemporary American culture continues to be characterized by a heavy emphasis on wealth as a basic symbol of success, without a corresponding emphasis upon the legitimate avenues on which to march toward this goal." [5]

Now, given this societal condition of anomie, not all of us would respond to it in the same way. Many lower-class persons, as the foregoing discussion has implied, respond to it by accepting the success goal while rejecting the use of legitimate means for realizing that goal. Merton refers to this deviant behavior as *innovation*. But many other individuals of various social strata may adapt differently to that same anomic condition. So, in addition to innovation, Merton lists other types of adaptation (see Table 2.1).

1. *Conformity* is the most popular mode of adaptation. It involves accepting both the cultural goal of success and the use of legitimate means of working toward that goal. Presumably most of us choose this adaptation.

2. *Innovation* is largely found among lower-class people, who reject the use of legal means in favor of illegal ones in their attempt to achieve the high success goal that they have learned to accept. This form of deviant adaptation, which is the central subject of anomie theory and which Merton discusses much more than any other, has been presented above.

3. *Ritualism* is common among lower-middle-class Americans who lower their aspirations or abandon high success goals so that they can more easily realize their modest aspirations. But in their attempt to realize these modest aspirations, they almost compulsively—hence ritualistically—abide by the institutional norm of toiling as an honest worker.

4. *Retreatism* is a withdrawal from society into the shell of one's self. The retreatist does not care about success, nor does he or she care to work. Examples of such people are psychotics, autists, pariahs, outcasts, vagrants, vagabonds, tramps, chronic drunkards, and drug addicts.

5. *Rebellion* involves rejecting the prevailing social expectation that we work hard in the rat race to reach the goal of great success. The rebel also attempts to overthrow the existing system and put in its place a new one with new goals and new means of reaching those goals.

COHEN: STATUS FRUSTRATION

Another version of anomie theory was proposed in 1955 by Albert Cohen. [6] This version is fundamentally the same as Merton's. Like Merton, Cohen suggests that American society encourages all classes of people to achieve status while at the same time making it difficult for lower-class people to really achieve it. As a consequence, lower-class people are compelled to

Table 2.1   A typology of modes of individual adaptation

MODES OF ADAPTATION	CULTURE GOALS	INSTITUTIONALIZED MEANS
I. Conformity	+	+
II. Innovation	+	−
III. Ritualism	−	+
IV. Retreatism	−	−
V. Rebellion	±	±

Note: (+) signifies *acceptance;* (−) signifies *rejection;* and (±) signifies "rejection of prevailing values and substitution of new values."

Source: Robert K. Merton, *Social Theory and Social Structure* (New York: The Free Press, 1957), p. 140.

achieve status in their own way—that is, to engage in deviant acts. Although the theme is the same as in Merton's theory, Cohen tells the story differently, replacing Merton's word *success* with *status.*

According to Cohen, lower-class boys are like their middle-class counterparts in their desire to achieve status. An important place for the youngsters to achieve status is the school, which they are forced to attend. But the school turns out to be a most unlikely place for lower-class boys, because it ensures their failure. How so? The school is run by middle-class teachers, promotes middle-class values and behavior, and judges the student's achievement by middle-class standards of behavior and performance. The school then is a middle-class status system. For a person to achieve the status of a successful, competent, or good student in the middle-class setting, he or she must possess the following middle-class values, virtues, and traits: motivation, diligence, verbal fluency, academic intelligence, the ability to delay gratification, courtesy, opposition to fist fights, and respect for property. In this status system, middle-class boys obviously have a good chance of becoming successful. Yet lower-class boys, who have not been socialized in the same way as middle-class boys, are thrown into a status system where they are expected to compete with middle-class boys. The result is not surprising: lower-class boys fail disastrously. Cohen describes their problem in this manner:

In particular, different patterns of socialization are associated with the different social classes and middle-class socialization is far more effective in training children for such success than is lower-class socialization.

For this and other reasons, lower-class children are more likely to experience failure and humiliation. In brief, they are caught up in a game in which others are typically the winners and they are the losers and the also-rans.[7]

Being a loser or also-ran is psychologically frustrating. Driven by this frustration, which Cohen calls *status frustration*, lower-class boys go back to their own lower-class neighborhood and set up their own competitive system, which Cohen refers to as *delinquent subculture*. In that subculture they can compete fairly among themselves for high status in accordance with their own criteria of achievement. Their criteria of achievement are in direct opposition to the "respectable" middle-class or conventional criteria. They judge as wrong whatever values and behaviors are considered right by conventional standards, and they judge as right whatever values and behaviors are considered wrong by conventional standards. So it is obvious that the lower-class boys' very attempt to achieve status within their own competitive standards is—according to conventional standards—delinquent. In their attempt to achieve status among themselves, they will engage in such so-called delinquent activities as stealing "for the hell of it," fighting, terrorizing "good" children, destroying property, and defying various conventional taboos. These delinquent activities are nonutilitarian, malicious, and negativistic in nature. As Cohen sums it up,

The delinquent subculture, we suggest, is a way of dealing with the problem of adjustment we have described. These problems are chiefly status problems: certain children are denied status in the respectable society because they cannot meet the criteria of the respectable status system. The delinquent subculture deals with these problems by providing criteria of status which these children *can* meet.[8]

You may notice some differences between Cohen's and Merton's versions of anomie theory. First, Merton is concerned with the *utilitarian* kinds of deviant behavior; for example, his juvenile delinquents and adult criminals would steal merchandise in order to possess, use, or sell it. In contrast, Cohen deals with the *non*utilitarian types; for instance, his delinquent boys would steal goods and then throw them away. Second, in Merton's theory, deviant behavior among the lower classes is an *individual's* attempt to solve his problem, which stems from his suffering the lack of opportunity for achieving his success goals. On the other hand, in Cohen's theory, the lower-class boys work together as a *group* to solve their common problem of status frustration, the solution being their delinquent subculture.[9] And, third, Cohen's theory may be considered an extension of Merton's, although this extension was not intended by Cohen at all. Merton's theory suggests that the discrepancy between success aspiration and opportunity pressures the lower-class person *directly* into deviance. But Cohen's theory suggests that the discrepancy between status aspiration and opportunity leads the lower-class boys *indirectly* toward the joint production of a delinquent subculture—that is, via the social-psychological mechanism of status frustration.

But underneath these differences, Cohen's theory is basically the same as Merton's. First, both Cohen and Merton assume that people of lower social classes are more likely than people of higher social classes to engage in deviant activities. And secondly, both suggest the same factor as the cause of the lower classes' greater tendency toward deviance. That causal factor is the society's failure to help lower-class people to fulfill the aspirations (for success or status) that it has induced in those people.

CLOWARD AND OHLIN: DIFFERENTIAL ILLEGITIMATE OPPORTUNITY

There is a third version of anomie theory, which is a direct extension of Merton's formulation. This third version was presented in 1960 by Richard Cloward and Lloyd Ohlin.[10] You may recall the way Merton formulates the theory: the lower classes tend toward deviant involvement because they, like the upper classes, have been encouraged to hold high success goals but, unlike the upper classes, are denied the legitimate opportunity or means of achieving those success goals. Cloward and Ohlin accept the general idea of this formulation. At the same time, though, they want to extend it by introducing the concept of differential illegitimate opportunity.

First of all, Cloward and Ohlin point out that Merton correctly directs our attention to the problem of differential legitimate opportunity—that the lower classes have lesser opportunity than the other classes for achieving success in a legitimate or conforming manner. But Merton wrongly assumes that the lower classes, when confronted with the problem of differential opportunity, would automatically and successfully engage in deviant activities. In other words, Merton fails to recognize the fact that the lower classes, after being confronted with the problem of differential *legitimate* opportunity, are further confronted with the additional problem of differential *il*legitimate opportunity. This additional problem is that some members of the lower classes have lesser opportunity than others of the same classes for achieving success in an illegitimate or deviant manner. What Cloward and Ohlin want to emphasize is that, while all lower-class people have the same lack of opportunity for engaging in legitimate and conforming activities, they do not have the same opportunity for participating in illegitimate and deviant activities. Thus, when a lower-class person is pressured toward committing a deviant act such as theft or robbery, there is no guarantee that he or she will actually do it. Whether or not the person will actually do it depends on the nature of his or her access to illegitimate opportunity in the lower-class neighborhood.

There are three types of illegitimate opportunity, each being provided by a deviant subculture. The *criminal* subculture provides the illegitimate opportunity for achieving success goals. If lower-class youngsters are integrated into this subculture, they are able to achieve their success goals by stealing, robbing, and selling loot to a fence. This is the kind of deviant activity to which Merton assumes all lower-class youngsters would turn when they are denied conventional opportunities in the larger society. But, according to Cloward and Ohlin, many of these lower-class youth are not integrated into the criminal subculture and therefore do not enjoy criminal opportunities.

Yet some of those youth may find themselves in another neighborhood where the *conflict* subculture flourishes. In this subculture, a youngster has the opportunity to achieve "rep" or status within a violent delinquent gang. But that opportunity is available only to those boys who can meet such requirements as possessing great fighting skill and demonstrating enthusiasm for risking injury or death in gang warfare. There are some lower-class adolescents who fail to meet these requirements and are therefore denied the opportunity for achieving status within the conflict subculture.

There is finally a third subculture—the *retreatist* subculture—in which the only requirement the candidate is supposed to meet is the willingness to enjoy the use of drugs. Persons who are recruited into this retreatist subculture are likely to be those who have failed to achieve success in the criminal subculture or to attain status in the conflict subculture. Because of this failure to achieve success or status in the delinquent underworld *and* in the conventional upperworld, the retreatists have been called "double failures."

In brief, Cloward and Ohlin have tried to extend Merton's anomie theory by specifying the social mechanism through which the aspiration-opportunity discrepancy leads lower-class people to engage in one of three different deviant activities. That social mechanism is the system of *differential illegitimate opportunity*. In addition, like Cohen, Cloward and Ohlin present each of their delinquents' activities as a *subcultural* or *group* adjustment, while Merton describes his deviants' behavior as an *individual* adaptation, to the problem of the gap between aspiration and opportunity. Yet Cloward and Ohlin basically agree with Merton. They uphold Merton's thesis that deviant behavior results from the discrepancy between success aspirations and the opportunity for realizing those aspirations. They also continue to support

Merton's idea that lower-class people are more likely than higher-class people to get involved in deviant pursuits.

EVALUATION OF ANOMIE THEORY

First, there is no reliable evidence to support the theory's claim that people of lower classes are more likely than those of other classes to engage in deviant behavior.[11] It is true that the official statistics on crime and delinquency, which anomie theorists rely on, do confirm the theory. But the official statistics are largely unreliable and invalid. They are unreliable because law enforcers are much more likely to catch lower-class criminals and delinquents. They are invalid because they do not reflect the total picture of deviance—they measure instead a very small portion of the totality of deviance, namely, the relatively serious types. If we modify the theory and say that lower-class people are more likely to commit what society considers *serious* types of deviance, then the theory does have adequate empirical support from both the official and unofficial reports on criminality and delinquency.

Second, there is no evidence to support the assumption of anomie theory that lower-class people tend to hold the same level of success aspirations as do upper- and middle-class people. On the contrary, both theoretical analysis and empirical data show that lower-class people hold a significantly lower level of success aspirations. It is true, as anomie theorists claim, that American society does encourage lower-class people to embrace high success goals. But it is not necessarily true, as anomie theorists assume, that lower-class people will in effect embrace high success goals. Merton and other anomie theorists appear to have ignored the fact that the manifest, intended function of success ideology (to get all classes of people to entertain high aspirations) is *not* the same as its latent, unintended consequence (people of higher social classes end up holding far higher aspirations than do people of lower classes).

Third, related to the preceding criticism is the doubt cast upon Merton's assumption of value consensus. Many sociologists question Merton's assumption that the same set of cultural goals (i.e., success goals) govern various groups of individuals in the society. They point out that this assumption fails to jibe with the pluralistic and conflicting nature of American society. Recognition of this *value pluralism* may reveal the limitation of anomie theory. Thus many minority groups in our society have their own cultural values, so they may engage in deviant acts without having been influenced by the cultural goal of success. Examples of these deviant acts are as follows:

"Violations of fish and game laws by Indians; common law marriage, statutory rape, marihuana use, and carrying concealed weapons by Mexican migrants; common law marriage, "totin'" (petty theft) and assault by rural Negro migrants; gambling and opium use by Chinese; informal sororal polygyny, gambling and statutory rape ("sex sixteen" cases) among Hawaiians; drunkenness among older Japanese in Hawaii; and cockfighting among Filipinos." [12]

Fourth, anomie theory has been criticized for overdrawing the picture of lower-class delinquents as sorry kids who are forced into unpleasant deviant activities by the lack of success opportunity. This, Gwynn Nettler argues, slights the fact "that lower-class ways of life may have a rationale and a definition of 'how things ought to be' that have their own validity." Nettler continues:

This structural explanation [anomie theory] is blind, therefore, to the
fun that is involved in being delinquent—fun like skipping school, rolling
drunks, snatching purses, being chased by the police, staying out till
all hours, going where one wants, and doing what one wants without
adult supervision.[13]

Fifth, despite all these shortcomings, anomie theory does have some very important redeeming value, aside from its being considered by many sociologists as highly interesting. For one thing, anomie theory has contributed greatly to the sociological idea that the society, not the individual, causes deviant behavior. Before the theory was presented in 1938, many sociologists tended to seek the causes of crime and delinquency within the individual rather than without. The fact that today many sociologists take for granted the notion of deviance being caused by society, is a testament to the contribution of anomie theory.

Also, anomie theory seems to have a valid premise: the discrepancy between aspirations and the opportunity to realize these aspirations produces pressures toward deviation. This premise appears valid as long as we do not do what Merton has done—use it to make the unwarranted generalization that the lower classes are more pressured toward deviation than are other classes. Instead, we may use the premise to suggest that anybody, regardless of his or her class, tends to engage in deviance if he or she experiences a significant gap between aspiration and opportunity. Indeed, research has shown that wherever the aspiration-opportunity gap strikes, it tends to generate deviation. This has occurred, for example, in such diverse areas as an interdisciplinary scientific research team, the professions, an orthodox Jewish community, and a military prison,[14] as well as in the army, a governmental bureaucracy, and a Soviet firm.[15]

DIFFERENTIAL ASSOCIATION THEORY

This theory is the brainchild of Edwin Sutherland. Long after it was first published, several sociologists attempted to improve it. Let us examine this in some detail.

SUTHERLAND: DIFFERENTIAL ASSOCIATION

More than forty years ago—about the same time when anomie theory was proposed by Merton—the theory of differential association was introduced by Edwin Sutherland.[16] Today it enjoys great popularity among many sociologists.

Sutherland developed his theory as an attempt to explain two sets of human phenomena. First, he wanted to explain why crime rates vary with different *groups* of people. He wanted to explain, for example, why city people are more likely to commit crimes than country people, why males are more delinquent than females, why blacks are more prone to criminality than whites, and why there are more crimes in poverty areas of cities than in other areas. To make sense of these different crime rates, Sutherland suggested the idea of differential social organization or differential group organization. By *differential group organization* he referred to the fact that a society is composed of different groups of people, some having a criminalistic tradition and others having an anticriminalistic tradition. Groups with a criminalistic tradition are thought to have a higher crime rate than those with an anticriminalistic tradition. As Sutherland said, "The formal statement of the theory indicates, for example, that a high crime rate in urban areas can be considered the end product of criminalistic traditions in those areas." [17] In other words, *criminalistic tradition* is theorized to be the cause of high crime rates or group criminality.

Secondly, Sutherland developed his theory in order to explain *individual* criminality—to explain why some individuals become criminal while others do not. He considered the cause of individual criminality to be what he called *differential association*. This concept of differential association is much more clearly and fully developed than the concept of differential group organization discussed above. As a result, Sutherland's theory has become popularly known as differential association theory; it has never been referred to as differential group organization theory. Differential association theory contains nine statements, which are intended to show how a particular individual comes to engage in criminal behavior.[18]

1. "Criminal behavior is learned." This means that nobody inherits criminality in the same way as you inherit the color of your skin, hair, and eyes.

Rather, a person has to learn how to commit crimes just as he or she has to learn how to become, say, a doctor or engineer.

2. "Criminal behavior is learned in interaction with other persons in a process of communication." Learning criminal behavior is like learning other things. It involves communication through the use of words and gestures.

3. "The principal part of the learning of criminal behavior occurs within intimate personal groups." Communication may occur through such impersonal agencies as movies and newspapers, or between members of an intimate personal group such as our buddies, boyfriends or girlfriends, and parents. Communication from one's parents plays a more important part in teaching a person the criminal way of behaving.

4. "When criminal behavior is learned, the learning includes (a) techniques of committing the crime, which are sometimes very complicated, sometimes very simple; (b) the specific direction of motives, drives, rationalizations, and attitudes." In learning the criminal way of behaving, individuals not only have to learn how to commit the crime, which may be very complicated or simple, but they also have to develop the kinds of motives, drives, excuses, and attitudes that are necessary for committing the crime.

5. "The specific direction of motives and drives is learned from definitions of the legal codes as favorable or unfavorable." Individuals acquire certain motives and drives—for or against criminal activities—from the way the people around them treat legal codes. They may acquire a distaste for crime if the people around them always respect the law. They may develop a taste for criminality if the people around them have a contempt for the law. Or, they may become ambivalent toward lawbreaking or law-abiding, as people often are in our American society, where we come into contact with all sorts of people—some favorable to the law, others unfavorable to it, and still others with mixed feelings about it.

6. "A person becomes delinquent because of an excess of definitions favorable to violation of law over definitions unfavorable to violation of law." Since this statement is the heart of differential association theory, many sociologists have virtually equated it with the entire theory. We may reword the statement or theory in this way: *if a person associates with criminal patterns more than with anticriminal patterns, he or she is likely to become criminal.* Because this theory has created a great deal of misunderstanding, Sutherland's student, Donald Cressey, has tried to clarify it by describing what it means as well as what it does not.[19]

First of all, according to Cressey, the term *criminal patterns* does not necessarily refer to criminal persons or persons with a criminal character. The theory does not mean that if you hang around with criminals more than noncriminals, you are likely to become criminal. *Criminal patterns* refers to more than criminal persons; it also includes *criminal behavior, criminal behavior patterns,* or *definitions favorable to violation of law.* By all these phrases, Sutherland actually meant the *idea* of committing crime. For example, if a father tells his children that "it's all right to steal when you are poor," he is giving them an idea of committing crime—or, in Sutherland's words, "presenting them with a criminal behavior pattern." On the other hand, if the father tells his children that "it's wrong to steal," he is giving them an anticriminal idea—or, in Sutherland's words, "presenting them with an anticriminal behavior pattern." We should note that the emphasis is on whether the father gives his children criminal or conventional ideas, less on whether the father himself is criminal or conventional. Therefore, the theory means that if a person is given more ideas of committing crime than ideas of performing conventional acts, he or she is likely to commit crime.

In addition, the theory does not refer to contacts or associations with criminals only. It does not mean that if a person has a lot of contacts with criminals he or she will become a criminal. For example, criminologists may have a lot of contacts with the criminals whom they are studying, but they will not necessarily become criminal themselves. The theory instead refers to both criminal and anticriminal contacts or, more precisely, to the *excess* of criminal over anticriminal contacts. This means that people may find themselves influenced by both criminal and anticriminal contacts. But if they are *more* influenced by the former than the latter, they are likely to become criminal. All this is suggested by the term *differential association,* which refers to the fact that a crime-prone person's *association* with criminal persons and ideas *differs* from (or, more precisely, is more than) his or her association with anticriminal ones. Defined in this way, differential association is theorized to be the cause of individual criminality.

7. "Differential associations may vary in frequency, duration, priority, and intensity." As we have noted, there are two contrasting types of associations: associations with criminal behavior and associations with anticriminal behavior. These two may differ from each other as to their frequency, duration, priority, and intensity. A person may associate with criminal behavior more frequently, more lastingly, more significantly, and more intensely than with anticriminal behavior, or vice versa. All this suggests that whether individuals will become criminal depends on how often they are exposed to criminal ideas, for how long a time they are thus exposed, how early in their life this exposure began, and how much prestige the source of those criminal ideas had as well as how much emotional commitment the source had toward the criminal way of life.

8. "The process of learning criminal behavior by association with criminal and anticriminal patterns involves all of the mechanisms that are involved in

any other learning." This means that although criminal behavior differs in *content* from other, noncriminal forms of behavior, the *way* of learning criminal behavior is basically no different from the way of learning any other form of behavior. Suppose a learning theory is able to tell us how a person has learned to become a good or poor student, a great or inept lover, a loving or unloving spouse, an efficient or inefficient worker, and so on. The same learning theory should be equally able to tell us how the individual has learned to engage in criminal behavior.

9. "While criminal behavior is an expression of general needs and values, it is not explained by those general needs and values, since noncriminal behavior is an expression of the same needs and values." Thieves generally steal because they need money, but honest laborers work hard also because they need money. So the need for money cannot tell us why some people steal while others do an honest job. It is like breathing. All people—criminals and noncriminals alike—have the ability to breathe. But this breathing ability cannot be said to cause criminal behavior.

In conclusion, Sutherland's concept of differential group organization (or, more precisely, *criminalistic tradition*) is designed to explain *group* criminality, while his concept of differential association is intended to explain *individual* criminality. Since these two concepts belong to the same theory, they must be related to each other. Thus, according to the theory as a whole, criminalistic tradition produces group criminality, which in turn generates differential association, which finally causes individual criminality. Put in another way, an individual is likely to get involved in criminal activities if he or she belongs to a group with criminalistic traditions, whereas another individual tends to stay away from criminal activities if he or she is a member of a group with *anti*criminalistic traditions.

You may recall that, long after Merton introduced *aspiration-opportunity discrepancy* as the cause of deviant behavior, Cohen unintentionally, and Cloward and Ohlin intentionally, extended Merton's anomie theory. Though basically agreeing with Merton's theory, they suggested that aspiration-opportunity discrepancy (the goal-means gap) produces deviant behavior not directly but rather through an intervening mechanism. Cohen called it "status frustration" while Cloward and Ohlin named it "differential illegitimate opportunity." In other words, Cohen specified status frustration, while Cloward and Ohlin pointed out differential illegitimate opportunity, as the mechanism by which aspiration-opportunity discrepancy produces deviant behavior.

What has happened to Merton's anomie theory has also happened to Sutherland's differential association theory. Long after Sutherland introduced differential association as the cause of criminal behavior, Daniel Glaser on the one hand, and Robert Burgess and Ronald Akers on the other hand, extended Sutherland's theory.[20] Though basically agreeing with Sutherland's theory, they seemed to suggest that differential association produces criminality not directly but rather through an intervening mechanism. Glaser identified that intervening mechanism as *differential identification;* Burgess and Akers singled it out as *differential reinforcement.* In other words, Glaser presented differential identification, and Burgess and Akers differential reinforcement, as the process by which differential association produces criminal behavior.

GLASER: DIFFERENTIAL IDENTIFICATION

Glaser first argues that Sutherland's theory "actually conveys a rather mechanistic image of criminality." [21] Such an image shows the individual as being mechanically pushed into criminal involvement by an association with criminals. It ignores the individual's role-taking and choice-making ability. Glaser, then, tries to correct this mechanistic image by suggesting that a person's association with criminals would not have the criminogenic effect on him or her, unless the individual identifies with them. Glaser states:

The theory of differential identification, in essence, is that *a person
pursues criminal behavior to the extent that he identifies with real or
imaginary persons from whose perspective his criminal behavior seems
accceptable.* Such a theory focuses attention on the interaction in
which choice of models occurs, including the individual's interaction with
himself in rationalizing his conduct.[22]

Glaser's theory may be taken to suggest that it is all right for you to associate with criminals in real life or in books and movies, as long as you do not take them so seriously that you identify with them, treating them as your heroes. If you do identify with them, you will likely become a criminal yourself.

BURGESS AND AKERS:
DIFFERENTIAL REINFORCEMENT

As Burgess and Akers see it, Sutherland's theory is inadequate in that it merely suggests, in very broad terms, the learning process which people must go through before they become criminal. It fails to specify what that learning process entails. In trying to correct this failure, Burgess and Akers offer the idea of *differential reinforcement* as the substance of that learning process.

Burgess and Akers derive their idea from a well-known theory in psychology, which has been variously referred to as *learning theory, behaviorist theory, operant behavior theory, operant conditioning theory,* and *reinforcement theory*. Generally, *reinforcement theory* says that we are motivated to continue behaving in a certain way if we have been rewarded for doing so, or to discontinue the behavior if we have been punished for it. For example, you are likely to kiss your date good-night if you have been satisfied by your past experience of kissing her (or him). When applied to criminal behavior, reinforcement theory says that a person will continue to engage in criminal behavior if he or she has been rewarded for doing so.

One aspect of reinforcement theory that is most relevant to the Burgess-Akers reformulation of Sutherland's differential association theory, is the Law of Differential Reinforcement. In technical language, the law states that "given a number of available operants, all of which produce the same reinforcer, that operant which produces the reinforcer in the greatest amount, frequency and probability will have the higher probability of occurrence."[23] This can be expressed in simple terms as follows: if you are given a number of options, such as saying good-night, handshaking, kissing, necking, and love-making after going out with your date, you will most likely choose the option that has been most (greatly, frequently, and probably) satisfying to you in the past. When applied to criminal behavior, the Law of Differential Reinforcement would explain that a person will choose criminality over conventionality if he or she finds criminality more (greatly, frequently, and probably) satisfying than conventionality. When this law is incorporated into Sutherland's differential association theory, the theory would explain criminal behavior in this way: a person will likely become criminal if he or she finds criminal patterns more satisfying, rewarding, or reinforcing than anticriminal patterns after he or she has associated with criminal patterns more than with anticriminal patterns. Thus Burgess and Akers supply what they seem to consider as the missing link in Sutherland's theory: differential association → *differential reinforcement* → criminal behavior.

To sum up the whole theory of differential association, we may present it in the form of a causal sequence: differential group organization (criminalistic tradition) → group criminality (high crime rates) → differential association → (Glaser's) differential identification or (Burgess's and Akers's) differential reinforcement → individual criminality.

EVALUATION OF DIFFERENTIAL ASSOCIATION THEORY

First, differential association theory is mainly applicable to criminals and delinquents who commit crime and delinquency in groups. The theory is less applicable to those who often commit crimes alone, such as "rural offenders, landlords, trust violators, check forgers, and white-collar criminals." [24]

Second, it is difficult to determine precisely what differential association or "excess of criminal patterns over anticriminal patterns" is in real-life situations. Many researchers have found that people often cannot identify the persons from whom they have learned criminal and anticriminal behavior patterns, much less determine whether one behavior pattern has exceeded another in their lives.[25]

The difficulty in finding an empirical indicator of differential association is, from the scientific point of view, extremely damaging to the theory. This is because the theory may become a useless statement of circular reasoning. As it is convenient to identify individual criminality as the empirical indicator of "the excess of criminal patterns over anticriminal patterns," then it is tautological to say that "the excess of criminal patterns over anticriminal patterns" *causes* individual criminality.

But Cressey does not accept this criticism. He says: "It should be noted that these damaging criticisms of the theory of differential association as a precise statement of the mechanism by which persons become criminals do not affect the value of the theory as a general principle which organizes and makes good sense of the data on crime rates. A theory accounting for the distribution of crime, delinquency, or any other phenomenon can be valid even if a presumably coordinate theory specifying the process by which deviancy occurs in individual cases is *incorrect*, let alone untestable."[26] In this quote, Cressey apparently believes that, if it cannot successfully explain *individual* criminality, the theory can at least account for *group* criminality. Can it? This leads us to the next point.

Third, it also appears difficult for the theory to account scientifically for group criminality. The theory can explain group criminality, but in a tautological way. As quoted earlier, Sutherland said: "The formal statement of the theory indicates, for example, that a high crime rate in urban areas can be considered the end product of criminalistic traditions in those areas."[27] Note that a criminalistic tradition is supposed to explain a high crime rate, or that the former is the cause and the latter the effect. It is difficult to observe criminalistic tradition. But it is easy to observe a high crime rate. We may use this as the observable indicator of a criminalistic tradition. Yet it would be an exercise in circular reasoning if we say that the criminalistic tradition is the *cause* of a high crime rate.

Fourth, in emphasizing the importance of learning how to become criminal or delinquent, Sutherland's theory may have assumed that some special skills must be learned in order to pull off a criminal or delinquent act. Some sociologists have severely criticized this part of the theory. Sheldon Glueck, for example, attacks it this way:

What is there to be learned about simple lying, taking things that belong to another, fighting, and sex play? Do children have to be taught such natural [delinquent] acts? If one takes account of the psychiatric and criminological evidence that involves research into the early childhood manifestations of antisocial behavior, one must conclude that it is not delinquent behavior that is learned; that comes naturally. It is rather *non*-delinquent behavior that is learned. Unsocialized, untamed, and uninstructed, the child resorts to lying, slyness, subterfuge, anger, hatred, theft, aggression, attack, and other forms of social behavior in its early attempts of self-expression and ego formation.[28]

You may see that the child's delinquent acts listed in this quote are basically so unsophisticated that one need not learn a skill in order to be able to commit them. You could add to that list some adult crimes which are also unsophisticated, such as murder, forcible rape, aggravated assault, and other such crimes of impulse and passion—which need not be learned, either.

Fifth, Glaser's differential identification theory appears to have been supported by some empirical data. Victor Matthews, for example, found that high school boys who identified with delinquent friends were likely to become delinquent themselves.[29] But there is no conclusive evidence that identification with delinquent friends is the cause of delinquency or occurs before a person becomes delinquent.

Sixth, the Burgess-Akers differential reinforcement theory cannot by itself explain why a person *initially* commits a deviant rather than conforming act. The theory cannot tell us the concrete nature of the reinforcing stimuli that are supposed to cause deviant behavior. This, as Akers admits, can be known only from other theories or from studies about the biological, psychological, and sociocultural factors in deviant behavior.[30]

But, once we have got the knowledge from other theories and studies as to what causes a person to commit a deviant act in the first place, differential reinforcement theory can become very useful for explaining why that person *continues* to commit that deviant act. According to differential reinforcement theory, a person continues to commit a deviant act because he or she has in the past been rewarded more than punished for that deviant act, whereas another person does not repeat a deviant act because he or she has been punished more than rewarded for the deviance.

Seventh, although it is difficult (as the second point has suggested) to determine the exact, empirical meaning of differential association, numerous sociologists have nonetheless found that their research data appear to support Sutherland's theory. But this need not be surprising. For those sociologists have found empirical support not exactly for Sutherland's theory, but instead for their own interpretations of the theory. As James Short, who has done much research attempting to test the theory, concludes: "Much support has been found for the principle of differential association *if* the liberties taken in the process of its operationalization [translation into empirical or testable terms] are granted." [31] Most frequently, researchers have translated the principle of differential association into an intellectualized version of the popular "bad companions" theory, which says in effect that a person who runs around with bad companions will more likely become bad than another who does not.[32] This seems to be what those researchers have found out in their empirical studies. For example, one of them gives this concluding statement about his research: "On the basis of this research, it is clear that adolescents who associate extensively with delinquent friends report more delinquent behavior than those whose contact with delinquent peers is minimal." [33] At any rate, all this shows that Sutherland's differential association theory has inspired a good deal of research, which may make the theory more empirically testable and thus a better scientific theory.

CONTROL THEORY

Control theory differs from the other major theories discussed above. First, both anomie and differential association theorists approach the problem of explaining deviant behavior head-on and ask: What causes deviance? But control theorists approach the problem in a roundabout way and ask: What causes conformity? They figure that if they can find out what causes conformity, they will automatically find out what causes deviance. For what causes deviance is simply the *absence* of what causes conformity. Second, both anomie and differential association theorists reject the Freudian idea that deviant behavior can naturally or by itself burst forth from our inborn animal impulses. They instead theorize that deviant behavior is produced by an anomic social condition or has to be learned by the individual. But most control theorists seem to accept the Freudian idea to one degree or another. So they argue that deviant behavior need not be learned and that the inborn animal impulses, if not properly controlled, will naturally turn into deviant behavior.

Generally, in the eyes of control theorists, what causes conformity is social control over the individual and therefore *the absence of social control causes deviance*. As for the more specific nature of social control, various control theorists tell the story a little differently. There are two groups of control theorists, one telling the story with original research data to back it up and the other telling the same story but without the data. Let us discuss only the first group. It consists of three sociologists—Walter Reckless, Ivan Nye, and Travis Hirschi.[34]

RECKLESS: CONTAINMENT

In his version of control theory, which he calls *containment theory*, Reckless assumes that there are powerful forces pushing the individual to a deviant course of action. This assumption is apparently derived from sociology, psychology, and common sense. From sociology and common sense, Reckless gets the idea that the individual is propelled to deviancy by such external or sociological forces as "poverty or deprivation, conflict and discord, external restraint, minority group status, and limited access to success in an opportunity structure . . . the distractions, attractions, temptations, patterns of deviancy, advertising, propaganda, carriers of delinquent and criminal patterns (including pushers), delinquency subculture, and so forth." [35] From psychology and common sense, Reckless gets the idea that the individual is motivated to deviancy by such inner or psychological forces as "the drives, motives, frustrations, restlessness, disappointments, rebellion, hostility, feelings of inferiority, and so forth." [36]

Being caught up in those inner and outer forces, people have a strong tendency to violate social norms. Yet not all people in this situation are equally successful in turning their deviant tendencies into deviant *action*. Reckless's containment theory is designed to explain why some people are successful while others are not.

According to the containment theory, in addition to the above-mentioned inner and outer forces that pressure and provoke the individual toward deviance, there are inner and outer forces that protect and insulate the individual against deviance. Since the latter forces protect and insulate the individual against deviance by containing those deviance-generating forces, they are referred to as inner and outer containment. *Inner containment* is found within the individual. It consists of such personal qualities as "self-control, good self-concept, ego strength, well-developed superego, high frustration tolerance, high resistance to diversions, high sense of responsibility, goal orientation, ability to find substitute satisfactions, tension-reducing rationalizations, and so on." [37] *Outer containment* exists outside the individual. It is composed of such social factors in the person's immediate environment as "a presentation of a consistent moral front to the person, institutional reinforcement of his norms, goals and expectations, the existence of a reasonable set of social expectations, effective supervision and discipline (social controls), provision for reasonable scope of activity (including limits and responsibilities) as well as for alternatives and safety-valves, [and] opportunity for acceptance, [for] identity and [for] belongingness." [38] If a person's inner and outer containments are strong, he or she will most likely engage in conforming behavior. If a person's inner and outer containments

.are weak, he or she will most likely engage in deviant behavior. If one of the containments is strong while the other is weak, he or she will have medium likelihood of engaging in deviant behavior.

Reckless and his associates have collected some data that apparently support the containment theory.[39] In 1955 they studied two groups of sixth-grade boys in the highest delinquency areas in Columbus, Ohio. One group consisted of "good" boys—who were considered by their teachers as likely to stay out of trouble with the law. Another group was made up of "bad" boys—who were regarded by their teachers as headed for trouble with the law. During the next four years, a much smaller proportion of the good boys than bad boys (4 percent vs. 39 percent) were found to have committed delinquent acts. Direct evidence shows that the good boys had strong inner containment such as positive self-concept and adequate sense of responsibility, while the bad boys had weak inner containment such as negative self-concept and little sense of responsibility.[40] Moreover, there is some indirect evidence that suggests that the good boys were insulated against delinquency by strong outer containment such as close parental supervision of the boys' activities and friends, while the bad boys were made vulnerable to delinquency by weak outer containment such as the lack of parental supervision.

NYE: SOCIAL CONTROL

Like Reckless, the second control theorist Ivan Nye assumes that there are powerful forces pushing all of us toward deviance.[41] Unlike Reckless, Nye simply relies on Freudian psychology and singles out our animal instincts as the motivating force of deviance. Since all of us are born with the same animal instincts, we all have the same natural tendency to behave like an animal by breaking social norms. Yet most of us do not actually break the norms, while some of us do. In order to explain this difference between conforming and deviant behavior, Nye, like Reckless, uses the concept of control.

According to Nye's version of control theory, society uses social control to help us check our animal instincts or deviant tendencies so that we will become law-abiding citizens. Social control, then, is seen as preventing us from deviation or ensuring our conformity, and the lack of social control is seen as creating the opposite result. Nye divides social control into four types.

The first type is *internal control*. Society, particularly through the parents as its control agents, socializes the child in its values and norms so that he or she will internalize them and turn them into a conscience. The conscience is the internal control that prevents the person from getting involved in deviance.

The second type is *indirect control.* The development of affection and respect for his or her parents serves as the indirect control over the child.

The third type is *direct control.* Society relies on the police, parents, friends, and other conforming groups to impose direct control on the individual. Direct control entails the threat and application of ridicule, ostracism, and various forms of punishment.

Legitimate need satisfaction is the fourth type of social control. Society provides legitimate means for satisfying the individual's need for affection, recognition, and security. This serves to protect the person against involvement with deviance.

Social control of one form or another can be exercised over adolescents by the family, peer groups in neighborhoods, schools, churches, law enforcement agencies, and other formal and informal groups. Nye has focused his empirical research on the family. His findings overwhelmingly support control theory in that they show a negative relationship between family control and delinquent behavior.

HIRSCHI: BOND TO SOCIETY

Like Nye, the third control theorist, Travis Hirschi, assumes that we are all animals endowed with the ability to commit deviant acts.[42] Most of us do not take advantage of this ability—as Hirschi's control theory suggests—because of our strong *bond* to society. Our strong bond to society, then, ensures our conformity; conversely, if our bond to society is weak or broken, we will commit deviant acts.

You may have perceived that Nye looks at our relations to society from the sociological standpoint of how society controls us as individuals. In contrast, Hirschi looks at the same relations from the psychological standpoint of how we as individuals tie or *bond* ourselves to society. According to Hirschi's theory, there are four ways that individuals bond themselves to society.

The first is by *attachment to others.* Individuals attach themselves to conventional people and institutions. In the case of juveniles, they may show this attachment by loving and respecting their parents, making friends with conventional peers, liking school, and working hard to develop intellectual skills. A *commitment to conformity* is the second way. Individuals invest their time and energy in conventional types of action, such as getting an education, holding a job, developing an occupational skill, improving a professional status, building up a business, or acquiring a reputation for virtue. At the same time, people show a commitment to achievement through these activities. The third way is *involvement in conventional activities*. People simply keep themselves so busy doing conventional things that they do not have time for partaking in deviant activities or even for thinking about deviant acts. A *belief in the moral validity of social rules* is the fourth way that people bond themselves to society. Individuals have a strong moral belief that they should obey the rules of conventional society. A young person may show such moral belief through a respect for the police or through a positive attitude toward the law.

If these four elements of the individual's bond to conventional society are strong, the individual is likely to get stuck in conformity. If these four elements of the bond are weak, the individual is likely to slide into deviance. Hirschi has tested such a version of control theory on schoolchildren. His findings support the theory very well. More specifically, his findings show that the youngsters with stronger attachment to others, stronger commitment to conformity, deeper involvement in conventional activities, or deeper belief in social rules are more likely to engage in conforming activities.

In summary, all the control theorists suggest that containment, social control, or bond to society prevents individuals from committing deviant acts, and the lack of it prompts them into committing them.

EVALUATION OF CONTROL THEORY

First, as we have indicated, control theory has generally enjoyed a good deal of empirical support. But we should note that these supporting data are largely about adolescent, unsophisticated delinquent behavior. There is no evidence that the theory can also explain adult or more sophisticated deviant acts. In fact, we may argue that the theory cannot. Let us elaborate on this as our second point.

Second, control theory has used lack of ambition as one explanation of juvenile delinquency. It is true, as Hirschi's data have pointed out, that juvenile delinquents are more likely than nondelinquents to lack ambition. But this does not necessarily mean that the lack of ambition, which reflects the lack of social and intellectual skills, causes delinquency. Instead, it simply means that for an adolescent to become delinquent he or she does not have to be ambitious or to acquire social and intellectual skills. Why not? Because of the simple fact that delinquent acts are so uncomplicated and unsophisticated that children can easily commit them.[43]

Now, there is a big difference between the world of childhood and that of adulthood. Generally, adults' deviant acts are more complicated and sophisticated than those of juveniles. In order to commit the complicated and sophisticated acts, adult deviants cannot afford to be like juvenile delinquents, namely, unambitious or lacking in social and intellectual skills. For example, far different from the unambitious and unskilled juvenile delinquents, such adult deviants as former Attorney General John Mitchell, former Presidential Assistants John Ehrlichman and Bob Haldeman, and other Watergate criminals are extremely ambitious and highly skilled.

Also, it is true, as demonstrated by Hirschi's data, that frustrated aspirations do not provoke juvenile delinquency.[44] But this may be false if generalized to more sophisticated, adult deviance. There is research to suggest that frustrated aspirations do provoke adult deviance.[45] This is not to imply that all adults will engage in relatively sophisticated deviant acts if they experience frustrated aspirations. Indeed, it seems that, just as the experience of frustrated aspirations does not provoke delinquency among juveniles, neither does it provoke deviance among *some* adults. This is likely to be true on two conditions: if the word *deviance* refers to such unsophisticated acts as murder, forcible rape, and aggravated assault—namely, acts that are quite similar to the unsophisticated ones committed by juvenile delinquents, and the word *adults* refers to those who are quite like juveniles in being powerless members of society—namely, poor, socioeconomically deprived, or socially and intellectually unskilled adults. In other words, powerless or childlike adults do not have to experience frustrated aspirations in order to commit deviant acts that are as unsophisticated as juveniles' delinquency. Yet frustrated aspirations may easily provoke many relatively powerful adults into sophisticated forms of deviance such as tax evasion, fraudulent advertising, and the like. In sum, although it is useful for explaining juveniles' unsophisticated delinquent acts, control theory is less useful for explaining adults' sophisticated deviant behavior.

Third, control theory presents an inadequate view of social control. This view may accurately reflect the world of childhood but not that of adulthood. Again, there is a big difference between the world that juveniles live in and the world that adults live in—the former being comparatively simple and the latter complicated. In the more simple world of childhood, it is often the case that things are either black or white, people are either good guys or bad guys, and rules are so clear-cut that the distinction between obeying them (conformity) and violating them (deviance) can be easily established. It is somewhat like the wonderful world of Walt Disney movies, Lassie, and John Wayne Westerns—all of which tend to portray a clear contrast or contest between good and evil. In such a simple world, the nature of social control is unmistakably clear: social control works against evil so that good will prevail.

Thus, in attempting to control juveniles' animal—evil or deviant—impulses, parents as society's social control agents socialize their charges to become civilized: to dress properly, to eat properly, to respect property, to be polite, considerate, and well behaved—in other words, to acquire conforming behavior. In this process of acquiring conforming behavior, juveniles do not simultaneously acquire the tendency to perform deviant acts. This is because conformity and deviance, or good and evil, are clearly distinguishable from and clearly opposed to each other. The acquirement of conformity is categorically the prevention of deviance.

On the other hand, the world of adulthood is far more complicated. In the adult world, the acquirement of conformity is *not* categorically the prevention of deviance. When adults learn some conforming behavior, they simultaneously acquire the tendency to perform deviant acts. There are two reasons for this. One is that the ability and opportunity to perform deviant acts depend on the ability and opportunity to perform conforming acts. For example, when adults learn how to manage a bank, they also acquire the ability and opportunity to embezzle money from the bank; when adults become government officials, they also acquire the ability and opportunity for bribery; when adults become physicians, they also acquire the ability and opportunity to get involved in medical malpractice. So, unlike a juvenile, an adult must learn and have the opportunity to become deviant, and this ability to be deviant and the opportunity for it result from becoming an accomplished conformist.

Another reason for the overlap between conforming and deviant behavior is that social rules pertaining to adults are comparatively ambiguous. It may be easy for us to define a juvenile's behavior (say, stealing or buying an apple) as either absolutely delinquent or absolutely nondelinquent, but it is far more difficult to define an adult's behavior (say, giving a gift to a public official or to a friend) as either a criminal act of bribery or a noncriminal act of friendship. Consequently, when an adult appears to be performing a conforming act, he or she may actually be perpetrating a deviant act.

But, as has been implied before, not all adults have the same problem. There are adults who are almost as powerless as juveniles, such as the poor, uneducated, unsophisticated, and unskilled. Having been thrust by birth and socioeconomic circumstance into a world very much like the juvenile's world, the powerless adults do not have to learn how to commit such unsophisticated deviant acts as murder, forcible rape, and aggravated assault. Also, the rules which the powerful establishment applies to powerless adults are like those applied to juveniles. Those rules are generally so clear-cut that it is easy for a social control agent to establish what constitutes the observance of them (conformity) as opposed to what constitutes the violation of them (deviance). For example, the law against homicide is far more clear-cut than the law against corporate tax evasion. As a result, it is much easier—assuming that there is evidence for the act—for the court to determine the guilt or innocence of a powerless adult accused of homicide than to determine the guilt or innocence of a powerful adult accused of corporate tax evasion.

Yet most adults, being unlike powerless juveniles, are constantly faced with ambiguous rules and constantly exposed, through conforming activities, to deviant opportunities. There is, then, a difference between the complex world of adults and the simple world of juveniles. We may conclude that the view of social control as presented by control theory may be relevant to juveniles, but less so to adults.

SUMMARY

In this chapter we have discussed three major scientific theories of deviance. As scientific explanations, they focus on the *causes* of deviant behavior.

Merton's anomie theory suggests that lower-class people are more likely to get involved in deviant activities because the society has encouraged them to pursue a high success goal without providing them with the necessary means of achieving it. Cohen unintentionally extends this theory by proposing that when their aspirations for status are frustrated in the middle-class milieu, lower-class boys tend to set up a delinquent subculture. Cloward and Ohlin intentionally extend Merton's theory by suggesting that whether the potentially delinquent lower-class youth will actually become delinquent depends on the factor of differential illegitimate opportunity. Anomie theory has been criticized for lacking empirical support, for ignoring value pluralism, and for slighting the fun of delinquency. But the theory has been praised for replacing the psychological with the sociological approach to deviance and for offering a valid premise concerning the aspiration-opportunity gap.

Sutherland's differential association theory states that a person will become criminal if he or she associates more with criminal than with anti-criminal people and ideas. Glaser extends this theory by suggesting that differential identification is the determining factor for turning the differential association into criminal action, while Burgess and Akers identify that determining factor as differential reinforcement. Sutherland's theory has been criticized for its failure to explain the behavior of lone criminals, for offering an empirically vague concept and a tautological explanation, and for wrongly assuming the learning of special skills as necessary for committing crime and delinquency. But the theory has inspired substantial empirical research. It has also been pointed out that Glaser's theory has received some but not conclusive empirical support, while the Burgess-Akers theory can explain repeated but not initial deviance.

Control theory reasons that what causes conformity is control and there-fore the lack of control causes deviance. Reckless refers to this causal factor of conformity as *containment*, Nye, *social control*, and Hirschi, *bond to society*. This theory has been well supported by empirical data, but it is applicable to unsophisticated delinquent behavior only. The theory seems unable to explain more sophisticated adult deviant behavior, aside from presenting an oversimplified view of social control.

SUGGESTED READINGS

Burgess, Robert L. and Ronald L. Akers. "A Differential Association-Reinforce-ment Theory of Criminal Behavior." *Social Problems* 14 (Fall 1966): 128–147.

Clinard, Marshall B., ed. *Anomie and Deviant Behavior: A Discussion and Cri-tique.* New York: Free Press, 1964.

Cloward, Richard A. and Lloyd E. Ohlin. *Delinquency and Opportunity: A Theory of Delinquent Gangs.* Glencoe, Ill.: Free Press, 1960.

Cohen, Albert K. *Delinquent Boys: The Culture of the Gang.* Glencoe, Ill.: Free Press, 1955.

Glaser, Daniel. "Criminality Theories and Behavioral Images." *American Jour-nal of Sociology* 61 (March 1956): 433–444.

Hirschi, Travis. *Causes of Delinquency.* Berkeley and Los Angeles: University of California Press, 1969.

Merton, Robert K. *Social Theory and Social Structure.* Rev. ed. New York: Free Press of Glencoe, 1957; pp. 131–194.

Nye, F. Ivan. *Family Relationships and Delinquent Behavior.* New York: John Wiley, 1958.

Reckless, Walter C. *The Crime Problem.* 5th ed. New York: Appleton-Century-Crofts, 1973; pp. 55–57.

Sutherland, Edwin H. and Donald R. Cressey. *Criminology.* 9th ed. Philadelphia, Pa.: Lippincott, 1974; pp. 71–93.

Thio, Alex. "A Critical Look at Merton's Anomie Theory." *Pacific Sociological Review* 18 (April 1975): 139–158.

3 HUMANISTIC THEORIES OF DEVIANCE

In this chapter I shall discuss three major theories that are of a different character from those presented in the preceding chapter. The theories here do not focus on the causes of deviant behavior. Instead, they concentrate on the meanings of deviance, as well as on how people behave in keeping with those meanings.

LABELING THEORY

In the early 1960s, a group of humanistic sociologists, especially Howard Becker, John Kitsuse, and Kai Erikson, interpreted deviance as a process of symbolic interaction.[1] They should have referred to this interpretation as symbolic interaction theory—which had been used for many years to analyze the social psychology of human behavior in general. But they did not. So, much to their chagrin today, both their followers and critics have often applied a new label to the old theory. The new label is none other than *labeling theory*. Kitsuse, for example, reveals his chagrin this way:

Ironically, we . . . face the problem of labels. Proponents as well as critics have referred to the approach by several names from the straight-forward "the labeling approach to deviance" and "the new conception of deviance" to the more grandiose "labeling theory of deviance." Labeling, in its many variations, is an unfortunate term that has more confused than clarified the distinctive perspective that has developed around this approach. The most unfortunate aspect of the term is that it invites if not encourages a vulgar acceptance as well as rejection of the approach; for example, the simple-minded ways in which Howard Becker's definition of deviant and deviant behavior has been used and misused.[2]

It is obviously too late now for Kitsuse and Becker to change the label by which their theory is popularly known.[3] Yet in order to get an accurate view of their so-called labeling theory, we should discuss it as a version of symbolic interactionism.

A VERSION OF SYMBOLIC INTERACTIONISM

Symbolic interactionists hold the same belief about human beings as do the humanists, whom we discussed in the first chapter. The belief is that a human being is a conscious, feeling, thinking, and reflective subject rather than a nonconscious, unfeeling, unthinking, and unreflective object. As Herbert Blumer, the chief proponent of symbolic interactionism, says, "In place of being a mere medium for operation of determining factors that play upon him, the human being is seen as an active organism in his own right, facing, dealing with, and acting toward the objects he indicates." [4] Such a humanist view of people has led symbolic interactionists to interpret human behavior in the following way.

Human behavior is not a static entity but rather a dynamic action that occurs in the fluid and ever-changing context of social interaction. In this context of social interaction, people, as conscious and active individuals, "take into account what is going on around them and what is likely to go on when they decide what they will do." [5] In other words, when people interact with one another, they actively impute meanings to one another's acts, so that they can rely on those meanings to act and react toward one another in the future. Thus, whatever meanings people impute to each other's acts will have consequences for one another's future behavior. For example, if your friend interprets the manner of your speech as indicative of your being an intelligent person, this interpretation may, on the one side, make you happy and proud, and on the other side, make your friend respect and admire you.

In their attempt to interpret deviant behavior, labeling theorists take advantage of the two central ideas in symbolic interactionism. These two ideas are implied in the preceding paragraph or suggested by the very two words that make up the name of the theory. First, as suggested by the word *interaction*, deviance—like any other kind of human activity—is a collective action, involving more than one person's act. Thus, according to labeling theory, we should not focus on the deviant person alone but rather on the *interaction* between the supposed deviant and conformists. As Becker says,

The conventional [scientific-deterministic] style of studying deviance has focused on the deviant himself and has asked its questions mainly about him. Who is he? Is he likely to keep being that way? The new [labeling] approach sees it as always and everywhere a process of inter-action between at least two kinds of people: those who commit (or are said to have committed) a deviant act and the rest of society, per-haps divided into several groups itself. The two groups are seen in complementary relationship. One cannot exist without the other.[6]

Second, as suggested by the word *symbolic*, the interaction between the supposed deviant and the conformists is governed by the meanings that they impute to each other's actions and reactions. Blumer puts it this way: "Symbolic interaction involves *interpretation*, or ascertaining the meaning of the actions or remarks of the other person, and *definition*, or conveying indi-cations to another person as to how he is to act." [7] All this clearly suggests that the meaning (variously referred to as symbol, significant gesture, inter-pretation, definition, or label) that people attach to an act is much more important than the act itself. Thus labeling theorists apply this symbolic interactionist idea to deviant behavior. As Kitsuse puts it, "Forms of be-havior per se do not differentiate deviants from non-deviants; it is the responses of the conventional and conforming members of the society who identify and interpret behavior as deviant which sociologically transform persons into deviants." [8]

In short, labeling theorists interpret deviance not as a static entity whose causes are to be sought out, but rather as a dynamic process of symbolic interaction between both deviants and nondeviants. Consequently, labeling theorists do not ask as scientists do: What causes deviant behavior? Instead, they ask three major questions: Who applies the *deviant* label to whom? What consequences does the application of this label have: for the person labeled? And for the people who apply the label? (These questions can be expressed in terms of symbolic interactionism: Who interprets whose be-havior as deviant? And how does this interpretation affect the behavior of both parties involved in the matrix of interaction?)

WHO LABELS WHOM?

According to labeling theorists, people who represent the forces of law and order as well as conventional morality apply the deviant label to those who have allegedly violated that law and morality. Examples of the *labelers* are the police, judges, prison guards, psychiatrists, mental hospital attendants, and similar social control agents. On the other hand, examples of the *labeled* are criminals, juvenile delinquents, drug addicts, prostitutes, homosexuals, mental patients, mental retardates, and the like. Generally, the rich, white, or powerful are more able to label others as deviant. As Becker says, "a major element in every aspect of the drama of deviance is the imposition of definitions—of situations, acts, and people—by *those powerful enough or legitimated to be able to do so.*" [9] (Emphasis added.) On the other side of the same coin, the poor, black, or powerless are more likely to be labeled deviant. Thus a poor or black person is more likely than a rich or white person to be arrested, prosecuted, or convicted as a criminal, even if both have committed similar crimes; to be declared insane or committed to a mental institution, even if both suffer from similar psychiatric conditions; and so on.

CONSEQUENCES OF LABELING

Labeling a person deviant may have some consequences for the person so labeled and also for the labelers. Labeling theorists have a great deal to say about the consequences of labeling for the labeled but little to say about those for the labelers. Let us take a look at these two aspects of the consequences of labeling.

FOR THE LABELED According to labeling theorists, being labeled deviant produces *negative* consequences for the individual so labeled. A major consequence is that once people are labeled deviant, they tend to see themselves as deviant, which in turn leads them to continue the so-called deviant behavior. The issue here is not whether they have actually committed deviant acts, but rather that, whatever the nature of these acts, whenever they are defined as deviant by others, they also define them as deviant, then continue to engage in them, and finally become confirmed deviants. This process of becoming deviant was long ago discussed by Frank Tannenbaum, whom the proponents of labeling theory are fond of quoting. In Tannenbaum's view, a child may engage in many forms of activities—such as breaking windows, annoying people, climbing over the roof, stealing apples, playing truant— and innocently consider all these as a way of enjoying him- or herself. But the parents, teachers, and police may and often do define these activities as a type of nuisance, delinquency, or evil. So they would "dramatize the evil" of these activities by admonishing, scolding, spanking, hauling into court, or jailing the child. In thus dramatically labeling the child a delinquent, he or she will become one, and later a criminal.[10]

In discussing the process of becoming a criminal, Tannenbaum merely implied that there are two types of criminal act. One is the *first* act, which the child considers as innocent but which adults define as delinquent, and, second, the *final* behavior, which both child and adults define as delinquent. Edwin Lemert later made explicit the distinction between these two forms of behavior. He called the first one *primary deviation* and the second, *secondary deviation*.[11]

Like Tannenbaum, Lemert sees the difference between primary and secondary deviance to be more than temporal—more than the fact that one occurs earlier than the other, or that primary deviance is committed for the first time while secondary deviance is continued or repeated deviance. Thus Lemert sees primary deviance as a matter of value conflict—namely, as any behavior that the society may define as deviant but that the performer of that behavior does not so define. This behavior becomes secondary deviance, only when the person comes to agree with the society's definition of the behavior as deviant, and sees him- or herself as a deviant.

Labeling theorists are mostly interested in analyzing the process of becoming a secondary deviant—of how a person goes from primary to secondary deviation. They refer to this analysis as a sequential, career, or identity-stabilizing model of deviance. Here is an example of the model described by Lemert:

> The sequence of interaction leading to secondary deviation is roughly as follows: (1) primary deviation; (2) social penalties; (3) further primary deviation; (4) stronger penalties and rejections; (5) further deviation, perhaps with hostilities and resentment beginning to focus upon those doing the penalizing; (6) crisis reached in the tolerance quotient, expressed in formal action by the community stigmatizing of the deviant; (7) strengthening of the deviant conduct as a reaction to the stigmatizing and penalties; (8) ultimate acceptance of deviant social status and efforts at adjustment on the basis of the associated role.[12]

So by the time an individual reaches the stage of accepting the social status of being a deviant, he or she is a secondary deviant. As such, the individual repeatedly engages in deviation as a way of life. All this may be more concretely illustrated. If a man is released from prison after serving a sentence for the crime of robbery, he is likely to be stigmatized as an "ex-con." As a stigmatized ex-con, he will find it difficult or impossible to get a good job. For that reason, he will be compelled to commit another robbery and thus launch his career as a robber.

In short, once labeled a deviant, the individual tends to suffer the negative consequence of continuing to engage in deviant activities as a secondary, confirmed, or career deviant. In this process of becoming a secondary deviant, the person also suffers other related types of negative consequences, such as being ridiculed, humiliated, degraded, harassed, beaten, imprisoned, or otherwise dehumanized—treated as an object, animal, or nonperson. The deviant is, in Becker's well-known words, "more sinned against than sinning."

FOR THE LABELERS   As has been mentioned, most labeling theorists have very little to say about the consequences of labeling for the labelers. But from Erikson's works, we can see that labeling others as deviant creates positive consequences for the community, group, or individuals that apply the label. Erikson writes:

As a trespasser against the group norms, he [the deviant] represents those factors which lie outside the group's boundaries: he informs us, as it were, what evil looks like, what shapes the devil can assume. And in doing so, he shows us the difference between the inside of the group and the outside. It may well be that without this ongoing drama at the outer edges of group space, the community would have no inner sense of identity and cohesion. . . . Thus deviance . . . may itself be, in controlled quantities, an important condition for *preserving* stability.[13]

If some individuals are periodically singled out to be convicted and punished as criminals, conventional members of the community will know better the distinction between good and evil so that they will align themselves with good and against evil. This is another way of saying that the deviant does us a great service by teaching us what evil is like, presenting him- or herself as an object lesson for what we shall suffer if we do evil, and thus encouraging us to avoid punishment and do good. The deviant is similar to what the Russians are to the Chinese. The Chinese single out the Russians as bad, deviant, revisionist communists, and often sarcastically boast that they are very grateful to the deviant Russians for serving as their "negative example" so that they can more easily succeed in building a "pure," "true" communism in China.

In sum, when some individuals or groups are labeled deviant, there will then follow some positive consequences for the labelers, such as the community, the most important consequence being the preservation and strengthening of social cohesion and social order.

EVALUATION OF LABELING THEORY

Labeling theory has enjoyed tremendous popularity among sociologists. But it has also drawn considerable criticism. I shall first discuss two of the most common criticisms by other sociologists, and then present my own.

First, many sociologists criticize labeling theory for not being able to answer the etiological question about (primary) deviance—the question being: What causes deviance? Jack Gibbs, for example, points out that labeling theory cannot provide adequate answers to these three etiological questions: "(1) Why does the incidence of a particular act vary from one population to the next? (2) Why do some persons commit the act while others do not? (3) Why is the act in question considered deviant and/or criminal in some societies but not in others?" [14]

This is actually not a criticism. Though not intended to do so by its author, this criticism simply pinpoints the central characteristic of labeling theory, namely, that the theory is basically humanistic—antideterministic or voluntaristic. This is why the original proponents of the theory did not even ask, let alone answer, the largely scientific—deterministic or causal— question.

But some of the more recent advocates of labeling theory seem to have changed the originally humanistic, voluntaristic content of labeling theory into a more scientific, deterministic one. This shift is especially apparent in their empirical studies on secondary deviance. As we have noted, the original proponents, Lemert in particular, strongly emphasized the voluntaristic element in the process of a person's becoming a secondary deviant—through *active* interaction with the labelers. But many of Lemert's followers have tended to present the image of the secondary deviant as a *passive* object whose behavior is totally determined by the labelers. So this has prompted David Bordua to observe that labeling theory "assumes an essentially empty organism, or at least one with little or no autonomous capacity to determine conduct. The process of developing deviance seems all societal response and no deviant stimulus." [15] Instead of describing the *process* of interaction between the labelers and the labeled that eventually leads to the latter's secondary deviance, these revisionist followers of labeling theory tend to define, operationalize, or measure labeling as a *causal variable* of secondary deviation.[16]

Second, labeling theory has been criticized for grossly oversimplifying and distorting the real world, as well as for exaggerating the significance of labeling in the making of a deviant career.[17] Relatedly, Nanette Davis has also pointed out what she considers as its defect: "Labeling theory, characteristically oriented within a symbolic interaction framework, has suffered from a 'methodological inhibition' often associated with this social psychological approach. Conceptual impoverishment is facilitated by an absorption with general imagery, with unsystematic, elusive, and suggestive empirical presentations, rather than definitive tests of interaction framework." [18]

These criticisms are indeed well taken. But they simply point out that labeling theory is largely humanistic in character. The things that have been pointed out—oversimplification, distortion, exaggeration, elusiveness, suggestiveness, vagueness, lack of definitive tests, and the like—are normally the by-products of a humanistic work.[19] But they do not necessarily diminish the value of a humanistic theory. According to Robert Bierstedt's humanistic viewpoint, a work, argument, or theory should be judged for its *cogency* rather than truth.[20] If we accept this humanistic criterion, we may have to regard labeling theory as a very good theory. For it seems highly cogent, as its acceptance by numerous sociologists can testify. The cogency of labeling theory seems to lie primarily in the fact that its core idea—namely, that the use of a label, definition, or symbol in social interaction has significant influence on human behavior—is something that all of us can feel and witness in our daily lives.

I will now present my critique in regard to each of the three points of labeling theory that we have discussed earlier.[21]

The first point of labeling theory is that the more powerful impose the deviant label on the less powerful. The problem here is that it is logically impossible for labeling theorists to study powerful people *as deviants*. This is largely due to the way labeling theorists define deviant behavior. They define it not as the intrinsic quality of an act but as a consequence of labeling by powerful, superordinate parties, such as the ruling classes and their social control agents. A deviant, then, is whomever the powerful define as such. Now, it is obvious that the powerful will not define themselves as deviant but will so define comparatively powerless people.

All this suggests that, according to the logical implication of labeling theory, since the ruling classes and their social control agents do not define themselves as deviant, they are not and can not be deviants—only the powerless and subordinate people can be deviants. Therefore, the first problem with labeling theory is its inability to deal with powerful people as deviants. Related to this problem are the next two.

The second point of labeling theory is that being labeled deviant produces negative consequences for the person so labeled. More specifically, the deviant label tends to induce the person into further deviant involvement. This point is well taken and even well supported by research findings, but it seems largely applicable to powerless, not powerful, deviants. The experience of being labeled deviant may have a deviance-encouraging effect on the powerless, but the same experience may have the opposite, deviance-discouraging effect on the powerful. For example, as suggested by research evidence, legal punishment such as imprisonment may provoke powerless deviants such as drug addicts and public drunks to more deviance, while similar punishment discourages powerful deviants such as corporate and other white-collar criminals from further deviance.[22]

The third point of labeling theory is that labeling others as deviant creates positive consequences for the individuals, groups, or communities that apply the label. The major positive consequence is the preservation and consolidation of social order and social stability. This appears to be true, but true only because of two significant factors. (1) The labelers represent the more powerful forces of society, while the labeled are such powerless deviants as robbers, murderers, rapists, and other so-called common criminals. (2) By recruiting and punishing these powerless deviants, the more powerful, conventional members and law-enforcing agents of the society champion law and order, so that they themselves would not commit robbery, murder, rape, and other crimes commonly perpetrated by powerless people. Thus the third point of labeling theory is correct insofar as labeling some powerless people as criminals may ensure social order and thereby deter the more powerful people and their law-enforcing agents from committing those dangerous crimes.

But labeling theorists fail to mention that, behind the facade of social order that is maintained in part by labeling some powerless people as criminals, the more powerful persons, the lawmakers, and the law-enforcing agents may be tempted to commit various crimes. Of course, they would not commit those dangerous crimes commonly perpetrated by powerless individuals. They would instead commit more sophisticated, more devious, and more undetectable types.

PHENOMENOLOGICAL THEORY

Many sociologists have been influenced by labeling theory since the early 1960s. But toward the end of that decade, some sociologists took a step beyond labeling theory and developed a new one called *phenomenological theory.*[23] While labeling theory focuses on *societal* reaction to deviance and on the impact of this reaction upon deviants and their labelers, phenomenological theory concentrates on the deviants' own reaction to their behavior.

CRITIQUE OF POSITIVISM

Phenomenologists start out by launching a philosophical attack on sociologists who adopt the positivist view of deviance. As was discussed in Chapter 1, the positivists, whom we referred to as scientists, assume the objective and deterministic approach to deviance. They view the deviant person as if he or she were an object whose behavior is determined by various forces in the environment. Consequently, in order to study deviant behavior, they are primarily interested in seeking out those causal forces, thereby ignoring how the deviant person thinks and feels about his or her own deviant experience. In contrast, phenomenologists consider the deviant's subjective experience as the heart of deviant reality. At the same time, they regard positivists' supposedly objective notion of deviant behavior as unreal. Thus, according to phenomenologists, positivists' supposedly objective notion of deviance has nothing to do with deviant phenomenon as such, but merely has to do with their own preconception of a human being as an object. As phenomenologist Jack Douglas says:

[Positivists have followed the] practice of substituting phenomena of their own construction for those of common-sense, everyday life and then studying their own ad hoc phenomena as if these constituted "reality." They have done this in part to avoid the complexities and "biases" of common-sense terms, but the study of their ad hoc reality has simply created another level of complexity: since they have still wanted their studies to be ultimately related to everyday life, they have had to shift back and forth between their ad hoc phenomena and the everyday phenomena, constructing post hoc systems of translating devices and other devices.[24]

What Douglas means is that positivists do not study a phenomenon as it really is but rather study *their own conception* of what the phenomenon appears to them. For Douglas and other phenomenologists, the real phenomenon and the positivist conception of it are not the same as positivists have traditionally presumed them to be. The real phenomenon, in phenomenologists' view, is the immediate experience and consciousness of the person under study. In order to know what the real phenomenon is, one has to rely on the person's subjective experience—to discover how the person feels and what he or she thinks about his or her, say, deviant experience. Thus deviant reality is the *subjective meaning that the deviant person imputes to his or her own deviant experience.* This subjective method contrasts sharply with the positivists' objective method of applying their own scientific concepts to deviance. For example, psychiatrists may objectively (in consonance with psychiatric theory and knowledge about insanity) diagnose a man as insane, but the "insane" man himself may actually be sane or feel himself to be so. According to phenomenologists, the person's subjective experience constitutes the real phenomenon, while the psychiatrists' conceptualization as well as objective observation of his mental condition do not.

SUBJECTIVISM AS KEY TO DEVIANT REALITY

Why, then, do phenomenologists insist that only the person's subjective experience constitutes real phenomenon, while psychiatrists'—and for that matter—sociologists' and other social scientists' conceptualizations as well as objective observations do not? There may be two reasons. One is that phenomenologists and positivists simply hold different philosophical views of humanity. While positivists regard human beings as if they were passive objects whose behavior is determined by forces in their environment, phenomenologists consider people active subjects who are capable of intending and carrying out their own behavior. As Douglas argues, "it is primarily intentions at any time—our purposes at hand—that order human thought, that determine the relevance of information and ideas about the world and ourselves." [25] Another phenomenologist, Matza, especially wants us to appreciate "man's causal capacity, his activity, his tendency to reflect on himself and his setting, and his periodic struggles to transcend rather than succumb to the circumstances that allegedly shape and constrain him." [26]

Now, the issue here is voluntarism versus determinism. But since this is a philosophical issue, there is no way to prove one view true and another false. A philosophical view is an expression of one's personal values and preferences; it directs one's attention to whatever facet of reality one wants to see or appreciate, and at the same time it diverts one's attention away from other facets of reality which one does not want to see or appreciate. So the attempt to establish the empirical truth or falsehood of either philosophical view is as futile as the attempt to determine your preference for, say, coffee as true and my preference for tea as false. At any rate, we may argue over which beverage tastes better and still insist that our preferred drink is better. In like manner, phenomenologists argue about the two philosophical views and insist that their own view is more convincing. Therefore, in keeping with their philosophical view of human beings as conscious and active subjects, phenomenologists naturally insist that only a person's subjective experience constitutes real phenomenon.

Another reason for that insistence is more empirical, more amenable to factual proof. This has to do with phenomenologists' observation that the meanings of a deviant phenomenon are *fundamentally problematic*—that is, there is a great deal of uncertainty and disagreement over the meanings of deviance. These uncertainties and disagreements are very common among scientists or positivists in their attempt to "objectively" observe and explain an individual's deviant behavior. In his analysis of suicide, Douglas finds that doctors, coroners, and official statisticians—on whom positivistic sociologists rely heavily for their definition of suicide—often disagree among themselves as to whether a given death is "suicide." [27] They may generally agree that a self-caused death should be interpreted as suicide if there is "intention to die." But since the *"intention* to die" is difficult to determine after the person is dead, they may disagree whether a given suicide has actually intended to die. Those who believe there is intention to die would define the self-caused death as "suicide"; those who do not, would interpret it as "accidental death."

All this implies that since the meanings of deviance are fundamentally problematic, uncertain, and conflicting for scientists, their positivistic conception of deviance cannot possibly, positively, and accurately get at the essence of a deviant phenomenon. Yet positivists, as phenomenologists critically point out, have failed to see the problematic and uncertain nature of their scientific conception of deviance. They have instead assumed that deviance such as suicide would mean the same thing to all people and especially to scientists themselves, thereby erroneously considering their so-called objective study of deviance as valid.

The observation that the meanings of deviant phenomena are essentially problematic is, of course, not new. It is a major part of the assumption behind labeling theory.[28] But phenomenologists take a step further by elaborating on the nature of meanings. According to Douglas, there are two types of meanings: abstract meanings and situated meanings. *Abstract meanings* are "the meanings imputed to [deviant behavior such as] suicide *independent of* concrete situations in which the communicator is involved," and *situated meanings* are "the meanings imputed to concrete situations in which the communicator is involved."[29] In other words, *abstract meanings* refer to the *objective* idea that positivists apply to the behavior of a subject under study, while *situated meanings* refer to the subject's *subjective* interpretation of his or her own behavior. Positivists' objective idea about deviance is actually their *own* scientific idea, which is far removed from the context of the deviant subject's immediate experience. In this sense, then, positivists' objective idea about deviance cannot possibly get at the real meaning of the subject's deviant experience. Only the deviant person's subjective interpretation of his or her experience can penetrate into the reality of deviance. As a result, phenomenologists strongly emphasize that in order to understand the real phenomenon of deviance, we should rely heavily on the people's subjective interpretations of their own deviant experiences.

But phenomenologists' commitment to the subjective view is not total and absolute. They cannot always concur with the subject's own interpretation of his or her deviant experience. Taking the subject's interpretation at face value may distort the deviant reality, for the subject does not always know what he or she is talking about. So phenomenologists must "objectively" evaluate the subject's interpretation and experience, separating out truths from untruths. Phenomenologists, in Douglas's words, "must not simply describe and analyze everyday experience from a common-sense subjective standpoint, but must objectively observe and analyze that experience to turn it into scientific data to be used in constructing and testing scientific theories of everyday life."[30] Nevertheless, phenomenologists contend that their objective stance differs from positivists'. In order to objectively observe and analyze an experience, positivists try to make full use of their scientific preconceptions, propositions, methods, and knowledge. In contrast, phenomenologists attempt to expunge from their minds not only all these scientific notions but also their own personal ideas and beliefs—so as to become totally receptive to the true meaning of the subject's experience.[31] Phenomenologists have referred to this "objective" approach of theirs as *phenomenological reduction, phenomenological bracketing,* or *theoretic stance.*

USES OF PHENOMENOLOGY

Douglas and Matza have used their phenomenological theory to analyze a specific type of deviant experience. In his analysis of suicide, Douglas searched for the meanings that various people attach to suicide.[32] Although religious, legal, and other cultural values of our society condemn the act of suicide, most people do not hold a person morally responsible for self-killing. They blame instead the family, relatives, lover, employers, or society for having somehow caused the individual to commit suicide. Awareness of this moral meaning makes it possible for people to flirt with suicide as a means of appealing for help, or to resolutely kill themselves as a way of making others feel guilty. Throughout his analysis, Douglas clearly implies the phenomenological philosophy of voluntarism, namely, that human beings are capable of exercising free will, intention, and purpose—such as reflected in their constructing the meaning of suicide and behaving in accordance with this meaning.

In analyzing marijuana use, Matza explicitly describes how a person willfully, intentionally, and purposefully gets involved in the process of becoming deviant.[33] There are three steps in the process of becoming deviant: affinity, affiliation, and signification.

Affinity refers to the attractive force that tends to draw a person to deviant involvement. The attractive force may come from such circumstances as family life, social class background, adolescent turmoil, search for identity, or whatever scientific sociologists may think of. In a concrete way, however, all these circumstantial forces cannot irresistibly propel the individual to a deviant career. For people have the capacity to withstand and transcend them. These forces are merely a stage on which individuals can decide for themselves whether to move toward, or to back away from, the prospect of being deviant. If they decide on the former, they may seek out some concrete deviant opportunity and persons, such as marijuana and its users. At this point, the individuals consider and reconsider whether or not to *affiliate* themselves with—to get converted into—the deviant career. If they decide to do so, they will smoke marijuana regularly, but may not necessarily see themselves as deviants. They may acquire the deviant self-identity, only if they collaborate with the society's *signification* of the behavior as deviant. To signify the behavior as deviant, the society imposes a ban on it and employs its law-enforcers to apprehend the violators of that ban.

Through awareness of the ban and through the experience of being apprehended, deviants still have to decide whether or not to see themselves as the
society sees them, namely, as deviants. Even if they decide to see themselves
as deviants, they may later reverse that decision. At bottom, then, the
process of becoming deviant is fluid and unpredictable. As Matza says
toward the end of his lengthy analysis: "Even at the conclusion of the signification process—imprisonment and parole—the process of becoming deviant
remains open. Reconsideration continues; remission remains an observable
actuality." [34]

EVALUATION OF PHENOMENOLOGICAL THEORY

First of all, phenomenologists have offered a very convincing argument
about the inadequacy of positivism; namely, that positivists cannot get at the
essence of deviant reality. But phenomenologists' contention that they themselves can, is less convincing.

As we have observed, phenomenologists argue that they can penetrate
into the essence of human phenomena because they strive to keep a totally
open mind, to suspend all beliefs and judgments about the phenomena in
question, and that positivists cannot because their analysis is distorted by
their pre-existing concepts and knowledge. The issue that we could raise
is this: Can phenomenologists themselves keep a totally open mind so as to
experience, observe, and depict the essence of reality? We could argue that
they cannot, either.

It is difficult to see how one can really escape the human fate of having
one's experience of observation influenced by one's beliefs, judgments, ideas,
and words. It is difficult to see how one can really empty one's mind so
that it can absorb the essence of a phenomenon. Some Zen Buddhists have
methodically tried for their whole lifetime to empty their minds in the
hope of achieving satori, enlightenment, ultimate truth, or ultimate reality.
It is doubtful that they have ever succeeded. [35] In his pilgrimage to the East,
the American Trappist monk Thomas Merton found that a Tibetan Buddhist
priest, despite his thirty years of meditation, still could not achieve "the
ultimate emptiness." Neither could Merton himself. [36] We may as well conclude that it is impossible for any human to grasp the essence of reality.
Positivists cannot do it. Neither can phenomenologists.

What phenomenologists actually attempt to do is only to create a version
of human reality. The phenomenologist version may be unique, but it is
not necessarily superior to the positivist or other versions. Since sociologists,
whether they be phenomenologists, positivists, or others, differ as to their
value systems, ideological inclinations, observational methods, and sensitivity
to human experience, they are bound to create different, conflicting, and com-
peting versions of human reality. In this regard, we may point out the

contribution of phenomenological theory. Its view of deviant behavior as understandable through the individual's subjective experience does differ, conflict, and compete with the positivist emphasis on the objective side of deviant reality, thereby enabling us to look at the subject with a broader perspective and understanding. But let us critically examine the content of the phenomenological version of deviant reality.[37]

As they personally cherish individual autonomy, personal freedom, or free will and possibly consider themselves as enjoying such freedom, phenomenologists tend to see their deviant subjects as in possession of the same freedom in their own lives. Consequently, phenomenologists overreact to, and thereby dismiss, the deterministic perspective of human behavior—which treats human beings as if they were objects rather than subjects. They do so in an abstract philosophical way, without perceiving the latent *political* meanings of the determinists' empirical contributions.

The determinists have accumulated a massive amount of facts that we simply cannot pretend don't exist. If we look at these facts, we may discover that they by and large support an implicit scientific-sociological law. The implicit law is that relatively powerless people live their lives as oppressed, controlled, or manipulated objects rather than as free subjects. Thus the determinists' assumption about human beings as being uninfluenced by their free will is indeed correct. More precisely, it is correct in a tautological sense. The determinists first assume people to be uninfluenced by free will, then seek out for their study powerless people whose free will has been much suppressed or underdeveloped, and finally discover these people's behavior as supporting the initial deterministic assumption that people are, after all, uninfluenced by free will.

On the other hand, phenomenologists go to the opposite extreme. They like to emphasize the importance of free will, but only in the abstract sense of free will being found in all human beings. They then impose this abstract notion of free will upon the day-to-day world of powerless people. In doing so, phenomenologists fail to recognize that powerless people have very little free will; in the concrete world their free will is suppressed by the powerful and they have a substantially smaller range of available choices in comparison to the powerful. Phenomenologists in effect mistake the *potentiality* for the *actuality* of exercising free will, not realizing that powerless people may have the potentiality but do not experience the actuality. As a result, phenomenologists have created a picture of powerless deviants as highly sophisticated, free-thinking, and choice-making philosophers, very much like phenomenologists themselves. An example of this can be found in Matza's "rendition" of the supposedly true nature of deviance.

Preoccupied with what he calls "the philosophical inner life" of his subject, Matza has elevated the deviant to the status of a profound philosopher. These philosopher-deviants are constantly engrossed in analyzing the intricate meanings of all that happens or threatens to happen to them. We may wonder how his deviants, being bogged down with such heavy philosophizing, could ever find time for, or be interested at all in, deviant *action*.

CONFLICT THEORY

More than thirty years ago, a number of sociologists began to point out the pluralistic, heterogeneous, and conflictive nature of modern society.[38] In a traditional or simple society, people share the same cultural values and therefore carry on a harmonious relationship with one another. Such value consensus and social harmony are absent in modern industrial societies, particularly in the United States. Instead, there is a great deal of social and cultural conflict. *Social conflict* has to do with the incompatible interests, needs, and desires of such diverse groups as business companies versus labor unions, conservative versus liberal political groups, and so on.[39] *Cultural conflict* has to do with the discrepant norms and values concerning the definition of right and wrong—what is considered right in one subculture is considered wrong in another. For example, in the 1930s a Sicilian father in New Jersey, after killing his daughter's sixteen-year-old seducer, felt proud of having defended his family honor in a traditional way, and he was very surprised when he was arrested.[40] Either social or cultural conflict brings about criminal behavior. Therefore, conflict as well as its resulting criminality is an inherent, normal, and integral part of modern society. Those sociologists who held this view thirty years ago can be regarded as conflict theorists.

But conflict theorists failed to systematically develop the notion of conflict as the source of criminal definition rather than behavior. They were still very much tied to the traditional concern with the scientific explanation of criminal behavior. Occasionally, they did suggest the definitional rather than behavioral aspect of criminality. One of them, for example, said: "Social problems are social conditions of which some of the causes are felt to be human and moral. Value judgments define these conditions as social problems. Value judgments are the formal causes of social problems, just as the law is the formal cause of crime." [41] But this and other earlier conflict theorists did not try to follow through with that kind of idea. Only very recently have a group of sociologists emerged to systematically explore criminality as strictly a matter of definition. These sociologists are the new conflict theorists; three of them will be discussed in the following.

TURK: ELEMENTS OF CRIMINALIZATION

Austin Turk wants us to understand criminality, not by searching for the causes of criminal behavior, but rather by finding out how some people come to acquire a criminal status.[42] For a person to acquire a criminal status does not depend on what he or she is or does; rather, it depends on the legal authority's definition of the person as a criminal. To be defined as a criminal is to be criminalized. Turks attempts to show how people may come to be criminalized. Thus he calls his theory a *theory of criminalization.*

According to Turk's theory, the greater the cultural difference between authorities and subjects, the greater the probability of their conflict. The authorities are the lawmakers and law-enforcers, while the subjects are the ordinary people who are supposed to be controlled by the law. If these two parties cannot agree on the content of a law or on what constitutes a criminal act, they are likely to argue and fight over their disagreement. But such disagreement or cultural difference does not always result in an argument, fight, confrontation, or conflict between the two parties. So Turk describes some conditions under which the cultural difference is likely to result in conflict.

If both parties actually do as they say, their disagreement will result in conflict. On the other hand, if there is a discrepancy between words and action for both parties, then their disagreement will not result in conflict. For example, if a police officer has a strong prejudice against marijuana smoking and is determined to enforce the law against it, and if a student believes there is nothing wrong with smoking marijuana and insists on his right to smoke it, then we have a situation where the two individuals are very likely to come into conflict. But if neither of them puts his belief into practice, conflict between them is very unlikely. Now, since the authorities have the power to criminalize the subjects rather than the other way around, criminalization of the subjects is likely to occur in the event of conflict between the two parties. So, if there is a conflict between the police officer and the student over marijuana smoking, the former is likely to arrest the latter.

Yet conflict does not always result in criminalization. The probability of criminalization depends upon the following conditions: (1) If authorities consider a law highly significant and important, they are likely to assign criminal status to the subjects who violate that law. (2) If law enforcers find the subjects' legally prohibited behavior to be greatly offensive, the subjects are likely to be treated as criminals. (3) The greater the power difference in favor of the authorities, the greater the probability of their criminalizing the opposing subjects. And (4) the more realistic the moves of a conflict, be it the authorities or the subjects, the more likely the party is to be successful. The last point should be explained.

The realistic moves on the part of authorities involve avoiding the use of brutality, showing respect for normal legal procedures, guarding against the demonstration of their hostility for the opposition, and doing whatever they can to prevent the opposition from increasing its size and power. Such realistic moves may increase the authorities' chances of successfully eliminating the opposition's resistance. On the other side, the opposition may increase its chances of successfully ending the authorities' enforcement efforts if it engages in these realistic moves: concealing its offensive behavior, decreasing the offensiveness of whatever behavior cannot be concealed, refraining from any actions that may increase consensus among various law enforcers, and doing whatever is possible to ensure that the power difference in favor of the law enforcers does not increase.

Basically, Turk deals with the immediate context of the conflict between legal authorities and their subjects. His conflict theory conveys the image of a dogfight, involving the legal authorities as the topdog and their subjects as the underdog. The next conflict theorist is more concerned with the *broad* context of the conflict; he provides a commentary on the historical and organizational background of the dogfight.

CHAMBLISS: REALITY OF LAW

William Chambliss reminds us that there are many legal scholars and social scientists who are not even aware of the dogfight.[43] These people hold the value-consensus view of society; they assume that the law is based on the widespread consensus of the citizenry, represents the public interest, treats all citizens as equal, or serves the best interests of the society. Such a legal perspective can be supported by the study of the *law in the books*, because the law in the books as represented by the American Constitution, the common law, and the statutes does proclaim equal treatment for all. But this simply means that legal authorities ought to be fair and just. Whether they are fair and just is another matter. Such a matter can be determined by studying the *law in action*, which entails observing how legal authorities actually discharge their duty. As a result of studying the law in action, Chambliss concludes that legal authorities are actually unfair and unjust, favoring the rich and powerful over the poor and weak. Chambliss and his associate Robert Seidman sum it up this way:

We have shown by example and study that complex, stratified societies are inevitably pluralistic. As such, the law will always represent the interests of one group as against the interests of another. . . . In addition to shattering the myth that the law rests on value-consensus, the empirical study of the law in action also makes it abundantly clear that the State is hardly a value-neutral arena in which conflicts are worked

out for the "good of everyone." Rather, these studies have shown that
the upshot of the conflicting interests is such that law comes to
represent the entrenched power groups.[44]

There is, then, a significant discrepancy between the law in the books and
the law in action or between the ideal of law and the reality of law. The
discrepancy lies in the legal authorities' unfair and unjust handling of their
subjects, which Turk has also described in his conflict theory. Many people
may wrongly blame the discrepancy on the evil character of lawmaking and
law-enforcing individuals. Chambliss rejects such individualistic interpretation. He shows how those individuals are heavily influenced by the historical
and organizational background of the law.

Modern Anglo-American law stems from the legal system of early
England. The English legal system was established in the eleventh century.
Its central feature is that personal wrongs are considered as transgressions
against the state and that only the state has the right to punish the transgres-
sors. This legal principle replaced the earlier nonlegal norm that personal
wrongs, being a highly personal matter, should be settled through reconciliation by the private parties concerned. To carry out the new legal principle,
the government used force and coercion as the means for handling wrongs
and disputes; created two separate bodies, the lawmakers (legislature) and
law-enforcers (judiciary); appointed judges to settle disputes between the
state and individual citizens or between individual citizens themselves; and
relied on peers (juries) for ultimately deciding disputes.

Such is the general structure of the legal system in early England and it
still prevails in contemporary American society. But the specific content
of the laws as well as the specific manner of enforcing them has often
changed to reflect the interests of the ruling classes. For example, the
vagrancy laws in fourteenth-century feudal England reflected the powerful
landowners' need for cheap labor, because the law required poor able-bodied
men to work at low wages, made it unlawful for them to move from one
place to another to avoid the low-paying jobs or to seek higher wages, and
prohibited giving alms to able-bodied beggars. Then, in the sixteenth century, the vagrancy laws were changed to protect the interests of prosperous
merchants who had to transport their goods from one town to another, as
the new vagrancy laws were applied to the rogues, vagbonds, and highway-
men who often preyed upon the traveling merchants. Today in both
England and the United States, the vagrancy laws are meant to control the
down-and-outers, the undesirable, the criminal, and the nuisances, thereby
reflecting the desire of the influential middle and upper classes to make their
streets safe and peaceful. Historically, then, criminal law has in effect, if
not in intent, served the interests of the rich and powerful rather than the

interests of the poor and powerless. Under this historical influence, the legislators of today understandably tend to make laws that favor the rich and powerful.

Law enforcers such as the police, the prosecutors, and the judges also tend to become the tools of power and privilege. This tendency should scarcely be attributed to individual law enforcers. Rather, it is mostly the consequence of *organizational imperative*. It is in the nature of any organization that its members are compelled to perform tasks that will maximize rewards and minimize trouble for the organization. The reward to be sought by the law-enforcing agency is public support; the trouble to be avoided is the withdrawal of such support or worse. Thus it is rewarding for the law-enforcing officials to arrest, prosecute, and convict such powerless skid-row drunkards, vagrants, gamblers, prostitutes, rapists, thiefs, and robbers. But it will likely cause trouble for their agency if the law enforcers make the same effort to process the respectable middle- and upper-class members for their white-collar offenses. In view of such organizational imperative, the law-enforcing officials are very likely to make the law serve the interests of the rich and powerful.

QUINNEY: SOCIAL REALITY OF CRIME

Unlike Chambliss, Richard Quinney blames the unjust law directly on the capitalist system. He says, "Criminal law is used by the state and the ruling class to secure the survival of the capitalist system, and, as capitalist society is further threatened by its own contradictions, criminal law will be increasingly used in the attempt to maintain domestic order." [45]

Such a critical view of capitalism, however, is based on Quinney's conflict theory of criminality. Quinney calls his theory "the social reality of crime." [46] By this term he means that there are four interrelated factors that produce high crime rates but also help to consolidate the established legal order as well as the dominant class. First, the dominant class *defines* as criminal those behaviors that threaten its interests. Secondly, it *applies* these criminal definitions or laws to ensure the protection of its interests. Thirdly, members of the subordinate class are compelled by their unfavorable life conditions to engage in those *actions* that have been defined as criminal. And fourthly, the dominant class uses those criminal actions as the basis for constructing and diffusing the *ideology* of crime that, in effect, works against the subordinate class because the latter is thought to contain the dangerous criminal elements.

More recently, Quinney has tried to go beyond the mere description of his conflict theory. He has tried to turn his theory into a call for political action. As his conflict theory implies, there is something terribly wrong with existing society—not only in this country, but also in what Quinney calls "state-socialist countries" such as the Soviet Union and some East European nations. What is wrong is that members of the powerful class inevitably criminalize those of the powerless so as to exploit, oppress, and subjugate them, thereby preserving, consolidating, and perpetuating the status quo of social inequality. Thus Quinney calls for our development of a revolutionary consciousness that should eventually lead to the creation of a democratic-socialist society—so that it will end the oppression of the powerless by the powerful.[47]

Other conflict theorists, who call themselves the *new criminologists*, have tried to go in the same direction. For example, Ian Taylor, Paul Walton, and Jock Young declare:

For us, as for Marx and for other new criminologists, *deviance* is normal—in the sense that men are now consciously involved (in the prisons that are contemporary society and in the real prisons) in asserting their human diversity. The task is not merely to "penetrate" these problems, not merely to question the stereotypes, or to act as carriers of "alternative phenomenological realities." The task is to create a society in which the facts of human diversity, whether personal, organic, or social, are not subject to the power to criminalize.[48]

EVALUATION OF CONFLICT THEORY

A number of sociologists have criticized conflict theory. First of all, their most common criticism is the same as that which has been directed against labeling theory. Thus they insist that conflict theory is inadequate because it fails to explain deviant behavior—it does not tell us the *causes* of deviant behavior. As Gibbons and Jones argue, "the principal inadequacy of conflict theories on deviance and criminality lies in the area of causal or etiological hypotheses.. . . In short, complete, detailed conflict theories regarding the social origins of deviant conduct have not yet been developed." [49] As we have mentioned, this is not really a criticism. It merely points out, though unintentionally, that conflict theory is basically humanistic. For the reasons discussed in Chapter 1, conflict theorists as humanists do, indeed, reject the search for the causes of deviant behavior.

Second, a more pertinent criticism suggests that, contrary to what its proponents seem to imply, conflict theory cannot apply to *all* kinds of deviant behavior. As Ronald Akers observes, "the conflict approach seems more appropriate to the analysis of the behavior of groups and individuals involved in *ideological and political confrontations*. It is less appropriate to the analysis of the behavior of those involved in many types of common-law crimes, usual deviations, and vices." [50]   In this quote, Akers means that conflict theory is correct if it is taken to suggest that political crimes emerge from group conflict, but that the theory is not correct if it is taken to mean that such nonpolitical, ordinary crimes as murder, theft, burglary, rape, and arson result from group conflict. At first glance, this criticism appears perfectly valid. It certainly was many years ago, but today it seems less valid. For today an increasing number of "common criminals" tend to see their crimes as essentially political in nature. Nonetheless, Akers is correct in observing that conflict theory is not applicable to trivial deviations and vices —because they are not serious enough for the powerful to get politically excited and to pass laws against them.

Third, conflict theory seems to hold the unconvincing assumption that in the utopian, socialist society, such nasty human acts as killing, robbing, raping, and otherwise hurting one another will disappear after the power to criminalize them is abolished. We may argue that the abolition of the power to criminalize does not necessarily lead to the abolition of the human capacity to hurt one another. It may be more realistic to assume that if full social equality were achieved, the serious forms of human nastiness would greatly decrease rather than completely disappear. With the abolition of poverty in a fully egalitarian society, there would not be any poor people to produce, as they do now, a comparatively large volume of serious crimes and thus this volume would greatly decrease. This is because the formerly poor people in the new, fully egalitarian society would have as small a tendency to commit those serious crimes as the rich in the present, inegalitarian society do.

Fourth, from the standpoint of understanding the making and enforcing of norms, rules, or laws, conflict theory does offer us a solid contribution. As Akers says, "This perspective leads us to ask and suggests why certain values and norms become dominant and others do not. For this reason the conflict approach is *potent as an explanation of the formation and enforcement of the norms themselves*." [51]

SUMMARY

In this chapter we have discussed three major humanistic theories of deviance. As humanistic interpretations, they deal with the meanings of deviance and with the impact of these meanings on people's behavior.

The first was labeling theory. According to labeling theory, super-ordinate parties apply the deviant label to subordinate parties; being labeled deviant produces unfavorable consequences for the individual so labeled; and labeling others as deviant generates favorable consequences for the individuals, groups, or communities that do the labeling. But labeling theory has been criticized by some sociologists for being unable to tell us the causes of deviant behavior and for oversimplifying and exaggerating the influence of labeling on the development of a deviant career. In addition, I have criticized it for neglecting powerful deviants.

The second one, phenomenological theory, claims that positivistic sociologists cannot capture the essence of deviant phenomenon, while phenomenological sociologists can cut into the heart of deviant experience with the scalpel of subjective interpretation and phenomenological reduction. Phenomenologists' argument that positivists cannot get at the essence of deviant reality is highly persuasive. But their claim that they themselves can is excessive and unjustifiable. What they themselves can get at is only their own version of deviant reality, not the essence of that reality itself. In addition, although they offer us a much needed subjective version of deviant behavior, phenomenologists have so far applied their concept of free will to largely powerless deviants, not to the more powerful.

Conflict theory, the third one discussed, systematically describes how the powerful segment of society imposes the criminal definition upon the powerless. This theory has been criticized for its failure to explain deviant behavior. It has been considered highly applicable to political crimes, but less so to ordinary deviations and vices. And it seems to hold the unconvincing assumption that the abolition of the power to criminalize would end all crimes—including killing, robbing, and raping. Yet the theory is very useful for understanding how the powerful segment of society makes rules and carries them out.

SUGGESTED READINGS

Becker, Howard S. *Outsiders: Studies in the Sociology of Deviance.* New York: Free Press, 1963.

Chambliss, William J. *Crime and the Legal Process.* New York: McGraw-Hill, 1969.

Douglas, Jack D., ed. *Deviance and Respectability.* New York: Basic Books, 1970.

Erikson, Kai T. *Wayward Puritans: A Study in the Sociology of Deviance.* New York: Wiley, 1966.

Kitsuse, John I. "Societal Reaction to Deviant Behavior: Problems of Theory and Method." *Social Problems* 9 (Winter 1962): 247–256.

Krisberg, Barry. *Crime and Privilege: Toward a New Criminology.* Englewood Cliffs, N.J.: Prentice-Hall, 1975.

Lemert, Edwin M. *Human Deviance, Social Problems, and Social Control.* 2nd ed. Englewood Cliffs, N.J.: Prentice-Hall, 1972.

Matza, David. *Becoming Deviant.* Englewood Cliffs, N.J.: Prentice-Hall, 1969.

Quinney, Richard. *The Social Reality of Crime.* Boston: Little, Brown, 1970.

Schur, Edwin M. *Labeling Deviant Behavior: Its Sociological Implications.* New York: Harper & Row, 1971.

Thio, Alex. "The Phenomenological Perspective of Deviance: Another Case of Class Bias." *The American Sociologist* 9 (August 1974): 146–149.

Turk, Austin T. *Criminality and Legal Order.* Chicago: Rand McNally, 1969.

4 TOWARD AN INTEGRATED THEORY OF DEVIANCE

It is possible to integrate the scientific and humanistic theories into an overall, holistic theory. In order to do so, we must seek out the key concepts of these conflicting theories and then reconcile and combine them into a new theory. But what can possibly be the key concepts? Different sociologists offer different answers. I would like to offer my own for your critical consideration.

On the one side, from Chapters 1 and 2, we can perceive the underlying scientific concept of *social constraint*. At the extreme, analysis in terms of social constraint tends to picture human beings as objects at the mercy of such forces as other people, events, and circumstances. Such a picture seems to accurately capture those individuals who in their lives often experience being treated by others as objects or being pushed by various social circumstances into behaving in certain ways. Taking everything into account, we may say that those people are likely to be relatively *powerless* in society. On the other side, from Chapters 1 and 3, we can identify the humanistic concept of *individual freedom*. This humanistic concept portrays human beings as very much in command of their selves, wills, and actions, as well as blessed with the ability to influence people, events, and circumstances. Such a portrait seems accurate in representing those people who usually enjoy the ability to act as subjects rather than react as objects or to freely choose certain actions rather than be compelled to do them. Taking everything into account, we may say that these people are more likely to be relatively *powerful* in society.

In considering these two concepts, we can reconcile them because they suggest different degrees of the same thing, namely, power—the scientific concept suggesting lesser power and the humanistic, greater power. Thus we can integrate these two theories by showing how the difference in the amount of power relates to deviant behavior. I shall call the result of this integration *power theory*.

POWER AS DIFFERENTIA OF DEVIANCE

It is a truism that social inequality exists in all societies all over the world. There may be less social inequality in some societies than in others, but it is never completely absent in any society. Various people may define social inequality by different criteria, but it seems best to define it by power. Political scientist Andrew Hacker says:

We know America has classes, and that they are more than temporary way stations. No matter how we divide up Americans according to culture, career, even income, *power is at the heart of the question*. Some people have more freedom, more independence, than others. Some are buffeted about from birth to death, never in a position to bend events or answer back to authority. Class may confer power over others; in personal life it affects how you can make the world work on your behalf.[1] [Emphasis added.]

But the concept of social inequality need not be applied to the inequality between upper and lower classes alone. It can be applied as well to the inequality between upper and middle classes or between middle and lower classes. It can even be applied to the inequality between whites and blacks, between men and women, between parents and children, between judges and defendants, between psychiatrists and patients, and so on. This is because any two groups can be considered unequal insofar as one is, on the whole, more powerful than the other. For the sake of simplicity and convenience, I shall often refer to one group as *the powerful* and the other as *the powerless*. At the same time, I shall mainly discuss the difference in deviance between the upper and the lower classes merely as an illustration of how power theory works. So the same discussion may be generalized, in one degree or another, to almost any other two unequal groups such as those mentioned above.

Now, power inequality does not only affect the quality of a person's life in general, as the above quote has implied. It also affects the quality of deviant activities likely to be engaged in by that person. We may propose that *the more power people have, the more likely they will engage in lower-consensus deviance*—the "less serious," more profitable, or more sophisticated type of deviance—*with lower probability of being labeled deviant.* This proposition can be easily supported by observation of the crime problem in any unequal society. Even in our society where social inequality may not be as great as in many other countries, we can easily observe that the rich and powerful tend to commit more relatively profitable crimes (such as fraudulent advertising and commercial bribery) with impunity, while the poor and powerless are more likely to get involved in the less profitable type of crimes (such as murder and mugging) with higher risk of legal retribution.

We have, in effect, proposed that the amount of power differentiates people into two contrary groups on the basis of the *type* of deviance each is likely to commit.

POWER AS CAUSE OF DEVIANCE

In view of the first proposition presented above, we may state the second proposition that *it is more likely that the powerful will engage in lower-consensus deviance than the powerless will commit higher-consensus deviance.* For example, it is more likely that a rich man will commit tax evasion than a poor man will perpetrate armed robbery. The implication is that, if the type of deviance is held constant by treating lower-consensus deviance (say, tax evasion) and higher-consensus deviance (say, armed robbery) as though both were the same deviance, the powerful are more prone to deviance than are the powerless. In other words, the proneness of the powerful to lower-consensus deviance is greater than the proneness of the powerless to higher-consensus deviance.

There are at least three important factors that can explain why the powerful are more prone to deviance. These factors are greater deviant opportunity, greater subjective deprivation, and lesser social control.

GREATER OPPORTUNITY FOR DEVIANCE

It seems like a paradox of human life that the more legitimate opportunities there are for an individual to attain success, the more deviant opportunities there are to do so. This is primarily because, as Albert Cohen has observed, "there are *not* some things that are legitimate opportunities and *other* things that are illegitimate opportunities, but that the *same* things are typically, and perhaps always, both." [2] Thus, since they have more legitimate opportunities than do the powerless, the powerful have also more (illegitimate) opportunities for deviant activities.

It is obvious, for example, that the powerful have far greater opportunities for getting a good education, a well-paying job, social influence and prestige, and other amenities of life. But at the same time, if they want to commit some deviant acts, they will enjoy far more and better (illegitimate) opportunities to do so than will the powerless. Suppose a rich banker and a poor laborer want to illegitimately acquire a large sum of money. The former has access to more and better opportunities than does the latter. The rich banker can easily defraud the Internal Revenue Service as well as his many customers and still have an excellent chance of getting away with it. In contrast, the poor laborer would find his illegitimate opportunity limited to crudely robbing the banker; such illegitimate opportunity being further limited by his excellent chance of getting arrested, convicted, or imprisoned.

Therefore, given their greater deviant opportunity, the powerful can be said to be more likely to engage in deviant activities. But the temptation to take advantage of the deviant opportunity may not be strong enough to get the powerful individuals involved in deviant activities. Another factor may be needed to motivate them into deviant involvement, and this motivating factor may come from their experience of greater subjective deprivation.

GREATER SUBJECTIVE DEPRIVATION

Subjective deprivation can be defined as the feeling of not being able to get what one wants. It is a feeling of the discrepancy between what one wants and what one actually has. It has been referred to by Emile Durkheim as anomie, and by Robert Merton as the gap between the goal and the means or the disjunction between aspiration and opportunity.[3]

Once again, it seems like a paradox of human life that subjective deprivation stems largely from too many opportunities for success. The reason is that too many opportunities tend to raise one's aspirations so high that they cannot be easily realized. If aspirations cannot be easily realized, one is motivated to resort to some illegitimate means of actualizing the aspirations. This, then, is tantamount to the perpetration of deviant acts.[4]

People who enjoy too many opportunities and consequently suffer great subjective deprivation are more likely to be the powerful members of society. This is essentially because, when compared with the powerless, the powerful are more heavily influenced by the pervasive ideology of success to entertain very high success goals. These success goals, not being easily attainable, tend more to generate frustration in powerful persons. As Merton writes: "An observer of a community in which annual salaries in six figures are not uncommon, reports the anguished words of one victim of the American Dream: 'In this town, I'm snubbed socially because I only get a thousand a week. That hurts.' " [5] Therefore, though far from being *objectively* deprived as are the powerless, the powerful are *subjectively* deprived. On the other hand, objective deprivation tends to suppress the aspirations of the powerless so that they are relatively free from subjective deprivation. All this has been explained by Emile Durkheim many years ago:

> Poverty protects against . . . [subjective deprivation] because it is a restraint in itself. No matter how one acts, desires have to depend upon resources to some extent; actual possessions are partly the criterion of those aspired to. So the less one has the less he is tempted to extend the range of his needs indefinitely. Lack of power, compelling moderation, accustoms men to it. . . . Wealth, on the other hand, by the power it bestows, deceives us into believing that we depend on ourselves only. Reducing the resistance we encounter from objects, it suggests the possibility of unlimited success against them. The less limited one feels, the more intolerable all limitation appears. [6]

In short, the more power one has, the higher one's aspirations are, and the greater one's subjective deprivation is. As has been suggested in Chapter 2, subjective deprivation is positively related to deviant behavior. Now, since the powerful are more likely than the powerless to experience subjective deprivation, the former can be said to be more motivated to deviant action. But one more factor may be needed to make deviant motivation result in an actual deviant act. That factor is the relative lack of social control imposed on the powerful, to which we shall turn next.

LESSER SOCIAL CONTROL

Given both their access to greater deviant opportunity and their stronger motivation toward deviance by their greater subjective deprivation, the powerful are indeed more prone to deviant action than are the powerless. Logically, then, the society should exercise stronger control over the powerful. But, once again, it seems like a paradox that the society does just the opposite—exercising lesser control over the powerful. Consequently the powerful are even more inclined to engage in deviant activities.

The seeming paradox can be explained by the condition of social inequality. By virtue of their condition, the powerful have more influence in the making of laws and in their enforcement. It is no wonder that the laws against higher-status criminals are relatively lenient and seldom enforced, but the laws against lower-status criminals are harsher and more often enforced. For example, no corporate criminal has ever been sentenced to death for manufacturing untested drugs that "cleanly" kill many people, but there have been many lower-class criminals sentenced to death for "messily" killing only one person.

Moreover, the condition of social inequality has the tendency to perpetuate itself, so that the powerful continue to face lesser social control. If the society decided to exercise more control over the powerful, it would threaten the very structure of inequality. Suppose the society imposed as harsh a punishment (say, the death sentence) on powerful deviants for their "unserious" crimes (such as illegal banking practices) as on powerless deviants for their "serious" crimes (such as bank robberies). This would kill the incentive of many higher-status persons to seek ingenious, original, creative, or bold means for achieving greater success and power. If those higher-status persons were too scared to try anything ingenious in their success-seeking activities, the society would stop being dynamic, creative, prosperous—and, most importantly, inequalitarian—as it is now. Thus, the existing condition of social inequality requires that lesser social control be exercised over the powerful. In this way the powerful are encouraged to resort to some deviant means for aggrandizing their fortune and power. In view of this, we need not be surprised, for example, to be told the following by economist Alexander Cockburn: "There is a market for stories about people violently robbing banks, less of one for stories about banks peacefully robbing people. Yet contemplation of banking practices would lead one to suppose the latter to be the more thriving and popular of the two industries." [7]

On the other hand, the same society apparently cannot afford to encourage the powerless as it does the powerful to engage in deviant activities. This is because their criminal acts are much more "dangerous," as they may seriously threaten rather than support the existing structure of inequality. Therefore, in order to ensure the security of the life and property of the powerful, the society carries out relatively strong preventive and punitive measures against powerless deviants by containing them either in prisons or in prisonlike ghettos and slums. In this way the powerless deviants can more easily victimize one another or their nondeviant fellows—and leave the powerful ones alone—as we shall see later. At the same time, the huge majority of the powerless who are *not* deviants may feel too scared by the law to commit crimes. All this may explain the relatively small volume of lower-class crime. As observed by Andrew Hacker, "My own considered—and by no means capricious—view is that we ought to count ourselves fortunate that so small a part of our population has taken to thievery. That so many [poor] Americans remain honest, while being treated so shabbily, has never ceased to amaze me." [8]

To sum up the entire discussion on power as the cause of deviance: due to the condition of social inequality, the powerful are more likely to enjoy

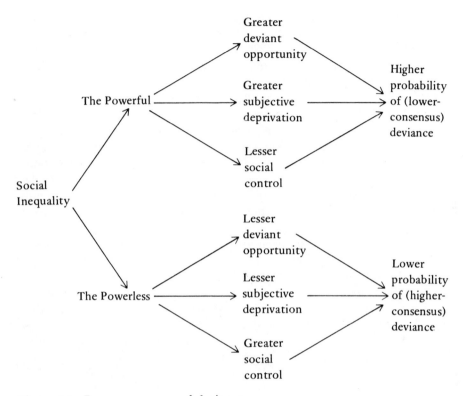

Figure 4.1   Power as a cause of deviance.

greater deviant opportunity, experience greater subjective deprivation, and encounter lesser social control, as compared with the powerless. In consequence, the powerful are more likely to engage in deviant activities. (See Figure 4. 1.)

SYMBIOSIS BETWEEN POWERFUL AND POWERLESS DEVIANCE

It appears that powerful and powerless people with their opposing types of deviance tend to reinforce each other—so as to help preserve the status quo of social inequality in both deviant and legitimate opportunities. This symbiotic relationship between deviance by the powerful and deviance by the powerless can be expressed in the form of the third proposition of power theory: *Deviance by the powerful induces deviance by the powerless that, in turn, contributes to deviance by the powerful.*

Powerful people's deviance contributes to powerless people's in at least three ways. First, the powerful exert a *direct impact* upon the powerless in leading the latter to criminal activities. For example, a nation's war-making leaders may directly coerce the powerless citizens to participate in killing; leaders of the business, political, and law-enforcement communities may directly produce crimes and vices in the ghettos and slums by running an organized crime syndicate;[9] and American farm entrepreneurs in the Southwest may become "antilaw entrepreneurs" by actively hiring "wetbacks" (illegal immigrants from Mexico), thereby maintaining an abundant supply of cheap labor as well as turning the wetbacks into a population of powerless "criminals." [10]

Second, the powerful contribute to deviance by the powerless through the *trickle effect* of deviance from powerful to powerless. For example, when a nation's leaders so indiscreetly commit a crime that it is widely publicized, such as in the case of the Watergate conspirators, ordinary citizens may also be encouraged to engage in criminality. This trickle effect is well described by journalist Sydney Harris:

It is immorality and illegality at the top levels of society that filter down their dubious ethic and set the tone for attitude and action in the lower strata of society. It has always been this way, and always will be. What the king does—whoever the king may be—gives the commoners their cue for conduct, both privately and publicly. When elected officials are flagrantly crooked, when police are venal or responsive to political pressures, when large corporations grossly violate laws against conspiracy or price-fixing, then the general public turns sour and cynical and opportunistic and amoral.[11]

A third way in which the powerful's deviance induces the powerless to commit deviance is indirect, subtle, and hidden. Many powerful people discreetly and surreptitiously carry on deviant activities in order to serve their huge self-interest, to realize their personal ambition, or to achieve great success for themselves. Numerous people with power and influence in government and business, for example, routinely commit such covert deviant acts as spying, eavesdropping, misrepresenting, conspiring to obstruct justice, conniving against enemies, or otherwise ingeniously getting around the law, all for the purpose of serving their engrossing self-interest. In so doing, they help to *reinforce the inequality* of society, with its resulting unfavorable social conditions that tend to provoke powerless individuals into criminality.

We have just seen how the powerful's deviance helps bring about the deviance of the powerless. Let us now see how the latter, in turn, influences the former.

The first way is that the deviant activities of the powerless help to deflect, weaken, or nullify the *social control* over the powerful, thereby freeing the powerful to engage in their own deviant pursuits. Generally, it will cost much more time and effort for social control agents such as the police, prosecuting attorneys, and judges to catch a powerful deviant than it will a powerless one. It will also threaten their job security if they are equally zealous in catching and punishing both the powerful and the powerless ones. As a result, social control agents are busy netting the smaller fish in the safe shallow waters and avoiding the bigger fish in the dangerous open sea. This is why social control agents end up hauling into courts, jails, and prisons a huge number of mostly powerless deviants who have committed public drunkenness, vagrancy, disorderly conduct, robbery, rape, and murder. While doing all this, social control agents tend to leave the more powerful deviants alone with their income tax evasion, private drunkenness, corporate price-fixing, fraudulent advertising, and governmental corruption. The message of all of this can hardly be missed by the more powerful members of society. Therefore, by preoccupying the attention of social control agents, deviant activities by the powerless help to deflect, weaken, or nullify the social control over the powerful and thereby encourage the powerful to pursue their deviant interests.

Second, the deviant activities of the powerless, by providing a contrast effect that sets off the powerful as morally superior in their own eyes, tend to weaken the powerful's *self-control* over their own deviant propensities, thus leading them into deviant pursuits. Powerless persons' deviant acts, such as homicide and armed robbery, enable powerful individuals to set up a standard for judging who is moral and who is immoral. Since they are unlikely to commit these serious deviant acts, powerful members of society tend to consider themselves as highly moral. This positive self-image inevitably prevents these powerful individuals from applying to themselves the *other* moral standard that they are *more likely* to violate—namely, the moral standard against the "less serious" deviant acts, such as violations of the antipollution law. In fact, powerful persons do not take this moral standard as seriously as they do the one that the powerless are more likely to violate. For example, the powerful would not approve of sentencing a wealthy violator of antipollution law to life imprisonment or death, but would readily approve of such punishment for a poor violator of anti-homicide law. Censequently, while they would exert a lot of control on the powerless to prevent them from committing "serious" crimes, the powerful would not exert as much control on themselves to prevent their

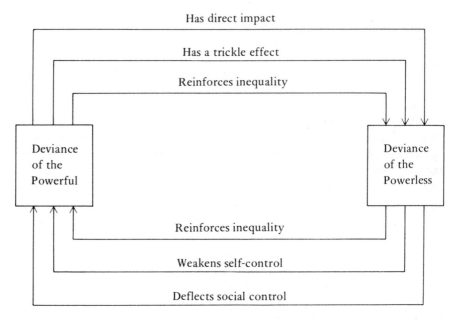

Figure 4.2 Symbiosis between the deviance of the powerful and the deviance of the powerless.

own commission of "unserious" deviance. Lacking this self-control, powerful individuals are very apt to commit their brand of deviant acts.

Third, deviant activities on the part of the powerless help to maintain the practice of *inequality* in the larger society as well as in the criminal justice system, thus encouraging the powerful to commit their own deviant acts with relative impunity.

Powerless criminals typically kill, assault, and rob people in their own neighborhood. As the President's Commission on Law Enforcement states:

One of the most fully documented facts about crime is that the common serious crimes that worry people most—murder, forcible rape, robbery, aggravated assault, and burglary—happen most often in the slums of large cities. Study after study in city after city in all regions of the country have traced the variations in the rates for these crimes. The results, with monotonous regularity, show that the offenses, the victims, and the offenders are found most frequently in the poorest, and most deteriorated and socially disorganized areas of cities.[12]

Two things follow from this. One is that the poor people's life becomes even more oppressive. Another is that the rich, because their own life and property are far from being seriously threatened, can complacently keep on using police action against the poor deviants, rather than applying the far more effective but costly method of abolishing their oppressive, criminogenic life condition. The continuation of this oppressive life condition for the powerless helps to consolidate the structure of social inequality. And within this structure, the general public as well as the law-enforcement agencies will continue to exercise far less social control over the powerful. This then will encourage the powerful to engage in what they consider as less serious deviant activities.

We have so far discussed the complementary relationship between deviance by the powerful and by the powerless. This relationship takes the form of one causing the other and vice versa. It is illustrated in Figure 4.2.

EVALUATION OF POWER THEORY

First, from the scientific standpoint, power theory can be judged worthless, because there are no empirical data nor will there be any to support it. For example, in order to confirm its second proposition, that the powerful are more prone to deviance, we may have to show that the proportion of the powerful population committing "unserious" deviant acts is greater than the proportion of the powerless population perpetrating "serious" crimes. There are at present no data to show this.

But it may be impossible to obtain this kind of information through the use of the currently popular *consensus methodology*. For the powerful, when compared with the powerless, are characteristically less inclined and less able to be coerced to divulge their deviant activities. This is further compounded by the fact that the powerful's deviant activities are typically carried out in a more sophisticated, surreptitious, indirect, and consequently undetectable manner. Perhaps only the unconventional *conflict methodology*—such as the use of lawsuit by Ralph Nader, investigative journalism by Jack Anderson, and the use of intelligence and counterintelligence techniques developed by the FBI and CIA—could produce data on the powerful's deviant activities.

Second, although it is not directly supported by existing data, power theory may be confirmed by indirect evidence and logical reasoning. There is some evidence, as has been suggested before, that the powerful are more likely than the powerless to have greater deviant opportunity, to experience greater subjective deprivation, and to face lesser social control. From this evidence, along with the additional evidence that deviance is positively related to deviant opportunity, subjective deprivation, and lax social control, we may logically conclude that the powerful are more likely than the powerless to engage in deviant activities. This has to do with the power theory's second proposition. What about the theory's first proposition concerning the two deviant *types,* and third proposition regarding the *symbiosis* between these deviant types? The former can be supported by ample impressionistic observations, and the latter by some evidence showing the different ways in which the deviance of the powerful and the powerless influence each other. All this evidence, however, has largely been derived from uncontrolled impressions and insights rather than from scientifically controlled research. Hence power theory should be taken as a sensitizing rather than definitive, empirically testable theory.

Third, power theory assumes that middle-class people, being more powerful than lower-class ones, are also more likely to participate in deviant activities. Critics may question this assumption by offering the following argument: middle-class people have been known to work hard to make themselves feel and look respectable and morally upright. They tend to do such things as "going to church, taking pride in property, being neat and orderly, showing a capacity for moral indignation against corruption." [13]

However, what all this means is basically that middle-class people are not likely to engage in those deviant activities typically carried out by lower-class people; namely, those deviant activities—such as rowdy drinking, indiscreet fornication, mugging, robbery, rape, murder, and the like—that can easily bring disrespect to the deviant. This is obviously because the middle classes have a strong desire to feel and look respectable. Yet this selfsame desire can powerfully induce them to choose the more respectable deviant acts to commit. Sociologist Edward Ross's description of such deviants in 1907 may still be relevant today:

The criminaloid [i.e., middle-class criminal] counterfeits the good citizen. He takes care to meet all the conventional tests—flag worship, old-soldier sentiment, observance of all the national holidays, perfervid patriotism, party regularity and support. . . . Nor will he fail in that scrupulous correctness of private and domestic life which confers respectability. . . . The criminaloid must perforce seem sober and chaste, "a good husband and a kind father." The criminaloid, therefore, puts on the whole armor of the good. He stands having his loins girt about with religiosity and wearing the breastplate of respectability. His feet are shod with ostentatious philanthropy; his head is encased in the helmet of spread-eagle patriotism.[14]

Therefore, insofar as they enjoy greater deviant opportunity, suffer greater subjective deprivation, and experience lesser social control, the middle classes can be said to be *more* likely to engage in ("respectable") deviance than are the lower classes (likely to get involved in "disrespectable" criminality).

Fourth, power theory can also be employed to explain why, *within the same class,* some individuals are more likely than others to commit certain deviant acts. For example, power theory can explain why some members of the lower class are more likely than others of the *same* class to commit homicide, rape, robbery, and other "street crimes." More specifically, power theory would suggest that some lower-class people (e.g., lower-class *men*) are more likely than other lower-class people (e.g., lower-class *women*) to commit those crimes, because the former—due to their greater power—have greater deviant opportunity, greater subjective deprivation, and lesser social control.

These three explanatory concepts of power theory have actually been suggested in one way or another by anomie theory and control theory, discussed in Chapter 2. The only difference between these two scientific theories and power theory is in the way these three explanatory concepts are used. The scientific theorists have explicitly or implicitly used the concepts to explain their traditional assumption about the lower classes being more inclined to criminality than are middle and upper classes. But I have earlier used the same concepts to explain the contrary assumption about the higher classes being more deviant—and here to explain the assumption that some individuals are more deviance-prone than others within the same class.

Fifth, the presumed validity of power theory is limited by the fact that there are some lower-consensus deviant acts that the powerful may be *no* more likely than the powerless to commit. In other words, contrary to what is suggested by power theory, the powerless may be just as likely as the powerful to perform these lower-consensus deviant acts. The lower-consensus deviant acts in question can best be exemplified by the mundane, ordinary acts such as violating etiquette, lying a little, cheating a little, or otherwise sinning that occur in the daily life of any fallible human. It is also quite probable that critics may find other forms of deviant behavior that cannot be attributed to power at all. Thus we have to conclude that just as human beings do not live by bread alone (however important it may be), so they do not deviate by power alone (however important it may be).

SUMMARY

The highly abstract concepts in the scientific and humanistic sociological philosophies—that have influenced the perspectives and theories of deviance discussed in the preceding three chapters—are brought down to a more concrete level. At this concrete level, the scientific concept of social constraint is taken to apply to the life condition of powerless people, and the humanistic concept of individual freedom is taken to apply to the life condition of powerful people. The resulting two concretized concepts are then integrated into a theory called *power theory*.

The theory consists of three propositions. One, the powerful and the powerless are different in the type of deviant behavior each is likely to commit. Two, the powerful are more prone to deviance than are the powerless. Three, there exists a symbiotic relationship between the deviance of the powerful and of the powerless. These three propositions are tied together by the concept of social inequality.

Power theory can be considered scientifically worthless because of its lack of empirical support, but this merely reflects the reality of the power-deviance relationship as one that is not amenable to standard empirical tests. There are, nevertheless, indirect evidence and logical reasoning to support the theory, which may sensitize us to the relative prevalence of the largely undetectable and unmeasurable deviant acts of more powerful people. Further, the theory can explain the difference in deviance between the middle and lower classes, because the former are more powerful than the latter. The explanatory concepts of power theory can also be used to explain the difference in deviance among individuals within the same class. But the theory cannot be applied equally well to all forms of deviant behavior.

SUGGESTED READINGS

Comfort, Alex. *Authority and Delinquency in the Modern State*. London: Routledge and Kegan Paul, 1950.

Gordon, David M. "Capitalism, Class, and Crime in America." *Crime and Delinquency* 19 (April 1973): 163–186.

Sorokin, Pitirim A. and Walter A. Lunden. *Power and Morality: Who Shall Guard the Guardians?* Boston: Porter Sargent, 1959.

II SPECIFIC FORMS OF DEVIANT BEHAVIOR

We have so far dealt with general analyses of deviant behavior. Chapter 1 has discussed how various sociologists define the nature of deviance in a general way. Chapters 2, 3, and 4 have shown how various sociologists theorize about deviance, also in a general way.

These general analyses, however, as they involve the use of general perspectives and general theories, assume that all forms of deviant behavior are in some respect similar to one another. This necessarily ignores the numerous unique aspects of each specific form of deviant behavior. Thus, in the following chapters, we shall discuss these unique aspects. This will give a closer view and deeper understanding of each deviant behavior.

5 MURDER

Murder is a relatively rare form of criminal act. As shown by Table 5.1, the murder rate is the lowest in comparison with other major crimes. Also, a person is five times more likely to die in a car accident than to be murdered.[1] It is even more likely for us to kill ourselves than to be killed by others.[2] Aside from its being rare, murder is the most serious offense—its cost to the victim is forever irreparable and its cost to the victim's loved ones is incalculably high.

In spite or because of its rarity and seriousness, murder fascinates many of us. Thanks to a legion of novelists as well as television and movie producers, we often entertain ourselves with a murder mystery, trying excitedly to figure out "who done it?" But our morbid fascination with murder may have led some of us to a mistaken view of the crime. We may fear strangers as our potential murderers, while in reality most murders are committed not by people unknown to us but by our acquaintances, friends, lovers, or relatives. We may also imagine that most murders are fascinating mysteries, while in real life most murders are no mysteries at all—the police can easily find out from the people at the murder scene who the culprit is. Let us, then, examine in greater detail the real nature of murder.

THE NATURE OF MURDER

To understand murder we shall first look at the profile of murderers as a group, to discover where they come from, who they are, and where, when, and how they do their killings. Then we shall see various social contexts

Table 5.1 Crime rates, United States, 1975

CRIME INDEX OFFENSES	NUMBER	ESTIMATED CRIME 1975 RATE PER 100,000 INHABITANTS
Murder	20,510	9.6
Forcible rape	56,090	26.3
Robbery	464,970	218.2
Aggravated assault	484,710	227.4
Burglary	3,252,100	1,525.9
Larceny-theft	5,977,700	2,804.8
Motor vehicle theft	1,000,500	469.4

SOURCE: *Uniform Crime Reports*, 1976, p. 11.

in which murder is likely to occur. Finally, we shall examine some studies showing murder as a passion undeterred by capital punishment.

COLLECTIVE PROFILE OF MURDERERS

Proportionately more murderers can be found in less economically developed countries. They are also more likely to be found in societies where the culture of masculine violence flourishes. In the United States, murderers are typically poor, black, male, and aged twenty-six or older. Most of these murderers have had some previous experience in assaulting others. When they do their killing, murderers tend to do it at certain times and places and to choose certain methods of killing. We can learn more about this collective profile of murderers from the facts discussed below.

ECONOMIC UNDERDEVELOPMENT   In general, less industrialized countries, such as Colombia, El Salvador, and Mexico, have been found to have high rates of homicide, while more industrialized countries, such as Norway, the Netherlands, and Ireland, have been found to have low rates. The United States, however, has higher rates than most other industrialized countries in Europe.[3]

CULTURE OF MASCULINE VIOLENCE   The unusually high rates of murder in Latin American countries have been attributed to the "culture of violence." As Marshall Clinard and Daniel Abbott write, "The extremely high rate of homicide in Colombia represents a striking example of large-scale cultural violence, often called *Violencia Colombia.* There the use of violence has increased fantastically since 1948. . . . Originally rural in nature, these [murderous] activities permeate the cities, and despite army measures of control the homicide rate continues to be high." [4] It has also been said that motivating this cultural violence is the common desire of Latin American males to prove their *machismo* (manliness). Very often they prove their machismo by resorting to violence, which may result in murder. They are expected to be violent when they are insulted, cursed, scolded, jostled, or fail to win an argument.

CLASS   Studies by the National Commission on Violence in the United States in the late 1960s clearly indicated that homicides are concentrated heavily in the lowest class category.[5] Further, in his analysis of police data on homicide in Philadelphia, Marvin Wolfgang estimates that 90 to 95 percent of the offenders come from the lower end of the occupational scale.[6]

RACE   It is very clear from the National Commission's survey on homicide offenders that although there are fewer blacks than whites in the general population, blacks are involved in a much larger proportion of homicides. Specifically, despite the fact that blacks constitute only 11 percent of the general population, they commit 72 percent of the homicides. The killing is *intra*racial. Blacks kill their fellow blacks more than they do whites, and whites murder fellow whites more than they do blacks.[7]

SEX   Compared with females, males are far more likely to commit murder. As reported by the National Commission, 80 percent of the murders in 1967 were committed by men, while only 20 percent by women. It has also been found that men are more apt to do away with members of their own sex, while women tend more to murder members of the opposite sex.[8]

AGE   The greatest proportion of all killings in 1967 involved the age group of twenty-six and over. These older people are more prone to kill each other than younger victims. But in the few cases where older people quarrel with younger people, the former are more likely to end up dead.[9]

PREVIOUS EXPERIENCE IN VIOLENCE   Wolfgang hypothesizes that murderers tend to have violent pasts. These violent pasts usually began with minor assaults against others, gradually escalated to more and more serious assaults, finally culminating in homicide. In analyzing his data on homicide offenders in Philadelphia, Wolfgang finds evidence to support his hypothesis. He discovers that a relatively high proportion (64 percent) of homicide offenders have previous arrest records. He further finds that most of these murderers' previous offenses were aggravated assaults (66 percent), which throws additional support to the hypothesis of accumulated violence.[10]

TIME OF KILLING   Most murders are committed in the heat of passion, and there does seem to be some connection between season of the year and murder. Wolfgang discovered that the number of homicides increases during the hot late spring and summer; decreases slightly during the cool early spring and autumn; and drops even more during the winter.[11] Far stronger than this association, however, is the connection between homicide and days of the week as well as hours of the day. For homicide occurs most frequently during the weekend evenings, particularly on Saturday night.[12] This may be why the handgun most often used in murder is popularly called the "Saturday Night Special."

PLACE OF KILLING   Men are equally likely to commit murder in and outside the home, while women are more likely to do so at home than outside.[13] In the home, women most often do the killing in the kitchen. This may be because the kitchen is the place where women use butcher knives—which can become a weapon when a quarrel flares up. But the bedroom is the most dangerous place for women, as they are most frequently killed there by their husbands. This is perhaps because in the bedroom men are accustomed to demonstrating their "manliness" by sexually subjugating women—and so it is the place to physically subjugate them to death.

METHODS OF KILLING   Killing a human may appear extraordinary, when compared with, say, killing a rabbit. This consequently fires up the imagination of many mystery writers, who help spread the popular notion that murderers often use mysterious, exotic, ingenious, or superclever methods. Yet the data show that there is nothing special about the methods used for ending another person's life. Most objects can be readily turned into murder weapons, as long as they are conveniently accessible when the burst of anger occurs. In our society such firearms as handguns, rifles, and shotguns are easily available and so they are most often used as murder weapons.[14] Perhaps, seeing a gun while embroiled in a heated argument may incite a person to murderous action. As Shakespeare said, "How oft the sight of means to do ill deeds, makes ill deeds done." Of course, firearms in themselves can not cause homicide, nor can their absence reduce the motivation to kill. Still, were guns less available, many heated arguments would have resulted in aggravated assaults rather than murders, thereby reducing the number of fatalities. It is no wonder that the use of less dangerous weapons (such as knives) in attempted murders has been estimated to cause 80 percent fewer deaths.[15]

Table 5.2 Victimization by strangers, by type
of crime in seventeen United States cities, 1967
(by percentage)

TYPE OF CRIME	VICTIMIZATION BY STRANGERS
Unarmed robbery	86
Armed robbery	79
Forcible rape	53
Aggravated assault	21
Homicide	16

SOURCE: *Crimes of Violence*, Staff Report to the National Commission on the Causes and Prevention of Violence, 1969, 11, 217.

MURDER AS FAMILY AFFAIR

Many Americans are apparently afraid of getting attacked and killed by strangers, particularly in big cities. But, of the major crimes in this country, homicide is the least likely to be committed by strangers, as shown in Table 5.2. A closer examination of this table reveals that the less severe the bodily harm inflicted on the victim, the greater the likelihood of the crime being committed by a stranger. For example, unarmed robbery inflicts the least physical harm on the victim, and it is most frequently committed by strangers. On the other hand, homicide is the most harmful to the victim's body, and it is the least often perpetrated by strangers. Thus it appears that when we are surrounded by strangers, we had better watch out more for our money than for our bodies.

But in the company of our acquaintances, friends, dates, lovers, and spouses, we may have to watch out for our bodies more than our money. If they commit a crime against us, they are likely to do the ultimate harm to our person. Murder, then, can be considered the most personal crime. In fact, one national survey shows that the largest percentage of murders involves family members.[16] So murder can be called a family affair.

This sort of family affair is not unique to our society. It is found in many other countries as well. A study of homicides in an African country, for example, concludes:

People, in general, do not kill strangers except in cases of robbery and other felonies in which material gain is the prime motive. This reveals a strange contradiction. In these societies people are afraid and suspicious of strangers or of those with whom they are not related. Thus, they fear them and think they are safer with those they know and even safer with those to whom they are related, especially biologically. And yet it is through these intimate interpersonal relationships that one is most likely to meet his slayer.[17]

MURDER AS DOING THE VICTIM A FAVOR

The general public often has more sympathy for the murder victim than for the offender, because it assumes that the murder victim is weak and meek, helplessly slain by the strong and aggressive offender. This assumption is not always correct. At least one out of four homicides involves the victim being the first to attack his or her subsequent slayer. Wolfgang has called such murder "victim-precipitated homicide," and found in his study of Philadelphia murders that 26 percent of them were victim precipitated.[18] The following are typical cases of victim precipitation:[19]

• A drunken husband, beating his wife in the kitchen, gave her a butcher knife and dared her to use it on him. She warned him that she would use it if he should strike her again. At the very instant he heard this warning, he slapped her in the face—and he was fatally stabbed.
• A husband accused his wife of giving money to another man, and attacked her with a milk bottle, then a brick, and finally a piece of concrete block, while she was making breakfast. Having a butcher knife in hand, she stabbed him in his chest.
• A drunken man with knife in hand approached a person during a quarrel. When this person showed a gun, the drunk dared him to shoot. He did.
• A man struck his girlfriend repeatedly on her head, because she refused to let him shove his penis into her rectum. Finally, she grabbed a butcher knife and shoved it into his body.

Because they provoke another person to kill them, Wolfgang assumes that these self-precipitated murder victims may have secretly wanted to kill *themselves*.[20] This assumption of suicide wishes may well be correct. But if they have suicide wishes, why do they not take it upon themselves to end their own lives? Perhaps they have been influenced by what may be considered a culture of showy masculinity, characteristic of any sexist society. This culture encourages males to show off their toughness and hide their tenderness, to act like a "man" and avoid acting like a "woman," or to engage in manly braggadocio and shun feminine quietism. Under the pressure of this culture, suicidally inclined males would not reveal their "sissy cowardice" and beg for condescending sympathy from others by quietly ending their own lives. Instead, they would display masculine bravado and earn from others some "respect" as the worst person imaginable, by making an ostentatious assault upon another person that is secretly designed for their own annihilation—the result being a victim-precipitated murder.

MURDER AS FOREPLAY TO SUICIDE

From the preceding discussion, we see that the so-called victims of victim-precipitated homicide are actually people with suicidal tendencies, who contribute greatly to their own deaths. There is yet a different group of offenders with the same suicidal tendency. They are homicide-suicide offenders, people who first kill another person and then finish themselves off. The difference between these two types of offenders is obvious. While the "victim" of victim-precipitated homicide conceals the suicide wishes, the homicide-suicide offender reveals them.

Homicide-suicide accounts for about 4 percent of the murders in our country but at least 30 percent in England. There are two conflicting views on the nature of homicide-suicide. One is held by a sociologist; the other by a psychiatrist. The sociologist sees homicide-suicide as a form of *normality;* the psychiatrist views it as a symptom of *abnormality.* According to the sociologist, the murderer-suicide is a normal person, because, after killing the loved one, he or she is able to feel remorse, just as we would expect normal people to feel after they had done such a horrible thing. On the contrary, the psychiatrist diagnoses the murderer-suicide as a psychotic, because he or she does not feel remorse—instead he or she joyfully anticipates a reunion with the victim in another world, and therefore kills him- or herself in order to achieve that goal.[21]

Those two conflicting views can be reconciled. It is true that there are some murderer-suicides who are "normal." It is also true that there are some murderer-suicides who are "psychotic." But these two types of murderer-suicides may have one thing in common—both are unaffected by the culture of showy masculinity discussed above. Instead of acting like "tough guys," as required by that culture, both behave like "weaklings." In effect, the normal one begs the mortally wronged victim (who is usually a wife or sweetheart) for pardon, and the psychotic one dreams for happy reconciliation in another world. Both are equally like characters portrayed in soap operas on television.

MURDER AS WINNING TRIVIA

Murder is an extremely serious human act, yet the motive for committing it often appears to be downright trivial. Ordinary quarrels, which often seem to be over nothing at all, are the most common reasons for poor people to kill. The following are some typical examples: [22]

• A man was fatally shot in front of a tavern because he had refused to lend his assailant a dollar.

• Two men were arguing over a five dollar bet and became involved in a scuffle. Then one took out a gun and pulled the trigger on the other.

• Two fellow workers were drinking beer; they argued over a one dollar pool bet. One wound up in a morgue.

• A man was drunk when he came home. He told his uncle to move over in bed. Seeing that his uncle would not, he stabbed him to death.

• "Hey, you're lookin' at me."
"No I ain't."
"Yes you are. Why you lookin' at me?"
Minutes later one of them lay still in a puddle of blood.

Murder, then, is a quick and effective way for the poor to win an argument—over trivia. Middle-class people usually use a much less drastic means such as verbal ability to settle an argument. But the poor suffer from a lack of verbal ability. So they are more often compelled to use their physical strength to end an argument with—and sometimes the life of—another person.

We may also note that arguments such as those illustrated above may appear trivial to us. Yet the same arguments are apparently taken by the poor as reasons for defending their honor as men. A dirty look, a little insult, a jostle would not usually get middle-class people into a little argument, let alone spill another person's blood. But the same is perceived differently by the poor. Why do the poor make such a mountain out of a molehill with deadly consequences for themselves?

The explanation can be found in the economic and social oppression of the poor, which the upper and middle classes are free from. The poor man's honor as a man—or, for that matter, as simply a human being—has been substantially diminished by the frustrating and humiliating forces in his life. Some of these forces are impersonal, such as the general condition of poverty, so that the poor man cannot fight back, even though these impersonal forces have turned him into a violent-prone person by making him live almost like an animal. Other humiliating forces, however, can be found in people, such as the police, the bureaucrats in a welfare or unemployment office, and employers—who usually treat him with far less respect than they do the more successful higher-status persons. But since these people are more powerful than he is, the poor man cannot fight back at them either.

In consequence, he has extremely little honor left to him, and so, in order to live at least more honorably than an animal, he dearly hangs on to it. Although he cannot maintain this fragile honor in the larger society or in the presence of those more powerful people, he certainly can in his immediate neighborhood or among his equally honor-deprived friends and acquaintances. But because his honor as a man is already extremely fragile, the pressure of daily frustration and tension weighing on him can easily threaten or destroy it. Thus an insult from his relatives, friends, or acquaintances (who are, after all, his last straw of hope for keeping his honor) may mean to him the threat that all his honor will be taken away. If you are a man, try to imagine yourself in a situation where your friend threatens to take away all your honor by cutting off your penis. You would probably fight like mad to defend your honor even at the risk of killing him. So would the poor man, when he feels all of his honor is being threatened by what may seem—to us—a trivial insult.

MURDER AS UNDETERRED PASSION

Many sociologists have observed that as a crime of passion, murder is not deterred by the death penalty. The evidence supporting this observation has come in different forms.

First, there is the evidence that comes from comparing the homicide rates in those states that still retain capital punishment, with the homicide rates in those states that have abolished it. Generally, such comparisons show the homicide rates to be two to three times higher in the retentionist than abolitionist states.[23] This would suggest that the death penalty does not work. But the much higher homicide rates in the retentionist states are not necessarily caused by capital punishment, but are probably the result of the distinctive cultural and population characteristics of the region. For example, the South, where all the states retain the death penalty, has the largest black population and a culture of violence as reflected by its traditionally high murder rates. Thus the population and cultural characteristics, rather than the death penalty itself, may be responsible for the high homicide rates.

In consequence, sociologists have excluded the Southern states from analysis of the relationship between capital punishment and murder. Instead, they focus on Northern and Western states that share about the same population composition and cultural tradition. The result has consistently shown that the death penalty states still have slightly higher homicide rates than their neighboring states that have abolished the death penalty. Although this finding does not prove that the death penalty encourages murder, it does at least clearly show that the death penalty does not deter murder.

Another type of evidence that shows the nondeterrent effect of capital punishment comes from comparing the homicide rates that occurred before and after abolition of the death penalty within the same states. Such comparisons have shown no significant difference in homicide rates before and after the states abolished capital punishment. Furthermore, the restoration of the death penalty in eleven states that had earlier abolished it, has not led to any significant decrease in homicide. So all this suggests that the death penalty does not deter people from committing murder.

Finally, there is yet another piece of evidence. It comes from comparing the numbers of homicides shortly before and shortly after one or more executions of convicted murderers were widely publicized. If the death penalty has a deterrent effect, the execution should so scare potential killers that they would refrain from killing, and the number of homicides in the area would decrease. But this is not the case. In Philadelphia during the 1930s, for example, the number of homicides remained about the same sixty days prior and subsequent to a widely publicized execution of five murderers. This finding suggests that the death penalty, even when the state shows people that it means business with it, apparently does not frighten potential killers from killing. In fact, it may do the opposite—indirectly encouraging them to kill. For instance, in California between 1946 and 1955, the state always chose Friday mornings to carry out executions. Surprisingly, there were more murders during the weekends following executions than during weekends when there were no Friday morning executions.[24]

It may be concluded that the death penalty does not deter murder, or, more precisely, that the death penalty is no more effective than other existing measures to deter murder. This is because murder is a crime of passion most often carried out under the overwhelming pressure of a volcanic emotion, while capital punishment can be effective only if murder is a calmly calculated act.[25] Despite its being an ineffective deterrent to murder, however, capital punishment can be very effective for other purposes. It is particularly effective in (1) preventing the murderer from ever doing harm to others again, and (2) satisfying the emotion of outrage against the murderer. These may be the real reasons for the advocacy of capital punishment by some people. But these people often like to appear civilized by calmly arguing about the presumed deterrence of the death penalty, rather than admitting they are really screaming for the blood of the murderer.

THEORIES OF MURDER

In general, there are three kinds of theory for explaining why some people commit murder. They differ in telling us *where* the cause of murder can be found. Biogenic theories say that it can be found inside the human *body*. Psychogenic theories maintain that it can be located within the human *psyche*. And sociogenic theories argue that it can be sought in the *social environment*—outside both the human body and psyche. Let us visit each of these three places and see how murder is produced.

BIOGENIC THEORIES

There are three biogenic theories of murder. They are more specifically referred to as the racist theory, the ethological theory, and the genetic theory.

THE RACIST THEORY You may recall that blacks have considerably higher homicide rates than whites. Since being black is a biological trait, does this mean that murder is biologically determined, and blacks are therefore born to be more homicidal than whites? Modern biologists do not think so. But some people, being influenced by white racism, equate blackness with criminality in general. If they are shown the data that link high homicide rates to blacks, they may believe that blacks are instinctively homicidal.

There is no evidence to support the idea that blacks have a more powerful instinct to kill than whites. Of course, there is evidence that shows American blacks to have a higher homicide rate than American whites. But this evidence does not mean that blacks as a racial group are instinctively more homicidal. To get at the real meaning of that evidence, we should note at least two facts. One is that so-called black Americans are actually not a pure racial type—neither are so-called white Americans. This is because most blacks in this country have "white blood" in them. Another fact comes from anthropologist Paul Bohannan's study of homicides in central Africa.[26] If the higher homicide rate among American blacks is due to their black genes, then we should expect their blacker brothers and sisters in Africa to be even more homicidal. Yet this is not the case at all. As shown by Bohannan's study, African blacks have lower homicide rates than not only American blacks but also the general American population. This leads Bohannan to conclude: "If it needed stressing, here is overwhelming evidence that it is a cultural and not biological factor which makes for a high homicide rate among American Negroes." [27]

THE ETHOLOGICAL THEORY This theory has been put forth by ethologists, who are for the most part zoologists specializing in the study of animal behavior. According to these scholars, humans are not just biologically the same as other animals in having the instinct to kill. Humans are far more homicidal. This is evidenced by the fact that while other dangerous animals *rarely* kill other animals of the same species (for example, tigers rarely kill other tigers and wolves rarely kill other wolves), humans *often* kill other humans. At least one hundred million humans have been killed by other humans since the First World War in 1914—in addition to the much smaller scale of interhuman killing carried out by private citizens in predominantly lower-class neighborhoods. Ethologists have attempted to explain why this intraspecies aggression is so much more common among humans.

Their explanation is that while such ferocious animals as tigers, wolves, and ravens are endowed with the *instinct to inhibit* their killing instinct, humans are not. Why not? Because unlike ferocious animals that can easily kill other members of their own species, unarmed humans are like such harmless animals as doves, rabbits, and chimpanzees in not being physically capable of killing their own kind. Thus in prehistoric times there was no natural selection pressure at work to breed into humans the instinctual mechanism for inhibiting their instinct to kill their own kind. Suddenly, however, humans developed artificial weapons, analogous to, and even far more dangerous than, the bodily built-in weapons of the ferocious animals. This weapon development was just too sudden for evolution to cope with it. The result was that the mechanism of inhibition against their killing instinct failed to evolve in humans. Without this inhibiting mechanism, humans have often used their artificial weapons such as knives and guns and bombs to kill each other.[28]

All this may explain why the human race as a whole is the most homicidal in the animal kingdom. But it cannot explain why some humans are more homicidal than other humans. All of us, the ethological theory implies, have the same evolutionary past, the same killer instinct, and the same lack of instinctual inhibition against killing. Then, if the theory is consistent, all of us should have the same likelihood of killing others. Yet this is not the case. As we have observed, the black, the poor, and the male are more homicidal than the white, the rich, and the female.

THE GENETIC THEORY Most of us genetically normal human beings are born with 23 pairs of chromosomes—46 in all—in each of our body cells. Twenty-two of these pairs are called autosomes, while the remaining pair is referred to as sex chromosomes. In normal males, there are two sex chromosomes, named X and Y. The X is inherited from the mother; the Y from the father. The X is believed to be gentle and passive and the Y tough and aggressive. Normal males, then, are described as XY—whose gentle and tough characteristics supposedly balance each other.

Now, a very small percentage of our male population (about one-seventh of one percent) are born with an extra Y chromosome, and so are called XYY males. With the extra Y, which is supposed to make a man tough and aggressive, the XYY males are considered genetically abnormal. The major characteristics of these people are that they are a little mentally retarded, have too much acne on their faces, stand taller than the average normal male (6 feet 1 inch vs. 5 feet 7 inches), and—most importantly—have a strong tendency to be unusually aggressive. Thus it has been theorized that the extra Y chromosome can drive the XYY male into committing a dangerous, violent crime such as murder. To test this theory, some geneticists have studied the inmates in prisons as well as hospitals for the criminally insane, and have found that an unusual number of them have the extra Y chromosome.[29]

This theory has extremely limited validity, however, for several reasons. One, the sample of XYY criminals studied by the geneticists was a biased one, because these criminals were confined in the institutions, whereas many, perhaps most, XYY criminals are not. Two, while some murderers have an XYY chromosome, most murderers do not. Three, the XYY chromosome may at best serve only as a potential, not determinant, of violence. Even though an XYY chromosome has the potential of leading its carrier to violence, social-cultural factors may largely determine whether the potential will turn into actuality. As one geneticist admits:

A social mechanism is entirely possible. Large, possibly slightly retarded, males [with XYY chromosomes] may be ridiculed for their height and may respond aggressively. In any case, it would appear that of the total amount of violence in our society only a very small part is contributed by XYY individuals.[30]

PSYCHOGENIC THEORIES

There are two psychogenic theories of murder. One is the psychoanalytic theory. The other is the psychological theory of frustration-aggression.

THE PSYCHOANALYTIC THEORY   According to psychoanalysts, our psyche consists of three parts: the id, the ego, and the superego. The id is the basic drives that we were born with. Technically, the id has been referred to as Eros, libido, life instinct, or sex drive. Very simply, the id is our inborn desire to live, enjoy ourselves, make love, or celebrate life in one way or another. But such desires cannot be successfully fulfilled unless we have learned *how* to fulfill them. Thus we have learned innumerable ways to live as best we can. The knowledge that results from this learning becomes our ego. In trying to make us enjoy ourselves, our ego tells us that there is a limit to our id satisfaction or self-enjoyment. For example, if we want to satisfy our sexual desire, we cannot simply grab a man or woman in the street and make love right there. This limit to our self-enjoyment is imposed upon us by society in the form of rules and injunctions—"You should not do this. . . . You should not do that." Our acceptance of these rules and injunctions becomes the cornerstone of our superego—which is in a way similar to our conscience.

Our id and superego are always at war with each other—both, after all, are equally emotional and quite often unreasonable. Our id may make us want to satisfy *all* kinds of sexual fantasies, and our superego may say no to *any* kind of sexual fantasy. If we fail to satisfy our id, we feel unhappy; if we fail to obey our superego, we feel guilty. So we are always caught between these two conflicting parts of our psyche, with a good chance of feeling unhappy or guilty. Fortunately though, the rational part of our mind, the ego, can resolve the conflict between the id and the superego. Thus the ego serves as a mediator, attempting to find a way to satisfy the id without disobeying the superego or to obey the superego without frustrating the id. If the ego often fails in this mission, unhappiness or guilt feelings may so overwhelm the individual that he or she becomes mentally ill. This in turn may lead him to such violent acts as murder.

The ego has yet another problem to cope with, the failure of which would also lead to violence. In Freud's view, we were born with not only Eros (the life instinct) but also Thanatos (the death instinct). Part of this death instinct is an aggressive drive directed against other people rather than oneself.[31] Since this aggressive drive is as normal as the sex drive, it also demands to be expressed. But the superego also demands that the aggressive drive be suppressed as much as the sex drive is. Here we see once again a war threatening our psychic land. For example, our aggressive drive may want us to cut up another person's body or to defeat him by taking away his life, but our superego prevents us from doing it. Our ego has to step in and play the mediating role. In order to reconcile the two warring parties, our ego usually employs the sublimation approach—which enables us to satisfy our aggressive drive in a socially acceptable way. So both our aggressive drive and superego are satisfied when our ego tells us to cut another person's body as a surgeon or to defeat him or her in sport, politics, business, or intellectual activity.

If, though, we were deprived of love or subjected to brutal attacks during our childhood, our aggressive drive would become too irrational for our ego to cope with—and too powerful for our superego to subdue. Consequently, we could engage in an extremely violent and bizarre murder. A case in point is Edmund Emil Kemper III, who, as a child, bitterly resented the separation between his parents and hated living with his quarrelsome mother. At the age of twenty-one, Kemper murdered eight young women by shooting, stabbing, and strangulation, then cut off their heads and hands, had sexual intercourse with the corpses, and ate flesh from some of them. Finally he went home and killed his mother. He chopped off her head, and then cut out her larynx and dumped it down the garbage disposal. "This seems appropriate," he said later, "as much as she'd bitched, screamed, and yelled at me over the years."[32]

On the other hand, if our parents tried too hard to transform us into being "good" by severely punishing us for expressing even the mildest form of aggression, we would have developed a superego so powerful that it would completely suppress our aggressive drive. Without the normal release of aggressive energy, we would gradually build up a reserve of that energy until it reached such a high-pressure point that it blew off the heavy lid of the superego. This may explain why a normally "very nice" person suddenly commits murder—to the great shock and disbelief of family, friends, and neighbors.

Anthony Barbaro, age seventeen, seemed to be like that type of nice guy. He "was the kind of son parents brag about. Quiet, considerate, a former Little Leaguer, altar boy and Boy Scout, he studied hard, worked twenty hours a week as a busboy and still managed to make it into the top 2 percent of his high-school senior class." He was, according to one of his friends, "very straight. . . . He didn't drink, he didn't take drugs, he didn't smoke— he mostly just studied all the time." His neighbor said he indeed came from a good family. During the Christmas holidays in 1975, this nice boy took a rifle and shotgun to the top floor of his high school building. From there he opened fire on the people in the street. Within two hours, three people lay dead and eleven injured.[33]

A study on thirteen "sudden murderers" like Barbaro concludes: "There are consistent patterns in their life histories and offenses. Such persons appear to be quite different from the usual delinquent or criminal. *They come from cohesive family backgrounds, where conformity to the rules of the social system was emphasized.*" [34] [Emphasis added.]

The psychoanalytic theory has very little applicability as less than 5 percent of all murders are committed by the mentally ill.[35] Further, the theory cannot be empirically tested. For example, it is impossible to observe and measure the so-called id, ego, and superego, as well as the aggressive instinct. But the theory is sufficiently supported by logical reasoning and anecdotal illustrations, as have been presented above.

THE PSYCHOLOGICAL THEORY Although they do not necessarily reject the psychoanalytic theory as false, psychologists prefer to offer their own theories that are more amenable to empirical testing. Examples of these theories are the frustration-aggression theory, behaviorist or social learning theory, and personality theory. The most popular and pertinent to murder is the theory of frustration-aggression.

The frustration-aggression theory was first proposed by John Dollard and his fellow psychologists at Yale University in 1939. It was stated as follows:

This study takes as its point of departure the assumption that *aggression is always a consequence of frustration*. More specifically the proposition is that the occurrence of aggressive behavior always presupposes the existence of frustration and, contrariwise, that the existence of frustration always leads to some form of aggression.[36]

These psychologists define *frustration* as the blockage of one's attempt to achieve a goal—whatever goal that may be. Suppose a male student attempts to have sexual relations with his date but she refuses, he can be said to have been frustrated. If she expects to turn him away from sex by firmly saying "No, thanks!" but he still strongly insists, then she can be said to have been frustrated, too. As for aggression, it can be any act that hurts a person in any way. Thus, that male student and his date may be led by their frustration to behave aggressively in one way or another. For instance, they may blame themselves for having dated the wrong person, call each other names, or hit each other.

Although the Yale psychologists stated that aggression is always a consequence of frustration, they did not mean that every time you experience frustration you are sure to respond aggressively. In order to get an accurate impression of what they meant, one must read carefully the entire book in which the theory is discussed. In fact, their statement quoted above is not completely categorical or unqualified. Note that they said "aggression is always *a* [not *the*] consequence of frustration." This implies that aggression is only one consequence of frustration and that there are numerous other kinds of consequences. Nevertheless, the above-quoted statement has created a great deal of misunderstanding among psychologists and sociologists. They have therefore criticized the theory by pointing out the obvious fact that not *all* frustrated people aggress against others.[37] To avoid misunderstanding, the Yale psychologists should have stated their proposition in a different way, such as in the way Leonard Berkowitz has recently stated it: "A frustrating event *increases the probability* that the thwarted organism will act aggressively soon afterward." [38] (Emphasis added.)

Although the theory has been generally supported by various kinds of research evidence,[39] it has rarely been applied to murder. Sociologist Stuart Palmer, however, has tested the theory by comparing fifty convicted murderers with their brothers who had not committed murder. He found that the murderers had experienced a greater amount of frustration in their early lives than their nonmurderer brothers. More specifically, the murderers had suffered the following frustrations more than the nonmurderers: "extreme birth traumas; serious diseases in infancy and childhood; accidents of various kinds; physical beatings; severe training practices at the hands of the mother; psychological frustration due to the emotionalizing of the mother; and traumatic incidents outside the home, as well as social frustration in school and recreational situations." [40]

Palmer is well aware of the methodological limitation of his study. His sample of murderers, drawn from the prison population in New England, is not necessarily representative of murderers across the United States. Most of the data are based on interviews with the murderers' mothers, and so the mothers may have distorted what actually happened to their sons in the early years. Besides, we should point out that frustration *rarely* leads to murder. For frustration can be expressed in many nonmurderous ways: fast driving, fierce competition in sports and academic work, active vying for favor from the opposite sex, high-pressure salesmanship and politics, and so on. Compared with these relatively harmless expressions of frustration, murder is indeed extremely rare.

SOCIOGENIC THEORIES

There are two sociogenic theories of murder formulated by sociologists. One has been called the external restraint theory. The other has been referred to as the subculture of violence theory.

THE EXTERNAL RESTRAINT THEORY   As we have observed above, the psychological theory of frustration-aggression is useful only in suggesting aggression as a possible consequence of frustration. But the theory does not tell us specifically what kind of aggression. We saw that Palmer does show murder as a specific kind of aggression that frustration is likely to bring about. But Palmer does not specifically tell us *why* frustration may lead to murder rather than to other forms of aggression, such as suicide. The reason for murder as a result of frustration is provided by Andrew Henry and James Short's theory of external restraint.[41]

The external restraint theory is intended to show why some people who are frustrated commit suicide, whereas others who are just as frustrated turn to homicide instead. The implication here is that while suicide and homicide are basically the same, in that both are acts of aggression resulting from frustration, they differ in that suicide is aggression directed inward against oneself, while homicide is aggression directed outward against another person. The theory, then, attempts to explain why an intensely frustrated individual will be likely to choose one type of aggression rather than the other. Such an individual would choose *self*-directed aggression (suicide) if he or she experiences *weak* external restraint, but would choose *other*-directed aggression (homicide) if the person suffers *strong* external restraint.

Henry and Short define the *strength of external restraint* as "the degree to which behavior is required to conform to the demands and expectations of other persons."[42] In other words, the strength of external restraint is the amount of social control imposed upon a person so as to limit his or her individual freedom and range of behaviors. According to the theory, then, people who suffer a great amount of that kind of social control are more inclined toward homicide than suicide, because they can legitimately blame others for their frustration.

Martin Gold extends the theory of external restraint to include a factor that mediates between strong external restraint and murder.[43] The mediating factor is the *socialization in aggression by physical punishment*. Gold believes that there are two types of socialization—or techniques of bringing up a child. One involves the parents' using *physical* punishment (for example, spanking, slapping, hitting, punching, or slugging) to deter their misbehaving child from further misbehavior. The other involves the parents' employing *psychological* punishment (for example, threatening withdrawal of love or lecturing to induce guilt) to correct their child's misconduct. Gold theorizes that physical punishment leads to outward aggression against another person, while children punished psychologically turn their aggression against themselves. When they become frustrated adults ready for aggressive action, those who have been physically punished will likely choose murder over suicide, while those who have undergone psychological punishment would choose suicide.

Henry and Short have offered some data to support their theory. Most important are the findings that the lower classes and blacks have significantly higher homicide rates than do the middle classes and whites. These findings are thought to support their theory because Henry and Short assume that the lower classes and blacks suffer stronger external restraint. This assumption is highly plausible. But from the scientific point of view, the validity of the theory has to depend on more than the assumption. It has to depend on empirical data directly supporting the relationship between strong external restraint itself and homicide. Such data, however, do not exist. Neither are there data to directly support Gold's theory that physical punishment causes one to choose homicide over suicide. Instead, Gold's theory is based on the assumption that lower-class people and blacks, who have higher homicide rates than do middle-class people and whites, are also more likely to have been subjected to physical punishment during their childhood. But even this assumption has been refuted by recent data showing that there are no class or racial differences in the use of physical punishment by parents.[44]

THE SUBCULTURE OF VIOLENCE THEORY   After analyzing his abundant data on homicide, Wolfgang reaches the following conclusion:

Our analysis implies that there may be a subculture of violence which does not define personal assaults as wrong or antisocial; in which quick resort to physical aggression is a socially approved and expected

concomitant of certain stimuli; and in which violence has become a
familiar but often deadly partner in life's struggles.[45]

Wolfgang then theorizes that the subculture of violence is the basic cause
of high homicide rates in the poor neighborhood and black ghetto.

Wolfgang further clarifies the nature of the subculture of violence. According to him, the violent subculture in the lower-class neighborhood is
actually a part of the larger, dominant culture of society. So members of
the violent subculture do not necessarily express violence in *all* situations. If
they did, they would have killed off their entire group and totally destroyed
the subculture of violence itself—for the dead obviously could not sustain
a subculture. But the subculture of violence has such an impact on the poor
that they engage in a wider range of violent behavior than do members of
the larger society. This is because those who live in the subculture have gone
through the process of associating and identifying with the model of
violence. At the same time they are discouraged from following the counter-
model of nonviolence from the larger society. Consequently, violence becomes a part of their lifestyle and their way of solving interpersonal problems. It is little wonder, then, that they do not consider the use of violence
as immoral nor feel guilty about their aggression.[46]

In short, except for its emphasis on violence, the subculture of violence
is basically the same as any other subculture. The fact that this particular
subculture emphasizes violence—which may appear to be a highly undesirable
behavior to many of us—should not prevent us from seeing the subculture
of violence as a normal part of living for the people deeply affected by it.
This is why Wolfgang suggests, as his data have shown, that most murderers
are normal rather than emotionally disturbed.

However, Wolfgang has exaggerated the notion that murderers and residents in a high-crime area are far more committed to violence than are
nonmurderers and the general population. This notion has been shown to
be false by a recent national survey. The survey showed that in the general
population people who engage in violence do not value violence any more
than those who do not engage in violence, and that convicted murderers in
prison do not value violence any more than nonviolent inmates.[47] Also,
people in the South, where homicide rates are unusually high, do not value
violence any more than do people in other, low-homicide regions.[48] All
these findings imply that there is not a *sub*culture of violence largely restricted to the lower-class neighborhood. There is instead a *culture* of
violence affecting all classes of people to about the same degree. Being
influenced by the same culture, the poor are nonetheless more likely than
the rich to resort to homicide, because, as power theory would suggest, the
poor are deprived of the wherewithal that the rich have for expressing their

violence in a more "civilized," nonhomicidal way. Let us explore further the application of power theory to murder.

POWER THEORY APPLIED

From the perspective of power theory, we can see that all the theories discussed above have one thing in common: they all focus on one type of murder. With power theory, we can divide killing into two types. One is relatively unprofitable to the killer because it carries a high risk of legal punishment, and the other is more profitable because it carries a high probability of reward. It is the unprofitable type of killing that all the above theories have concentrated on. Once we understand better the nature of these two types of killing, we will understand, perhaps better than the theorists themselves, why most homicides occur in the lower-class neighborhood.

The unprofitable type of killing can be viewed as "beastly"—in the descriptive rather than condemnatory sense of the word. For it typically entails the use of crude weapons, a lot of physical and emotional energy, face-to-face encounter with the victim, personally witnessing the victim's death, and having only one victim. This kind of killing, popularly called murder or homicide, is roughly comparable to the way a beast kills another animal. In contrast, the profitable type of killing requires the use of sophisticated weapons, very little physical and emotional energy, some distance between killer and victim, seeing the victim's death from afar or not seeing it at all, and taking many victims. Only human beings are capable of doing this kind of killing and so it may be called "civilized killing."

Now, as power theory would suggest, due to the unequal distribution of life's resources in society, people with more power could satisfy their killer instinct, take advantage of their XYY chromosomes, resolve their psychic conflicts, vent their frustration, or express their culturally induced commitment to violence—assuming that each of these motivating forces exists as other theorists suggest—by engaging in profitable, civilized killing. For example, the powerful may make war, manufacture and market untested drugs or unsafe cars, or ignore industrial safety and antipollution laws, which ends up bringing death to many people. On the other hand, people with less power such as the poor and the black are more likely to be pressured by any of the above-mentioned motivating forces into unprofitable, beastly killing— namely, homicide.

Thus power theory can simply attribute the overconcentration of homicides in the lower-class neighborhood to the underconcentration of power in that neighborhood. At the same time, power theory is superior to the other theories because it says that, even if all these motivating forces are real, they by themselves cannot cause a person to commit homicide; they merely create a potential for violence in a person. Whether or not an individual will activate that potential into some *unknown* form of violence depends on many other factors. But whether or not the person will become *homicidal* may depend very much on whether he or she is powerful or powerless. As for the external restraint theory, it is basically compatible with power theory in that its concept of strong external restraint is similar to the idea of socio-economic oppression suffered by the powerless members of society.

In addition, with power theory we may assume that powerful people's profitable, civilized killing is more prevalent than powerless people's unprofitable, beastly killing, because the former is much less severely controlled by society than is the latter. We may also perceive the underlying symbiotic relationship between these two types of killing. On the one side, the beastly killing tends to divert the public's attention from the more invisible and more complex civilized killing. "Our psychological makeup," as Ralph Nader says, "allows us to react with very quick indignation to the more primitive kinds of violence, but we have not caught up to the period of time whereby we can react similarly to the violence of radioactive substances, carcinogenic substances, machine violence, whether it's in our plants, foundries, or on the highway." [49] This lack of social control is likely to encourage the civilized killing to continue. In return, civilized killing—by averting the high cost of complying with safety and antipollution laws—is likely to strengthen the corporate high-profit structure and thereby preserve the wide gap in power between rich and poor. Further, the greater concentration of pollutants in the poorer areas of the city—by slowly killing some of the poor residents—would contribute further to the disruption of their own and their families' lives. The result of all this is that the poor will continue to be more likely than the rich to commit homicide rather than other, milder forms of violence.

SUMMARY

Murderers are likely to come from countries marked by economic underdevelopment and supported by the culture of masculine violence. In the United States, murderers are likely to be poor, black, male, and over twenty-five. Having committed a series of assaults against others, most of these people commit murder on Saturday evenings by using firearms. Male murderers tend to do the killing either in or outside the home, while female ones are more likely to kill inside their homes. For both males and females, their acts of murder involve relatives, friends, and acquaintances more often than they do strangers. The killing is sometimes precipitated by the victim; it is sometimes committed so as to be followed by suicide; and it often results from a trivial argument. Being a crime of passion, murder is not effectively deterred by the death penalty.

Various theories have been offered to explain murder. Racist theory blames murder on "black blood"; ethological theory attributes intraspecies killing among humans to the killer instinct; genetic theory posits the XYY chromosome as the causal factor in violent crimes like murder; psychoanalytic theory views murder as the consequence of unresolved psychic conflict; psychological theory traces violence to frustration; and one sociological theory points to strong external restraint as the cause of murder, while another sociological theory considers a subculture of violence as the breeding ground of homicides. Power theory, on the other hand, divides murder into two contrary types and shows the symbiotic relationship between them.

SUGGESTED READINGS

Bensing, Robert and Oliver Schroeder, Jr. *Homicide in an Urban Community*. Springfield, Ill.: Charles C. Thomas, 1960.

Bullock, Henry Allen. "Urban Homicide in Theory and Fact." *Journal of Criminal Law, Criminology and Police Science* 45 (January-February 1955): 565–575.

Gold, Martin. "Suicide, Homicide, and the Socialization of Aggression." *American Journal of Sociology* 63 (May 1958): 651–661.

Henry, Andrew F. and James F. Short, Jr. *Suicide and Homicide*. New York: Free Press, 1954.

Morris, Terrence and Louis Blom-Cooper. *A Calendar of Murder*. London: Michael Joseph, 1964.

Palmer, Stuart, *A Study of Murder*. New York: Thomas Crowell, 1960.

Quinney, Richard. "Suicide, Homicide, and Economic Development." *Social Forces* 43 (March 1965): 401–406.

Wolfgang, Marvin E. *Patterns in Criminal Homicide*. Philadelphia: University of Pennsylvania, 1958.

Wolfgang, Marvin E. ed. *Studies in Homicide*. New York: Harper & Row, 1967.

Wolfgang, Marvin E. and Franco Ferracuti. *The Subculture of Violence: Towards an Integrated Theory in Criminology*. London: Tavistock, 1967.

6 RAPE

$\mathbb{R}$ape or forcible rape is usually defined as a man's carnal knowledge of a woman without her consent. According to the FBI's *Uniform Crime Reports*, there were 56,090 cases of forcible rape reported to the police in 1975. But primarily because of fear or embarrassment on the part of the victims, forcible rape is one of the most underreported crimes. Some survey studies have estimated that only 20 percent of all forcible rapes are reported to the police. One small survey showed that only 2 out of 30 rape victims reported their experience.[1] It is therefore accurate to say that the actual number of forcible rapes is much greater than that reported to the police. One national survey conducted in 1965 estimated that the actual number is far more than three and a half times the number known to the police.[2] If we take this into account, we may roughly estimate that one out of 500 females of all ages was raped in the United States in 1975.

Compared with the other serious crimes, rape does not appear to be a very common offense. (See Table 5.1 in the preceding chapter.) But it does appear to be one of the fastest growing crimes in the United States (see Table 6.1).

THE NATURE OF RAPE

Like murder, rape is popularly considered one of the most serious crimes. But rape is not always looked at in the same way as murder is. When the police see a dead man reported to be a murder victim, they are generally

Table 6.1 Percentage of increase between 1970 and 1975 by type of crime

TYPE OF CRIME	INCREASE (%)
Forcible rape	48
Burglary	47
Aggravated assault	45
Larceny-theft	41
Robbery	33
Murder	28
Motor vehicle theft	8

SOURCE: *Uniform Crime Reports,* 1976, pp. 16, 21, 23, 25, 29, 32, 36.

sure that he is; yet when they see a live woman reporting herself to be a rape victim, they are less sure that she is what she says. The type that the police are sure is rape may be referred to as *officially recognized rape;* the other type, which the police are not sure about, may be called *officially unrecognized rape.* Underlying these two types of rape is a pervasive hidden culture that encourages men to assault women sexually. There are also other kinds of rape, such as homosexual rape and child molesting. All these types of rape, along with the hidden culture of rape, are to be discussed in this chapter.

OFFICIALLY RECOGNIZED RAPE

This is the type of rape that most people think of when they mention or hear the word *rape.* It is also the type of rape that most behavioral scientists refer to when they write about rape. Let us first examine some aspects of officially recognized rape. Then we shall see the impact that this kind of rape has on its victims.

SOME ASPECTS OF RAPE Sociologist Menachem Amir has done a detailed analysis of 646 rape cases from the Philadelphia police files for the years 1958 and 1960.[3] He found that most rapists are black and lower-class people. More significantly, he found that, contrary to the myth of black men being more likely to rape white women than black, rape is mostly an intraracial event—black men raping black women and white men raping white women. In about 95 percent of the rapes in Philadelphia, both offender and victim were of the same race; in only 3 percent was the rapist black and his victim white. According to a survey of rape victims in seventeen American cities in 1967, only about 10 percent of the rapes involved black men assaulting white women.[4] Amir estimated that black men are 12 times as likely as white men to be rape offenders; black women are also 12 times as likely as white women to be rape victims.

It appears that the phenomenon of blacks raping blacks is due to the far more severe legal punishment for raping white women than for raping black ones. As Attorney Haywood Burns points out:

National Prison Statistics show that of the 19 jurisdictions that have executed men for rape since 1930, almost one-third of them—six states— have executed *only* blacks. There have been some years in which everyone who was executed for rape in this country was black. Detailed state-by-state analysis has shown that the discrepancy in death sentences for rape is related to the race of the victim. Blacks raping blacks is apparently less serious than whites raping whites, and certainly less serious than whites raping blacks. But the black man today convicted of raping a white woman can be as certain of receiving the harshest treatment as was a Kansas black convicted of an interracial sex crime in 1855.[5]

It also appears that the phenomenon of blacks raping blacks is largely a matter of availability. Just as handguns are relatively available for expressing one's aggression in murder, black women are relatively available for expressing the black man's aggression in rape. In recent years, however, the availability of white females for victimization by black rapists has perceptibly increased. After finding that 21 percent of the rapes in Washington, D.C. in 1969–1970 (as compared with 10 percent or less in previous years) involved black men raping white women, Charles Hayman and his associates state that "there has apparently been a shift toward a larger proportion of adult white victims assaulted by strange black males."[6]

Rape may occur to females from the age of one all the way up to above the age of eighty. The age group most vulnerable to rape, according to Amir's data, is fifteen to nineteen years of age, and the second most vulnerable, ten to fourteen. In the intraracial rape events, offenders are generally older than their victims. But in cases where blacks rape whites, black offenders tend to be ten years *younger* than their white victims. This does not necessarily mean that the black offenders prefer older white women. It seems largely a matter of availability, because, as Amir's data show, most of these black-white rape episodes involve the commission of burglary or robbery in addition to rape. Perhaps the burglars and robbers feel that "if you rob a woman, you might as well rape her too—the rape is free."[7]

Rape follows the same temporal pattern as homicide. Amir's findings show that the number of forcible rapes, especially multiple rapes (two or more offenders taking turns raping one victim), tended to increase during the hot summer months. The most significant is the finding that most of the rapes occurred on weekends. But unlike homicide, in which alcohol plays an important role, most rapes do not involve drinking on the part of offenders and victims. Only in the few cases where they behave like murderers— inflicting more than the usual amount of violence on their victims—do the rapists tend to have been drinking. All this may be taken to mean that rape does not require the use of alcohol as does homicide, because rape is a less violent crime and thus one's inhibition against it is less. Furthermore, since rape is a less violent crime, less violent persons tend to commit it. Indeed, rapists have been found to be less likely than murderers to have previous arrest records, particularly for aggravated assault.

Most rapists do not randomly, impulsively, or explosively assault their victim. Instead, they do some planning before they strike; such planning accounted for 71 percent of the rapes analyzed by Amir in Philadelphia. In choosing their victim, the rapists do not show any special preference for a stranger or for someone that they know—such as their neighbor or acquaintance. This may explain why, as Amir found out, about half of the rape cases involved strangers and the other half nonstrangers. But most rapists do look for a certain type of female as well as a certain type of location to carry out their plan.

Rapists ordinarily choose females who they believe are vulnerable to attack. Such a female is somehow handicapped or cannot react appropriately or swiftly to the threat of rape, such as a retarded girl, an old woman, a sleeping female, or a girl who is under the influence of alcohol or drugs. Rapists are generally not acquainted with these females. In cases where they do know their potential victim, they will likely select one who has the reputation as "a loose woman," "a wild one," or "an easy lay." If they cannot easily determine the vulnerability of a female, the rapists work out a strategy to test her. They first try to determine whether or not their selected target is a friendly and helpful person. A man might, for example, approach a woman on the street and ask her for a light or street direction. If she provides it, he may proceed to ask her an intimate question, make some sexually suggestive remarks, put his arms around her, or touch her in a sexually provocative place in order to see how she reacts. If she reacts submissively or fearfully, he knows that she can be intimidated into submitting to his sexual demands. Other rapists might ask a woman to let them in her house for making an emergency phone call or for any other bogus reason. If the woman falls for such a ploy, the rapists establish her as their candidate for rape. Here is an example of how a rapist operates:

The rapist would walk into an apartment house and ring several door-bells asking for "Sally." When he found a woman who was helpful, attractive and presumably alone, he would explain how hot and tired he was and ask for a drink of water. Then he asked to use the bathroom so he could look around and make sure the victim was alone. Finally he would ask for a second drink of water and then approach the victim as she stood at the kitchen sink. With a knife at her throat and cut off from help, the victim usually capitulated.[8]

As for the location of rape, the assailants would look for places that can be easily entered and are relatively safe. Usually these are old houses and apartments in rundown areas of the city, where many women live alone. Rapists may also search empty streets, laundromats, and theater restrooms to find their unsuspecting victims.[9]

After they have successfully identified a victim for rape, the attackers do not need to resort to intimidation with such violent means as brandishing a weapon or brutal beating. Indeed, according to Amir's data, the majority of rapes (87 percent) involved only verbal coercion and nonphysical aggression, such as "Don't scream or I'll cut you to pieces," and "If you don't take your clothes off, I'll kill you!" But when they are ready to carry out the crime, rapists ordinarily become more violent. Amir found that while only 15 percent of the rapes did not entail any force, 85 percent involved some degree of violence including roughness, beating, and choking. The rapists would not merely subject their victims to forced intercourse; they would also force them to submit to such acts as fellatio, cunnilingus, anal penetration, and repeated vaginal intercourse, all of which occurred in 27 percent of the rape cases analyzed by Amir. Sometimes they make jokes at their victims' expense. After he was through, one rapist proclaimed to his victim: "I'll marry you if you get pregnant." [10]

Felony rape—rape as an adjunct to such felonious acts as burglary and robbery—is relatively rare. It accounted for only 4 percent of Amir's cases. Rarer still is lust murder or *rape murder*—rape followed by murder—which probably occurs in less than one percent of all murders or rapes. But multiple rape, which is sometimes referred to as group rape, gang rape, or gang bang is almost as common as single rape. Of all the rape cases studied by Amir, 43 percent were multiple rapes.

The most significant fact about multiple rape, as shown by Amir's data, is that its offenders are largely adolescents from ages ten to nineteen. There seems to be a similarity between multiple rape and whoring in that both involve sexual exploitation of one female by many males. The difference is that multiple rape involves the use of force by young boys or adolescents who cannot afford to buy a prostitute's time, while whoring does not require the use of force by adults who can. Moreover, multiple rape offenders are not particularly different from most single rapists in the way they choose their victims. Like most single rapists, multiple rapists tend to victimize the kind of vulnerable females discussed above—especially those with a "bad reputation."

Amir found that 19 percent of the rapes in Philadelphia were precipitated by the victims themselves. Amir refers to this kind of offense as "victim-precipitated rape," explaining that "the victim actually—or so it was interpreted by the offender—agreed to sexual relations but retracted before the actual act or did not resist strongly enough when the suggestion was made by the offender." A common victim behavior that Amir interprets as an invitation to sexual intercourse occurs when a woman agrees to have a drink or ride with a stranger. The implication here is that the victim is at least as much to blame as her offender. The following case has been given as an example of victim-precipitated rape:

An 18-year-old girl was standing in the parking lot of a hamburger drive-in when some men in a car called to her to come over to the car. When she reached the car, she thought she recognized one of the men so she sat in the front seat and started talking to them. Suddenly the driver started the car and drove off. They explained that they were looking for a friend. As they were driving, one of the men asked, "Do you want to fuck?" She laughed and said no. After stopping briefly at another drive-in, the man sitting alongside her put a gun to her head and said, "Are you scared?" She replied, "I don't like having a gun to my head and I am scared shitless, but I don't feel like crying and begging you because I don't feel like hassling you. You won't get any enjoyment out of being sadistic to me." The man turned to the men in the back of the car and said, "Well, what about it, do you want to or not?" They agreed to go ahead and rape her.[11]

But it may be pointed out that the idea of victim-precipitated rape is more a *male's* biased view than an accurate description of the crime. Even in the example quoted above, the girl cannot be said to have "asked for it." As attorney Camille LeGrand says:

The concept of victim precipitation hinges primarily on male definitions of expressed or implied consent to engage in sexual relations, and is shaped by traditional restrictive stereotypes of women. Thus, hitch-hiking and walking alone at night in a rough neighborhood may be considered behavior encouraging a sexual attack. This view of what a *man* can assume to be a sexual invitation is unreasonable. . . . When the female hitchhiker first sets out to get a ride, she normally is not expecting—or hoping for—a sexual encounter. A woman should not be made to feel guilty for acts that do not involve express sexual invitation, nor should she be denied the right to change her mind. In its failure to accord any consideration to the woman victim's intentions, victim precipitation becomes nothing more than a male view of the circumstances leading up to the incident.[12]

THE IMPACT OF RAPE An important way of understanding the nature of rape is to appreciate its impact on its victims. This impact varies from one victim to another. At one extreme are the victims who show a lack of concern. One such victim, when asked what happened between the two attacks of rape by her assailant, replied, "We went out for hamburgers." Other examples: some simply fall asleep after the rape; others are more upset over the theft of a purse, a ring, a transistor radio, or other similar property than over the rape; some victims may voluntarily engage in sexual relations with their assailant when they meet him again after the rape; other victims may later marry their rapist, whom they may or may not have met prior to the rape.[13] At the opposite extreme are the victims who are so traumatized by the rape that they sink into deep depression, attempt to commit suicide, or succeed in committing suicide. In between these two extremes are the great majority who initially experience shock, disbelief, anger, anxiety, or depression, but who eventually pull themselves out of it. This diversity of reactions to rape is apparently related to such factors as the degree of violence, the age of the victim, her social class or cultural background, and prior sexual experience. If she has been violently raped, is relatively young, comes from a middle- or upper-class family, or has had no or little previous sexual experience, the victim is likely to suffer relatively severe consequences.

Most victims of rape go through two phases of disorganization before they gradually and finally regain their ability to live normally.[14] From the time immediately following the rape to a few days or weeks thereafter is the acute phase of disorganization. During this phase most of the victims succumb to such feelings as fear, shock, humiliation, embarrassment, self-blame, or anxiety. These feelings are not only directly caused by the rapist but also indirectly brought about by the prevailing myth in a sexist society that "nice girls don't get raped."

After the initial, acute phase is over, the victims generally go through a longer, lingering phase of disorganization, which often lasts for a few months. In this phase victims may have frightening dreams. More commonly, victims experience what one writer calls *traumatophobia*—a phobic reaction to a traumatic event.

Ann Burgess and Lynda Holmstrom found the following phobic reactions to be the most common among their sample of rape victims:[15] (1) Fear of indoors was found in women who had been raped while sleeping in their beds. (2) Fear of outdoors occurred in those who had been attacked outside their homes. These victims would not go outside without the protection of another person or unless absolutely necessary. (3) Fear of being alone overwhelmed nearly all the victims after the rape. One of them gave this typical report to the interviewers: "I can't stand being alone. I hear every little noise—the windows creaking. I am a bundle of nerves." (4) Fear of crowds was common to many of the victims. (5) Fear of people walking behind them was a frequent complaint of some victims when they went out. This fear was particularly common among women who had been approached by their rapist suddenly from behind. One such victim said, "I can't stand to have someone behind me. When I feel someone is behind me, my heart starts pounding." (6) Sexual fears disrupted many victims' relations with their boyfriends, fiancés, or husbands. One victim was still dominated by these fears five months after the assault: "There are times I get hysterical with my boyfriend. I don't want him near me; I get panicked. Sex is OK, but I still feel like screaming."

You may notice the nature of these victims' feelings: fear and anxiety. They are inward-directed. Other possible feelings are outward-directed, such as anger and revenge. While most rape victims are gnawed by the inward-directed feelings discussed above, a few others express outward-directed feelings. But since 1970 in the United States, primarily as the result of the women's liberation movement, an increasing number of rape victims do not only express their outward-directed feelings. They also actively try to combat rape by setting up such antirape organizations as Anti-Rape Squad, WAR (Women Against Rape), Rape Crisis Center, Rape Hot Line, and Rape Action Coalition. The function of these organizations is to help the rape victim, organize Speak-Out on Rape conferences, teach self-defense classes, get special rape squads established in the police departments, encourage rape victims to report offenders, and pressure the legislatures to pass laws that would make it easier to convict the rapist who is now very likely to go scot-free.

This movement against rape got its major impetus in 1971 when a topless dancer in California came to a local feminist meeting with a complaint: she had been hired to dance at a stag party given in honor of a man about to be married. After the performance, all the men raped her and then threw her out—without paying her for dancing. The feminists later picketed the wedding with signs that read: "THE BRIDEGROOM IS A RAPIST." Word of this incident traveled across the country.[16]

In some cities, notably Los Angeles and Washington, D.C., women have organized special civilian antirape squads of their own. They swear to track down rapists, shave their heads, cover them with dye, photograph them for posters saying things like "THIS MAN RAPES WOMEN," and put the posters up all over the neighborhoods where the rapists live.[17] At a Speak-Out on Rape meeting in New York, one rape victim advocated a drastic measure against rapists: "The gun is taken from the murderer, the bottle taken from the alcoholic, the needle taken from the addict. Why isn't the weapon taken from the rapist? . . . I personally would like to see castration for rape." [18] But most women who are involved in the antirape movement are not that militant. They are more concerned with offering such postrape services as getting the victims to the hospital, providing venereal disease prevention, pregnancy tests, and, if necessary, abortion and psychiatric help, as well as helping the victims with moral support at the police station and with legal aid in the courtroom.

They also offer courses in self-defense against prospective rapists. These courses may require formal training in one of the martial arts such as judo, karate, or kung-fu. Or the courses may instruct the women on how to deal with potential and actual rapists. For example, women who live alone should not put their first names on mailboxes or in telephone directories but should use their first initial, such as "C. Jones;" if a woman is alone and hears an unexpected knock on the door, she should first yell "I'll get it, Jack" to her nonexistent husband; women might use an object in their purse or on their person—such as a comb, a nail file, an umbrella, high-heeled shoes, hairspray, or perfume—to temporarily stun or blind the rapist and thus give themselves time to flee; a woman should scream, bite, claw with the fingernails, pull the rapist's hair, or kick his crotch if he is unarmed; if he is armed and dangerous, women might learn something from the following:

The best job of amateur rapist-trapping I know of was accomplished by a woman who kept her wits about her even while being forced to the roof of her building at knife-point. The struggle was hopeless. She waited. When the man had finished, she told him, "That was the most marvelous experience I've ever had. I never knew it could be like this. I can't wait for the next time. Please, please promise you'll call me." She gave him her phone number. Unaccustomed as he was to such flattery, the rapist called first thing the next day. The woman invited the police to join their liaison. This time the rapist left with the police.[19]

It may reasonably be expected that the impact of rape will change its character in the future. More and more women who are raped will likely stop plunging into the traditional, passive, or self-destructive feelings of fear, anxiety, and guilt. They will instead take modern, active, and constructive steps to give peace to themselves but none to the rapist.

OFFICIALLY UNRECOGNIZED RAPE

It seems that most rapes are not officially recognized as such, even when they are reported to the police and other law-enforcing officials. There are a number of reasons for this official nonrecognition: absence of vaginal penetration; lack of bruises, cuts, or blood on the alleged victim's body; no witness to corroborate the alleged rape; the alleged rapist being known to the victim; and law enforcers' sexist attitude toward rape victims.

The law enforcers' sexist attitude can often be seen in the reactions of the police when a woman reports that she has been raped. The policeman may show disbelief, ridicule, or just plain lack of interest. For example, a woman who gave a calm, rational account of the rape, was asked, "What are you, some kind of sociologist?" If the woman is not pretty, her report of rape is dismissed as just another fantasy of a sex-starved female. A middle-aged mother who reports having been raped may be asked by a young policeman: "Did he have a climax?" [20] Many officers, especially the oldtimers, may say, "Unless a woman's a virgin, what's the big deal?" Regarding an old woman who reports that she has been raped, they may chuckle among themselves: "That's the best thing that has happened to her in many years!"

The officially unrecognized rape may be divided into two types. One involves old women, unattractive females, drunken women, women with "bad reputations" (who are known to have voluntarily slept with men before), and so forth. This type may be referred to as *double rape*—combination of actual rape by the rapist(s) and metaphorical rape by law enforcers who treat the victim as if she were a criminal responsible for provoking the rape. Although it involves neither the use of brutal force, nor the threat of violence with a knife or gun, nor the unwelcome insertion of a penis as does actual rape, metaphorical rape can be much more painful and traumatic to the victim, particularly if it happens in the courtroom. This is what they mean when many victims of double rape report on their experience in the courtroom: "It was worse than the rape itself!"

A case in point is a woman who brought charges against a thirty-six-year-old man in a San Francisco Superior Court.[21] According to her, the accused, along with three other men, forced her into a car at gunpoint. She was taken to the accused's fashionable apartment where he and the three other men first raped her and then subjected her to other forms of sexual humiliation. The police who later searched the apartment discovered four address books containing the names of hundreds of women. One of those names was the accuser's, which had been crossed out. In the court several women testified that the accused had lured them to his apartment and then forced intercourse on them. But the defense attorney argued that his client was a playboy who often picked up girls in bars and took them to his house where sexual relations took place with their consent—and that the accuser was simply one of those willing playmates.

Then the same attorney, through clever questioning, tried to portray her as a loose, sex-crazed woman. He in effect accused her of "being familiar with liquor," "having left her job as a secretary after it was discovered that she had sexual intercourse on a couch in the office," "having a sexual affair with a man while she worked as an attendant at a health club," "living with a married man," "having spent the night with another man who lived in the same building," and "encouraging her two children to have a sex game in which one gets on top of another." The rape victim protested, "Am I on trial? . . . I did not commit a crime. I am a human being." Although she also protested that all those accusations by the defense attorney were lies, the jury did not believe her. Instead, they believed the defense lawyer's portrayal of her as a "bad" woman, and so they acquitted the rapist of both the charges of rape and kidnapping. Thus her courtroom experience had made the woman a victim of double rape. As a leaflet passed out by women in front of the courtroom pointedly stated, "Rape was earlier committed by four men in a private apartment; now it has just been done by a judge and a lawyer in a public courtroom."

The other type of officially unrecognized rape may be called *date rape*, which many males may consider as the hallmark of a great lover but which is nonetheless engaged in without the woman's consent. Date rape may or may not involve forced penetration of the vagina. It may include such less serious acts as forcible necking, forcible petting above the waist, and forcible petting below the waist. The underlying characteristic of all these acts is that the offender resorts to force and disregards the woman's refusal to submit to him. Date rape probably happens to all women at one time or another in their lives, especially in the more sexually permissive societies.

In 1957 Clifford Kirkpatrick and Eugene Kanin asked a sample of 291 college girls whether they had been sexually offended during the academic year. More than half (55.7 percent) of the girls replied that they had been—*at least once during the academic year*. Their experiences of the offenses ranged from the relatively trivial to the serious—from forced necking to forced petting to forced vaginal penetration "in the course of which menacing threat or coercive infliction of physical pain was employed." Kirkpatrick and Kanin did the study more than twenty years ago, and found then that those girls expressed "considerable fear and guilt reactions" subsequent to the assaults by their dates.[22] Today, due to their lesser amount of fear and guilt feelings, a much larger proportion of college females may be expected to see and report their dates' behavior as a sexual offense. If we take into account the fact that these women date for more than one year, the reported incidence of date rape may be expected to be even higher than the 55.7 percent reported by Kirkpatrick and Kanin.

The following are typical cases of date rape:

A high school girl reports: The boy that brought me home stopped outside my house and wouldn't let me get out of the car. I tried to leave, but he grabbed me and wouldn't let me go until I would kiss him. I struggled, but he forced me to kiss him while he ran his hand over me. Then he let me go.[23]

In the words of another high school girl: After a few quiet walking dates we obtained a car and went for a ride. He stopped the car, and suddenly he was wild and raving. We struggled and fought, and I screamed to no avail. After biting him on the back three times so that blood came through, I used my shoe. He then came to his senses in his pain. . . . . I can't understand our first quiet dates.[24]

A woman describes what happened after she went out with her date and invited him to her apartment for coffee. He said, "Hey, let's make it." I said, "Oh, no. No way." He said, "Listen, I think you'd better. You better be a good girl and cooperate," and he grabbed at me. I tried to argue. I said, "Look, I don't want to. How could you enjoy it if I don't want to? We're the educated type, right? We're worried about whether we'll enjoy it." He pushed me on the bed and, when I started to cry, he said, "Be a good girl, or something bad will happen," and he held his fist in front of my face. I felt in real danger. I gave in. Later I walked into the police station without a mark on me and said, "I've been raped." They gave me that leer—you know, that New York Cop Leer. They brought in the guy for questioning. He said, "She was perfectly willing," and that was all there was to it.[25]

THE HIDDEN CULTURE OF RAPE

It is obvious that many societies openly condemn rape as a serious crime. It is less obvious that the same societies have a hidden culture of rape—a culture that secretly encourages males to assault females. This culture can be seen through the prevailing attitudes toward and beliefs about females, as well as through the concept of male and female sex roles.

WOMEN AS MEN'S PROPERTY   On the face of it the law against rape appears to protect the interests of the female. But actually it protects to a larger degree the interests of the male. This is because the female is treated like a piece of property that, before marriage, belongs to her father, and after marriage, belongs to her husband. If a man rapes an unmarried girl, he is actually committing the crime of vandalism against her father. If a man rapes a married woman, he is actually committing the crime against her husband. Thus statutory rape laws "help preserve the 'market value' of virginal young women as potential brides, rather than the protection of the naive girls from sexual exploitation." [26] As for forcible rape laws, feminist poet Susan Griffin writes:

The laws against rape exist to protect rights of the male as possessor of the female body, and not the right of the female over her own body. Even . . . the laws themselves are clear: In no state can a man be accused of raping his wife. How can any man steal what already belongs to him? It is in the sense of rape as theft of another man's property that Kate Millett writes, "Traditionally rape has been viewed as an offense one male commits against another—a matter of abusing his woman." In raping another man's woman, a man may aggrandize his own manhood and concurrently reduce that of another man. Thus a man's honor is not subject directly to rape, but only indirectly, through "his" woman.[27]

Moreover, the fact that women are treated as the property of men may be indicated by the following arguments.

When a female has been raped, we often say that she has been "ravaged," "ravished," "despoiled," or "ruined." These words connote the idea that a raped woman is like a piece of property that has been damaged.

When a man's wife has been raped, he tends to regard her as of lesser worth than before—in about the same way as he would regard a piece of damaged property. If he regarded her as a human being who has feelings rather than an object that does not, the husband presumably would show her more love and affection—because after being raped, she as a human being needs love and affection the most. Instead, her husband shows her less love and affection as if she were merely a piece of damaged property that has no feeling and has very little value. This is why many men say something like "I can't see how I can face my wife again if she has been raped." It is also little wonder that rape has the tendency to ruin the victim's marriage or strain her relationship with her husband, fiancé, or boyfriend.

The more often an object has been used, the less valuable it is considered to be. Similarly, in a society where women are treated as sex objects, the more often a woman has been sexually used—with or without her consent—by men other than her husband, the less valuable she is considered to be. A woman with very little value is referred to as a "cheap woman," "loose woman," "easy lay," "slut," "whore," and so on. Thus, just as a man who steals or damages another's relatively worthless property can easily get away with it, so can a man who ravages another's relatively "cheap" woman. For example, it is very difficult for a rapist to get convicted if his victim is known to have engaged in sex relations with more than two men, and it is almost impossible for the rapist to get convicted if his victim is known to be a prostitute. Also, since black or poor women are considered as less valuable sex objects than white or rich women, raping the former carries a lesser risk of getting convicted than raping the latter.

Throughout human history, when conquering armies confiscated or destroyed the conquered population's property, they also raped the women as if they were a part of the property. For example, not too long ago, when the Pakistani army invaded Bangladesh, the invaders raped at least two hundred thousand women. "They did it purposefully, as a matter of military strategy, to destroy the people's will to resist. These were rapes planned in advance and efficiently carried out under orders. . . . The troops were often shown pornographic films before being turned loose on women rounded up in buildings, in order to stimulate them enough to carry out their orders to rape." [28] After having been raped by the soldiers, these women were apparently considered as irreparably damaged property and therefore worthless junk, for their husbands threw them out of their homes.

Since women are culturally defined as men's property, men may find it difficult to respect women as human beings. It is through a lack of respect for women that men are encouraged to rape women, as rape expresses the very essence of this lack of respect for a woman.

WOMEN AS OBJECT OF MASCULINITY CONTEST   In a society that places a high premium on competition, men are pressured to engage in what may be called a masculinity contest. In order to come out as a winner, a man has to make out with the largest number of women possible.

And that means sex under whatever conditions the particular man can stand. Whether in a whorehouse or the back seat of a Toyota, the object is to score. However, your score counts more if you don't pay for it in cold hard cash. The most respected player in the game is the one who best outwits the most females by coaxing, lying, maneuvering; the one who, with the least actual cost to himself, gets the most females to give him the most sex. [29]

This masculinity contest is comparable to such competitive sports as football, baseball, soccer, and tennis. In any one of these sports, the players need an object—namely, a ball—to grab, hit, kick, or smash. Their goal is to score, and they could not care less whether they hurt the ball. Similarly, in the masculinity contest, the male participants need an object—namely, a woman—to grab and then just whang! bang! They don't care whether they humiliate, degrade, hurt, or terrify her as a human being. Instead, they see her as merely an object; they often refer to her as a piece of meat, a piece of ass, a box, or a whore. A victim of a gang rape reported that she was indeed treated in that way. After they had finished with her, the rapists said, "Let's dump this one and find another piece of meat." [30] Such a dehumanizing attitude toward women can be found in many men who engage in the masculinity contest.

But the dehumanizing attitude may not be sufficient for getting a man to actually play the masculinity game. At least two more things are necessary. One is the social pressure to play the game, and the other is the learning of some basic pointers for playing it.

The social pressure often comes from friends who ask something like the following: "Did you score?" "Had any lately?" "Did you screw her?" "Does she put out?" If you answer no, they may say, "What's the matter? Are you a sissy? Are you queer or something?" Such social pressure tends to make many men afraid of showing any sign of "femininity"—being soft, gentle, and considerate—in themselves. It also tends to make them want to show off their "masculine" qualities, such as aggressiveness, forcefulness, and violence. The likely consequence is that these men would engage in sexual violence, of one degree or another, against women.

In regard to the pointers for playing the masculinity game, they are found in the masculine role that men have been taught to play. This role requires that the male take an active part in achieving the social and then sexual relation with a female. He should be aggressive and use whatever force necessary to carry out his sexual conquest. He need not concern himself with how much force he is allowed to use. Our culture puts that burden on the female; it is she who has to determine the limit of the force he is allowed. But even when the female bluntly tells him to stop or puts up a fight to ward off his sexual advances, he may still ignore her resistance. Men often get this lesson in sexual conquest from the stereotype of the television, movie, and pulp-magazine hero who forcefully, persistently embraces and kisses the heroine despite her strong resistance and is finally rewarded by her melting in his arms. In real life such sexual aggression may easily lead to forcible rape.

"WOMEN WANT TO BE RAPED"   There is a popular myth that women consciously or unconsciously want to be raped. This myth is sometimes explicitly expressed and sometimes not.

Rapists, understandably, are the most likely to express the myth explicitly. As one study on rapists concludes, "Unfortunately most rapists can neither admit nor express the fact that they are a menace to society. Even convicted rapists who are serving long prison terms deny their culpability. *They tenaciously insist women encourage and enjoy sexual assault.* These men will tell you they are the greatest lovers in the world." [31]   (Emphasis added.) Relatively uneducated men are also likely to express the popular myth in an explicit way. As a member of the jury at the trial of a woman charged with murder, a factory worker was asked whether a woman could be acquitted for killing her rapist in self-defense. He answered, "No, because the guy's not trying to kill her. He's just trying to give her a good time. To get off, the guy will have to do her bodily harm, and giving a girl a screw isn't doing her bodily harm." [32]

Less explicit expression of the willing-victim myth can be found in the courtroom. A man charged with rape is supposed to be on trial, and he is presumed innocent until proven guilty of the alleged rape. But it is the woman, the alleged rape victim, who is often put on trial, and to add insult to injury, she is presumed guilty until proven innocent of provoking the rape. The prosecuting attorney is often not allowed to present evidence concerning the alleged rapist's past sexual conduct. But the rapist's lawyer is always permitted to question the victim about her past sexual conduct and to present evidence pertaining to it—in order to confirm his presumption of her as having provoked the rape. Quite often the rapist's lawyer argues that it is impossible to rape a woman if she resists. He may say something like "You can't thread a moving needle"; or "You can't put a pencil through a moving doughnut." So he insists that the rape victim has actually asked for it.

There are numerous other indications of the willing-victim myth. When a woman rejects a man's sexual invitation, he will likely keep on pressuring her—"What's the matter, are you frigid? Oh, come on, you know you really want to." If he eventually rapes her, he will assume that she has consented, even though she has strongly resisted all along. As one male attorney says, "So many chicks say no when there's yes yes in their eyes, and their thighs seem to spread at a mere flick of the finger." [33] Or more poetically, as Lord Byron wrote, "A little still she strove, and much repented/and whispering, 'I will ne'er consent'—consented." [34] Many men believe this so strongly that they show diminished respect for their wives or girlfriends who have been raped, suspecting that they may have "asked for it."

SOCIALIZING RAPE VICTIMS   To make it easier for males to rape females, the hidden culture of rape teaches girls to play the stereotypical feminine role. In learning this sex role, the girl acquires two things that make her a potential victim of rape. One is to be "feminine"—passive, gentle, weak, childlike, and economically dependent on men. The other is to be submissive to men.

To be feminine means that she is physically unaggressive and psychologically unprepared to defend herself in hand-to-hand combat. Thus, when she encounters her rapist-to-be, she is unlikely to gouge his eyes, kick him in the groin or genitals, or otherwise blind, maim, or kill him.[35] If she momentarily forgets being a "lady" and tries to fight off her attacker, she will be hampered by her "feminine" clothing. As Griffin says, "To be feminine is to wear shoes which make it difficult to run; skirts which inhibit one's stride; underclothes which inhibit circulation. Is it not an intriguing observation that those very clothes which are thought to be flattering to the female and attractive to the male are those which make it impossible for a woman to defend herself against aggression?" [36]

Being ladylike also involves being submissive to men. A "lady" does not shout, scream, scratch, hit, or otherwise make a scene when she is offended by a man. Thus, in public places such as buses, subways, elevators, and theaters, many women are not likely to react to sexual harassment. They will find it too embarrassing to make a public scene in response to such "sex grabs" as fondling of their legs, buttocks, or breasts by a molesting male.[37]

HOMOSEXUAL RAPE

The raping of an adult male by another is very rare in our society.[38] The risk of a man being raped by another man is apparently far less than the risk of a woman being raped by a man. But the homosexual rape is much more common within the prison than the heterosexual rape outside. Alan Davis estimates that in the Philadelphia prison system in the late 1960s, about 1 out of 30 inmates was raped. This estimated incidence of homosexual rape is indeed very high when compared to our earlier estimate that only 1 out of 500 females was raped in the larger society in 1975.

Davis found that virtually every slightly-built young man is sexually approached within one or two days after he has arrived in the prison. Many of those young men are repeatedly raped by gangs of inmates. Others manage to escape gang rape by seeking protection from a more powerful inmate, but they have to pay for that protection by serving as the target of their protector's homosexual assault. Only the tougher and more hardened young men are able to escape both single and gang rape.

In addition to single and gang rape, there is what Amir has called "victim-precipitated rape." To commit such a rape in the society at large, the offender usually offers his would-be victim a drink at a bar, a ride in a car, or a dose of sweet talk, and then forcibly demands sex favors from her. In other words, the rapist puts the victim in a vulnerable position first, and then uses force or threat of force to rape her. This, in essence, also happens in the prison. An old-time inmate offers a new inmate such goodies as candy, cigarettes, sedatives, stainless-steel blades, or extra food stolen from the kitchen, and after a day or so the gift giver will demand sexual repayment. Or the old-timer lures the young inmate into gambling, has him roll up large debts, and then tell him to "pay or fuck."

The characteristics of homosexual rapists and victims are comparable to those of male rapists and female victims outside prison. Homosexual rapists are more like men, and their victims are more like women. Specifically, the rapists are heavier, taller, and more violent, while their victims look less athletic and are better looking in a frail rather than husky way. Also, as is true outside prison, the rapists within it are generally older than their victims. But unlike the *intra*racial pattern of heterosexual rape outside the prison, the largest proportion (56 percent) of homosexual rapes in the prison are *inter-racial*—blacks raping whites. Still the two types of rape are similar in one sense—both involve members of the *dominant* group (the males outside the prison and the blacks inside) raping members of the *subordinate* group (the females outside and the whites inside).

In society at large, a woman is usually considered fair game for rape if she flouts the dominant sexist norm by being free and independent, engaging in sexual relations with different men, going to a tavern without a male escort, or hitchhiking alone. Within the prison system, a man also becomes fair game for rape if he rejects the dominant heterosexual norm by being a homosexual. Moreover, just as the sexist society encourages its inmates to rape the "bad" woman, so too the prison system encourages its inmates to rape the homosexual man. In fact, one known homosexual, when assigned to a prison, was given as a present to a gang of inmates in return for their good behavior.[39]

As for the nonhomosexual men who are as powerless within the prison as the powerless women without, once they are raped they are discouraged from reporting it to the authorities. According to Davis's report, one victim screamed for more than an hour while being gang-raped in his cell, and the guard who heard the screams did not bother to do anything. After the rape was over, the guard did do something—he laughed at the victim.

In cases where the victim files a complaint, he is likely to be subjected to the same kind of official "protection" that the female victim outside the prison is subjected to. As we have observed, the legal protection that the female victim is subjected to at the police station and in the courtroom makes her feel that the protection is worse than the rape itself. Many rape victims in the prison feel the same way about the protection that they get from prison administrators. Davis reports that the usual procedure for protecting the complaining victim is to place him on "lock-in feed-in." This means that after the victim files the complaint, he is locked up in his cell all day, fed in his cell, and not permitted any recreation, television, or exercise. But he is permitted to do at least one thing: look forward—when released—to being terrorized by his rapist's friends and by the rapist himself. Many victims consider all this worse than the homosexual rape itself.

On top of this tormenting experience, the victim is stigmatized as a homosexual. This stigma weighs on him for the duration of his confinement and follows him from one prison to another. As for the rapist, he does not consider himself a homosexual. He does not even consider himself to have engaged in homosexual acts; to him, it is his victim who has. There is nothing unusual about the homosexual rapist's holding such a view. It merely reflects the "blame the victim" syndrome, comparable to the heterosexual rapist's belief that his victim "asked for it."

From his findings Davis concludes that the primary motive for homosexual rape is *not* to relieve one's sexual deprivation. If an inmate simply wants to relieve his sexual deprivation, masturbation would be a much more convenient and normal method of relief than homosexual rape. Instead, the primary motive for homosexual rape is the need to subjugate and humiliate the victim. This is evidenced by the fact that homosexual rapists often use such language as "Fight or fuck"; "We're going to take away your manhood"; "You'll have to give up some face"; and "We're gonna make a girl out of you."

CHILD MOLESTING

Child molesting or *pedophilia* may be considered a form of rape, because the victim is not legally capable of giving her consent. The average molester is about thirty-seven years of age and his victim nine. Both are likely to be acquainted with, rather than strangers to, each other; the molester may be the victim's grandfather, uncle, parent's friend, or neighbor. Compared with the rapist, the molester is much less likely to resort to physical force or vaginal penetration. Typically, the molester plays with the girl's private parts or tells her to play with his.[40]

Although this is the popular mode of operation among the molesters, the general public seems to associate child molestation with violent sexual intercourse. This may explain why many people view the crime with extreme horror and are determined to get the "dirty old man" arrested and imprisoned. When a child is discovered to have been molested there is great fear and hysteria in the family, outrage in the neighborhood, and excitement and vengefulness among the police. But all this may come as a complete surprise to the child victim, because she lacks the adults' sexual sophistication, does not suffer any bodily injury, and may have found her molester's behavior amusing.[41] It is thus not surprising that child molesting does not have the same effect on its young victims as forcible rape does on its older, mature victims. One study of molested children indicated "remarkably little evidence of fear, anxiety, guilt, or psychic trauma" in those victims. Another study found that female adults who had been molested twenty years before—while they were between the ages of nine and thirteen —were none the worse for the experience.[42]

Just as the victims of child molesting differ from the victims of forcible rape, so the molesters also differ from the rapists. First, molesters are considerably older than rapists; most of the former are over thirty-five years of age while most of the latter under twenty. Second, molesters are more sexually repressed or less sexually aggressive; they started masturbating and engaging in sexual intercourse at a later age. Third, molesters are comparatively gentle and passive while rapists are tough and aggressive.[43] Fourth, molesters are much more incapable than rapists of getting along with adult members of the opposite sex.[44] Fifth, most molesters admit their guilt,[45] while most rapists refuse to do so. And sixth, homosexual molesters (those who molest boys) are even more likely than heterosexual molesters (those who molest girls) to admit their offense and to do so very frankly.[46]

Taken as a whole, the preceding data suggest that child molesters disastrously fail to meet the cultural standard of masculinity. This may explain why they are scorned, and, if young enough, are raped by their more "masculine" fellow inmates in prison. Their lack of masculinity may also explain why, unlike forcible rapists who tend to be violently aggressive and attack women in order to subjugate and humiliate them, child molesters refrain from violent aggression against their victims—and apparently they do not intend to subjugate and humiliate the children. Moreover, while the hidden culture of rape—which is related to the ideal of masculinity and to the males' domination over females in society—encourages rapists to blame their adult victim, this same culture fails to compel molesters to blame their child victim. This is why, unlike rapists, most molesters either fully and frankly admit their guilt or indirectly blame themselves rather than their victim. They usually attempt to do the latter by blaming their own drunkenness for having caused the offense, as can be shown by the following comments from various molesters of young girls:

• "I was intoxicated and I couldn't account for myself."
• "I was drunk. I didn't realize their age and I was half blind. I've always been a drinker." (The victims were six and seven years old.)
• "When I drink I get that 'I don't give-a-damn' attitude. I had no intention of hurting them. . . . Every time I committed a crime I was drunk; I'd never do it if I were sober."
• "My biggest problem is drinking; that's why I'm here in the prison." [47]

It may be noted that we have largely discussed one type of pedophiliac —men who molest young girls. There is yet another type of molester— women who molest young boys. Scholars have failed to study these female molesters. Like most lay people, scholars may believe that there are too few of them to be a significant subject for a study. Again like most lay people, scholars may feel that women are not as interested as men are in sexual activities, and that even if a woman did molest a young boy she could hardly do any harm without a penis.[48] Although the public is not interested in finding and punishing female molesters, their number may well be a significantly large one. After all, they have at least one thing in common with the other type of child molester as well as the rapist—they all occupy the dominant position vis-à-vis their victim.

THEORIES OF RAPE

Scholars in various disciplines have tried to explain why some individuals commit rape or why some groups or societies have a higher incidence of rape than others. They have produced at least four different explanations, which may be identified as (1) sexual inadequacy theory, (2) subcultural violence theory, (3) relative frustration theory, and (4) differential control theory.

SEXUAL INADEQUACY THEORY

In general, psychologists, psychiatrists, and psychoanalysts agree that rapists suffer from some personality defects or emotional disturbance. As one group of psychologists state, "It is true that classic neurotic symptoms are a rarity, but all types of character neuroses, character disorders, and more severe borderline and psychotic states are represented in rapists. It is equally clear that there are some specific characteristics present in rapists which differentiate them from other criminals and from other sexual offenders." [49] But these behavioral scientists disagree as to the *specific* personality characteristics that are supposed to reside in rapists.

A group of psychiatrists who studied rapists and other sex offenders in Sing Sing Prison concluded that none of these inmates had a normal personality and that most of them (70 percent) showed symptoms of schizophrenia. One psychiatrist who investigated the convicted sex offenders at the New Jersey Diagnostic Center suggested that "underlying or overt hostility was particularly evident" in these offenders. Other psychiatrists and psychologists have offered one or more of the following opinions in regard to the rapist's psychological problems: (1) The rapist suffers from some feelings of castration or sexual inadequacy that drives him to hide those feelings by engaging in overassertive and overaggressive sexual behavior; (2) he is troubled by inner conflict, inner disharmony, and social isolation; (3) he is afraid of revealing his homosexual tendency that he can only suppress by being overly aggressive toward women; (4) he can be sexually aroused only by women who put up a fight against his advances; (5) he is led by his Oedipus complex—sexual desire for his mother—to rape a woman who would resist just as his own mother would if she were attacked by him; and (6) he has been sexually overstimulated in his childhood by his mother, who combined her seductive behavior with cruelty toward him.[50]

Although all these specific characteristics appear different from each other, they seem to fit a pattern. The rapist is a man who, as the result of his unpleasant childhood experiences, has developed such a personality defect that he cannot relate successfully to women, which is often referred to as "sexual inadequacy." A common way for rapists to express their sexual inadequacy is to indulge in fantasy and then act out this fantasy by raping a woman. Here is how a rapist describes his fantasy.

I had a complete fantasy life that involved my being stronger than all men, irresistible to all women, a doer of great things. . . . I had fantasies about the women I was raping, how she felt physically, where she had been in life, some resentment that she's done things in life without me. I had a longing to do things in general with people. Sometimes I'd verbalize these fantasies if the woman was quite submissive, otherwise I'd just take the trip within myself.[51]

This theory of sexual inadequacy, with its assumption of personality defect or emotional disturbance, has very limited applicability. It may be applied to those imprisoned, emotionally disturbed rapists who are, after all, the typical sample studied by the psychological investigators. It is doubtful that most rapists, particularly those who are not imprisoned, are emotionally disturbed. The next theory may have somewhat broader applicability in that it assumes rapists to be free from psychological problems.

SUBCULTURAL VIOLENCE THEORY

In his sociological study of rape, Amir attempts to explain his major finding that lower-class blacks have the highest rate of forcible rape. He finds the explanation in Wolfgang's theory of subcultural violence, which, as we observed in the preceding chapter, was applied to homicide. Amir apparently believes that rape and homicide are alike in being acts of violence that stem from the lower-class black subculture—the subculture of violence. But Amir adds the sexual component to that subculture.

According to Amir, the lower-class black subculture has the following characteristics: (1) It emphasizes the importance of seeking thrills through aggressive actions and sexual exploits; (2) its male members are obsessed with their masculinity and feel the need to display and defend it by engaging in brief and transitory sexual activities with women; (3) it idealizes personal violence and prowess in its male members' social and sexual life; and (4) it encourages sexual permissiveness, early sexual experiences among boys and girls, the use of sex by boys for achieving status in their peer groups, and promiscuous behavior on the part of girls.[52] Amir further traces this black subculture to its source:

The Negro male's aggressive sexuality seems . . . due to the strong need to overcome problems of masculinity and of sexual identity. This is so because of the Negro family structure (mother-based family) and the need to overcome general social disadvantages, by substituting sexual aggressive masculinity for failures as a man in the economic and social status spheres.[53]

Unlike the theory of sexual inadequacy, which considers rape as the symptom of individual abnormality, subcultural violence theory assumes that the rapist himself is normal. Like normal people, the rapist does what he is expected to do by his culture, a subculture of violence, which encourages him to engage in rape. Thus the theory of subcultural violence, when compared with the sexual inadequacy theory, may be applied to a larger number of rape cases. But it is perhaps still of limited applicability, because it is based on Amir's possibly untenable assumption that lower-class black rapists are the typical rapists. Since the great majority of rapists are not known to the police, they may be quite different from Amir's sample of largely lower-class black rapists, who are known to the police. The fact that the great majority of rapists do not get arrested may indicate that they are like average males who are not too violent or immersed in a subculture of violence.

RELATIVE FRUSTRATION THEORY

Sociologist Duncan Chappell and his colleagues try to explain why the rape rate is much higher in Los Angeles than in Boston, or why there are more rapes in some societies than in others.[54] They first present an argument that they disagree with. The argument is that the lack of opportunities for nonmarital sexual activities, such as in a sexually restrictive society, generates a high rate of forcible rape. This means that in a more sexually permissive society, where there are abundant opportunities for nonmarital sex, the rape rate should be lower. In direct contrast to this argument, Chappell and his associates contend that the more sexually permissive society has the higher rate of forcible rape. They use the concept of relative frustration to explain why sexual permissiveness causes forcible rape.

Chappell and his colleagues believe that, compared with a male who is rejected by a female in a sexually restrictive society, a rejected male in a permissive society feels much more frustrated. It is in this sense that the *relative frustration* of the male is much higher in the more permissive setting than in the less permissive situation.

In the restrictive setting, the rejected male is more able to protect his ego by rationalizing that the female has rejected him not because he is unattractive but because the restrictive setting itself prevents her from accepting his sexual invitation. He may point out that girls are afraid of premarital sex, church rules are too oppressive, parents are too strict, or laws against nonmarital sex are too stringent. It is no wonder, he may conclude, that many girls cannot accept sexual overtures from an attractive man like himself. But in the permissive setting, the rejected male cannot use the rationalization just described. Instead, he is more likely to see that it is he himself who is responsible for his own failure to win the girl's favors. The consequence is that he may easily feel hurt, thereby increasing his sexual frustration. This sexual frustration, then, drives many men in the permissive society to resort to rape. Chappell and his associates use the same reasoning to explain why there are many more rapes in Los Angeles, which they consider to be a permissive city, than in Boston, which they regard as a restrictive city.

The theory of relative frustration may on the face of it appear to be quite persuasive. But its validity has yet to be tested. First, as Chappell and his colleagues have cautioned, we have yet to determine whether the reported difference in rape rates between Los Angeles and Boston reflect the *real* difference in rape rates or merely the difference in police efficiency between the two cities. Second, we have yet to determine whether the sexual climate in Los Angeles is *actually* more permissive than that in Boston. Third, even if it is true that the permissive city has a higher rape rate than does the restrictive city, we still have to find out whether a permissive setting *actually* causes relative frustration that in turn leads to rape. Finally, Chappell and his colleagues' assumption that *sexual* frustration causes rape is hardly tenable because *non*sexual frustration has much more to do with rape.[55]

DIFFERENTIAL CONTROL THEORY

After analyzing the sexual norm and behavior of the Gusii people in Kenya, anthropologist Robert LeVine reaches the conclusion that there are four factors that may explain the unusually high incidence of rape among the Gusii: (1) More severe social restrictions on females' nonmarital sexual activities than on males'; (2) stronger sexual inhibitions in females than in males; (3) economic or other barriers that prolong some males' bachelorhood and in the process generate great sexual frustration in these males; and (4) the absence of physical segregation between the sexes.[56]

You may notice that the last two factors merely set the stage for some form of sexual interaction—which may or may not be rape. The first two factors, however, apparently help ensure the occurrence of rape. For if females are highly restricted and inhibited but males are not, rape is likely to occur. On the other hand, if both sexes are equally restricted and inhibited, sexual abstinence would be prevalent. And if both sexes are equally unrestricted and uninhibited, promiscuity would be rampant. In other words, it is the *differential control*—females' sexual activities being more strongly controlled by society than are males'—that is a key cause of rape.

POWER THEORY APPLIED

Given their different degrees of power, members of the higher social classes are more likely to engage in officially *un*recognized rape while those of the lower classes tend more to commit officially recognized rape. The basic difference between these two types of rape can be illuminated further by feminist journalist Susan Brownmiller's observation:

> We know, or at least the statistics tell us, that no more than half of all reported rapes are the work of strangers, and in the hidden statistics— those four out of five rapes that go unreported—the percent committed by total strangers is probably lower. The man who jumps out of the alley or crawls through the window is the man who, if caught, will be called "the rapist" by his fellow men. But the known man who presses his advantage, who uses his position of authority, who forces his attentions, who will not take "No" for an answer, who assumes that sexual access is his right-of-way and physical aggression his right-on expression of masculinity, conquest and power is no less of a rapist—yet the chance that this man will be brought to justice, even under the best of circumstances, is comparatively small.[57]

It seems clear that more of the powerful or higher-status rapists are known to their victims than in the case of powerless or lower-class rapists. This may largely result from the lesser social control imposed on the former than on the latter. There may also be a symbiotic relationship between these two types of rapists. On the one hand, the powerful are likely to condemn the lower-class rapist. This serves to strengthen the stereotyped notion of the average rapist as a lower-class person, with the consequence of lower-class men being more likely to be officially recognized as rapists when they rape women in a crude, life-threatening way. On the other hand, the official recognition of these lower-class men as rapists, along with the popular view of these officially recognized rapists, make it difficult for law enforcers and the general public to label as rapists higher-status men who employ nonlife-threatening methods to force their attentions on their unwilling female acquaintances and girlfriends. This is particularly true in the case of those higher-status men who commit date rape. It is also true in the case of more powerful higher-status men who use threat of layoff to demand sexual favors from their unwilling female employees. As they are not defined by others nor by themselves as rapists, these higher-status rapists are encouraged to continue their raping escapades.

SUMMARY

Rape can be divided into two types: officially recognized rape and officially unrecognized rape. Some aspects of the first type are as follows: it is largely a lower-class or black crime; it is mostly intraracial; rape offenders and victims are mostly black; females most vulnerable to rape are between fifteen and nineteen years of age; most rapes occur during the weekend; most rapists plan their assault rather than act it out impulsively; gang rape is about as common as single rape; and victim-precipitated rape is not uncommon but the notion of victim precipitation is open to challenge. The rape has two types of impact upon its victims: (1) Most victims are beset with anxiety and guilt, and (2) a few, but increasingly more, victims feel outraged and revengeful. As for officially unrecognized rape, there are two kinds: double rape and date rape. Double rape refers to the experience of getting humiliated first by the rapist(s) and then by the law enforcers. Date rape, which is the most common sexual offense, is the type committed by a male against his date.

The hidden culture of rape is made up of the prevailing male attitudes toward females. In this culture, women are treated as if they were men's property; women are used as sex objects so that men can play their masculinity game; women are believed to have the conscious or unconscious desire to be raped; and girls are conditioned to play the feminine, submissive role. All this helps induce the male to rape the female.

Homosexual rape is rare in society but common in prison. In many respects, homosexual rape in prison is comparable to heterosexual rape in the larger society. It is basically a phenomenon of a more powerful man raping a less powerful one.

Compared with rapists of women, child molesters are generally older, less physically violent, less likely to engage in vaginal intercourse with their victims, and more willing to admit their guilt. It has also been pointed out that female adults who molest young boys have escaped the attention of the public and scholars alike.

There are four theories of rape. (1) Sexual inadequacy theory attributes rape to the offender's feeling of sexual inadequacy that is a part of his defective personality or which stems from his unpleasant childhood experiences.

(2) Subcultural violence theory blames the cause of rape on the lower-class black subculture that emphasizes the importance of seeking status through sexual violence. (3) Relative frustration theory traces the origin of rape to a sexually permissive culture that intensifies the male's feeling of rejection by a female and thus increases his sexual frustration. And (4) differential control theory explains rape as the result of the female's sexual desire being more strongly controlled by society than is the male's. Power theory can also be used to explain the two types of rape and to show the symbiosis between them.

SUGGESTED READINGS

Amir, Menachem. *Patterns in Forcible Rape*. Chicago: University of Chicago Press, 1971.

Brownmiller, Susan. *Against Our Will: Men, Women and Rape*. New York: Simon and Schuster, 1975.

Chappell, Duncan, Gilbert Geis, Stephen Schafer, and Larry Siegel, "Forcible Rape: A Comparative Study of Offenses Known to the Police in Boston and Los Angeles." In James M. Henslin, ed. *Studies in the Sociology of Sex*. New York: Appleton-Century-Crofts, 1971, pp. 169–190.

Griffin, Susan, "Rape: The All-American Crime." *Ramparts* 10 (September 1971): 1–8.

Kirkpatrick, Clifford and Eugene Kanin. "Male Sex Aggression on a University Campus." *American Sociological Review* 22 (February 1957): 52–58.

LeGrand, Camille E. "Rape and Rape Laws: Sexism in Society and Law." *California Law Review* 61 (May 1973): 919–941.

LeVine, Robert A. "Gusii Sex Offenses: A Study in Social Control." *American Anthropologist* 61 (December 1959): 965–990.

McCaghy, Charles H. "Child Molesters: A Study of Their Careers as Deviants." In Marshall Clinard and Richard Quinney, eds. *Criminal Behavior Patterns*. New York: Holt, Rinehart and Winston, 1967, pp. 75–88.

Medea, Andra and Kathleen Thompson. *Against Rape*. New York: Farrar, Straus and Giroux, 1974.

Weis, Kurt and Sandra S. Borges. "Victimology and Rape: The Case of the Legitimate Victim." *Issues in Criminology* 8 (Fall 1973): 71–115.

7 ROBBERY

Like murder and rape, robbery is considered by law enforcers as one of the most serious crimes. But there is something unique about robbery. Law enforcers classify crimes into two categories: (1) violent crimes, including murder, rape, and assault, and (2) property crimes, comprising robbery, burglary, larceny theft, and auto theft. Although they formally classify robbery as a property crime, law enforcers practically consider it a violent crime. Similarly, some sociologists treat robbery as a violent crime while others believe it to be a property crime.[1] All this is due to the fact that robbery has both characteristics—violence or threat of violence against the victim and theft of his or her property—as can be discerned from the *FBI Uniform Crime Reports'* definition of the crime: "Robbery is a vicious type of crime which takes place in the presence of the victim to obtain *property* or a thing of value from a person by use of *force* or threat of force."[2] (Emphasis added.)

THE NATURE OF ROBBERY

Given the above-mentioned dual nature of robbery—as both property and violent crime—we shall first examine both these aspects of it. Then we shall look at the statistical background of robberies and the personal background of robbers. Finally, we shall discuss the various types of robberies and robbers.

ROBBERY AS PROPERTY CRIME

As a property crime, robbery is a relatively rational, calculated act. As such, it requires making decisions. The decision making consists usually of a sequence of three elements. (1) Would-be robbers decide that they will rob in order to have more money than they can legitimately acquire; (2) they decide what target to rob; and (3) they decide how the robbery is to be carried out.[3]

FEELING THE NEED FOR MONEY   For most robbers the decision to rob is based on their desire for money. Money may not be the only motive for robbery, though. As one former bank-robber argues,

> I do not agree with the common assumption that all banks are robbed
> solely for money. I believe that money, in most cases, is only a
> secondary motive, and in many cases the man who commits the crime is
> not always fully aware of the primary factors motivating him. At least
> this was true in my case, and after seven years of associating with
> bank robbers I have become convinced that, like me, their reasons for
> robbing a bank were far more complicated than just a sudden need
> for money. . . . What I was searching for was not just any robbery, but
> one that would bring the indignant outcries from the so-called respect-
> ables. This bank robbery was my way of spitting in society's face;
> and I robbed their bank, and there was a strange, exciting pleasure after
> it was all over.[4]

This may be true for some bank robbers. But most robbers are not bank robbers. The fact is that the majority of robbers do express their need for money as the primary motive for their crime. One study in Oakland, California, for example, shows that two-thirds of robbery offenders gave money as their reason for robbing.[5]

Nevertheless, the desire for money varies in strength from one robber to another. In the Oakland study adult offenders mentioned the monetary motive much more often than did juvenile offenders (74 percent of adults as compared to 45 percent of juveniles). The juveniles seemed more likely than did the adults to be confused about the reasons for their robberies; they frequently seemed uncertain as to why they had got involved in the robberies in the first place. Another study, conducted in Boston, shows that adults are more likely than juveniles, and whites more likely than blacks, to have greater monetary ambition. Consequently, adults and whites tend to rob such commercial establishments as banks, grocery stores, variety stores, gas stations, and bars, which involve relatively large sums of money. Juveniles and blacks, on the other hand, tend to commit cab holdups, purse snatching, and mugging, which are less profitable.[6]

DECIDING WHAT TARGET TO ROB   Once an individual has decided to rob, he or she has to select a certain target. The target selection is generally based on these factors: the amount of money available, the risk of arrest, and the vulnerability of the victim-to-be.[7]

A robber usually knows that banks, grocery stores, department stores, and other commercial establishments have relatively large sums of money, but commercial establishments of the same type do differ in the amount of money that can be stolen. Thus in cases where the robber lacks information about the amount of money in a store, he or she obviously has to make an effort to find out. One professional robber, for example, wanted to estimate the amount of money he might steal from a company on the day when it paid its employees in cash. To make an accurate estimate, he sought information about the organization of the company, including the number of persons working at each level and the amount of each employee's salary. In another case, one group of robbers who specialized in robbing jewelry stores always sent their most conventional-looking member into the store to examine its most expensive jewelry. Then they were able to determine how much they could expect to steal, taking only the most expensive jewelry and fencing it for as much as half its price listed in the store.

In addition to looking for a lucrative target, the robber considers the risk of the criminal venture. A major risk is the police officer on the street or in a patrol car. To minimize this risk, most robbers choose to hold up stores in outlying commercial districts and thoroughfare streets, rather than in the central business districts. Another risk facing the robber is the possibility that the victim will put up resistance. To reduce this possibility, many offenders carry weapons. Also, they know that victim resistance is more likely to come from individuals who are forced to part with their own money than from those who are compelled to give up their employers' money. For this reason, a number of robbers avoid small stores that they think are owned and run by the clerks themselves.

Not all robbers are as calculating and methodical as has been indicated above. It appears that those who aim for a relatively big score tend to carefully calculate the amount of money to be stolen and weigh the risk of arrest. Many other robbers, particularly those who are blacks and juveniles, are less calculating and methodical. They nonetheless make a rational decision on their choice of a victim. In general, they tend more to choose a victim who they believe is clearly vulnerable. Thus they will rob individuals who wear expensive clothes or flash a large wad of money in poor sections of the city; women who are sixty or older; individuals who walk alone in deserted streets; and drunks, homosexuals, and prostitutes' customers in the vicinity of late-hour bars or in areas of prostitution.

DECIDING HOW TO ROB After robbers have decided that they need some money, that they will steal it, and have decided on the target, they then decide how to execute the crime. This last decision involves varying degrees of planning. At one extreme, some robbers, particularly professional ones who are after a big score, plan their crime with great care and minute detail. At the other extreme, some robbers, especially amateur ones who suddenly feel the need for a small sum of money, commit robbery on the spur of the moment.

One convicted robber said that once, while he and his friend were in a taxi, his friend suddenly grabbed the driver around the neck, menacingly flashed a knife before his eyes, and demanded his money. The convicted robber claimed that he or his friend had not considered any robbery until the very moment of its occurrence. In another instance, two robbers who had carefully planned most of their capers became involved in one that they had not planned. One of these two robbers went into a liquor store to buy some wine, but the clerk refused to sell it to him because he was drunk. Angered, he pulled out a pistol and demanded money. His partner, waiting outside in the car, was taken by surprise but nonetheless ran into the store to help. Later they were apprehended because the clerk succeeded in identifying the license number of the car. If they had planned the robbery, they would have used a stolen car or license plate in order to prevent that sort of identification.[8]

Such random, unplanned robberies have been reported to be quite common. The Oakland study, for example, indicated that over half of the adult robbers under study reported no planning at all.[9] This may be true for robbers who get convicted for their unplanned—and thus failed—robberies. But it seems doubtful that most acts of robbery happen randomly. If this were the case, the average robber would have been arrested for most of his or her robberies. Instead, the average robber usually commits many robberies before being caught; even the average unskilled robber—the mugger in the street—strikes many times before being arrested.[10] This low probability of arrest may suggest that most robberies are planned rather than unplanned, if the assumption is correct that unplanned robberies are more likely than planned robberies to result in arrest. At any rate, it seems reasonable to conceive of most robberies as being planned to one degree or another.

The degree of planning depends on the choice of a target. When robbers snatch purses from elderly women on the street, they ordinarily know the area well, which makes their escape easier. If the intended victim is young or a male, the robber usually works with friends to neutralize the victim's resistance. In choosing a cab driver as a victim, the offender "will hire a cab, ask to be driven to a place isolated from public view, pull a weapon or grab the driver from behind, demand his money, and run from the scene, often into a housing project or alley he knows well." [11] Finally, the choice of a commercial establishment requires even more planning. As one robber states, "The detailed planning and preparation . . . is the most important part of the heist. If this layout is done well, the mark is in the bag. The robbery itself becomes a simple transaction lasting but a few moments—sometimes less than thirty seconds." [12]

The planning of a holdup has two important elements. One is *casing*, which involves a careful examination, survey, or study of the mark. In casing a mark, say, a bank, the "heistmob" (robbery gang) would study the floor plan, arrangement of furniture, location of doors and windows, position of cameras and alarms, and so on. The heistmob may also take an advance look at the employees, guards, and customers. All this is designed to minimize the possibility of obstacles, resistance, and interference during the robbery. The second element of planning the crime is *role allocation*, which involves the assignment of a particular task to each member of the robbery gang. The gang may consist of two or more members. One member performs the role of "wheelman" (driver)—steals the getaway car, plans the escape route, sometimes doubles as "peekman" (lookout), and drives away from the scene of the robbery. The other member or members are called "inside-men" or "rodmen" (gunmen), whose function is to case the mark, enter the building, and execute the robbery.

In the process of executing the robbery, one inside-man will control the situation with pistol-backed authority while the other will swiftly gather the loot. In the words of an experienced robber:

The mob enters as casually as any other visitors. Melodramatics are for the movies. One man does the talking: "All right, folks, stay where you're at! Keep quiet! Keep your hands where I can see them! Nobody but the insurance company is gonna get hurt, so take it easy." Generally this fellow stands near the door where he can keep the whole room under observation as well as intercept anyone who may come in while the robbery is in progress. He is an authoritative figure, the center of attention. Most witnesses hardly notice the other insidemen, who go about their job of collecting the score as quickly and with as little fuss as possible. [13]

Such an efficient execution of the job, however, can be disrupted by store managers and other loyal employees who may try to become heroes by defending their bosses' business interests. Sometimes customers—particularly if they become hysterical—present what one robber calls "an occupational hazard of the first order." This hazard is further aggravated by none other than the robbers themselves. For they are not inclined to use violence against their victims. If their victims scream hysterically, they do not silence them by knocking them unconscious, strangling them, or cutting their throats. The fact that they generally prefer to avoid the use of violence indicates that their type of robbery is a property crime.

There are, however, some situations where robbers are compelled to use violence, and there are also some robbers who employ a significant degree of violence. These facts make robbery appear to be primarily a crime of violence, as discussed in the following section.

ROBBERY AS VIOLENT CRIME

After finding that the average robber has a prior arrest record that shows him to have committed more violent crimes than property crimes, John Conklin prefers to see him as a violent criminal.

The robbery offender should be seen as one who *often employs criminal violence in a nonutilitarian manner*. He frequently has been arrested for assaultive crimes in which no attempt was made to steal property, although he is no more prone than the general criminal population to arrest for such criminal violence. However, when he does commit theft from a person, he creates a situation in which force or threat of force is used against the victim.[14] [Emphasis added.]

It seems more accurate to say that robbers have a great *potential* for violence, but that this violent potential seldom results in *actual* violence when they are committing robbery. Several studies have indicated that only about half or less than half of all robberies involve some degree of force, violence, or injury.[15] In considering robbery as a violent crime, then, we should note (1) its element of *actual* violence, and (2) its element of *potential* violence. Actual violence in robbery is physical force that usually does not involve the use of a weapon, while potential violence is the threat of force buttressed by the use of a weapon.

THE ELEMENT OF ACTUAL VIOLENCE   Strong-arm or unarmed robberies are often viewed by the public as less dangerous than armed robberies. Yet they are far more likely to result in some injury to the victims. The Oakland study, for example, shows that 66 percent of unarmed-robbery victims, compared to only 17 percent of armed-robbery victims, were injured.[16] This can be explained by the following three reasons.

First of all, the use of physical force is itself a weapon of sorts, which the FBI has aptly referred to as a personal weapon. Thus it can function in a similar though less threatening way as a knife or pistol, namely, to intimidate the victim so that the robbery can be successfully carried out. Above all, the use of physical force—which often results in injuring the victim—is simply a necessary part of the act of taking away the property from its owner.

Second, the characteristics of robbery offenders may have something to do with the use of violence in their crime. Juveniles are much more likely than adults to harm their victims. As Conklin found in his study of Boston robberies, 32 percent of all juvenile offenders injured their victims so badly that they had to be taken to the hospital, while only 15 percent of adult offenders inflicted that much injury. Blacks are also more likely than whites to send their victims to the hospital. The same Boston study by Conklin shows that 26 percent of black robbers caused their victims to require hospital treatment, while only 10 percent of white robbers did that much harm to their victims. In brief, such offender characteristics as being young or black have been shown to be associated with the use of violence against robbery victims. All this may, in turn, be related to the following findings from the Boston study.

Robbers, particularly the youthful and black ones, are more likely to hurt their victims if the robbery incident occurs on the street than if it takes place in a commercial establishment. Muggers and purse snatchers on the street, for example, hurt their victims far more often than do professional robbers in a bank or store. The youthful and black offenders are further encouraged to injure their victims if they commit their crime in a group rather than alone, and if they find their victims alone rather than in a group. It thus appears clear that robbers who are likely to engage in violence against their victims tend to do so because they, being relatively inexperienced and socially disadvantaged, are driven toward the kind of robberies—street, unarmed robberies—that basically requires the use of physical force.[17]

Third, the offender's perception of victim resistance seems to be related to the use of violence in unarmed robberies. Many robbery offenders apparently believe that their victims are more likely to resist if no weapon is involved than if a weapon is involved, since their victims are less frightened by the absence than by the presence of a weapon. Thus, believing that they will encounter more victim resistance than will armed robbers, unarmed robbers are more likely to engage in violence against their victims.[18]

THE ELEMENT OF POTENTIAL VIOLENCE   It is largely in *armed* robberies that potential violence—threat of violence that is rarely realized—becomes very important in ensuring the successful execution of the crime. The use of a firearm, then, can be said to serve an *instrumental* function for the robber; it is a tool enabling the robber to achieve a material goal, namely, money. Many sociologists look at the use of a weapon in instrumental terms. But some psychologists and psychiatrists believe that the weapon serves an *expressive* function—enabling robbers to intimidate and control their victims so that they can fulfill a psychological need for dominating others.

One psychiatrist, for example, has conducted a study on the role of a gun in robbery, and suggested the expressive function of the gun for the robber. He reports that most of the convicted robbers whom he interviewed associated their use of a gun with their feeling of manliness. For them the gun represented the means to demonstrate their masculinity, to control others, and to command others to do their will. Although the actual acquisition of money was important to them, they relished more the brief moment when they were able to use the gun to make their victims obey their commands. "It was this mastery over others, a desire to control, a sense of omnipotence—and not a desire to hurt—that appeared to characterize these persons." [19] One robber describes what the gun does for him:

The gun is a symbol of power, of phallic omnipotence, and it is capable
of striking terror into the hearts of the weak and strong alike. It's
very difficult to explain all the queer, fascinating sensations pounding
and surging through me while I'm holding a gun on a victim, watching his body tremble and sweat. Any moment I expect his eyes to come
popping out of their sockets; and in that moment of terror-filled
realization I feel like God because I know and my victim knows that I
command the power of life and death.[20]

But sociologist Conklin, in his interview with convicted robbers, found only a few of them to have used the gun in order to satisfy their psychological need for dominance. Most of them talked about the weapon as simply a means for robbing people of their money. Moreover, Conklin argues that armed robbers, when compared with unarmed ones, manifest greater rationality in their robbery activities, as can be seen in their selection of lucrative targets to rob, their attempts to prevent victim resistance, and their allocation of tasks to members of the robbery gang. Such rationality seems to indicate that robbers use firearms because the weapons help ensure the successful stealing of money, rather than because they help express the robbers' masculinity.[21]

Perhaps the gun serves both an instrumental and an expressive function for most armed robbers. It is like a case of killing two birds with one stone, except that one bird is more desirable than the other. It is quite apparent that most armed robbers find the victim's money more desirable than the act of dominating the victim with a weapon. This is evident from the fact that most, if not all, armed robbers always take away their victim's money, and rarely, if ever, return it. It seems best to consider the expressive function of the gun as a "fringe benefit" that some armed robbers may enjoy. But the gun as an instrument is almost a necessity if they are to perform efficiently.

According to Conklin, a weapon may serve four instrumental functions in the process of efficiently performing a robbery. The first function is that the weapon creates a *buffer zone* between offender and victim. Many robbers believe that the firearm is most effective because it frightens the victim the most. With the firearm being able to hold the victim at a distance, the robber can cover a great area and can also control many victims at the same time. The second function of the weapon is to *intimidate* the victim. This function makes it unnecessary for the robber to resort to violence. In fact, many robbers use a weapon to avoid the need for violence. If the show of a weapon fails to intimidate the victim enough to give up his or her money, the offender often tries to increase the level of intimidation by cocking the pistol or holding it to the victim's head. If this attempt fails also, the robber may be compelled to use the weapon for the third purpose—to *make good the threat*. A few robbers stab or shoot the victim, but most simply strike—without seriously hurting—the victim on the side of the head or in the stomach to show that they "mean business." And the fourth function of the weapon is to *insure escape* after the completion of the crime, as robbers use the weapon to keep the victims, witnesses, and even police officers from interfering with their escape.[22]

It may be noted that these four functions have to do with the weapon as a warning signal of potential violence. The weapon can be effectively employed to carry out these four functions, primarily because its mere presence is so threatening that it makes it unnecessary for the robber to resort to its use. This may explain why robbers who are armed with a weapon tend to commit their crime without using violence. According to Conklin's Boston study, older and white robbers are more likely than younger and black ones to use weapons, and thus they usually avoid injuring their victims. Also, robbers who operate alone tend more to use weapons than do those who commit crimes in groups.[23] Let us learn more about these robberies and robbers by taking a brief look at the statistical background of robberies and the personal background of robbers.

BACKGROUND OF ROBBERIES AND ROBBERS

Robbery is chacteristically a big city crime.[24] In 1973, for example, the robbery rate in the large cities (with over 250,000 population) was about eight times greater than in rural areas. Relatedly, the more urbanized a region, the higher the rate of robbery. Thus, as the Northeastern states are much more urbanized than the Southern states, the former in 1973 had a robbery rate of 254 per 100,000 inhabitants as opposed to only 142 per 100,000 people in the latter. Usually about half of the robberies are committed on the street and the other half in commercial establishments. Most of the offenses are armed robberies (66 percent in 1973), while the rest are strong-armed robberies such as mugging, yokings, or other violent confrontations where physical force alone is used by the offender to subdue the victim. Over the years, armed robbery has increased faster than strong-armed robbery. Most armed robberies involve the use of firearms, and, as has been noted above, are more likely to be committed by older than younger men. The fact that younger men are more apt to commit *un*armed robberies may explain why most robbery offenders *arrested* are under the age of twenty-five, as unarmed robbers are less sophisticated and less efficient than armed robbers. Finally, in contrast to murder and rape, which are predominantly *intra*racial in nature, robbery has a high *inter*racial component—mostly involving young black males robbing older white males.

In comparing a sample of incarcerated black armed robbers with other black inmates who had committed other types of crime, Julian Roebuck and Mervyn Cadwallader found that the black armed robbers more frequently had similar backgrounds. They had been brought up in slum neighborhoods where they were heavily influenced by unfavorable home and street life. They had grown up in different homes—foster homes and relatives' homes—where criminality, conflict, and parental irresponsibility prevailed. Their mothers often entertained various lovers; their fathers were generally heavy drinkers; and their sisters were frequently prostitutes. They themselves had expressed hostility toward their fathers, been disciplinary problems in school, often stayed away from school, and frequently run away from home. They had become juvenile delinquents, working at such street trades as mugging and purse snatching; they had often been leaders of delinquent gangs. As they grew older, they engaged more and more in such crimes as petty thefts, rolling drunks and homosexuals, and holdups with a pistol or knife. After they were arrested and imprisoned, they demonstrated little insight into the nature of their past difficulties, placed the blame for their own mistakes on others, expressed bitterness toward the police and judges for their sentences, and insisted that they were technically not guilty of their crimes.[25]

TYPES OF ROBBERIES AND ROBBERS

From their study of robberies in London from 1950 to 1960, F. H. McClintock and Evelyn Gibson divide robberies into the following types:

1. Robbery of persons who, as part of their employment, were in charge of money or goods;
2. Robbery in the open following sudden attack;
3. Robbery on private premises;
4. Robbery after preliminary association of short duration between victim and offender (mainly for heterosexual or homosexual purposes);
5. Robbery in cases of previous association of some duration between victim and offender, e.g., friends, lovers, workmates.[26]

McClintock and Gibson further distinguish the first type from all the others combined, by describing it as robbery that "includes the premeditated, and carefully planned, raids on banks, post offices and large stores, and the seizure of money in transit from banks or business premises." [27] This implies that people who are likely to commit the first type of robbery are *professional* robbers, for they usually plan their crimes and rob relatively lucrative targets such as those just mentioned. It also implies that people who tend to perpetrate the other four types of robbery are *amateur* robbers, because they are less calculating and more inclined to rob individuals of smaller sums of money.

In his study of robberies in Boston during the first six months of 1964 and 1968, Conklin further divides *amateur* robbers into three types: (1) the *opportunist* robber, (2) the *addict* robber, and (3) the *alcoholic* robber. Conklin has provided a description of each of these three types, as well as of the professional robber.[28]

THE PROFESSIONAL ROBBER   This type carefully plans their crimes, executes them with one or more accomplices and with skill, and makes away with large sums of money. They have a strong commitment to crime as a way of earning a living, and seek a series of big scores to support an expensive, hedonistic lifestyle. There are two types of professional robbers; one is more specialized in robbery than the other. The more specialized ones commit robbery almost exclusively; the less specialized, being also committed to other forms of crimes, commit robbery only occasionally but nonetheless with professional skill. The first type of professional robber was more common in the 1930s, while the second type increased in number in the 1960s, and possibly in the 1970s as well.

Professional robbers are committed to the crime of robbery because it is often very profitable and thus enables them to enjoy an expensive lifestyle. As one professional robber, who often committed the crime with his friend, said:

> When we started with our first robbery, if it hadn't been successful we
> would have probably quit. A lot of times people will hit a place and
> get just $40 or $50. We got $7,200 on the first one. . . . If it had been
> someplace where we got $30 or $50 we might have hung it up right
> there and said, "The bother isn't worth it . . ." When you get that kind
> of money it's awful hard to do without it. Especially when you can
> spend it however you want and you don't even have income tax to
> pay. You want to go down and buy yourself a cashmere sports coat.[29]

Professionals, after executing a robbery, will often leave the city for a few weeks, perhaps taking a trip to such resort areas as Florida. Once there, they will spend the money like spendthrift millionaires, to satisfy luxurious whims and pleasures. When they have exhausted their supply of cash, they will start developing specific plans for other robberies. At other times they just keep their eyes open, watching for possible scores. Since they are interested in big scores, they will typically rob commercial establishments that contain large sums of money. As these targets generally take greater precaution against theft than do private citizens, professional robbers usually have developed considerably more skill and do more careful planning than other types of offenders who usually rob private citizens of smaller sums of money.

THE OPPORTUNIST ROBBER   This type is probably the most common. Unlike professionals, opportunists do not exhibit a long-term commitment to robbery. They may frequently commit such forms of theft as larceny and shoplifting, but they infrequently rob. When they do rob, they are quite unlike professionals. Opportunists usually choose individual persons rather than commercial establishments as targets. The criteria for this choice of target are easy accessibility and great vulnerability rather than large sums of money. Typical examples of such targets are elderly ladies with purses, drunks, cab drivers, and people who walk alone on dark streets.

Given the characteristics of their targets, opportunists commonly net small amounts of money—mostly less than twenty dollars—from robbery. But they are satisfied with the small loot, because they, unlike professionals, do not aspire to achieving a big score and enjoying an expensive lifestyle.

Most opportunists simply want—in their own words—"a little extra spending money," "a few nice clothes," or "some cash in the pocket," just so they are able to show their peers that they are "doing all right." Opportunists' low level of aspiration may be linked to the fact that, in contrast to professionals, who are usually white, in their midtwenties or older, and from middle- or working-class backgrounds, opportunists are often black, in their teens or early twenties, and from lower-class families. Since they select highly vulnerable victims to rob, opportunists do not feel the need for the use of a weapon. Thus this type of robber rarely carries firearms and often has no weapon of any kind. Yet they are likely to form a gang with two or three other opportunists to overpower the victim in a strong-arm robbery. So the group itself may operate as a weapon of sorts, comparable in threatening power to the use of a knife.

Conklin's view of the opportunist robber, presented above, may be enhanced by John Irwin's observation of the same type of robber, whom Irwin refers to as the *disorganized criminal*. According to Irwin, the disorganized criminal pursues "a chaotic, purposeless life, filled with unskilled, careless, and variegated criminal activity." [30] This type engages in a variety of simple and uncomplicated property crimes including unarmed robberies, holdups, burglaries, and larcenies. They are then "jack-of-all-trades" offenders. In early life, they often broke rules and got into trouble as if they were committed to "doing wrong." They may spend most of their time riding around with friends, and if they come across an easy mark to rob, they will commit the crime without hesitation. Instead of purposefully and actively planning their crimes, they often hang around various locations in the city waiting for some robbery opportunities:

They are always looking for a "set-up man," someone to plan jobs
and tell them exactly what to do. Since no "set-up man" would have
anything to do with people so obviously inept, unlucky, and unsuccessful, they go on cooling off as dishwashers, soda jerks, waiters, occasionally robbing a drunk or a timid queer, looking, always looking
[futilely], for the "set-up man" with a big job who will say, "I've been
watching you. You're the man I need for this set up. Now listen. . ." [31]

THE ADDICT ROBBER   This category includes heroin addicts as well as other regular users of drugs such as speed (amphetamine), LSD, and an assortment of pills, who commit robbery as a result of their drug use. Like the opportunist, the addict rarely plans a lucrative robbery and thus commits robberies that yield small sums of money. But due to the high cost of a drug habit, the addict desperately commits more acts of property crimes than does the opportunist. Obviously the addict also differs from the opportunist in the motivation of the crime; the addict is driven to steal money in order to maintain a drug habit. Somewhat less obviously, addicts have an even lower commitment to robbery, tend more to avoid the use of physical force when compelled to commit robbery as a last resort, do more planning prior to their crimes, and are more likely to carry a firearm, which, however, is not always loaded. The infrequent use of loaded firearms by addict robbers is related to their characteristic desire to avoid the use of physical force.

Addicts frequently are compelled to acquire money illegally, as they often run out of funds and need them to buy their next "fix." Consequently, they are driven to engage in various forms of criminal activities, but only occasionally do they turn to robbery. There is also an acute sense of desperation in their attempts to get money in whatever way they can. As one addict, who has robbed some cab passengers, says:

For me, the only hard part is keeping in H, paying my connection man.
I know these rich cats who can get good smack and shoot it for years
and nothing happens, but me, you know, it's a hustle to stay alive. I
run about a $100-, $150-a-day habit, so I have to cop twice that much to
keep my fence happy. I was driving cabs in 1970; I'd stage these robberies, and keep the receipts. Now, me and my partner are into burglary; no strong-arm stuff—you feel quiet on dope—just boosting TV
sets from houses where we know the people are away. And I do a skin
flick once in a while. But it's a hassle, believe me. Everybody on
the street wants to rip you off; you can get burned from pushers who
try and sell you sugar or rat poison. Then there is always the threat
of the law.[32]

THE ALCOHOLIC ROBBER   Of the four types, alcoholic offenders are the least committed to the crime of robbery and the most likely to be caught by the police when they rob. They do not plan their crime, neither do they try to make their crime easier by seeking a vulnerable victim. Instead, they often get involved in a situation that unexpectedly leads to committing a robbery. They may, for example, get into fist fights, or drunkenly assault people, and then take away their victims' money as an afterthought. Unlike the other types of robbers, whose crimes are always motivated by their desire for money, alcoholics often rob because they are drunk. The random nature of the alcoholic's crime may be illustrated by one alcoholic who walked into a liquor store to buy a bottle of whiskey. After he had given the clerk the money to pay for the whiskey, the clerk asked whether he wanted anything else. At that instant, the alcoholic decided that he did— and told the clerk that he wanted all his money. Surprised and angered, the clerk refused to cooperate. During the ensuing fight, the alcoholic managed to take some money and then fled from the scene.

SOCIAL ORGANIZATION OF PROFESSIONAL ROBBERS

The preceding discussion has primarily focused on the *individual* characteristics of each type of robbers, such as the degree of commitment to robbery as a source of livelihood, selection of a certain type of victim, and the techniques employed for carrying out robbery. What has not been discussed is the *group* life of each type of robber. Amateur robbers—the opportunist, the addict, and the alcoholic—are not committed to crime in general or to robbery in particular as a way of life. So they cannot be said to have a group life organized around a criminal or robbery system. But this is not the case with professional robbers. Having a deep, long-term commitment to robbery, professionals belong to a relatively cohesive system of robbery, which may be called the social organization of professional robbers. This social organization has been analyzed by Werner Einstadter on the basis of his interview with twenty-five professional robbers in California in 1966. The following discussion is based on Einstadter's analysis.[33]

PARTNERSHIP OF EQUALS   The relationship among members of a professional robbery gang is characterized by equality. Any member may present a robbery plan to his associates, and before it is acted upon, a consensus must be reached. The robbers are obviously aware that the success of their partnership depends on cooperation and that forcing an unwilling member to participate in a heist would only endanger the whole group.

Although there is no leader giving orders and assigning positions, the members' differences in previous experience, skills, and abilities may make the emergence of leadership possible. Such a "leader," however, acts as a planning consultant; he guides rather than directs, helping to ensure that each member likes his part of the job and will do it well. Prior to a robbery, the strengths and weaknesses of various members are discussed and decisions reached as to who will best do which part of the job. Although the leader may influence these discussions and decisions, each member of the group has a voice in them. The following is a member's account of how a decision was reached so that he would do the wheelman's part, which he preferred, rather than the inside-man's, which he did not like.

For one reason, I wasn't going in, that was the first reason. I told them that, but they wanted me to go in. Then they got talking about that he (another partner) was going to drive the car [but he] couldn't see good, and the second one, he's so damn nervous he'd probably take the key out and put it in his pocket and then couldn't find the key. . . . Then we didn't know how to trust the fourth guy that just came in; we didn't know whether he might run off and leave all of us, if all three of us went in. . . . Well, anyway, it all boiled down to that I should be driving the car because I don't get excited and I drive well.[34]

The fact that professional robbers operate as equals may have something to do with the following: compared with professional thieves, who usually have a hierarchical organization, professional robbers are more likely to form a temporary partnership for a specific heist only, more tolerant of each other's boastfulness and blunders, and less inclined to help each other when arrested. These facts imply that being an equal in a robbery gang means being independent and being one's own boss.

PATTERNS OF ACTIVITY   The success of a professional robbery depends largely on the coordination of various tasks. As mentioned before, there are two types of tasks, the wheelman's and the inside-man's. The typical robbery group consists of three persons: the wheelman and two inside-men. Of the two inside-men, one is the "backup," whose function is to watch the employees and customers in the establishment and keep the situation under control, while the other inside-man gathers the loot. In addition to the proper differentiation and efficient coordination of these tasks, the element of surprise and momentary domination of the scene are maximized to ensure the successful completion of the job.

According to Einstadter, there are three robbery tactics. The *ambush* is the least planned of all robberies and is most characterized by its element of surprise. The professional group considers this the lowest form of robbery, which the amateur is most likely to commit. But the professional may sometimes be driven to commit it as a desperate measure. In other words, the professional will resort to the ambush only when an emergency arises, such as when money for flight must be raised immediately for the group threatened with capture. The *selective raid* involves more, but still a minimum of, planning. Typically a series of this type of robberies are committed in rapid succession. The professionals ordinarily do not engage in the selective raid. But they resort to it in order to finance a more lucrative robbery. The *planned operation* is a carefully executed robbery, with all aspects of the crime clearly delineated and all members of the group knowing their parts well. This robbery tactic is most commonly carried out by professionals. Planning skills largely determine the success of the robbery operation, for the act of robbery itself often requires little or no skill. Thus the mark of professionalism in robbery is great skill in the planning.

IDEOLOGY OF ROBBERY Legitimate professional groups generally have a positive attitude toward their career. To some degree this is also true in the case of professional robbers. The professional robber sees his type of crime as an honest enterprise. Unlike theft and other property crimes, which involve furtiveness or deception, robbery calls for an open, direct, face-to-face confrontation with the victim. It is this quality of candor which, in the eyes of the robber, transforms robbery into an honest activity. One robber who considered himself very honest tried to explain why he preferred robbery to stealing: "Well, I just—I couldn't steal anything. You know—behind someone's back. When I took something I'd make no bones about it. I don't know, I guess it's just sorta being yourself—you just take it in front of the guy; you don't pussyfoot it around and do a lot of pretending. . . . And something else—it's a lot cleaner." [35]

Another robber even considered his crime more honest than the business activity of the companies that he victimized. "To me this is perfectly honest, because these companies are cheating people anyway. When you go and just take it from them, you are actually more honest than they are. Most of the time, anyway, they are insured and make more money from the caper than you do." [36] This attitude may partly explain why most professional robbers choose large commercial establishments as their targets.

It may, however, be pointed out that although they seem to believe in the ideology of robbery as an honest profession, most robbers are not totally committed to it. They often hope that they will someday hit the "big job" —the most profitable robbery—so that they can embark on a new, *conventional* business career.

THEORIES OF ROBBERY

Two sociologists, John Conklin and Leroy Gould, have independently tried to account for the increase in robbery rates. Both men have about the same basic idea, but they have developed it in different ways.

RELATIVE DEPRIVATION THEORY

Conklin attempts to explain the tremendous increase in robbery rates in Boston and other major cities in the United States between 1960 and 1969. He evaluates eight possible explanations and decides that the most adequate is relative deprivation theory.[37]

Since he attributes most of the increase in robbery rates to black offenders, Conklin posits that "changes in race relations in the United States have resulted in higher crime rates." This means that as black Americans improved their social condition in the 1960s, they were also more inclined to commit robbery. Conklin believes that the theory of relative deprivation provides the most adequate explanation for the presumed causal link between improved social condition and increased robbery rates. To demonstrate the adequacy of the theory, Conklin first points out the fact that the proportion of black robbery offenders increased from 56 percent in 1960 to 80 percent in 1969, though the black proportion of the American population changed only slightly—from 11 to 12 percent over the same period. Then, Conklin contends that blacks became more prone to robbery because they suffered from a large degree of *relative deprivation*. In other words, the absolute improvement in the life of blacks induced them to hold high expectations of enjoying an equal position with whites, but when they failed to realize that expectation, they experienced a great sense of frustration. One consequence of this was their tendency to commit robbery.

ECONOMIC ABUNDANCE THEORY

Although he also considers relative deprivation as an important factor in robbery, Leroy Gould holds the idea of economic abundance in particularly high regard. As he states, "abundance alone may explain a sizeable portion of the variation in rates of property crime." [38]

Gould derives the economic abundance theory from his observation that rates of property crime remained relatively low during the period of economic scarcity (from 1930 to 1943 in the United States), but the rates rose sharply during the period of abundance (from 1944 to 1965). In discussing this changing phenomenon, Gould suggests two key factors as intervening between abundance and crime: relative deprivation and the ease with which property can be stolen. As he says, "increases in the amount of property would serve to increase the relative deprivation of those who were still not sharing in the ownership of the property, while at the same time making it easier for these people to steal the property for their own use." [39]

According to Gould, individuals who are prompted by their relative deprivation to commit bank robbery are desperate for money. This desperation results from some threat to their livelihood, such as pending business failure, financial foreclosure, unpaid gambling debts, or inability to get ahead in their profession. Unlike robbers of the 1930s who robbed banks as a livelihood, modern robbers are driven by desperation to become amateurs—hence, their robbery is essentially "a crime of desperation." They are further encouraged to commit the crime of desperation, because it is easier, for example, to rob a bank today than it used to be. Unlike banks of thirty or forty years ago, which separated tellers from customers or robbers by iron bars and which were often protected by armed guards, banks today are open, usually isolated such as in the case of many branch banks, seldom watched by armed guards, and frequently without adequate alarm systems.[40]

It may be pointed out that Gould's assumption of the trend toward *amateur* robbery has been supported by André Normandeau's study in Philadelphia. But another study, conducted in London, has indicated the opposite trend—robbery has become increasingly *professional*.[41] Apparently there is a difference between American and British robberies. But this does not necessarily destroy the central point in Gould's theory that economic abundance boosts robbery rates by increasing relative deprivation and making it easy to rob.

POWER THEORY APPLIED

Power theory can be used to put robbery and the preceding theories in proper perspective. The kind of robbery discussed above is typically committed by relatively poor and powerless people. What has escaped discussion is the far more sophisticated and profitable type of robbery that the rich and powerful characteristically engage in. This type of robbery is often referred to as *white-collar crime*. It includes tax evasion, price-fixing, consumer fraud, embezzlement, swindling, and the like. These crimes, however, represent only one aspect of the dual nature of robbery: they are basically *property* crimes. They involve stealing money without the use or threat of force against their victims.

There is another, much neglected aspect of sophisticated and profitable robbery, however. This has to do with its being in fact a *violent* crime, but the threat of force involved is often so subtle that it is not popularly recognized as such. For example, some physicians use the threat of nontreatment (which is in effect a threat of bodily harm in the form of worsening sickness or death) to demand high fees from their patients; slum landlords use the threat of exposure to the elements (which is in effect a threat of bodily harm) in order to collect exorbitant rents from their tenants; and the government uses the threat of imprisonment (which is in effect a powerful threat of force) to demand payment of high taxes from its ordinary citizens.

The powerful's sophisticated and profitable robbery may be more prevalent than crude and unprofitable robbery by the powerless. This is particularly because there exist more opportunity for and less legal control over the former than the latter. In addition, there may be a symbiotic relationship between the two types of robbery. By committing robbery without getting punished for it, powerful people help to create a social climate of disrespect for the law. This, in turn, may encourage the powerless to commit robbery with the justification that "the rich do it, why can't I?" Such robbery by the powerless, however, very often enables the powerful to complain about it. In so doing, the powerful can dissociate themselves from "common criminals" and thereby reinforce their self-image as respectable people. This may make it easier for the powerful to see nothing wrong with the more sophisticated and profitable form of robbery. Such a lack of moral sensitivity to this form of robbery, further abetted by the relative lack of social prohibition against it, is likely to encourage the powerful to commit robbery.

SUMMARY

Robbery has a dual nature; it has the characteristics of a crime against property as well as those of a crime against the person.

As a crime against property, robbery is a rational act. To commit such an act, would-be robbers have to make rational decisions. These are usually decisions on three related matters. One, individuals decide they will rob because they feel the need for financial gain. Two, they decide what targets to rob. Three, they decide how the robberies are to be successfully carried out.

As a crime against the person, robbery may be committed with actual or potential violence against the victim. Actual violence often occurs in strong-arm robbery, because without the aid of a weapon robbers usually have to resort to physical force to subdue and then rob their victims. Potential violence is implied by the presence of a dangerous weapon, so that the victims feel threatened enough to let the robbers execute their crime efficiently and nonviolently.

Most robberies occur in large cities. Most involve the use of firearms, but younger men tend more to resort to unarmed robberies. Robbery is more interracial than intraracial, as it often involves young black men robbing older white men. Most robbers come from poor neighborhoods where they have had much experience in delinquent activities.

There are two broad categories of robbers, professionals and amateurs. In terms of the robbery types listed by McClintock and Gibson, professionals are likely to rob people in charge of a commercial establishment, while amateurs tend to rob individuals on the street, on private premises, after brief sexual encounter with victims, and after long association with victims. But while recognizing the professionals, Conklin further divides the amateurs into three types: the opportunist robber, the addict robber, and the alcoholic robber. Moreover, Einstadter elaborates on the social organization of professional robbers.

Conklin evaluates eight possible explanations of increasing robbery rates, and considers relative deprivation as the most adequate. Gould regards economic abundance as the key cause of high robbery rates, but theorizes that abundance generates relative deprivation and the ease of robbing so as to create high robbery rates. Power theory can put these theories and the nature of robbery in proper perspective.

SUGGESTED READINGS

Conklin, John E. *Robbery and the Criminal Justice System.* Philadelphia: Lippincott, 1972.

DeBaun, Everett. "The Heist: The Theory and Practice of Armed Robbery." *Harpers*, February 1950, 69–77.

Einstadter, Werner J. "The Social Organization of Armed Robbery." *Social Problems* 17 (Summer 1969): 64–83.

Gibson, W. B., ed. *The Fine Art of Robbery.* New York: Grosset and Dunlap, 1966.

Gould, Leroy C. "The Changing Structure of Property Crime in an Affluent Society." *Social Forces* 48 (September 1969): 50–59.

McClintock, F. H. and Evelyn Gibson. *Robbery in London.* London: Macmillan, 1961.

Normandeau, André. "Patterns in Robbery." *Criminology* 6 (November 1968): 2–15.

Roebuck, Julian B. and Mervyn L. Cadwallader. "The Negro Armed Robber as a Criminal Type: The Construction and Application of a Typology." *Pacific Sociological Review* 4 (Spring 1961): 21–26.

Sagalyn, Arnold. *The Crime of Robbery in the United States.* Washington, D.C.: Government Printing Office, 1971.

8 PROSTITUTION

There is no precise definition of prostitution; it would be futile to attempt one. Consider, for example, this seemingly simple definition: prostitution is the selling of sexual favors for money. This definition is so ambiguous that it may include marrying for money, may exclude the exchange of sexual favors by a high-class call girl for a mink coat, and may exclude a streetwalker's whipping her masochistic customer for money. Thus it is impossible to find a clear, precise definition of prostitution—one that excludes all acts and persons not intended to be included and that includes all acts and persons not intended to be excluded.[1] The best we could do is to find an operational definition that most people might agree with. Such a definition has been offered by anthropologist Paul Gebhard: "A prostitute is an individual who will engage in sexual activity with strangers or other persons with whom the individual has no affectional relationship in exchange for money or other valuable materials that are given at or near the time of the act."[2]

Prostitution is illegal in the United States, except in some counties of Nevada. In many other countries, prostitution is legal but the prostitute's public solicitation is not. Prostitution is big business, especially in the United States. It has been estimated that American men spend somewhere between seven and nine billion dollars a year on the sexual favors of prostitutes. The amount of this profit—which is obviously tax free—is ten times the annual budget of the U.S. Department of Justice. Although it is obviously impossible to know the exact number of prostitutes, there have been reports that full-time professional prostitutes in the United States number as high as half a million—not considering the fact that many more are part-time prostitutes. It has been estimated that there are 315 million acts of commercial sex per year.[3]

THE NATURE OF PROSTITUTION

Prostitution has long been a subject of great interest to many people. Thousands of books, articles, and stories have been written about it. Movies and television shows have portrayed it, often attracting large audiences. As a consequence, a number of popular beliefs concerning prostitution—which are mostly false—have been created or reinforced. In order to understand the nature of prostitution, let us first examine these popular beliefs, checking them against some research evidence. Then we shall look at the various types of prostitutes, the way female prostitutes learn their trade, the occupational ideology of female prostitutes, and the various people—madams, pimps, and customers—who are closely involved with prostitutes.

PROSTITUTION: FACT VS. FICTON

As prostitution has a very long history, it is popularly believed to be the oldest profession in the world. But this belief is a myth, for the priesthood is the oldest profession. Similarly, most popular beliefs about the nature of prostitution are false. Let us look at nine of them.[4]

First, many people hold the "white slavery" idea that young girls are often lured away or kidnapped and then forced into prostitution. It is true that some actual cases of white slavery can be found, as the following account by a fourteen-year-old girl of her introduction to prostitution will testify:

I was grabbed in a store by this guy and this chick who said they were taking me for a ride. They said they wanted me to meet a friend.
He was a pimp. They sold me to him for $100. He locked me up in this hotel room and ran in cheap tricks—$10. . . . I got away after a week, but he followed me and gave me a line I fell for, so I went back with him. He grabbed my hair, so I kicked him between the legs—boom!
He called in another guy and they took my clothes off. They began to heat up this coat hanger with matches and burn my ass with it. Then the pimp put his foot on my face and stomped it. I figured, well, you've got to take some bad things in life.[5]

Such an experience, however, is rare among prostitutes. In fact, only a very small proportion—no more than 4 percent—of prostitutes could be said to have been coerced into prostitution. Even among these prostitutes, many have the choice not to sell their bodies. When they say that their husband or boyfriend forced them to enter prostitution, they are really saying that they chose prostitution rather than leave their mate.

Second, it is often mentioned in both folklore and scientific literature that women become prostitutes because they are nymphomaniacs who have an insatiable desire for sexual intercourse with numerous men. This is not substantiated by facts. While it is true that an occasional promiscuous female may decide to add profit to pleasure, most prostitutes have not been more promiscuous than their nonprostitute sisters. In addition, most prostitutes do not enjoy having sex with their customers, though they do with their husbands or boyfriends.

Third, since it is difficult to legitimately get huge sums of money to support an addiction to such hard drugs as heroin, some female addicts may turn to prostitution. But this link between drug addiction and prostitution has been exaggerated. The truth is that only a very small proportion of prostitutes (no more than 4 percent) are drug addicts.

Fourth, among men there are two contradictory beliefs about how prostitutes treat their clients. On the one hand, men view the prostitute as nasty and hard-hearted—as evidenced by the saying, "as cold as a whore's heart." On the other hand, men romanticize the prostitute as a sweet and warm-hearted woman—as exemplified by movie heroine Irma La Douce, "a whore with a heart of gold." In reality, however, the prostitute's attitude toward her clients is quite similar to that of anyone who provides services to a diverse clientele. Some clients she likes, a few others she dislikes, and toward most of them she simply feels neutral.

Fifth, perhaps influenced by the popular judgment that prostitution is a fate worse than death, the popular assumption is that prostitutes by and large find their profession extremely distasteful and thus deeply regret choosing it. This may prove to be a misconception. One researcher found that nearly two-thirds of the prostitutes in his sample reported no regrets at all. However, this finding should be put in proper perspective. Those prostitutes did not regret being "in the life," apparently because they recognized the fact that they, being unskilled or poorly educated, could not possibly get a legitimate job that would pay as well as prostitution.

Sixth, a number of clinical psychologists incorrectly assume that prostitutes are sexually frigid. Actually, when they have sexual intercourse with their friends or husbands, prostitutes as a group are somewhat more responsive than nonprostitute females—they are more able to achieve orgasm.

Seventh, it is widely believed that prostitutes are usually infertile. This popular belief is, indeed, well substantiated by evidence. Gebhard found that only 11 percent of the prostitutes in his sample reported pregnancy by their clients. The low incidence of this occupational hazard may be attributed to the high incidence of another type of occupational hazard—venereal disease. For the majority of the prostitutes in Gebhard's sample had contracted either syphilis or, more frequently, gonorrhea.[6]

Eighth, most people assume that prostitution is completely incompatible with religious belief and church attendance. The truth is that in many ancient societies prostitution was considered sacred—practiced in the temple as an act of worship.[7] Today, while it is true that most prostitutes rarely attend religious services, a substantial minority do so. Gebhard estimates that 3 to 10 percent of Protestant prostitutes and up to 14 percent of Catholic prostitutes attend church regularly. Particularly in Latin America and southern Europe, are prostitutes likely to go to church.

Finally, a common misconception is that prostitutes are basically either homosexual or, tiring of having sex with so many men, turn to homosexuality. This idea may seem logical, but it is not supported by evidence. The majority of the prostitutes (61 percent in Gebhard's sample) have had no homosexual experience whatsoever.

TYPES OF PROSTITUTES

There are a great variety of types of prostitutes. It has been reported, for example, that there are eighteen different types.[8] Most of them are relatively rare, so only the more common types are to be discussed here. These types are—in ascending order of status and the price they charge—the streetwalker, the bar prostitute, the brothel prostitute, the massage-parlor prostitute, and the call girl.

THE STREETWALKER   In prostitution, soliciting customers in the street is probably the most ancient method. The prostitute who uses this method is a *streetwalker*. Historically she has been considered as being at the bottom of the status system of prostitution. In general, she charges her customer about twenty dollars, which is less than the fee obtained by most other types of prostitutes. Furthermore, she is less attractive, less educated, more likely to contract venereal disease, and more often arrested by the police.[9] The streetwalker represents the largest number of prostitutes.

The streetwalker uses a standard method of soliciting. When she sees a potential customer, she smiles at him. She will say to him such things as: "Hi"; "Lonesome?" "How are you today?" "Which direction are you heading?" or "Are you a stranger in the city?" If the man responds, she will ask, "How would you like to do something?" Then she will tell him her price. Very often, however, the man himself will take the initiative and ask, "How much?" Once an agreement is made, she will take him to a hotel room.[10]

More recently, a violent new breed has emerged among streetwalkers. As journalist Gail Sheehy observes, "They work on their backs as little as possible. More often they work in cars, with partners, and in hallways and in the open on sidewalks running through the theater district and surrounding the grand hotels. The bulk of their business is not the dispensation of pleasure. It is to swindle, mug, rob, knife and possibly even murder their patrons."[11] One mode of operation, for example, involves two women driving around in search of a mark. When they spot a man stopping for a "Don't Walk" sign, they will wave, smile, and invite him into the car. As he slides in between them, they will drive toward a secluded area and park. While one girl is playing with him, the other will steal his wallet, remove the cash and credit cards, and return the wallet. If the man is too jumpy, the women may bite, slug, or knife him.[12]

THE BAR PROSTITUTE   This type of prostitute has remained largely unstudied by sociologists and other behavioral scientists.[13] But she is a very common sight, particularly in the South, Southwest, and Midwest of the United States. The vast majority of bar prostitutes look for their customers in lower-class taverns. Most of them are not full-time prostitutes, though. They are girls between seventeen and twenty-five, hustling to supplement their incomes earned as barmaids or waitresses. Some turn tricks only when they are between jobs or find themselves in financial emergency. Most of them have less than a high school education, come from low-income families, and are from very small towns or rural areas. They live mostly in cheap hotels and roominghouses. They often move from city to city; the move is often made on a whim, as when they are offered a ride.

They typically drink too much, exist on hamburgers and Coke and the high-calorie, low-nourishment snacks available in most bars. They seldom bathe, apparently losing interest in their personal appearance. Young, pretty, and shapely at the beginning of their careers, they often look years older in a matter of months, with "beer bellies" and other fatty accumulations spoiling their figures. Psychiatrist Harry Benjamin and philosopher R. E. L. Masters write:

There seems little doubt that it is the *modus operandi* that brings about the swift deterioration of this type of prostitute. Her method is to spend the evening in a bar (and sometimes the day, too), cultivating the acquaintance of a man who buys her drinks. Sometimes she must continue to drink for hours before the man asks her to leave with him— many of the girls, especially the younger ones, lack the courage to make the advance. Then, when she asks for money, he may decline—having mistaken her for a "pickup," not a prostitute; and the drinking must begin all over again with some fresh prospect.[14]

THE BROTHEL PROSTITUTE   A brothel is a place where prostitutes meet their customers and share their earnings with its operator. It has been variously referred to as a cathouse, whorehouse, parlor house, and bordello. Very often it is simply called a "joint" or "house." In the 1920s and 1930s there were many brothels in this country. But since 1945 most of them have been forced to shut down. Today there still remain some brothels that operate openly in Nevada and clandestinely in other parts of the country.

In Nevada, where prostitution is legal, brothel prostitutes are finger-printed and carry prostitute identification cards issued by the police or district attorneys. The women are generally required to have a weekly medical checkup. They usually sit at the windows and try to attract male passersby with smiles. When a client enters the house, the madam (proprietor) will direct a girl to him. The account by a visitor to a Nevada brothel in the late 1960s is fairly typical of how the girl conducts her business (except that her prices are much higher today):

She said, "I'll sit with you . . . Where are you from . . . ? I'm from Los Angeles. . . . Let's go to my room, so we can talk . . ." In her room she continued: I can give you a nice date . . . French (fellatio) for $15, or I can give you a straight (coitus) for $10. The price of a quickie is $5. For $20 and up, you could have a real good time. . . . You don't need to be afraid. . . . We get a smear examination once a week and a blood test once a month. . . . You won't have to worry—the doctor makes sure. . . . He checks us and we check everyone ourselves.[15]

In other states where the brothel is covertly operated, the madam usually makes sure that the potential client is not from the vice squad. She will, of course, readily admit a regular customer. But in cases where she does not know him, she will first meet him at a nearby bar or send a cooperating cab driver to size him up. When convinced he is a genuine customer, the madam or the taxi driver will take him to the brothel. The brothel is typically open from 10 A.M. to 6 P.M.; a few houses operate from approximately 6 P.M. to 11 P.M. The reason for preferring daylight hours is that vice squads in many cities are not likely to be active then. The few brothels that do conduct their business after dark usually have police connections.[16] The working girl may wait in the brothel or she may wait in her own apartment for phone calls from the madam, to whom she typically gives half her earnings. Since the clients often look for variety, the house prostitute does not work in a brothel for an extended period—the longest she will stay in one brothel is about six months. To minimize the risk of arrest, the madam also periodically changes her place of business.

THE MASSAGE-PARLOR PROSTITUTE   In the past, the massage parlor was mostly a legitimate establishment where skilled physical therapists rendered service to affluent health enthusiasts.[17] Today it is often used as a cover for prostitution. This is because most customers expect to obtain sexual pleasure of one type or another at a massage parlor. As one parlor girl explains, "If you're giving straight massages you might as well be on welfare. . . . You couldn't make it in this business without giving locals (masturbation)."

Masturbation is, indeed, the most popular form of sexual service requested by customers. When inquired as to the percentage of clients who ask for masturbation, one masseuse replied, "I kept track of that once. While working at this one parlor I did over 500 massages and only four guys *didn't* ask for a local." There are other types of service that the masseuse may perform. Each type has its own price. As one parlor girl explains, "It's $15 for an hour long massage including a local. An extra $5 will get my top off and $5 more takes my bottom off. For $10 more he can bathe with me for a half hour. (This is a rare practice.) Anything after that is negotiable between me and the customer. I have to soak him for $35 before negotiating a blow-job or a lay." If this masseuse agrees to perform fellatio on her client, she will probably charge between $30 and $40; for coitus, she may demand a fee of somewhere between $40 and $60.

In view of their relatively high fees, it is little wonder that massage-parlor prostitutes attract mostly white-collar businessmen rather than lower-class men. But these women themselves come from all walks of life. Some of them have had only a fifth-grade education while others are college graduates. Their ages range from fourteen to sixty-four, with the majority being in their twenties. They are usually paid on a commission basis; they receive about 40 percent of the earnings for each massage. They may earn generous tips from their customers for rendering special sex service.

To get employed in a massage parlor, a girl has to be trained as a masseuse and to get a license for practicing her profession. The training may involve reading a book on massage, putting it into practice on the body of the massage-parlor owner, or doing both. To become licensed as a professional masseuse, she has to—among other things—show proof of having received proper training and undergo a medical checkup. But authorities treat her as if she were a legalized prostitute. As a licensed masseuse says, "They made me feel like a whore while trying to get licensed. The medical check doesn't do any good. They don't care if I have infectious sores on my hands or TB. They simply want to assure that I won't give VD to my customers. Now what does that imply?"

THE CALL GIRL   Occupying the highest status in prostitution, call girls have been referred to as "the aristocrats of prostitution." [18] As befitting this title, they usually charge from fifty to a hundred dollars for each sexual intercourse and occasionally charge even more. They are better educated or more sophisticated than the other types of prostitutes. They dress expensively, and they live in the most affluent neighborhoods of our large cities. Call girls are acutely aware of their high status and will feel greatly insulted if they are treated like the ordinary streetwalker or brothel prostitute. In fact, some call girls will not apply the term *prostitute* to themselves.

It is typical for the call girl to get her clients by phone. Usually she acquires her clientele from other call girls, a procurer, or a madam. Her previously satisfied clients often recommend her to their friends, so she often receives calls from prospective customers, who say, "I'm a friend of John Doe; he gave me your number." Many call girls, however, do not use personal telephones; instead, they receive their calls from an answering service, which is the number that she gives to her clients. Such an arrangement serves two purposes. One is to minimize the risk of arrest or of being traced by the police. As for the other purpose, a call girl describes it thus:

The first prerequisite is a telephone in good working order, with an
answering service connected so that business can continue even when
the proprietor is out on a call—away from home. Usually as soon as
"business has been completed," the girl will call her answering service
for messages, thus enabling her to hop from one address to another
without wasting expensive time. If there has been a call at her residence
while the present job is in progress, and the phoned-in customer has
left a message or number with the girl's answering service, it is not unusual for the amenities of the current business to be completed quickly
(the passage of fee from "John" to girl) and a hasty departure for
the next destination made by the busy young lady.[19]

Unlike other, low-priced prostitutes, the call girl dresses neither poorly nor garishly but in good taste. She is skilled in making her commercial transaction appear noncommercial. Thus she knows how to obtain the promise of a fee without explicitly discussing it with her clients. She also knows how to get paid handsomely by playing the role of her client's girlfriend in public. She seems to adhere to a professional code of ethics. For example, if she meets her customers in public, she would not embarrass them by greeting them, unless they greet her first. Especially if the clients are prominent people, she would not even name them in her conversation with other call girls. She would not steal from her customers, nor let them overpay her when they are drunk and thus temptingly exploitable. She would do her best to satisfy her clients, even in cases where a client has difficulty in getting an erection. And she would not reveal the sexual inadequacies of any client to his friends.

LEARNING THE TRADE

As a profession, prostitution requires the learning of certain skills. "In order to survive," Travis Hirschi suggests, a prospective prostitute "must be able to 1) find the customers, 2) 'sell' them, 3) provide a suitable place in which to transact business, 4) please the customer, 5) collect her money, 6) protect herself from disease, pregnancy, and physical injury, and 7) avoid the police." [20] Hirschi is generally correct, except that his fourth point needs to be qualified.

Since prostitution is an illegitimate profession and thus not subject to scrutiny by the Consumer Protection Agency, its practitioners do not necessarily have to please the customer. Instead, they must learn how to shortchange him or, in the parlance of prostitution, they must learn how to "turn a trick." This is especially true in regard to low-priced street-walkers; less so with respect to the high-priced call girls—who are more apt to refer to their sexual transaction as a date. For most prostitutes, who are not handsomely paid, it makes good business sense to turn as many tricks as possible within the shortest period of time. Thus, to become successful in the profession, a novice must learn how to shortchange her customer, in addition to the other things that Hirschi has mentioned. The following shows what she has to learn to become a professional prostitute:

The minute Suede [an experienced prostitute] closes the door, her
trick's shoes hit the floor.
SHE: You have to pay me first, okay?
HE: I have to pay you now? Got any change?
SHE: No change.
HE: This okay?
SHE: Okay . . .
She doesn't even undress. She unzips. . . .
There is motion for less than a minute. "Okay?" She opens the door,
slaps on her shoes, scuffs down the hall with her hot pants open and
into the toilet with a contemptuous SLAM! Now she's out, washed,
zipped, and darting down the stairs to catch the next trick.
Time elapsed: eight minutes. Before the hour is out, Suede turns four
tricks. Through it all her face remains vacant as a potato.[21]

Less grossly exploitive toward the customer is the higher-priced prostitute —the call girl. James Bryan's study reveals that the novice call girl has to go through a training period.[22] She may receive her training either from a pimp or from another more experienced call girl. But more often she learns from the latter. Her training period may last from two to eight months, and usually this period is spent in the trainer's apartment.

She learns that call girls should be considered intelligent, self-interested, and honest individuals while their customers should be regarded as corrupt, dishonest, and exploitive. Thus the novice is encouraged to exploit the exploiters (customers) by whatever means necessary. However, she will merely become familiar with this philosophy of prostitution; she is not particularly inclined to adopt it. She receives instruction on such interpersonal techniques as how to engage in telephone conversations and how to discuss the fee and obtain it. She also receives information pertaining to personal and sexual hygiene, prohibition against alcohol and dope while with a client, and the sexual habits of particular customers. Sometimes she is told to bring a customer to her apartment, and the trainer eavesdrops on the sexual transaction and discusses it later with her. Specific sexual techniques, however, are rarely taught, though the trainee's previous sexual experiences may have been quite limited.

It appears that there is not much for the trainee to learn and that what needs to be learned can be easily and quickly acquired. Why, then, must the training period last for such a long time as two to eight months? Actually, the training period serves the crucial purpose of enabling the new call girl to develop a sizable and lucrative clientele. During the training period, the trainer introduces a stream of customers to the apprentice. For each new sexual encounter between customer and apprentice, the trainer receives forty to fifty percent of the total fee. But after that, the apprentice is free to sell her service to the customer without further kickback to the trainer. Once the apprentice has acquired an adequate number of clients, she terminates her apprenticeship.

IDEOLOGY OF PROSTITUTION

Like any other profession, prostitution has an ideology. The ideology of prostitution contains two basic elements; one is the idea that it performs a necessary, important service for society, and the other is the belief that prostitutes are morally superior to conventional people.

"PROSTITUTION IS NECESSARY TO SOCIETY" Some prostitutes believe that their profession helps to prevent sex crimes:

We girls see, like I guess you call them perverts of some sort, you know, little freaky people and if they didn't have girls to come to like us that are able to handle them and make it a nice thing, there would be so many rapes and . . . nutty people.[23]

I believe that there should be more prostitution houses and what have you, and then we wouldn't have so many of these perverted idiots, sex maniacs, all sorts of weird people running around.[24]

A number of prostitutes claim that their work contributes to the success of marriage:

I could say that a prostitute has held more marriages together as part of her profession than any divorce counselor.[25]

I think that the release of talking about an unhappy home situation may well have saved many a marriage, and possibly even lives, when nerves have been strained to a breaking point. It is well known that it is easier to unburden serious trouble onto a total stranger. . . . Easier still to tell a girl whose time you have bought, whom nothing will surprise, and who is in no position to despise you.[26]

Prostitutes also see their work as if it were no different from that of humanitarians, social workers, psychological counselors, and psychiatrists:

I could endure a surprising amount of humiliation for the handicapped person . . . most of the girls felt morally obliged to see the handicapped Johns and be usually kind to them.[27]

I don't regret doing it because I feel I help people. A lot of men that come over to see me don't come over for sex. They come over for companionship, someone to talk to. . . . They talk about sex. . . . A lot of them have problems.[28]

"PROSTITUTES ARE MORALLY SUPERIOR" According to their professional ideology, prostitutes are basically honest while many members of respectable society are dishonest. Professional prostitutes believe that many respectable women who marry for money (such as "the society girls who marry older men they don't love—who happen to have money") are actually prostitutes, except that they are not honest enough to consider themselves as such. Professional prostitutes also see their respectable customers as hypocrites. As one prostitute says, "We come into continual contact with upright, respected citizens whose voices are loudly raised against us in public, and yet who visit us in private." [29] Therefore, the prostitutes consider themselves morally superior to these "respectable" but dishonest men and women of conventional society.

The professional ideology, as described above, implies that the individual prostitute holds herself and her colleagues in relatively high esteem. Bryan's data, however, suggest that the call girl holds herself in much higher esteem than she does her colleagues. This is due to the extensive disloyalty, distrust, hostility, and exploitation among call girls. As one of them says, "But yet there's never a real close friendship. . . . I mean they will do anything for each other. But still at times when they're taking pills and things, they'll go against you. . . . They'll slit your throat at times." [30] Moreover, Bryan's findings suggest that although they are basically familiar with their professional ideology, they do not personally endorse or believe it. For example, the call girl generally does not despise her customers, other men, and straight women; on the contrary, she rates them as significantly more worthwhile than her fellow prostitutes.

Given the fact that the call girl does not behave in accordance with the ideology of her profession, what about other types of prostitutes? The answer can be sought in Norman Jackman and his associates' classification of prostitutes. According to this classification, there are three types of prostitutes. The *dual-world* prostitute is one who works in the world of prostitution and lives in the conventional world. She does not swear or use obscene language; professes religious beliefs; associates with straight people rather than prostitutes or criminals. The *criminal-world* prostitute is one who identifies herself with criminals and with those on the fringe of the criminal world. And the *alienated* prostitute belongs to neither the dual nor criminal world. Instead, she is friendless and bitter about the whole world. As one such prostitute says, "the world's been so screwed up by all the bastards in it." [31] Of these three types, the dual-world prostitute— whose characterization seems to fit the call girl—can be said to be more likely than the criminal-world and the alienated prostitute to personally reject the ideology of prostitution. This may be due to the fact that dual-world prostitutes, who are better educated and higher priced, feel themselves very much a part of conventional society. They are less often known and stigmatized as prostitutes by the public as well as less likely to be harassed by vice squads. Thus they feel less compelled to justify their prostitution.

On the other hand, streetwalkers and other lower-priced prostitutes tend more to believe in their professional ideology. Since 1970 an increasing number of them have even attempted to translate it into political action. They have also received support from some nonprostitute feminists. As one of the latter, Ti-Grace Atkinson, has proclaimed: "Prostitutes are the only honest women left in America, because they charge for their services rather than submit to a marriage contract which forces them to work for life without pay." [32] Thus, in 1973, the prostitutes in Marseilles, France went on strike for thirty days to protest police harassment; conducted a noisy march through the center of town; and listened attentively to their leader who loudly voiced their sentiment: "Considering the service we render, we are practically a public utility. If they want to tax us—all right. But don't prevent us from working. Most of us have children to bring up." [33] Then in 1975 the prostitutes in Lyons, France occupied a church, demanding a better deal from the government. They demanded that police harassment be stopped, and that prostitutes be officially recognized as socially useful workers who should be entitled to pensions and social security benefits. The prostitutes' revolt spread rapidly to many other French cities.[34]

A number of American prostitutes have also formed unions in some cities in the United States. Examples of these unions are ASP (The Associated Seattle Prostitutes), PONY (Prostitutes of New York), and COYOTE (Call Off Your Old Tired Ethics). Their main mission is to improve their working conditions as well as to fight for the legitimacy of their profession. For instance, COYOTE, otherwise called "The Loose Women's Organization," has advised its members how to detect undercover policemen ("Kiss them on the mouth—they won't kiss back"); picketed hotels that charged prostitutes double rates for a room but let vice-squad men use it for free; filed a class-action suit against the antiprostitution law in California; and persuaded the San Francisco Police Department to stop imposing on the arrested prostitute a mandatory three-day jail quarantine for VD examination.[35]

SUPPORTING PLAYERS IN PROSTITUTION

Aside from the prostitute herself, there are three kinds of people who get involved with her in one way or another. These people may be considered to be playing a supporting role in prostitution. They are the madam, the pimp, and the customer.

THE MADAM   The public uses the term *madam* to refer to the owner or manager of a brothel; brothel owners themselves call one another "landlady." Most of them are former prostitutes with a great deal of experience "in the life" behind them. They run their establishments in about the same way as legitimate business people run theirs, except that they have to deal with problems arising from the illegal nature of their trade. Thus there are three major forms of activities that the madam characteristically engages in. The first has to do with the employees, the second the customers, and the third the police.

To run a brothel, the madam obviously has to hire prostitutes. Very often she also employs a support crew of cooks, maids, and bouncers. She recruits her prostitutes largely through her current employees, the pimps, and the madams in other cities. She trains the new girls to become professional prostitutes. In this "turning out" process, she teaches them the importance of cleanliness, self-pride, social skills, and such old customs of prostitution as refraining from kissing the client, asking for payment before giving him the sexual service, and careful checking of the client for venereal disease. After the girls become professional, the madam supervises their work, keeps them happy, prevents quarrels and jealousy among them, and makes and enforces rules governing their behavior. The nature of her work is such that she usually functions as if she were the prostitutes' mother.[36]

The madam is responsible for getting customers. She keeps a "John Book," which contains the customers' names and telephone numbers; she uses it when there is not much business in the house. Usually the customers call her. When a client comes over, she receives him, encourages him to buy drinks, introduces the girls to him, and lets him pick whichever one he likes—or she simply asks one of the girls to entertain him. The madam's main concern is to make the client happy so that he will become a regular visitor. This means that the madam has to constantly find and hire new girls, for it is the variety of girls that keeps the customers happy.

The madam must also know how to deal with the police. She is typically skilled in recognizing a policeman, no matter how he disguises himself. As one madam says, albeit boastfully, "I could spot a copper a mile away—if I don't see him I can smell him." [37] However, in order to remain long in the business, she usually has to work out some stable arrangement with the law officers. She may have to periodically bribe them. But more often she develops an understanding with the police that they will go through the motions of arresting her every now and then—thereby keeping up the appearance of performing their duty to appease the public's moral outrage against prostitution—while allowing her to continue her business. One madam refers to such an understanding as "mutual respect." She says,

When the police come and take you to jail time after time, you can't help but develop a mutual respect; they are doing their job and doing it consistently well. But they see that you are doing your job and doing it well. They can see I run a clean place—no drugs, no thefts, no trouble, no minors in here—either girls or customers; the girls' weekly medical check-up forms are always in plain sight.[38]

THE PIMP   Many of the prostitutes who do not work for a madam work for a pimp. While the madam gets a large portion—usually about fifty percent—of her employees' earnings, the pimp typically gets all of them. Also, unlike the madam who has to find customers for her prostitutes, the pimp simply tells his prostitutes to go out in the street and hustle. He does not want to be bothered with the details of their working life. The pimp, then, is *not*—according to the dictionary—"a pander, a procurer, or a man who solicits customers for a prostitute in return for a share of the proceeds." Rather, he is simply a man who lives off the proceeds of one or more prostitutes. For this reason, he is generally considered "the lowest of the low," especially by middle-class whites.

Pimps themselves, however, are not particularly disturbed by the moral stigma. In fact, the majority of them being black, they enjoy fame and prestige among lower-class black males. This is because black pimps, through the hustling activities of their white or black women, are able to make a lot of money from white men. Such pimping represents a unique lower-class black adaptation to the common American desire for material success. The pimps proudly justify their high status by doing nothing except wearing expensive clothes, riding around in Cadillacs or Lincoln Continentals, and exercising awesome control over their women.[39]

A pimp may have anywhere from one to twenty women, who consider themselves as "wives-in-law," and are referred to by their master as his "stable." Most pimps, however, have only two or three women. According to anthropologists Christina and Richard Milner, pimps and their stables live in a subculture that is the exact opposite of the conventional culture. In the pimping subculture, *polygyny* (the union of one man with several women) is the norm; men are extremely dominant; women are extremely submissive; and the ideal union is between a black man and several white women. Also, the men are obsessed with their appearance, spending many hours a day on their hair, clothes, jewelry, and toilette in order to make themselves look beautiful. Their women are the economic providers, working very hard to support the household. There is a rigid separation between the sexes; at gatherings, men huddle in one corner while women talk only among themselves. These same women, however, frequently engage in sexual activities with other men, toward whom their own men show no jealousy. Consequently, paternity of their children often comes from outside the subcultural group. In such a subculture, men are expected to demonstrate great style and creativity in their dress, women generally sleep during the day and work at night, money is worshiped as a god, conspicuous consumption is indulged in every day, there is no concern for future security, and of course their major industry is the selling of sex to outsiders.[40]

As in any other culture, pimps adhere to a set of implicit codes of conduct. These codes tell them how to deal with their stable, fellow pimps, and male members of conventional society. The Milners have expressed the codes in the form of biblical commandments:

I. Man is the Lord God. He shall have dominion over women and control them; also, he shall stand with his fellow men against any bitch who puts herself before man.

II. Thou shalt have no other gods before money; for money buys affection, respect, and acceptance.

III. Thou shalt never fornicate in vain, without getting paid; for fair trade is no robbery.

IV. Thou shalt seek to avoid direct confrontation with thine enemy, and shalt trick or outwit him before resorting to violence.
V. Thou shalt not steal from thy friends. But thou shalt rob thine enemies blind. A man can't fool with the Golden Rule in a crowd that don't play fair.[41]

To effectively control his stable, a pimp often resorts to violence. As a former prostitute says, "I saw a girl walk into a bar and hand the pimp a $100 bill. He took it and burned it in her face and turned around and knocked her down on the floor and kicked her and said, 'I told you, bitch, $200. I want $200, not $100.' Now she's gotta go out again and make not another hundred, but two hundred."[42] Some pimps believe that the best way to secure a woman's loyalty is to beat her into unconsciousness and then reward her with his sexual favors.[43]

The pimp's violent method of exercising control over his women is apparently very effective. These women generally worship him as if he were a god, and they invest in him all their hopes, dreams, and goals for the future. They wear his beatings proudly as symbols of his love. Everything that he does to them is considered right, proper, or admirable. When a prostitute was asked what her pimp did to deserve all her earnings, she replied, "He doesn't do *nothing*. But the way he does nothing is *beautiful*." [44]

The prostitute's devotion to her pimp has intrigued or puzzled many psychologists, psychiatrists, and other experts. They ask, "Why would a woman engage in prostitution, risking arrest, disease, and mistreatment, only to hand over all her earnings to a man who often brutalizes her?" The answer that these experts offer is usually what we would expect from an ethnocentric person looking at the "strange" behavior of the natives of another society. These experts generally consider the prostitute as a masochist, a drug addict, or somehow abnormal, thereby implying that there is something wrong with her. According to anthropologists Christina and Richard Milner, however, few of these prostitutes are masochists or junkies, and most of them are quite "normal" human beings who actually enjoy their lives with pimps. The relatively frequent beatings of the prostitute by her pimp is, in fact, comparable to the beating of a nonprostitute wife by her husband in many a lower-class family. The Milners further suggest that these prostitutes may possibly have greater personal happiness than do the liberated or unliberated women of conventional society.[45]

THE CUSTOMER In the existing literature on prostitution, there is relatively little discussion on the prostitute's customer, who in the argot of the trade is called a "John" or "trick." This lack of interest in the customer apparently reflects the public's unconcern with him or the fact that the law often punishes the prostitute but not her client. In studies that do exist on the customer, these two topics have been discussed: reasons for visiting prostitutes and types of customers.

Numerous reasons have been given for a man's buying sexual favors.[46] They can be classified into three broad categories: quick, easy sex; untangled sex; and sexual variety.

To take the first category, a number of men may find themselves in various situations where they can count on a prostitute to give them quick, easy sex. Generally, seducing a female requires some time, effort, or ability. There are men who do not have the time to seduce a woman, particularly if they are too busy pursuing a career or simply being strangers in a city far away from their wives or girlfriends. There are also men who simply want to have sex—not conversation, not companionship, not cultivation of friendship or love. For these people, the ritual of dating—taking the girl to a restaurant, a movie, a bar, and possibly a bedroom—demands too much effort. They thus prefer a prostitute from whom they can effortlessly get what they want; besides, a prostitute may cost them less money than a date. There are yet other men who do not have the ability to attract and persuade a woman to go to bed with them. They may be too shy, emotionally insecure, mentally or physically handicapped, or too old. They, therefore, find it impossible to compete with other men for women. For such men, a prostitute can be easily gotten without risking rejection.

Second, some men do not want to get seriously involved with women. They want to dodge emotional entanglements, obligations, and interpersonal conflict. For example, they want to avoid getting entangled with a girl in courtship or marriage. They want to avoid being obligated to her if she becomes pregnant or contracts venereal disease. And they want to avoid the risk (in the case of seducing a married woman) of causing marital discord or breakup, being stigmatized as sex maniacs, or getting beaten up or murdered. What these men want, then, is impersonal, untangled sex, which can free them from the conventional strictures regarding the responsibility of sex. Such kind of sex is characteristically available from the prostitute.

Third, there are a large number of men who turn to prostitutes for the experience of sexual variety. Some of these men have unusual sexual tastes that are not shared by their wives or girlfriends. They may want to engage in the masochistic or sadistic type of sex that involves the infliction of pain on themselves or their partners. They may have a strong desire for fetishes—they may want, for example, to have coitus in a coffin, or to bring in a dozen or so panties of different shapes and colors and ask the woman to model each one of them. Some men may have a strong desire for anal intercourse or, far more frequently, for oral sex. These men's wives or girlfriends may consider any one of these sex acts as too bizarre or perverted—they may not want to cooperate or may even tell their men to see a psychiatrist. But prostitutes can be asked to engage in such sexual behavior. Also, there are many men who are bored with their wives or who want to experience sex with a variety of women. For these men, the availability of prostitution is an answer to their needs, as there are prostitutes of all physical types.

As for the types of customers, psychoanalyst Harold Greenwald has come out with three, with some overlap among them: the occasional John, the habitual John, and the compulsive John.[47]

The majority of the customers are perhaps the occasional type. Many of these men are away from home. They may be sailors who have been out at sea without women for long stretches of time; they may be businessmen attending sales meetings or conventions; they may be tourists who consider their trip incomplete without the services of a prostitute; and they may be soldiers on the move, traveling salesmen, and other similarly mobile individuals. Most of these men are married. But there are also occasional Johns among unmarried youths. These young men usually look for prostitutes in groups. They may have been drinking at a party and, if they fail to get sexual pleasure from their dates or other girls, they may decide to search for prostitutes. There are also cases in which a young man is brought by his father to a prostitute so that he will "learn the facts of life," "lose his pimples," "become a man," or "get rid of his effeminate characteristics or homosexual tendencies." Occasional Johns may also be men whose wives are ill or pregnant, whose girlfriends persistently refuse to engage in coitus, or who once in a while get the itch to try something different.

The habitual Johns are those who want to make friends with one special prostitute. Given the purely commercial transaction between themselves and a prostitute, habitual Johns may attempt to turn it into an affectionate relationship. They are fond of asking the prostitute many questions, telling her about their lives, offering to help her in whatever way they can, and trying to make her enjoy the sex or reach orgasm—which, to many prostitutes, is an occupational hazard for it takes the John too long to ejaculate. Some habitual Johns insist on giving the prostitute an expensive present that costs much more than her fee, rather than paying her the fee itself. In this way, they may enjoy the illusion of making love to a "nice girlfriend" rather than a "dirty whore."

The compulsive Johns are those males who cannot keep away from prostitutes. They may feel that sex is dirty and would not want to defile a "good" woman, so they copulate with "bad" ones only—namely, prostitutes. Some of the compulsive Johns can be sexually potent only with prostitutes;

they cannot have an erection with their wives. A number of compulsive Johns are strongly attracted to prostitutes because of the peculiar sex acts that they will perform.

THEORIES OF PROSTITUTION

There are two major theories of prostitution. One may be referred to as a social-psychological theory. The other may be called a sociological or functionalist theory. These two theories do not deal with exactly the same subject. The social-psychological theory explains why some females become prostitutes. The sociological theory explains why prostitution exists.

SOCIAL-PSYCHOLOGICAL THEORY

This theory of why a woman becomes a prostitute has been presented in one way or another by psychiatrists, journalists, and other nonsociological writers. It has been most neatly presented by psychiatrist Harry Benjamin and philosopher R. E. L. Masters. They list three factors that they contend cause a woman to enter prostitution: (1) predisposing, (2) attracting, and (3) precipitating factors. They further point out what is involved in each of these three factors:

Predisposing factors are such elements in the prostitute's background as the "broken home," parental (especially maternal) promiscuity, approval or tolerance of prostitution in the immediate social milieu, and trauma productive of (certain types of) neuroses.

Attracting factors are the comparative advantages of a prostitute's career for a particular individual: larger earnings, an easier life, a more interesting or exciting life, for some the expectation of sexual gratification and so on.

Precipitating factors include economic pressure, no chance for a desirable marriage, enticement or persuasion by a pimp or other prostitutes, an unhappy love affair, a good opportunity, etc.[48]

Benjamin and Masters further note that there are two types of prostitutes: the voluntary and the compulsive. Voluntary prostitutes are women who have entered prostitution on a relatively rational basis or mainly as the result of a free choice. Compulsive prostitutes are those who get into the life primarily because they are driven to it by their psychoneurotic needs. They are generally more impoverished, more inept, and more unintelligent than voluntary prostitutes. Benjamin and Masters argue that, as causes of entry into prostitution, attracting factors have a greater influence on voluntary prostitutes; predisposing factors have a greater impact upon compulsive prostitutes; and precipitating factors are about equally important for both.[49]

Since they believe that voluntary prostitutes are far more common than compulsive ones, Benjamin and Masters go on to elaborate on the attracting factors. The attracting factors in becoming a prostitute are what Benjamin and Masters call "the distinct and readily discernible advantages for a good many women." They are as follows: (1) The income from prostitution is much higher than that from most other occupations open to women. (2) There is a great deal of opportunity for adventure, excitement, and glamor in the life, because prostitutes may meet some intelligent, prominent, and affluent men—which is much more interesting and exciting than the experience of the average secretary, store clerk, and other working women. (3) To many prostitutes, their occupation is an attractively easy, undisciplined way of earning a living. These women often say, "I do as I please"; "I don't have to punch any damned timeclock"; or "I get paid for screwing a guy I like anyway." And (4) a few prostitutes are so highly sexed that they enjoy many or most of their sexual activities.[50]

While Benjamin and Masters emphasize the importance of the attracting factors, other writers stress the predisposing factors as causing a girl to enter prostitution. For instance, psychoanalyst Harold Greenwald contends that there are a number of "psychological and social factors influencing the choice of the [call girl] profession," which appear quite similar to what Benjamin and Masters have called "predisposing factors." Greenwald's list of the psychological and social factors includes the following: (1) Most call girls come from broken homes or from homes characterized by the absence of warmth and affection between the parents. (2) The call girls have suffered neglect and rejection at home and thus developed feelings of loneliness and unworthiness as well as hostility toward their parents. (3) The call girls learned early in life that they could get some measure of attention, interest, or affection by giving an adult sexual gratification. (4) As a result of these early experiences, call girls show such behavioral symptoms as anxiety, fear of homosexuality, sexual promiscuity, inability to establish stable relations with others, inability to conform to standards of society, distorted perception of reality, lack of self-control, and so on. (5) They use prostitution to prove that they are attractive to men. And (6) they have negative attitudes toward work. As for the economic reward that Benjamin and Masters consider as crucial for inducing a girl into prostitution, Greenwald discounts it:

While economic factors, such as the wish for a high income, may have
had some influence on the girls' decisions to become call girls, these
factors were apparently more useful to them as a way of rationalizing
their choice. They could deny the emotional problems that led them
to become call girls by asserting that it was just for money.[51]

In essence, Greenwald, as well as other writers,[52] suggests that if a girl
has been subjected to a good deal of emotional unrelatedness to other
people such as her parents, she is likely to become a prostitute—an occupation where emotional unrelatedness between people is characteristic.

In the absence of statistical data, it is impossible to judge which of the
three causal factors presented by Benjamin and Masters is more important
than the other. It seems only plausible that each of the three has some
effect on a woman becoming a prostitute.

SOCIOLOGICAL THEORY

This theory was first proposed by Kingsley Davis in 1937. Today it is
still very popular among sociologists, who refer to it as a *functionalist
theory* of prostitution.

Most writers, such as those discussed above, are interested in the question
of why some women become prostitutes. In contrast, Davis is interested in
why most women do *not* choose prostitution as their profession. As he states,
"The interesting question is not why so many women become prostitutes,
but why so few of them do." [53] The rationale for such a statement is this:
Given the fact that prostitution hardly requires any skill or effort and yet
pays more than ordinary women's work, why do so few women become
prostitutes? "The answer of course," Davis says, "is that the return is not
primarily a reward for labor, skill, or capital, but a reward for loss of
social standing. The prostitute loses esteem because the moral system—
especially when prostitution is purely commercial—condemns her." [54] In
other words, so few women become prostitutes because so many women
are deterred by the social stigma of prostitution. The assumption is that
the moral system of society is more powerful than the economic reward
of prostitution.

With such an assumption, Davis attempts to explain why prostitution
exists in society. To put it simply and bluntly, Davis's explanation is this:
The moral system of society causes prostitution. How is this possible?
According to Davis, by its very effort to make the sex drive part of a
meaningful social relationship, the moral system of society creates advantages for prostitution. This is because the moral system also condemns
prostitution as a meaningless sex activity. Thus, when a man is away from

home and cannot satisfy his sex drive with his wife, or when a man is a stranger in town and does not have enough time to seduce a respectable woman, he is driven into the arms of a prostitute who will satisfy his sex drive in—as the moral system would have it—a meaningless way. Also, by defining certain sex acts like fellatio and cunnilingus as immoral and hence not to be indulged in with one's wife or girlfriend, the moral order encourages males to turn to prostitutes for the enjoyment of these sex acts.

After discussing how the moral system causes prostitution, Davis reverses himself by suggesting that prostitution has a large effect on the moral system; in fact, it strengthens it. In other words, prostitution serves the function (hence Davis's theory is called "functionalist theory") of "protecting the family and keeping the wives and daughters of the respectable citizenry pure." [55] This is because, as Davis implies, prostitution encourages the husbands and sons of the respectable citizenry to go to prostitutes rather than persuade respectable women to engage in sexual promiscuity.

In sum, Davis's theory suggests that prostitution exists in society because the moral system paradoxically encourages it, and it in turn serves the important function of preserving the moral system—specifically, feminine virtue. Such a theory, as Davis observes, is contrary to the popular belief that "an evil such as prostitution cannot cause a good such as feminine virtue, or vice versa." [56] There is some evidence to support the theory. For example, in Asian societies where prostitution is common, sexual promiscuity of respectable females is uncommon, while in Western societies where prostitution is uncommon, sexual promiscuity of respectable females is common.

POWER THEORY APPLIED

We have so far dealt with the popularly recognized type of prostitution. It may be referred to as *overt prostitution*, as it is an overt act of renting one's body for monetary reward. The more subtle act of trading one's person for long-term financial security has not been popularly recognized as prostitution, and thus it has not been discussed by sociologists and other scholars. This *covert prostitution* may be found in marriages or liaisons where the wives or mistresses are about as equally subjugated by their husbands or lovers as are the overt prostitutes by their Johns. What underlies both forms of prostitution is more than the trading of one's body for financial reward. It is the subjugation and humiliation of the owner of the body by its user that is the essence of prostitution. Now, it appears that while lower-status women tend more to engage in overt prostitution, higher-status ones are more inclined to participate in covert prostitution.

Due to the great stigma attached to overt prostitution, very few lower-status women engage in it, unless they are forced—socially, economically, and psychologically—to do so. On the other hand, since covert prostitution is highly rewarding, many higher-status women willingly participate in it. This may suggest that higher-status women are *more* likely to become covert prostitutes than are lower-status women likely to become overt prostitutes. There may also be a symbiosis between these two types of prostitution. Being overtly treated as sex objects for sale rather than respected as human beings, lower-class prostitutes may fuel the male's sexist attitude toward women in general. This attitude, in turn, may influence males to treat their wives and other women as sex objects. All this, along with higher-status women's voluntary acceptance of male domination, may serve to reinforce sexual inequality and thus both forms of prostitution.

SUMMARY

There are a number of popular misconceptions about prostitution. First, there is the white slavery mythology. Second, prostitutes are believed to be nymphomaniacs. Third, most drug-addicted girls are thought to become prostitutes. Fourth, prostitutes are either criticized as nasty and hard-hearted or idealized as sweet and warm-hearted. Fifth, prostitutes are considered to be extremely unhappy with their work. Sixth, prostitutes are assumed to be sexually frigid. Seventh, prostitution is regarded as completely incompatible with religion. Eighth, prostitutes are believed to be homosexuals. There is, however, one popular belief that turns out to be true: prostitutes are usually infertile.

There are many different types of prostitutes. They are, in ascending order of status: the streetwalker, the bar prostitute, the brothel prostitute, the massage-parlor prostitute, and the call girl.

In order to become a prostitute, a female has to learn where to find customers, how to get them to buy her services for a certain fee, where to carry out the sexual transaction, and how to protect herself from such occupational hazards as VD, pregnancy, physical injury, and police harassment. Lower-priced prostitutes (such as streetwalkers) are generally more inclined than the higher priced (particularly call girls) to shortchange their customers. Prostitution is a relatively unskilled occupation; it can be learned very quickly.

In becoming a professional prostitute, a woman also learns the ideology of prostitution. According to this ideology, prostitution performs a necessary and important service for society, and prostitutes are morally superior to conventional males and females. As with most social ideals, prostitutes have become aware of the ideology but have not taken it too seriously. More recently, however, an increasing number of them have become militant, attempting to achieve legitimacy and respectability for their profession.

There are three supporting members of the prostitute's profession: the madam, the pimp, and the customer. The madam is the owner or manager of a brothel, and employs the prostitutes to serve her customers. The pimp is primarily a nonworking lover of a prostitute, who lives off her earnings and often beats her. And the customer is usually a member of conventional society, who visits prostitutes for quick and easy sex, for untangled sex, and for the experience of sexual variety. The customers have been divided into three types: the occasional John, the habitual John, and the compulsive John.

There are two major theories of prostitution. (1) The social-psychological theory essentially says that some females become prostitutes because they have suffered emotional unrelatedness to others in their past experiences. While considering this as a predisposing factor to entering prostitution, Benjamin and Masters further suggest that there are two other factors. They refer to these as attracting and precipitating factors: the former being the great economic reward of prostitution, and the latter the opportunity for entering it. (2) The sociological theory suggests that there are two factors that can explain the existence of prostitution. One is that prostitution is created by society's moral system; the other is that prostitution serves the function of preserving the sexual morality of respectable women. Finally, with power theory we may divide prostitution into overt and covert types, each influencing the other through their mutual reinforcement of sexual inequality in society.

SUGGESTED READINGS

Benjamin, Harry and R. E. L. Masters. *Prostitution and Morality*. New York: Julian Press, 1964.

Bryan, James H. "Apprenticeships in Prostitution." *Social Problems* 12 (Winter 1965): 287–297.

Bryan, James H. "Occupational Ideologies and Individual Attitudes of Call Girls." *Social Problems* 13 (Spring 1966): 441–450.

Greenwald, Harold. *The Elegant Prostitute*. New York: Walker, 1970.

Heyl, Barbara Sherman. "The Female House of Prostitution," in Irving Louis Horowitz and Charles Nanry, eds. *Sociological Realities II*. New York: Harper & Row, 1975, pp. 339–344.

Hirschi, Travis. "The Professional Prostitute." *Berkeley Journal of Sociology* 7 (Spring 1962): 33–45.

Milner, Christina and Richard. *Black Players*. Boston: Little, Brown, 1972.

Sheehy, Gail. *Hustling*. New York: Delacorte Press, 1971.

Winick, Charles and Paul M. Kinsie. *The Lively Commerce*. Chicago: Quadrangle Books, 1971.

9 HOMOSEXUALITY

I t is relatively easy to define homosexuality. Most sex researchers would define it as the feeling of sexual desire for members of the same sex, or the experience of engaging in sexual activities with persons of the same sex, or a combination of both the feeling and the experience. It is more difficult to define what a homosexual is. As Alfred Kinsey and his associates wrote in 1948,

[People] do not represent two discrete populations, heterosexual and homosexual. The world is not to be divided into sheep and goats. Not all things are black nor all things white. It is a fundamental of taxonomy that nature rarely deals with discrete categories. Only the human mind invents categories and tries to force facts into separate pigeon holes. The living world is a continuum in each and every one of its aspects. The sooner we learn this concerning human sexual behavior the sooner we shall reach a sound understanding of the realities of sex.[1]

Therefore, according to Kinsey and his associates, a person can be assigned a position on a continuum from one extreme of being exclusively heterosexual to the other extreme of being exclusively homosexual. (See Figure 9.1.)

It is impossible to know the exact incidence of homosexuality. There is great stigma attached to homosexuality, and many who have engaged in homosexual acts may not know or admit that they have, especially if they do not belong to the gay community. But in 1948 and 1953, Kinsey and his colleagues found that 37 percent of white American males and 13 per-

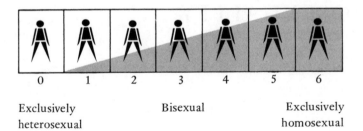

0. Exclusively heterosexual

Bisexual

Exclusively homosexual

0. Exclusively heterosexual
1. Predominantly heterosexual, only incidentally homosexual
2. Predominantly heterosexual, but more than incidentally homosexual
3. Equally heterosexual and homosexual
4. Predominantly homosexual, but more than incidentally heterosexual
5. Predominantly homosexual, but incidentally heterosexual
6. Exclusively homosexual

Figure 9.1 The Kinsey heterosexual-homosexual continuum.

Adapted from Alfred C. Kinsey, Wardell B. Pomeroy, and Clyde E. Martin, *Sexual Behavior in the Human Male*, W. B. Saunders, Philadelphia, 1948, p. 638.

cent of white American females had some homosexual experience between adolescence and old age, whereas 4 percent of the males and 1 percent of the females were exclusively homosexual throughout their entire lives.[2] The same findings emerged in a more recent study.[3] All this suggests that homosexuality is surprisingly widespread—given the fact that most Americans believe homosexuality to be a perversion, sickness, or harmful to American life, and the fact that there are harsh laws against homosexual conduct in most of the states in this country.

THE NATURE OF HOMOSEXUALITY

To understand the nature of homosexuality, we should first of all recognize the popular myths about it. According to one, male homosexuals are typically effeminate in that they walk like women, talk like women, or look like women, while female homosexuals are typically masculine in that they walk, talk, and look like men. Actually it is difficult to distinguish most homosexuals from their heterosexual counterparts. Another myth is that homosexuals characteristically play one role only—either as an active or passive partner in their sexual activities. The truth is that most homosexuals engage in a lot of alternation between those two roles. Still another myth is that the homosexual particularly likes to molest or seduce young children. The fact, however, is that the great majority of gay men have no more sexual interest in young boys than the great majority of "straight" men have in young girls. Finally, a myth has it that homosexuals are sick—their homosexuality is a symptom of mental illness. Some homosexuals, particularly those who go to psychiatrists, are perhaps mentally ill, but so are some heterosexuals, particularly those who also go to psychiatrists. Therefore, just as it is wrong to conclude that heterosexuality is a symptom of mental illness, it is also wrong to conclude that homosexuality is.

Perhaps because there are more male homosexuals than female, or because society reacts more strongly against male than female homosexuality, or because there is the sexist attitude that women are not important enough to deserve scholarly attention to their sexual problems, most of the existing literature is about male homosexuals. In the following, we shall therefore discuss mostly the studies on male homosexuals, who will often be referred to as simply *homosexuals*.

TYPES OF HOMOSEXUALS

As we have seen from Figure 9.1, Kinsey and his colleagues classify homosexuals into six types, ranging from the most incidentally to the exclusively homosexual. As these six types differ as to the degree of homosexual feeling and experience only, the typology cannot tell us other aspects of these homosexuals. For example, it cannot tell us what kinds of men they are, what they look like, how they act, what social classes they come from, and so on. Psychiatrist Martin Hoffman has asked these questions but only gives "the most general (and unsatisfactory) answer, namely, that these people run the entire gamut from the swishy faggot who can be identified a block away, to the husband, son, or brother whom even fairly sophisticated persons would not suspect of any homosexual interest. They include people who are handsome, clever, and rich, those who are ugly, stupid, and poor, and all combinations and gradations in between. Homosexuality penetrates into every conceivable socioeconomic, religious, and geographical classification." [4] Such an enumeration of various types of homosexuals is indeed useful; it shows that there is as great a variety of people among homosexuals as among heterosexuals. But it is, as Hoffman admits, unsatisfactory, because it implicitly deals with too many aspects of the homosexuals' lives. Let us then attempt to strike a balance between Kinsey's abstract and neat typology and Hoffman's concrete and chaotic enumeration.

We may roughly divide homosexuals into seven types, comparable to the six in Kinsey's classification but described in more concrete terms. They are, ranging from the most incidentally to the exclusively homosexual, (1) trade, (2) street hustler, (3) prison homosexual, (4) bisexual, (5) call boy, (6) closet queen, and (7) gay guy. Most of these terms come from the language of the homosexual world.

TRADE   This is the type whose sexual feeling and experience are predominantly heterosexual and only incidentally homosexual. He is, or has been, married, and seeks homosexual experience only as a means of releasing tension. Were cheap brothels easily accessible to him, he would frequent them. He only wants other males to go down on him and refuses to reciprocate. He refuses to go down on other males because he considers himself straight and has a masculine self-image. Defining himself as straight and masculine, he merely treats his partner's mouth as if it were a woman's vagina. Many trades find their male sex-objects in public toilets. In his study of homosexual activities in public restrooms, sociologist Laud Humphreys found that most trades come from the lower classes, are Roman Catholics, and do not get enough sex from their wives.[5]

STREET HUSTLER   This type is like the trade in having predominantly heterosexual feelings, but he engages in a greater volume of homosexual activity. He is usually a lower-class teen-age boy who considers himself heterosexual and masculine, and he frequently makes money from letting adults have fellatio with him, but, like the trade, refuses to reciprocate sexually. He abandons homosexual prostitution when he reaches adulthood.[6]

PRISON HOMOSEXUAL   This type, like the trade and street hustler, is predominantly heterosexual, sees himself as masculine, and is able to abandon homosexual activities if circumstances permit. But unlike the other two, whose heterosexual experience mitigates their homosexual activities, the prison homosexual is forced by his confinement in a one-sex institution to resort to homosexual release only. Thus, in terms of homosexual experience, the prison homosexual may be said to be closer to the homosexual pole of the Kinsey continuum.

BISEXUAL   This type is about equally heterosexual and homosexual. According to Humphreys, the bisexual is married and engages in as much sex with his wife as he does with other men. He enjoys homosexual experience for its own sake, rather than using it for release, money, or expression of masculinity. He does not consider it a loss of self-respect or of masculine self-image when he goes down on his male sex-partners. He treats his partners as potential friends rather than as sex objects only. But he shuns the gay bar and its patrons who are exclusively homosexual, so that he will not be publicly identified as a homosexual. This is because he usually comes from the higher social classes and wants to protect his family and his lucrative profession.[7]

CALL BOY This type has had some heterosexual experience, but is predominantly homosexual in sexual identification and activity. He is likely to be unmarried. The call boy seems to enjoy his homosexual work, and is willing to engage in a variety of sex acts with his customers. After his short-lived career is ended, he is likely to continue considering himself a homosexual and participate covertly in homosexual activities or openly join the gay community.[8] This, then, distinguishes him sharply from the street hustler, who usually becomes completely heterosexual after giving up his experience as a prostitute.

CLOSET QUEEN This is a male who keeps his homosexuality hidden from the public. He may be married or single, but the label *closet queen* is usually applied to the covert, single man. Although the closet queen is predominantly or exclusively homosexual, he is afraid to reveal this publicly. He conceals his homosexuality from the heterosexual world of which he is a part, and he also avoids associating with overt homosexuals in the gay subculture. He is, in turn, likely to be scorned by overt homosexuals because of his preference for teen-age boys, whom he often lures to be his sex objects.[9]

GAY GUY This type is exclusively and openly homosexual. As an overt homosexual, he is obviously not married to a woman, is well integrated into the homosexual subculture, associates mostly with other homosexuals, and is proud of being gay. Of all the homosexuals, the gay guy wants a permanent love relationship with another man.[10] Recently, an increasing number of gay guys have been politicizing their attempt to make homosexuality respectable.

THE EMERGENCE OF HOMOSEXUAL IDENTITY

With the exception of gay guys, the other types of homosexuals do not publicly identify themselves as being homosexual and thereby become gay guys. The trade, the street hustler, and the prison homosexual all engage in homoerotic activities but do not think of themselves as homosexuals; they would never become gay guys. Others—the bisexual, the call boy, and the closet queen—do conceive of themselves as being partly or completely homosexual, and thus have at least some possibility of eventually becoming gay guys. In the argot of the homosexual world, becoming a gay guy is called "coming out," as it involves a person's *publicly* identifying himself as a homosexual.

Long before they come out, however, many young gays do not even *privately* identify themselves as being homosexual. Such is the case, even though they are exclusively or predominantly attracted to persons of the same sex. In his study of homosexuality, sociologist Barry Dank asked his subjects whether, prior to their graduation from high school, they knew they were homosexual. Some of their typical responses are as follows:

SUBJECT 1:   I think I did but I didn't know how to put it into words.
I didn't know it existed. I guess I was like everybody else and thought
I was the only one in the world . . . I probably would have said
I didn't know. I don't think I really knew what one was. I would
have probably asked you to explain what one was.
SUBJECT 2:   I would have said, "No. I don't know what you are
talking about." If you had said "queer," I would have thought
something about it; this was the slang term that was used, although
I didn't know what the term meant.
SUBJECT 3:   I don't think I would have known then. I know now.
Then I wasn't even thinking about the word. I wasn't reading up on it.[11]

The major reason for homosexual teen-agers' failure to develop a homosexual identity is apparently that their parents and other socializing agents of society have taught them the meaning of heterosexuality but nothing about homosexuality. However, there are a number of social contexts where they can learn the meaning of homosexuality, and then privately or publicly identify themselves as being gay. As Dank points out, they may acquire the knowledge of homosexuals and homosexuality through meeting self-defined homosexuals, from straight persons who are knowledgeable about the subject, or by simply reading about it. Their homosexual identity is also likely to emerge in such one-sex environments as mental hospitals, YMCAs, prisons, the military, public restrooms, gay bars, and school dormitories.[12]

ACTIVITIES IN HOMOSEXUAL MARKET

Of all the one-sex environments, the gay bar and the public restroom are the most popular for homosexual encounters. The gay bar typically attracts males who want to *publicly* show off their homosexual identity, while the restroom characteristically entices those who wish only *privately* to identify themselves as being completely or partly homosexual. We will discuss these two homosexual locales further.

PICKUP IN THE GAY BAR   The gay bar is the most important, perhaps the only, place for a novice homosexual to come out. In the gay bar he may be pleasantly surprised to discover many homosexual men who are physically attractive and masculine, no different from their heterosexual counterparts in many ordinary bars. As he meets homosexuals from all walks of life, he may come to believe that the gay population is very large and diverse. Once he has come out in the gay bar, the homosexual—especially if he is young and attractive—is approached by eager tutors. They teach him the homosexual language, the variety of homosexual acts, and the special way of spotting vice-squad officers. They also instill in him the idea that the homosexual way of life is both legitimate and healthy.[13]

In thus receiving a good deal of social and moral support from veteran gays, the rookie homosexual is disabused of the negative stereotype that he has learned from straight society—he stops seeing himself as a "queer," "pervert," "sick," "dirty old man," and so on. He may also learn to accept himself as he is and to respect himself as he is respected by other gays, so that he develops a positive self-image. As one homosexual says, "I had this feeling of relief; there was no more tension. . . . I guess the fact that I had accepted myself as being homosexual had taken a lot of tensions off me." [14] In their study of homosexuals in several societies, sociologists Martin Weinberg and Colin Williams have discovered about the same thing. They found that, compared with those who were little involved with other homosexuals, those who were frequently involved reported fewer psychological problems, such as feelings of depression, loneliness, and guilt, shame, or anxiety about their homosexuality.[15]

The newly self-defined homosexual soon finds out the ways in which the gay bar is similar to and different from the straight, singles bar. One similarity is that both bars are basically sexual marketplaces, where patrons may ostensibly seek sociability but usually want to pick up a stranger to go to bed with. Another similarity is that the customers of both bars place a high premium on youthful appearance and physical attractiveness, so that the possession of these assets ensures success in the sexual market. As for the differences between the two kinds of bars, there is first the obvious one that the gay bar is almost exclusively patronized by males while the singles bar has both sexes. There are three less obvious differences.

First, compared to the singles bar, the gay bar seems to produce a larger quantity of "one night stands"—sexual activities without emotional involvement. In the singles bar, the males may strongly desire the one night stand but the females may be less eager, while in the gay bar all the males are about equally eager for sex without involvement. So the males have a tougher time seducing the females in the singles bar than do the men seducing other men in the gay bar. Hence, a greater amount of sexual activity without involvement is produced by the gay bar. This may also explain why there are fewer bars for female homosexuals than for male. Like straight women, but unlike gay men, lesbians have been socialized to appreciate sex with involvement rather than sex without involvement. Lesbians, then, are far less promiscuous than homosexual men.

Second, while they engage in a greater amount of sex without involvement than do the straight bar's customers, the gay bar's patrons do not seem to have as much uninvolved sex as one would expect—in view of the great opportunity for finding pickups in the gay bar. Thus, compared to the straight bar's customers, the gay bar's patrons tend more to stand around, silently throwing glances at one another. People unfamiliar with the gay bar scene may "imagine that if you are going to a place to seek a sexual partner, you go in, look around a little bit, walk up to somebody that you like, engage in a conversation, and then go out together. And sometimes this is precisely what does occur in the gay bar. Very often, in fact. But the bewildering problem which confronts the uninitiated observer is why this does not happen more often; why, in fact, all these good-looking and well-dressed young men are standing around uncommunicative." [16]

Hoffman suggests that the reason for the gay men's reluctance to make the initial overture is their fear of getting rejected—they are afraid that they may be considered physically unattractive by their desired sex partner. This seems to be a convincing explanation. Homosexual men place as much importance on the male's physical attractiveness as do heterosexual men on the female's. Thus a man trying to seduce another man in a gay bar would find himself in the same situation as a woman trying to seduce a man in the singles bar. For both the would-be male and female seducers would be equally fearful of getting rejected because they may not be attractive enough. At the same time, the sociological factor of sex role training should not be ignored: men have not been trained to seduce other men just as women have not been trained to seduce men.

Third, both the fear of rejection and the lack of training in the seduction of same-sex others may generate a unique, subtle method of making the initial overture to an intended sexual partner. Thus, instead of boldly walking up to a girl and directly flattering her with sweet words and amorous attention, as heterosexual men in the singles bar would do, the homosexual man would use the covert, silent, nonverbal, or "glancing" approach to pick up another man in a gay bar. Here is how Evelyn Hooker describes the way the homosexual man communicates his sexual intent to another:

Some individuals are apparently communicating with each other
without exchanging words, but simply by exchanging glances—but
not the kind of quick glance which ordinarily occurs between men.
It is said by homosexuals that if another catches and holds the glance,
one need know nothing more about him to know that he is one of
them. . . . Many men in the bar, then, are not engaged in conversation,
but are standing along a wall, or by themselves at a vantage point in
the room so that they may be seen as well as see, and are scanning faces
and bodies. Occasionally, we may see a glance catch and hold
another glance. Later, as if in an accidental meeting, the two holders-
of-a-glance may be seen in a brief conversation followed by their
leaving together. Or, the conversation may be omitted. Casually and
unobtrusively, they may arrive at the door at the same time, and leave.[17]

From this description, you may notice that the homosexual man's glancing approach is in some way similar to that often used by women who
want to get picked up by a man in a singles bar. By simply glancing at a
man in a seductive way, a woman may attract a man to approach and
initiate conversation with her—if she is physically attractive enough to him.
In yet another way, the homosexual man's glancing tactic is similar to a
heterosexual man's responding to a woman's seductive glance—by walking
toward the desired sex partner—except that the heterosexual man is far
more likely than the homosexual to initiate conversation, because the
former has been taught by society how to talk to a woman, while the
latter has not been taught how to talk to another man, for sexual purposes.
Thus the homosexual's seductive method is a highly complicated one, which
requires him to both initiate and respond to a seductive glance. In other
words, he attempts to play at the same time the role of the conventional
woman and the role of the conventional man, with the result that he plays
the seduction game in a uniquely unconventional way, as described in the
above quotation.

SEX IN THE MEN'S ROOM   While it is true that there is hardly any verbal
interaction in the gay bar, this is even truer in the case of homosexual
encounters in the public men's room. When two homosexuals who have
met in the gay bar retire to a bedroom to make love, they do strike up
some conversation. But when two men have sex in a restroom, they do not
exchange a single word. They are like two sex machines programmed to
do their thing, which involves one silently performing fellatio on the other
until orgasm is produced, at which point they separate without talking to
or looking at each other. As Humphreys observes:

Tearoom [public restroom] sex is distinctly less personal than any
other form of sexual activity. . . . What I mean by "less personal" is

simply that there is less emotional and physical involvement in restroom fellatio—less, even, than in the furtive action that takes place in autos and behind bushes. In these instances, at least, there is generally some verbal involvement. Often, in tearoom stalls, the only portions of the players' bodies that touch are the mouth of the insertee and the penis of the insertor; and the mouths of these partners seldom open for speech.[18]

Although they do not feel any emotional attachment to their sex partners, these "tearoom" participants may develop strong, sentimental attachment to the restroom itself. For example, when he asked a tearoom enthusiast whether he remembered one restroom that had been torn down, Humphreys got the following response:

Do I ever! That was the greatest place in the park. Do you know what my roommate did last Christmas, after they tore the place down? He took a wreath, sprayed it with black paint, and laid it on top of the snow—right where that [toilet] stall had stood. . . . He was really broken up![19]

Apparently the tearoom enthusiasts have an overwhelming need for anonymity; they do not want their parents, wives, children, friends, and workmates to discover their restroom escapades. While it is perfectly safe for them to get emotionally attached to a restroom, it is too risky for them to show even the slightest feeling for their homosexual partners. By not getting emotionally involved, they find it easy not to exchange words and glances with homosexual partners. In this way they can easily keep their homosexual identity to themselves, because, even to their tearoom partners, they are known merely as a penis or mouth rather than as a whole person with homosexual interest. Consequently, the homoerotic activity in the public restroom is the ultimate form of impersonal sex. Not surprisingly, the majority of tearoom participants are married men, trades, bisexuals, closet queens, and other covert homosexuals, who generally want to protect their public identity as being heterosexual. Restroom sex, however, tends less to interest overt homosexuals from the gay bar world, since they have come out and desire somewhat more personal sex.

There is a difference between the gay bar and the gay restroom world. Concerning the latter, Humphreys notes, "In these public settings . . . there exists a sort of democracy that is endemic to impersonal sex. Men of all racial, social, educational and physical characteristics meet in these places for sexual union. With the lack of involvement, personal preferences tend to be minimized." [20] In other words, since they are only interested in sex without involvement, the restroom gays do not care much what their sex partners look like, as long as the latter have a willing mouth or penis. This contrasts with the sexual market in the gay bar, where, as we have previously noted, homosexuals strongly emphasize the value of physical attractiveness in their intended partners.

Another difference between gay bar patrons and gay restroom visitors has to do with age. When two gay bar patrons pick each other up, they are usually about the same age. But in most cases of tearoom sex, the two participants are of different ages. This is probably because tearoom trade is restricted to fellatio only, while there is a greater variety of sex acts engaged in by gay bar partners. In general, the older man practices fellatio on the younger one. As a relatively old tearoom participant told Humphreys, "Well, I started off as the straight young thing. Everyone wanted to suck my cock. I wouldn't have been caught dead with one of the things in my mouth! . . . So here I am at 40—with grown kids—and the biggest cocksucker in (the city)!" [21]

HOMOSEXUAL PROMISCUITY

Terms such as *one night stand, sex without involvement, sex without commitment, impersonal sex,* and the like have been used to refer to the same action. This action is often associated with sexual promiscuity, which is usually defined as the readiness to have sex, or the experience of having sex, with a variety of partners. In the preceding section, several things have been suggested in regard to homosexual promiscuity.

Homosexual men as a group are no more promiscuous than heterosexual men—"promiscuous" in the sense of being ready to have sex with different partners. But homosexual men do have more promiscuous experience—in the sense of having engaged in sex with more partners than have heterosexual men. This is because homosexual men have greater opportunity for promiscuous experience, which stems from the fact that in a homosexual context two men attracted to each other are likely to be equally ready for impersonal sex, while in a heterosexual situation a man may be ready but his intended partner may not be. As implied by what has just been said, compared to females, males are more promiscuous—in both senses of the word—whether they be homosexual or heterosexual. This is due to the fact that men are more likely than women to have been socially conditioned to be easily aroused by sexual stimuli. And covert homosexuals are more driven to promiscuous sex than are overt homosexuals. This is because covert homosexuals feel greater need for anonymity than do overt homosexuals. In short, three factors in homosexual promiscuity have been suggested: opportunity for impersonal sex, sex role training, and need for anonymity.

Promiscuity makes it difficult for two homosexuals to establish a permanent relationship, which in turn compels them to become even more promiscuous. The ultimate cause of this is, according to Hoffman, conventional society's prohibition against homosexual union. Hoffman describes how the social prohibition operates:

Closeness between men is considered a sign of something wrong with the individuals involved . . . is thought of as indicating a fault in the masculinity of the two individuals. When such closeness is considered in the individual's mind, he immediately defines himself as a sissy, faggot, degenerate, etc. . . . [What society does] is give the individual a sense that his homosexual behavior is bad. How then is he expected to develop a warm, intimate relationship with a partner whom he unconsciously devalues as a person for engaging in acts with him which he defines as degraded? . . . Thus, the instability of relationship which is frequently used as grounds for condemnation of homosexuality is, in fact, the product of this condemnation.[22]

Hoffman also notes that another cause of the instability in homosexual relationships is our society's overemphasis on masculinity. To be masculine, one has to be rugged, independent. To the extent that homosexual males have internalized this masculine stereotype, they have also developed a fear of dependency. This fear of dependency makes it difficult for two male homosexuals to form a stable union, as both want to play the dominant role and inevitably find themselves in conflict with each other. Furthermore, by defining the gay man's sexual feelings as a problem, society forces him to concentrate on his sexuality and treat another man merely as a sex object rather than a person. Such sex fetishism also makes it difficult for two homosexuals to develop a lasting relationship, because their sexual attraction to each other can quickly diminish.[23]

In view of the problem of promiscuity or instability in homosexual relationships, many gay males simply give up the idea of a permanent union modeled on conventional marriage between a man and a woman. They believe that since conventional marriage is already unrealistic and impractical—because of the ensuing infidelity, jealousy, quarrels, and breakups—an attempted fidelity between two males is even more so. Thus two unique types of long-term relationships are common in the gay community. One type has been referred to as "marriage with an open arrangement." In this, partners are free to engage in one night stands with other men, as long as these casual and impersonal sexual activities do not become serious and personal. Another type of long-term relationships is "marriage with a three-way arrangement." In this kind of union, each partner is not free to go out by himself in search of casual sex, but instead both partners go out together to find a third man to participate in a three-way sexual experience. Sometimes those two partners will jointly participate in an orgy with two or more other men.[24]

The foregoing discussion should not lead us to stereotype the homosexual as a giant sex organ constantly in search of orgasm. In fact, his homosexual behavior constitutes only a small portion of his everyday activity—most of the things that he does everyday are essentially the same as those done by heterosexuals. But we may note that the problem of promiscuity is nonetheless more common among gays than among straights. This is not because promiscuity is inherent in homosexuality, but because of the various social and psychological factors discussed above.

LESBIAN BEHAVIOR

Compared with male homosexuals, lesbians are generally less promiscuous. One reason for this has been suggested before: lesbians have been socialized to be less interested in sex than love. Another reason is that lesbianism is less severely condemned than male homosexuality. While there are laws that condemn male homosexuality, there is no law that specifically prohibits lesbian behavior. Unlike men who engage in homosexual acts, women are rarely, if ever, arrested and convicted for homosexuality. When two women live together for a long time, most people would not suspect them to be lesbians and thus would not treat them with contempt—as they would males.

CONVENTIONAL ASPECTS OF LESBIANISM Since gay women are, as the above suggests, not too alienated from conventional society, they tend to share some characteristics with straight women. As sociologist Jack Hedblom concludes from his study of lesbian behavior: "The social career of the female homosexual occurs within a subcultural context that parallels closely the career of the heterosexual woman." [25] Let us look at the parallels that emerge from Hedblom's study.

The first parallel is that, compared with men, women are socialized to be less aggressive and less assertive. As a central part of this socialization, women are trained to be committed to marital fidelity. Gay women, like their straight sisters, are exposed to the same influence. One study reports:

The lesbian prided herself on the chastity of the lesbian group as
compared to the male homosexual. . . . It was not unusual for lesbians
to remain true to one woman. "Like other women," a lesbian
told me, "we think in terms of a monogamous ideal, even when we
don't practice it." [26]

Second, most lesbians are involved in a marriage arrangement, which is comparable to "living together" or common-law marriage in the heterosexual world. Obviously, lesbians' marriagelike relationships have no legal and social support from heterosexuals and are easier to establish than heterosexual marriages—for lesbian marriage does not need to be solemnized through formal announcement and public rituals. This may be the reason why, like common-law marriages in straight society, lesbian marriages tend to be impermanent.

Third, a majority of gay women are able to carry on a comfortable relationship with straight people. Although they belong to the gay community, lesbians have to work and associate with members of the straight community. The fact that they are comfortable with straights shows their effectiveness in passing as heterosexuals. Such a posture of heterosexuality is actually not difficult for lesbians to put on, because they—like straight women—have been strictly socialized to play the conventional female role.

Fourth, in addition to being a part of the straight community's social and occupational scene, the young lesbian usually remains in its sexual scene as well. Thus, regardless of her homosexual interest or her growing involvement with the homosexual community, the young lesbian typically continues to date men for a long period of time. This is largely because her heterosexual friends and family often pressure her into conforming to a conventional lifestyle, and make her feel that she may as well enjoy herself during the "fun period" of heterosexual dating. A large number of lesbians, in fact, have sexual intercourse with their male dates, which often results in orgasm.

Fifth, due to the covert nature of homosexuality or the need for putting on the appearance of being heterosexual, the style of lesbian dating differs from that of heterosexual dating. What lesbians do on dates is about what they and their straight female friends did when they were in their early teens. Instead of going out with boys, as young teen-age girls, they had house parties, group outings, and other collective activities. Now that they are older, lesbians continue that earlier pattern, except that there is the additional component of sexual interest. This may be why some lesbians like to call one another "kid." By doing the "kid stuff," gay women can easily hide their homosexuality.

Sixth, in their early experiences of homosexual dating, most lesbians engage in manual stimulation only. A minority of them try oral sex, but this does not always lead to orgasm. In large part, young lesbians' dating activities are similar to those of young heterosexuals who often resort to necking and petting as a substitute for "going all the way." Also, lesbians are similar to straight girls in that they tend to get involved in the "love first, sex later" pattern—rather than "sex first, love later maybe" that is more characteristic of males' dating behavior. The following is how a lesbian describes her typically female experience of graduating from non-sexual to sexual involvement with another person:

The fall after graduation from high school I started at (a residential school). I met a girl there who was extremely attractive. She had a good sense of humor and I was drawn to her because I liked to laugh. Many of the girls used to sit around in the evenings and talk. As our friendship grew, our circle narrowed and narrowed until it got to be three or four of us who would get together at night and talk. Then there was only three. Then two—us. And maybe after a couple of months of this, our relationship developed into something more. Starting out by simply kissing. Later petting. That type of thing. It didn't actually involve overt sexuality (genital contact) until February.[27]

UNCONVENTIONAL ASPECTS OF LESBIANISM   Although we have just discussed the similarities between the gay and the straight female, we should hardly ignore the differences between them. Gay women are stigmatized and discriminated against by conventional society much more than their straight counterparts. This creates some unique experiences for homosexual women.[28]

First, although they have engaged in homosexual activities, many lesbians in their adolescence are not aware of their being homosexual. Usually after two young lesbians finish playing some sex game with each other, they do not talk about it. Neither do they use such words as *homosexual* or *lesbian* to refer to each other. They usually restrict themselves to kissing and caressing, and only get involved in oral sex and other orgasm-inducing acts when they are in their early twenties. They tend to see their homosexual involvement in a nonsexual way, as the following description by a lesbian of her earlier experience suggests.

We started out just being friends and then it became something special. She taught me a lot of things. I love music and she taught me how to listen to it and appreciate it. She liked things I liked, like walking. We read a lot together. We read the Bible, we read verses to each other. We shared things together. We caressed each other and kissed. *I think it was a need to have someone there. And I was there and she was there and we just held on to each other.*[29] [Emphasis added.]

A second point is that heterosexuals like to stereotype the lesbian as a pseudo male—a woman who, desiring to be a male but biologically unable, ostentatiously behaves like a man. Such a stereotype has influenced some lesbians themselves, so that they tend to identify themselves as the "butch" type (who is supposed to play the masculine, aggressive role), as opposed to the "fem" type (who is supposed to play the feminine, passive role). Most lesbians, however, feel that they are emotionally and sexually attracted to another woman regardless of whether she is a butch or a fem.

When lesbians fall in love with one another, they simply want to respond to each other as women.

A third difference between straights and lesbians is that lesbians do not receive strong support from their family for their sexual preference, for their decision not to get married, and for their decision not to have children. Instead, they get either minimal or outright disapproval from their parents. Most lesbians maintain some partial family ties, while a few are forced to sever those ties when they are rejected by their parents. The parents who get along well with their lesbian daughters are not necessarily understanding and sympathetic. In fact, they frequently pretend that their daughter is not a homosexual. Many other parents neither know nor suspect that their daughters are lesbians because their daughters are careful in hiding their homosexuality from them.

Fourth, as they are unlikely to marry and depend on a man for support, most lesbians appear more seriously committed to work than are most straight women. Thus they are fearful that their bosses may discover their homosexuality and then fire them. One lesbian describes her fear of discovery as "living under a sword or with a time bomb." Even if they are not afraid of getting fired for their lesbian lifestyle, they still prefer to keep their workmates in the dark. As one lesbian explains,

I work very hard at not letting people at the office know. I don't think
I would get fired or anything. It's just the nervousness I know it
would start. The other girls look at you curiously. Any touching,
even accidental, is taken for a pass. I've had it happen before, when
I got careless and let someone know who talked. I got so that I'd wait
for the john to be empty before I'd go in. I don't want to go through
that again.[30]

A fifth difference is that it is relatively difficult for a lesbian to develop a durable friendship with another lesbian. This is because the lesbian is likely to choose her friends from the same group from which she selects her lovers or sexual partners. In such a situation, many lesbians end up having friends who are their ex-lovers, ex-rivals, or current rivals, which often makes for some uneasiness and mistrust. Despite all these problems, most lesbians claim that they manage their friendships fairly well—not in the sense of their friendships being permanent but in the sense of their being able to spend lesiure time together and to provide comfort in moments of distress. What is true of the lesbian's difficulty in developing a friendship, is also true of her problem with forming an enduring love relationship.

Sixth, without support from their surrounding social world, lesbians must make a great effort to learn to accept themselves—to live comfortably with their homosexual feelings and practices. In order to be successful in this regard, they have to deny the importance of conventional rewards and statuses, such as the approval of friends and family, a respectable position in the general community, a family of one's own, and the secure feeling that one is as normal as other members of the straight society. Since they are a product of conventional society, many lesbians fail to accept fully their homosexual identity and lifestyle. Thus many of them every now and then think of getting married to a man or feel that their homosexuality is unnatural, wicked, and sinful. But this problem of self-acceptance is likely to become less serious and less common, as more and more lesbians are acquiring the knowledge that lesbianism is nonpathological as well as a pride in being gay—especially from the women's gay liberation movements.

SITUATIONAL LESBIANISM In addition to the chronic lesbians discussed above, there are situational lesbians—heterosexual women who are encouraged by one-sex situations to engage in lesbian activities. One study by Charles McCaghy and James Skipper shows how the striptease occupation, which is a one-sex situation, induces strippers to play with one another after they have performed for largely male audiences whom they consider as degenerates.[31] McCaghy and Skipper found that the striptease occupation generates lesbian activity because of three major factors.

The first is that their working conditions prevent strippers from making friends and renewing acquaintances in the manner that ordinary people do. So they often complain about their loneliness while on tour. As one girl said, "When you are lonely enough you will try anything." The second factor leading to situational lesbianism is the unsatisfactory relationships with men. The stripper usually dislikes the men whom she meets in her occupation; she feels that they treat her like a piece of meat rather than a person. In the words of one girl: "If a guy took me out to dinner and showed me a good time, I'd sleep with him. But most of them just call up and say 'Let's fuck.'" Consequently, she finds great satisfaction from sexual contacts with her fellow strippers, who understand her and her job. And the third reason for the stripper's involvement in lesbian activities is the availability of opportunities for homosexual contacts. This is made possible by the atmosphere of permissiveness toward sexual behavior among the strippers. To them, sexual contacts with the right person are like having a martini after a hard day or night's work. As one stripper said, "I usually don't get kicks out of other women, not really, but there are times. Sometimes you come home and you are just too tired to work at it. Then it's nice to have a woman around. You can lay down on the floor, relax, watch TV and let her do it."

Another study that shows the relationship between one-sex situations and lesbian activity deals with women in prison.[32] According to this study, at least 90 percent of female inmates who engage in homosexuality are situational lesbians—more specifically, "jailhouse turnouts." They were not homosexual before they entered prison, and will return to heterosexuality after they leave prison. Unlike men in prison, women inmates do not resort to force to get sexual favors from others. Also unlike lesbians outside the prison who often alternate between the butch and the fem role, the jailhouse turnouts define themselves and are defined by others as being either butches or fems. There are fewer butches than fems in the prison population.

The butch looks and behaves like a man; she wears her hair close-cropped, wears no makeup, does not shave her legs, and walks with masculine gait. She is also "singularly unattractive," very fat or very skinny, and often has skin disorders. In contrast, the fem maintains a feminine appearance and does things to please her intended partner—in the same manner as a woman tries to please a man. A fem in prison puts it this way: "It's just like the outside. I flirted, I got things for her, I did her clothes, I woke her in the morning, we went to dances—the same things you do for a man on the outside." [33] When they are having sex, the fem simply lies still on her back and lets the butch go down on her, manipulate her clitoris, and fondle her breasts. In doing this, the butch may refuse to let the fem touch her, or may remain completely clothed so as to maintain her illusion of masculinity—which is difficult for her to do if she is naked and sees her own female body.

FIGHTING FOR RESPECTABILITY

Because they have been widely stigmatized and persecuted, many homosexuals have developed intense feelings of moral inferiority, self-hatred, and fear of having their sexual preference discovered by straights. It is no wonder that homosexuality has long been called "the love that dare not speak its name." But today the proclamation "gay is good" can be heard all over the United States. The once-closeted subject of homosexuality is now openly discussed, and many homosexuals themselves have come out of the closet. There are gay studies classes in at least fifty colleges, gay dances, gay parades, gay associations, gay political groups, gay churches, gay magazines and newspapers, gay synagogues, gay Alcoholic Anonymous groups, gay credit unions, and even a gay Nazi Party—along with a Jewish gay group organized to fight it.[34]

Why has all this come about? There are apparently three factors. The first is that in 1948 and 1953 the Kinsey Report, as we have suggested earlier, announced that millions of American men and women were exclusively or incidentally homosexual. This report attracted so much attention that many homosexuals became aware, for the first time in their lives, that they were not alone—that they belonged to one of the largest minority groups in the United States. Today the same Kinsey Report is still widely quoted and has the same impact on many homosexuals. Second, since the early 1960s, sexual permissiveness has been on the increase in our society. A great number of naked bodies and sexual acts have been casually portrayed in the mass media. Many people, particularly the young, have also got on the sexual bandwagon. There is, then, a growing toleration of various types of sexual activities and interests. And, third, the success of the black civil rights movement in the 1960s has encouraged numerous oppressed minorities to fight for freedom, equality, and respectability. Homosexuals consider themselves as one of these oppressed minority groups, and thus struggle to assert "gay power."

The first major homosexual organization was established in the early 1950s in San Francisco. It was called the Mattachine Society, named after medieval court jesters who told the truth while hiding behind masks. True to its name, the Mattachine Society was at first largely a secret organization concerned with teaching gays and their straight sympathizers about homosexuality. Soon afterwards the first all-female homosexual organization, the Daughters of Bilitis or DOB, was formed in San Francisco. Then chapters of these two organizations, along with other new homophile groups, were established all over the United States. By 1969, the number of homophile organizations had soared to about 150.[35] These organizations differed in their goals and activities, but they all were basically alike in being relatively nonmilitant. They chose the genteel word *homophile* rather than the cruder *homosexual* to refer to themselves. They were concerned with educating the public about homosexuality, counseling gays in trouble, and providing recreational services to gays. They quietly picketed such government agencies as the Department of Defense, the State Department, and the Civil Service Commission for their antihomosexual policies.

Then, in June 1969, the police raided the Stonewall Inn, a gay bar in New York. The patrons, who used to be cowed by such raids, reacted by throwing bottles and stones at the police. This violent reaction against police harassment soon led many young homosexuals to form a large number of militant organizations. No longer referring to themselves as *homophile*, these militant organizations chose more provocative names, such as the Gay Liberation Front and the Gay Activists Alliance. They tried to confront America with the fact that they are an oppressed minority group, whose aspiration for respectability is no different from that of blacks, Chicanos, American Indians, women, migrant farm workers, and the like. They marched in great numbers, shouting such slogans as "Two-four-six-eight, Gay is twice as good as straight!" "Three-five-seven-nine,

Lesbians are mighty fine!" and "Gay Power!" They also resorted to dramatic confrontation tactics in dealing with antigay political figures. One such tactic was "zapping"—disrupting, for example, a Foran for Governor rally in Chicago in 1971 by marching, dancing, and chanting, "Ho, ho, hey, hey, freaking fags are here to stay" as well as "Foran is a macho pig." [36] More recently the militant fervor has cooled, and there has returned the traditional show of concern with providing counseling and other social services to gays who need them.

The cooling of the gays' militancy may have been due to the many victories achieved by the gay power movement. Since 1970, eleven state legislatures have followed Illinois in allowing consensual sodomy between adults. The school boards in some cities have banned discrimination in the hiring of gay teachers, and a number of court decisions have upheld the gay's right to teach. A bill has been introduced in Congress to amend the 1964 Civil Rights Act so that it will prohibit discrimination against homosexuals. The Bank of America, IBM, NBC, AT&T, and other big corporations, as well as the Civil Service Commission have announced their willingness to hire homosexuals. The American Psychiatric Association has stopped listing homosexuality as a psychiatric disorder. More than three hundred gay marriages have been performed in a church in Los Angeles.

Nevertheless, there still remain widespread prejudice and discrimination against homosexuals. Many members of straight society also feel threatened by the gay's demand for respectability. They fear that if homosexuality becomes respectable, the gay will gain the legal right to marry, homosexual instruction will be included in school sex courses, gay love stories will be as popular as straight love stories in schools and libraries, and homosexuality will spread like a plague—especially among young people. Even normally liberal heterosexuals are enraged by the granting of marriage licenses to homosexual couples. Several years ago in Boulder, Colorado, many liberal straights were in an uproar over six legally sanctioned gay weddings—and one cowboy protested by trying to marry his horse. [37] Another way that liberals withhold respect from gays is to be condescendingly kind to them, pitying them as if they were blind or mute. [38]

THEORIES OF HOMOSEXUALITY

There are numerous theories in the existing literature on homosexuality. They may be classified into three major types: biological, psychiatric, and sociological theories.

BIOLOGICAL THEORY

Two biological factors have been singled out by some medical researchers as causes of homosexuality. One is genetic abnormality and the other hormonal imbalance.

GENETIC ABNORMALITY   It has been argued that homosexual men are genetically female—they have a female type of sex chromatin. But this argument has been refuted by most studies. An occasional finding of a female chromosomal pattern in a homosexual man can be attributed to pure coincidence. A somewhat more convincing argument is the general theory that homosexuality is an innate trait. Studies of twins are usually employed to support this theory. One study, for example, shows that if one of the *identical* twins is homosexual, the chances are one hundred percent that the other will also be homosexual, whereas if one of the *fraternal* twins is homosexual, the chances drop to only fifty percent.[39] Such findings have been taken to mean that homosexuality is largely determined by one's genes, as identical twins are more genetically alike than fraternal twins. This interpretation, however, is not acceptable to most social scientists. They would argue that social environment is largely responsible for causing homosexuality, because, when compared with fraternal twins, identical twins are more likely to be subjected to similar experiences.

HORMONAL IMBALANCE   Some medical researchers theorize that an imbalance between male and female hormones causes homosexuality. A few laboratory studies have been conducted to support this theory. One study found that young homosexual men had lower levels of male hormone than did young heterosexual men. Another study indicated that lesbians' daily secretion of androgens (male sex hormones) was considerably higher than their production of estrogens (female sex hormones). Nevertheless, a number of criticisms have been advanced against the hormonal theory. First, the findings in support of the theory have not been confirmed in many other laboratories and, in some cases, have actually been refuted. Second, even if all the laboratory results showed hormonal differences between gays and straights, we still could not conclude that hormonal imbalances are the *cause* of homosexuality. For hormonal imbalances could well be the *effect* of homosexual practice. Third, when attempts were made to "cure" homosexuality by administering testosterone (the male hormone), the homosexual's sex drive increased but it was still directed to homosexual partners. And fourth, since laboratory studies have been limited to very small samples of homosexuals, they cannot tell us how common the hormonal imbalance is among the gay population as a whole— as compared with the straight.[40]

PSYCHIATRIC THEORY

There are two related assumptions in this theory. One is that homosexuality is a form of mental illness. The other is that a poor parent-son relationship gives rise to homosexuality.

HOMOSEXUALITY AS MENTAL ILLNESS   As a form of mental illness, homosexuality is characterized by "hidden but incapacitating fears of the opposite sex." In their study comparing homosexual mental patients with heterosexual mental patients, psychiatrist Irving Bieber and his associates came to this conclusion: "Any adaptation which is basically an accommodation to unrealistic fear is necessarily pathologic; in the adult homosexual, continued fear of heterosexuality is inappropriate to his current reality. We differ with other investigators who have taken the position that homosexuality is a kind of variant of 'normal' sexual behavior." [41] By the pathological fear of heterosexuality, the psychiatrists actually refer to *castration anxiety*—the irrational fear, by the male homosexual, of the female genitals. More specifically, the male homosexual is seen as a man who perceives the vagina "as a castrating instrument capable of biting or tearing off the penis." [42] Such a perception is considered as unrealistic, presumably because the vagina, being toothless, cannot bite off the penis. Instead, the homosexual should be afraid of inserting his penis into another man's mouth, which after all does have teeth in it. And yet he is not afraid. Why not? Because he is mentally ill.

The psychiatric concept of homosexuality as mental illness has been widely and severely criticized. Most critics argue that the illness concept is usually based on the study of a biased sample, namely, psychiatric patients. In order to conduct a valid test of the pathological concept of homosexuality, one has to compare homosexual patients with homosexual nonpatients or to compare nonpatient heterosexuals with nonpatient homosexuals. This has not been done by proponents of the pathological view. "The few studies that *have* compared nonpatient homosexuals and nonpatient heterosexuals have not borne out the theory that homosexuals are sick or even different, except for sexual preferences." [43]

Not considering themselves mentally ill, militant homosexuals are the most severe critics of the psychiatric view of homosexuality. In 1973 they succeeded in forcing the American Psychiatric Association to remove homosexuality from its list of mental disorders. But the psychiatrists still do *not* say that homosexuality is normal. They in effect continue to imply that homosexuality is a mental disorder, though they now use the less harsh term *sexual orientation disturbance* to refer to homosexuality. Thus, with that new term, homosexuals are still viewed in a negative way, namely, as "individuals whose sexual interests are directed primarily toward people of the same sex and who are either bothered by, in conflict with, or wish to change, their sexual orientations." [44]

POOR PARENT-SON RELATIONSHIP   Related to the pathological concept is the notion that a poor parent-son relationship causes homosexuality. A young boy will become homosexual later in his life if he has a domineering, over-protective, and seductive mother and an ineffectual, detached, and hostile father. Being alienated from his father, the boy will not look upon him as a model for learning the masculine role. Instead, being driven by his hostile father into the arms of his loving mother, the boy will learn to identify himself with his mother. As a consequence, the boy will grow up to become homosexual. On the other hand, if there is a warm and affec-tionate relationship between father and son, homosexuality cannot occur.[45]

Studying homosexual patients, Bieber and his associates have produced findings to confirm their notion of disturbed parent-son relationships as the cause of homosexuality. But numerous other studies, relying on samples of *non*patient homosexuals, have either totally refuted or only partially supported the Bieber notion. As for the nature of the partial support, there are studies that have confirmed the causal importance of either the overprotective mother or the hostile father but not both, while other find-ings show that bad parent-son relations are slightly more common among homosexuals than heterosexuals, but characterize only a very small portion of the homosexual sample. After examining all these studies, Hooker con-cludes, "Thus it appears that disturbed parental relations are neither necessary nor sufficient conditions for homosexuality to emerge . . . the necessity of looking at other etiological factors should be underlined." [46] Further, Bieber and his associates' work may be criticized on theoretical ground. Their notion of "mama's boy" as a candidate for homosexuality is apparently based on the myth that the male homosexual is typically an effeminate, limp-wristed, "swishy" individual—just like his mother.

SOCIOLOGICAL THEORY

There are two types of sociological theory about homosexuality. One has to do with the etiology of homosexuality, so it may be called a causal theory. The other largely stays away from the etiological problem, hence is a noncausal theory.

CAUSAL THEORY   This theory basically suggests that homosexuality, just like heterosexuality, is the result of conditioning within a given context of social interaction.[47] It assumes that human beings are born with a diffuse or neutral sexual drive insofar as their sexual object choice is concerned. In childhood, they are not particularly attracted to the homosexual or heterosexual object choice—a same-sex partner is just as sexually exciting as is a different-sex partner. For that matter, they are equally capable of being sexually aroused by their rubber duck, pet cat, pet dog, or any other object. Only through constant interaction with parents and other socializing agents of society, are they conditioned to narrow, focus, and restrict their sexual interest to the sexual object choice approved by society—and simultaneously conditioned to kill off their interest in the other object choices disapproved by society. Since there is a powerful taboo against homosexuality and strong support of heterosexuality in our society, most American adults have been conditioned to heterosexual activity.

But some individuals may have been conditioned toward homosexuality by their sexual experiences with same-sex others during their childhood or adolescence. They may have engaged in homosexual acts as an experimentation to satisfy their curiosity or childhood naughtiness. They may have performed homosexual acts for money or other rewards. Or they may have been driven into homosexuality because they were rejected by their peers for being physically weak or uncoordinated, or because they were unsuccessful with members of the opposite sex. Whatever the reason that first led the youngster into homoerotic activity, if he or she repeatedly engaged in it and enjoyed it, he or she becomes homosexual.

NONCAUSAL THEORY   This theory is primarily critical of the other theories. First of all, it criticizes the biological and psychiatric theories for defining homosexuality as a pathological condition that must be cured. Then it suggests three related points as important for understanding homosexuality. One, homosexuality is not pathological but merely a variant of sexual expression. It is assumed that some homosexuals have more psychological problems than do others, but these psychological problems do not necessarily cause or result from homosexuality. Two, since homosexuality is a normal form of sexual expression rather than a sickness, there is no need to search for cures. Attention, then, should be directed to the similarities between the process of becoming homosexual and the process of becoming heterosexual. Three, contrary to the psychiatric theory, which overemphasizes the importance of early childhood, we should view one's adult experience as more important than earlier experience for understanding homosexual behavior.

The above three points are related to labeling theory. For this theory suggests that homosexuality is not a sickness in itself but only appears as such because it has been stigmatized by society. If it is not a sickness, homosexuality need not be cured. And since it is a social stigma, homosexuality significantly affects the life of the adult who engages in it.[48]

POWER THEORY APPLIED

With power theory, we may put the seven types of homosexuals mentioned earlier into two large categories, the *covert homosexual* and the *overt homosexual*. Bisexuals and closet queens may be considered as covert homosexuals, while trades, street hustlers, prison homosexuals, call boys, and gay guys may be regarded as overt homosexuals. Covert homosexuality is by definition less open to public observation and thus less subject to public condemnation, while overt homosexuality is more open to public observation and thus more subject to public condemnation. Since most people who are publicly known and officially harassed as homosexuals appear to have lesser prestige and influence in society, it may be observed that overt homosexuals are likely to be less powerful than covert homosexuals.

Although experts generally assume that homosexuality occurs at all social levels, we may speculate that covert homosexuality is more pervasive at the higher level than lower. There are at least two reasons for this. First, more powerful men are more prone to covert homosexuality because they tend more to experience subjective deprivation from their unrestrained and thus difficult-to-fulfill desire to become great winners in a highly competitive, "masculine" culture. This assumes that there is a connection between homosexuality and the cultural emphasis on masculinity. Some anthropological evidence seems to support this assumption:

Where male aspirations are cast in a noncompetitive mold, homosexuality tends to be low, but where perhaps the very same aspirations are rated individually with a consequent emphasis on such concepts as the winner and the hero, the homosexual potential is readily activated. For instance, among native peoples who live by hunting, if it is customary to share and share alike with little tendency to rate whose marksmanship is better or worse than that of somebody else, homosexuality is *always* low. But if it is customary to celebrate the expert hunter—perhaps count his trophies and compare them with those of the next man—then an enviable, individualized maleness is lionized and homosexuality can be high to very high. In fact, these trends are so pronounced that even in "heroic" societies which have instituted the strongest possible codes against homosexuality, there is more of it by far than in "non-heroic" societies which may not have even bothered to formulate any rules against it.[49]

Thus, under the pressure of the "heroic" culture, the more powerful men may hold too high an expectation for success in the institutionalized game of heterosexual conquest. Not being able to realize this expectation, they may be driven to achieve success in the deviant homosexual conquest.

Moreover, these more powerful men are more likely to be encouraged than are the less powerful to participate in the homosexual conquest, because they are less subject to social control. As sex researcher C. A. Tripp observes, "A person who has reached any sort of power position—be he the dean of a school, vice-president of a corporation, head of a department, or who holds power behind any throne—is often too dangerous to attack with anything less than tangible evidence [showing his homosexuality], and even then, at more risk to his attacker than to himself." [50]

There may also be a symbiosis between the more powerful and the less powerful homosexuals. The latter's overt homosexuality more often attracts public attention and official harassment, thereby distracting public scrutiny from the former's covert homosexuality. Being subjected to less public scrutiny, the more powerful feel freer to engage in homosexuality. But they are at the same time likely to publicly uphold the society's anti-homosexual morals or to avoid publicly giving support to the cause of homosexual liberation. This helps to force less powerful men to continue practicing homosexuality with as large a risk of public scorn and official harassment as they do now.

SUMMARY

Homosexuality is a relatively common phenomenon. There exist some myths about homosexuals: (1) Male homosexuals are effeminate while female homosexuals are manly; (2) the homosexual is restricted to either the active or passive role; (3) homosexuals often seduce young children; and (4) homosexuals are sick.

Seven types of homosexuals have been identified: (1) trade, (2) street hustler, (3) prison homosexual, (4) bisexual, (5) call boy, (6) closet queen, and (7) gay guy. They differ as to how strongly they identify with homosexuality or heterosexuality or both. The trade identifies most strongly with his heterosexuality, the gay guy identifies most strongly with his homosexuality, and the remaining types are somewhere between these two extremes.

Because of the social suppression of homosexuality, many young males who have developed sexual interest in other males do not see themselves as being homosexual. When they engage in homoerotic acts in such one-sex institutions as the YMCA and the Navy, they only privately define themselves as being homosexual. But when they find themselves being a part of a large group of homosexuals in a gay bar, they "come out"— identify themselves publicly as being gay.

Like the straight singles bar, the gay bar largely functions as a sexual marketplace where customers search for and pick up sex partners. Compared with the singles bar, the gay bar seems to produce a larger quantity of one night stands. Compared with singles bar customers, gay bar patrons stand around more, and use the nonverbal, glancing method to pick up their sex partners. Speech is even more rarely used in homosexual encounters in public restrooms. This "tearoom" sex is the ultimate form of impersonal sex—neither talking nor glancing interferes with the sexual exchange. But such impersonal sex serves to release the participant's sexual tension and to protect his identity.

Homosexuals apparently engage in a great amount of promiscuous sex. This seems to have resulted from society's stigmatization of homosexuality.

Lesbian behavior differs from male homosexuality in that the former is less sexually impersonal and promiscuous. Since they have been rigidly socialized in playing the conventional female role, lesbians are in some ways similar to straight women. But as they are nonetheless homosexual, lesbians do differ in some other ways from heterosexual females. Lesbian behavior also occurs among straight women who are deprived of normal heterosexual experiences by such one-sex situations as confinement in prison and in the occupation of stripping.

An increasing number of gays have tried to assert their power in the same manner as other more traditional types of minority groups have. Many gay organizations are now in existence. They have been successful in getting their rights recognized by some state legislatures, school boards, business corporations, and so on. But their fight for respectability is still far from being completely victorious; there is still widespread prejudice and discrimination against homosexuality.

Three types of theories have been proposed for explaining homosexuality. (1) Biological theory states that genetic abnormality and hormonal imbalance cause homosexuality. (2) Psychiatric theory assumes that homosexuality is a form of mental illness, and suggests that strained parent-son relations give rise to homosexuality in males. And (3) sociological theory suggests that homosexuality results from social conditioning and that it should be viewed as nonpathological. Power theory divides homosexuality into covert and overt types, showing why the powerful tend more to engage in the former type and how both may influence each other.

SUGGESTED READINGS

Bieber, Irving et al. *Homosexuality*. New York: Basic Books, 1962.

Dank, Barry M. "Coming Out in the Gay World." *Psychiatry* 34 (May 1971): 180–197.

Gagnon, John H. and William Simon. "Homosexuality: The Formulation of a Sociological Perspective." *Journal of Health and Social Behavior* 8 (September 1967): 177–185.

Gould, Robert E. "What We Don't Know about Homosexuality." *New York Times Magazine*, February 24, 1974, pp. 13, 51, 54, 56–58, 62.

Hoffman, Martin. *The Gay World*. New York: Basic Books, 1968.

Hooker, Evelyn. "The Homosexual Community," in John H. Gagnon and William Simon, eds. *Sexual Deviance*. New York: Harper & Row, 1967, pp. 167–184.

Humphreys, Laud. "Tearoom Trade: Impersonal Sex in Public Places." *Transaction* 7 (January 1970): 11–25.

Simon, William and John H. Gagnon. "The Lesbians: A Preliminary Overview," in J. H. Gagnon and W. Simon, eds. *Sexual Deviance*. New York: Harper & Row, 1967, pp. 247–282.

Tripp, C. A. *The Homosexual Matrix*. New York: McGraw-Hill, 1975.

Weinberg, Martin S. and Colin J. Williams. *Male Homosexuals*. New York: Penguin Books, 1975.

10 SUICIDE

Every year about 20,000 Americans die by their own hands. Seven times more Americans (140,000) try to do so but fail. These figures mean that suicide and attempted suicide are very rare when compared with other forms of deviant behavior. Suicide is more common than only one other kind of deviant behavior, namely, homicide. Attempted suicide, however, is much rarer than attempted homicide, assuming that aggravated assaults are in effect attempted homicides. Yet, despite its comparative rarity, suicide has fascinated so many sociologists, psychiatrists, and people in related fields that a tremendous number of books and articles have been written about it.

THE NATURE OF SUICIDE

According to a number of experts on the subject, most lay people hold the following false ideas about suicide. (1) People who talk about suicide do not actually want to, and will never, commit suicide. (2) Suicide happens without any warning at all. (3) Suicidal people always want to die. And (4) all suicidal individuals are mentally ill—suicide is always the act of a psychotic person.[1] These statements are false not because they do not contain any truth at all, but because they are overgeneralizations. For instance, it is true that a few individuals who commit suicide are mentally ill, but it is an overgeneralization to say that all people who do are mentally ill.

VARIETIES OF SUICIDAL EXPERIENCE

On the road to suicide can be found different types of travelers with different kinds of experience. Some *threaten* to kill themselves but do not make good their threats. Others *attempt* to take their own lives but do not succeed. And still others do *succeed* in committing suicide. Although they all share the same feeling that their lives are unbearably miserable, these three types of individuals differ in their approaches to suicide.

SUICIDE THREATENERS These individuals explicitly, directly, or loudly threaten suicide. They clearly want to live rather than die, as their suicide threats are intended as a means of achieving some objective in life. This does not necessarily mean that they will never carry out these threats. They might do so if their threats fail to achieve their objectives. In fact, several studies have shown that at least 40 percent of them have *seriously* attempted to kill themselves in the past.[2] Given the present lack of knowledge concerning them, it is not possible to know the percentage of suicide threateners who successfully, as opposed to those who unsuccessfully, carry out their threats. But it is obvious that those whose threats are heeded will more likely refrain from killing themselves than those whose threats are ignored. One study has indicated the various ways in which suicide threats can produce positive results for individuals:

The threat of suicide forces persons to marry, prevents marriage dissolution, coerces companionship between persons despite their mutual infidelity, prevents marriages, forces parents to acquiesce in their offsprings' vicious habits, precludes institutionalization, is rewarded by escape from further military duty, is used to obtain favored treatment over siblings, is employed as a device to avoid military induction.[3]

SUICIDE ATTEMPTERS Unlike the threateners who clearly want more to live than die, suicide attempters are more ambiguous in their intent. They are often seized with the mood of "I don't care whether I live or die." Thus, unlike threateners who issue their threats in unmistaken terms, the attempters are less explicit in communicating their suicidal feelings. They may simply show others how depressed they are, or tell others that they cannot sleep, but avoid using the word *suicide*. As a result, most of them do not succeed in conveying their distress signals to others. Only somewhere between 14 and 53 percent of suicide attempters are known to have forewarned others of even an ambiguous intention to die.[4] When they succeed in communicating their message, others do not take it seriously because of its vagueness. This is why suicide attempters eventually resort to dramatic and dangerous methods to express—still implicitly—their appeal for help.

The methods include wrist cutting, swallowing large amounts of sleeping pills, gas poisoning in the house or car, and so forth. Although these methods can be lethal, they are less foolproof than those used by successful suicides, such as shooting and hanging. In addition, most suicide attempts are carried out in a setting or in such a way that makes rescue possible, probable, or even inevitable. Attempters remain near others during the attempt, or call up a friend immediately afterward. This reflects their lack of determination to die, and most suicide attempts have therefore been described as "a road to life, not death." [5]

Suicide attempters are more likely to be women than men, to be young (between 24 and 44) than old (between 55 and 66), and to come from lower than upper classes. This is in contrast to those who successfully commit suicide. They are more likely to be men than women, to be old than young, and to come from upper than lower classes. [6]

SUCCESSFUL SUICIDES   From 7 to 33 percent of successful suicides are known to have had at least one prior attempt to kill themselves. Also, from 26 to 83 percent of them have openly or subtly communicated their suicidal ideas to others. [7] Successful suicides are a mixed category of people, including those suicide threateners who have failed to get what they desperately wanted, those suicide attempters who have not been rescued in time, and those individuals who were simply more determined to die. From notes left by successful suicides and from reports given by suicide attempters, we can discern at least four types of suicidal feeling.

First, suicides may feel *apologetic* toward their survivors. In the following suicide note, for example, the writer apologizes to her husband Tom, her father, and her mother for having to kill herself.

Tom, I love you so dearly but you have told me you don't want me
and don't love me. I never thought you would let me go this far, but
I am now at the end which is the best thing for you. You have
so many problems and I am sorry I added to them.
Daddy, I hurt you so much and I guess I really hurt myself. You
only wanted the very best for me and you must believe this is it.
Mommy, you tried so hard to make me happy and to make things
right for all of us. I love you too so very much. You did not fail,
I did. . . I love you all dearly and am sorry this is the way I have
to say goodbye. Please forgive me and be happy.

Your wife and your daughter[8]

Second, suicides may feel *vindictive* toward their survivors or themselves. Blaming others for his or her misery and self-destruction, the suicide seeks revenge by punishing them. This can be illustrated by the following suicide note from a thirty-eight-year-old divorced woman.

Bill,

You have killed me. I hope you are happy in your heart, if you have one which I doubt. Please leave Rover with Mike. Also leave my baby alone. If you don't, I'll haunt you the rest of your life and I mean it and I'll do it. You have been mean and also cruel. God doesn't forget those things and don't forget that. And please no flowers; it won't mean anything. Also keep your money. I want to be buried in Potters Field in the same casket with Betty. . . You know what you have done to me. That's why I did this. It's yours and Ella's fault, try and forget if you can. But you can't. . .

Your wife[9]

Some suicides may feel very angry with themselves for having done a wrongful act and then use self-killing to punish themselves. A common example of this suicidal experience is the person who kills him- or herself after murdering another person. This has been referred to as *atonement suicide*. Anthropologist Raymond Firth has described a clear case of atonement suicide, involving a man on a South Pacific island:

About the oddest [suicide] was that chosen by Pu Sao, who having broken wind in a public gathering, in his shame climbed a coconut palm and sat down on the sharp-pointed hard flower-spathe, which pierced his [anus] and killed him—a bizarre case of making the punishment fit the crime.[10]

Third, suicides may become *magnanimous* toward the world they choose to leave behind. In their suicide notes, some request that their bodies be donated to medical schools, other bequeath their property and money to charitable organizations, and still others forgive whoever has wronged them, as the following indicates.

Mary:

We could have been so happy if you had continued to love me. I have your picture in front of me. I will look at it the last thing. I do love you so much. To think you are now in the arms of another man is more than I can stand. . . I am giving my life for your indiscretion. Please don't let me pay too high a price for your happiness. All your faults are completely forgotten and your sweetness remembered. You knew I would do this when you left me— so this is no surprise. Good-bye darling—I love you with all of my broken heart.

W. Smith[11]

Fourth, suicides may become suffused with *surrealistic* feelings. This usually occurs in the very act of ending their lives. The stormy tension that has initially driven the individual to suicide dies down, and overwhelming calm takes over just before the suicide consciously breathes his or her last breath. In this state of calmness, they experience surrealistic feelings. A number of suicide attempters who cut their wrists report that wrist slashing was not painful at all. They felt that the sight and smell of their blood were anti-suicidal or therapeutic, leading them to "return to reality and life from the state of dead unreality" of this world. Some wrist cutters even likened the experience to orgasm followed by a soothing feeling of relaxation and then deeply comfortable sleep.[12]

GROUP DIFFERENCES IN SUICIDE RATES

In general, sociological, psychiatric, and other researchers have ignored suicide threateners and attempters, and focused instead on successful suicides. In their effort to find out the social characteristics of successful suicides, sociologists have relied heavily on suicide statistics compiled by coroners or other similar government officials. But at the same time sociologists have recognized, to one degree or another, that these official statistics are far from reliable. The following reasons have been suggested for the relative un-reliability of official suicide statistics.[13]

The first is that officials in different countries, states, or local areas use different procedures to determine what constitutes suicide. The result is that what is determined suicide in one place is considered a natural, accidental, or homicidal death in another. Even within the same country, state, or local area, coroners often disagree whether a given death is caused by suicide— or by homicide or accident. Thus when officials report a death as suicide, it may not be a suicide. On the other hand, when officials fail to report a death as suicide, it may actually be a suicide. When a corpse is found floating in a river, for example, it may be reported as a case of suicide when it is actually an accident, or vice versa. In short, official statistics on suicide are unreliable, not only because different officials define suicide differently, but because it is sometimes difficult to distinguish a suicide from a homicide, an accident, or a natural death.

Second, even if all the official investigators, using different procedures, found the same suicide rate for a given population, the rate would still be unreliable. The reason is that suicide victims or their relatives may conceal the evidence of the deaths as suicide. This is particularly the case if suicide is considered a disgrace for the self-killer and his or her family. Thus the consistent official statistics tend to consistently falsify (underestimate) the suicide rate. (*Suicide rate* refers to the number of suicides for every 100,000 people of a given population.)

Although sociologists recognize the unreliability of official suicide statistics, there are no data showing the *amount* of the unreliability. Consequently sociologists differ in their estimation of how unreliable the official statistics are. Scientific sociologists, who want to seek out the causes of suicide, claim that the official statistics are fairly reliable or the best available for studying suicide. In contrast, humanistic sociologists, who want to search for the social meanings rather than causes of suicide, assert that the official statistics are grossly unreliable. It would seem prudent, then, to look at the following suicide rates with caution and skepticism [14]—allowing for the possibility that they might well be fairly reliable, grossly unreliable, or somewhere in between.

SOCIETAL DIFFERENCES   In the past, anthropologists referred to the occurrence of suicide in non-European societies as either *common* or *rare*, rather than in the form of a suicide rate. Generally, anthropologists considered suicide as common in those societies where ritual suicide was known. Examples of ritual suicide include *suttee* (an Indian ceremony in which the widow threw herself onto the funeral pyre of her husband), *hara-kiri* (a Japanese ceremony in which a disgraced nobleman or defeated warrior plunged his sword into his stomach), and the Eskimo custom for an old man to do away with himself because he could no longer make an economic contribution. Since these ritual suicides were impressively exotic to Western anthropologists and socially approved in those societies, they were thought to be very common.

Today, however, sociologists believe that the suicide rates of non-European peoples were probably low on the average, when compared with Europeans. For example, the suicide rate for the whole of India in 1907 is estimated to be only about 4.8 (per 100,000), as compared, for example, with a rate of 32.6 for the north German province of Saxony in 1906–1910. Since European societies were generally more urbanized and industrialized, high suicide rates have also been attributed to high levels of urbanization and industrialization. Indeed, as suicide statistics for modern societies indicate, the more urbanized and industrialized countries, such as Denmark and Austria, have higher rates than the less urbanized and industrialized, such as Mexico and Nicaragua.

TEMPORAL DIFFERENCES   Probably because most countries have recently become more urbanized and industrialized, the suicide rates in most countries are higher today than around the turn of this century. But there have been marked fluctuations in suicide rates in highly industrialized countries between 1901 and 1960. On the whole, suicide rates in those countries were higher in times of economic depression and lower in times of war. Perhaps in times of economic depression, people were busy brooding over their own financial problems, while in times of war they were so busy trying to kill their common enemy that they did not have the time to brood over their personal problems.

URBAN VS. RURAL RESIDENCE   As suicide rates are positively correlated with urbanization, it is not surprising to see that during the nineteenth century and well into the twentieth, the urban suicide rate was higher than the rural rate in almost all countries. Similarly, as the difference between urban and rural life has recently decreased, the difference between the urban and rural suicide rates has also decreased.

RACIAL DIFFERENCES   In the United States, the rate of suicide among whites is much higher than among blacks, but the rate among Orientals is even higher than among whites. However, these differences in suicide rates are not due to racial backgrounds alone. The life in a certain region may also have a great impact on suicide. For example, during 1948–1952 the white suicide rate in Seattle, Washington was twice the Oriental rate, while the black rate in the same city was higher than the white rate in Mississippi. In other words, life in the Western states, which have consistently produced higher suicide rates than the Northern and Southern states, seems to exert powerful suicidogenic influences on whites and blacks. Furthermore, the varying rates among Orientals, whites, and blacks can partly be explained by the more urban backgrounds of Orientals, the more rural backgrounds of blacks, and the intermediate position of whites.

RELIGIOUS DIFFERENCES   On the whole, Protestants have higher suicide rates than Catholics, who in turn have higher rates than Jews. But it appears that the type of religion is not as important as the degree of religious liberalism. During the period 1900–1910 in the Netherlands, for example, the Jewish suicide rate far exceeded both the Catholic and the Protestant rate. Also, in New Zealand, among the Protestants, Congregational church members have the highest suicide rate, Baptists the next highest, and Church of Christ people the lowest. Most sociologists would explain the religious differences in suicide rates by referring to Durkheim's concept of social integration. Thus the higher Protestant rates are thought to be caused by Protestants' lesser integration into their church, when compared with Catholics or Jews. Perhaps religious liberalism and the lack of religious integration are in essence the same thing.

SEXUAL DIFFERENCE   In practically all countries, men are more prone to suicide than are women. But this male-female difference in suicide rates varies greatly from one country to another. For instance, around 1964–

1965, the male suicide rate was 23 times the female rate in Nicaragua, while the male rate was only 1.1 times the female rate in Luxemburg.

DIFFERENCES BY MARITAL STATUS   There are large differences in suicide rates by marital status. In general, divorced persons have the highest rate, the married the lowest rate, and the single and the widowed intermediate rates. Married couples, then, are most immune to suicide, but those without children are more prone to suicide than those with children. All this has been taken to suggest that the more and stronger ties you have to other people, the less likely you are to escape your problems through suicide.

AGE DIFFERENCES   The relationship between age and suicide has three patterns. One, the extremely young (below age ten) and the extremely old (above ninety) have extremely low suicide rates. This is a common pattern in many parts of the world. Two, the suicide rate consistently rises with increasing age, with a very low rate among the young and a very high rate among the old. This is also a common pattern in many parts of the world. A third pattern is that the suicide rate abruptly reaches a high level in the age group twenty- to twenty-four-years old, and then sharply declines at about age forty, after which the rate increases again with advancing age. This pattern, marked especially by the extraordinarily high rate of suicide among young people, is very uncommon. It occurs only in Japan and Okinawa.

OCCUPATIONAL DIFFERENCES   Various researchers have reported contradictory findings concerning occupational differences in suicide rates. (1) Some have reported that higher-status occupations (with higher prestige and income) have much higher rates than lower-status occupations. (2) Other investigators have found just the opposite—lower-status occupations have higher rates. (3) Still other investigators have found that both higher-status and lower-status occupations have high suicide rates, while middle-level occupations have lower rates. Sociologists generally accept the third finding, which actually reconciles the other two.

STUDENTS VS. NONSTUDENTS   Data have shown that college students in the United States and Great Britain have higher suicide rates than do people of the same age group in the general population. This has been attributed to the greater stress of college life. But there is no evidence that college life is any more stressful than noncollege, working life. It seems more plausible to argue that college students are more vulnerable to suicide when under stress because they are more likely than noncollege students to be unmarried.

We should note that none of the social factors presented above is fully correlated with suicide rates. There are always exceptional cases in which a given social factor does not have any impact on suicide rates at all. Take religion as an example. While it is generally true that Catholics have lower suicide rates than Protestants, there are some predominantly Catholic countries—such as Austria and Hungary—that have considerably *higher* suicide rates than most Protestant countries. In addition, although each has been discussed separately, the various social factors should be considered as working together to produce a certain suicide rate.

SOCIETAL RESPONSE TO SUICIDE

The way a society responds to suicide has been observed to influence self-destruction. As two experts on the subject said more than forty years ago, "Where custom and tradition accept or condone it, many persons will take their own lives; where it is sternly condemned by the rules of the Church and State, suicide will be an unusual occurrence." [15] Some support for this observation can be found in the fact that Moslem countries, which strongly condemn suicide, usually have lower suicide rates than Christian societies, which do not strongly condemn self-killing. Moreover, despite short-term fluctuations, the suicide rates in most Western countries on the whole increased between 1900 and 1960, and it is possible that suicide has been more common in the present century than in previous centuries. This can be partly attributed to the increasingly permissive attitude toward suicide. In the past, those who committed suicide were treated as criminals to be punished; today they are considered as victims to be sympathized with. For example, in medieval England and Europe suicides were punished by denial of Christian burial, by confiscation of property, or by burial at a crossroad with a stake driven through the heart. Today antisuicide law is a rarity, and in the few countries and states where it still exists, it is rarely enforced. Instead, an upsurge of posthumous love (or at least tender feeling) toward the self-killer typically fills the hearts of the surviving relatives, friends, and others—even if the person was not liked while alive.

Feeling guilty has become a characteristic response to suicide. Parents' suicide is particularly traumatic to young children, who may be so overwhelmed with guilt feelings that they become mentally disordered.[16] Mature adults, too, can hardly avoid the assault of guilt feelings. They often blame themselves for having failed to perceive the self-killer's suicidal intent, for having been unable to prevent the suicide, or for having done something that might have caused the suicide.[17] However, unlike young children, mature adults are capable of neutralizing their guilt. One study has shown that adults can rationalize their guilt in one or more of the following ways: (1) They regard themselves as having been good to the person who committed suicide. Thus they feel that they did not do anything that caused the suicide. (2) They view the suicide as inevitable. They believe that even if they had been extraordinarily nice to the suicidal person, they would have still been unable to stop the self-destruction. (3) They consider the suicide as a good thing for the person involved. They view the voluntarily deceased as being better off dead than alive—being free from previous suffering in this world.[18]

While sympathy, guilt, and the resulting rationalization are the stuff of modern attitudes toward those who have successfully killed themselves, the same elements have recently emerged to support those who are *contemplating* taking their own lives. This support has taken two forms working in seemingly opposite directions.

On the one side is the advocacy of the right to suicide. Such an advocacy has indeed gained favor with a growing number of Americans. In 1975, for example, a majority of young Americans (thirty years of age or younger) told Gallup pollsters that incurable disease or continual pain entitles individuals to end their lives. This has prompted the speculation that "we may one day institute the euthanasia parlors portrayed in the movie *Soylent Green*. In this picture of the future, people who wish to end their lives report to a government building, where beautiful girls welcome them and administer a lethal drug. As they lie dying, the volunteers watch movies of idyllic pastoral settings and listen to Beethoven's *Ninth Symphony*." [19]

Since suffering is a relative, subjective experience, what is today regarded as ordinary suffering could in the future be felt as too painful to bear. Then there would be too many people who would commit suicide rather than struggle to the end.

On the other side, there are those who also feel sympathetic to the distressed suicide-inclined person, but who consider his or her self-destruction, if it occurs, to be a tragic and unnecessary death. They would feel guilty if they did not try to prevent it. Thus, since the 1950s, there have been an increasing number of suicide-prevention organizations in various countries. There are now at least 150 such organizations in Great Britain and over 200 in the United States. The best known are the Samaritans in Great Britain and the Suicide Prevention Centers in the United States. Their primary function is to encourage the distressed, suicidal person to telephone them for help. They have friendly, compassionate, and dedicated volunteers working around the clock.

There is some evidence that these organizations, using the psychological method of counseling, can effectively deal with some individual cases of potential suicides. But they cannot substantially reduce suicide rates, because suicide is basically a sociological problem (caused by larger social factors) rather than a psychological problem (caused by factors within the individual). A British psychiatrist who has done much research on suicide seems to recognize the sociological nature of the problem:

It is true there are numerous public and private social agencies who come to the aid of people who ask for help, but their combined efforts amount to little in the face of the magnitude of the task, and they are too spasmodic. Also, their orientation and their limited resources enable them only to tide people over crises of which a suicidal act may be an alarm signal. They cannot create the psychological [or, more accurately, social] conditions which would prevent the occurrence of these crisis. To do this, *society would have to evolve a new approach to social responsibility and a new social morality.*[20] [Emphasis added.]

It may also be worth noting that people who are characteristically prone to suicide, such as older men, tend to stay away from suicide prevention centers, and, in the few cases where they do call the centers for help, tend to go ahead and kill themselves anyway. On the other hand, people who are less inclined to suicide, such as young women, constitute the majority of those who call up the centers and are very likely to refrain from taking their lives.[21] In other words, suicide prevention centers are comparatively useful to people who are *less* likely to commit suicide, but useless to people who are *more* likely to end their own lives. The reason for such misdirected usefulness of the suicide-prevention organizations is apparently this: the organizations cannot deal with the social factors that cause the older man and other seriously suicide-prone individuals to want to kill themselves. What, then, is the nature of these suicide-causing social factors? Some of the theories to be discussed below will give us the answer.

THEORIES OF SUICIDE

Theories of suicide can be divided into two very broad categories: psychiatric and sociological. Psychiatric theories generally assume that there is *something wrong* with the person who commits suicide; whereas sociological theories assume that there is *nothing* wrong with the person. More specifically, some psychiatrists believe that suicidal people are in one way or another mentally ill—hence, mental illness is considered the cause of suicide. Other psychiatrists hold the classical Freudian view that the death instinct, thanks to the breakdown of ego defenses, drives individuals to kill themselves. Still other psychiatrists theorize that the cause of suicide is mental depression, morbid anxiety, intense hopelessness, deep frustration, or a traumatic experience during early childhood.

Most sociologists find the psychiatric theories either invalid or useless.

They are invalid because there is no significant relationship between mental illness and suicide. They are useless in that they cannot explain why some individuals (who are, say, Protestants, men, or whites) are more likely to commit suicide than other individuals (who are Catholics, women, or blacks). Thus sociologists generally assume that there is nothing wrong with the suicidal person—in the sense that there is nothing wrong with being a Protestant, being a man, or being a white person. The causes of suicide, then, do not reside within the individual, but rather in the group to which he or she belongs. This idea underlies the sociological theories to be discussed below.

CLASSICAL DURKHEIMIAN THEORY

Although French sociologist Emile Durkheim presented his theory of suicide more than eighty years ago,[22] it remains the most influential theory in the field. If we examine it very closely, as we would the trees of a forest, we can get confused by its many ambiguities and inconsistencies. But if we look at it as a whole, as we would the forest, we may clearly see a very useful theory for explaining various types of group influences on suicide rates. Let us, then, look at the theory as a whole.

Durkheim theorizes that there are two major causes of suicide: one is *social integration* and the other *social regulation*. Social integration refers to individuals voluntarily attaching themselves to a group or society of which they are members. Social regulation involves the group's or society's coercively regulating (restraining, constraining, or controlling) the behavior of its members. Therefore, socially integrated individuals are those who have been socialized to the norms of their society; they are microcosms of their society, or enjoy being members of their society so much that they are happy and proud to follow its commands. They can be likened to puppets who enjoy giving up their freedom in exchange for love, affection, or moral support from others. In contrast, socially regulated people are those who, being unsocialized and thus distrusted by their society, are subjected to social control—because of which they become unhappy when forced to obey the society's commands. They can be compared to prisoners who are forced to give up their freedom to insure the protection of others from them. But obviously not all individuals attach themselves in the same degree to the society or are equally controlled by it. Compared with unmarried individuals, for example, married persons attach themselves more strongly to society, because of their being an important part of its basic social institution, namely, the family. Similarly, compared with the rich, the poor are more tightly controlled by the society, as indicated by, among other things, its greater law-enforcement efforts against them.

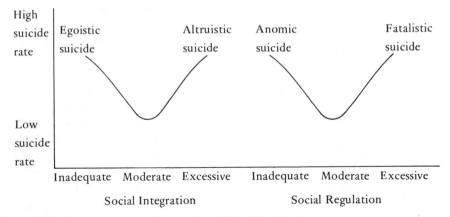

Figure 10.1   Schematic presentation of Durkheim's theory.

According to Durkheim's theory, people who experience *too little* social integration as well as people who experience *too much* integration are more likely to commit suicide, when compared with those who experience *moderate* integration. In like manner, people who are subjected to *too little* social regulation as well as people who are subjected to *too much* regulation are more likely to kill themselves, when compared with those who are subjected to *moderate* regulation. In other words, there is a curvilinear relationship between social integration and regulation, on the one hand, and suicide rate, on the other. Durkheim labels these types of suicide as follows: (1) the type caused by too little social integration is called *egoistic suicide;* (2) the type brought about by too much integration is named *altruistic suicide;* (3) the type generated by too little social regulation is termed *anomic suicide;* and (4) the type produced by too much regulation is branded *fatalistic suicide.* (See Figure 10.1.)

For example, compared with married persons, unmarried ones are more likely to commit *egoistic* suicide, because they, being *less socially integrated,* are less likely to receive love, affection, or moral support from others when deeply frustrated with their lives. Military personnel are more prone to *altruistic* suicide than are civilians working in a factory. This is because military personnel, being *more integrated* into their military unit, suffer greater dishonor when losing a battle, while civilian workers are more immune to dishonor when seeing their factory lose productivity. Rich countries have higher rates of *anomic* suicide than poor countries. The reason is that the citizens of rich countries, being *less socially regulated,* are more encouraged to expect too much from life, and thus become liable to greater frustration when their expectations are not fulfilled. Slaves in ancient societies were more likely to commit *fatalistic* suicide than free people in modern societies. This is because slaves were *more regulated* in that, in Durkheim's words, their "futures were pitilessly blocked and passions violently choked by oppressive discipline." [23]

Durkheim recognizes that egoistic and anomic suicide may appear similar to each other. For example, enjoying more freedom from social constraint and thus more prone to anomic suicide than are the poor, the rich are also likely to be individualists (less socially integrated) and therefore can be said to be more inclined to egoistic suicide. But Durkheim insists that these two types of suicide, along with their respective causes, do not always go together.[24] He may well be right. Consider, for example, these two cases: (1) Although Protestants are less integrated with their church group and thus more prone to egoistic suicide than are Catholics, they do not seem any less socially restrained, and therefore cannot be said to be more susceptible to anomic suicide than are Catholics. (2) Being less socially constrained and thus more liable to anomic suicide than are women, men do not seem any less socially integrated and consequently cannot be said to be more predisposed to egoistic suicide than are women. It should also be noted that social integration and regulation are basically distinguishable; the former being a largely *positive* experience for the individual and the latter a mostly *negative* experience, as was implied above.

Since Durkheim's writing is full of ambiguities, it is subject to various interpretations. One critic, Barclay Johnson, scrutinizes Durkheim's work and then concludes, contrary to our interpretation above, that egoistic and anomic suicide or social integration and regulation are actually identical.[25] Other critics generally suggest that Durkheim's key concepts of social integration and regulation cannot be measured and consequently his theory cannot be empirically tested.

MODERN DURKHEIMIAN THEORIES

There are a number of modern theories whose core concepts are derived from Durkheim's classical theory. Only two major ones are to be discussed here. One is what may be called *trifactor theory*, presented by Andrew Henry and James Short. The other is *status integration* theory by Jack Gibbs and Walter Martin.

Trifactor Theory   We already discussed this theory by Henry and Short in conjunction with homicide in Chapter 5. Here we will focus on the theory's explanation of suicide.[26]

Henry and Short define suicide as an act of aggression directed against oneself, the aggression having been induced by one's frustration with life.

Then they theorize that suicide as self-directed aggression results from three different factors, namely, (1) sociological, (2) psychological, and (3) economic factors.

There are two sociological factors that generate high rates of suicide. Henry and Short call one of them *weak relational system*, which means a lack of involvement in social relationships with other people. So the term *relational system* is identical to Durkheim's *social integration*. As Durkheim would have anticipated, Henry and Short point out that people who are inadequately involved with others are prone to suicide. To Henry and Short, these suicide-prone people include those who are unmarried rather than married, those who reside in urban areas rather than in rural areas, and those who live in the disorganized inner city rather than in the crime-free suburb, and those who are older (over sixty-five) rather than younger.

As for the other sociological cause of high suicide rates, Henry and Short call it *weak external restraint*. This term, once again, is identical to Durkheim's *inadequate social regulation*. Also, like Durkheim, Henry and Short argue that higher-status people are more likely than lower-status ones to commit suicide, because the former have lesser external restraints. By higher-status people, Henry and Short refer to white persons, males, individuals with high income, and army officers. By low-status persons, Henry and Short have in mind black persons, females, individuals with low income, and army recruits.

With respect to the psychological factor of suicide, Henry and Short suggest that a strong superego, which is thought to result from "internalization of harsh parental demands and discipline," produces a high "psychological probability" of suicide. The implied reasoning is that if people have been conditioned by their parents to develop strong consciences, they are likely to blame themselves rather than other people for their problems and frustrations. By blaming themselves (rather than others), they will likely kill themselves (rather than others).

As for the economic factor of suicide, Henry and Short show that suicide rates rise in times of economic depression and fall in times of prosperity. Economic depression, then, is a major cause of high suicide rates. Henry and Short also observe that, although people of both higher and lower statuses experience frustration that may lead to suicide, higher-status individuals experience considerably greater frustration and so are far more likely to kill themselves. This is because economic depression causes higher-status individuals, who by definition occupy a higher social position than lower-status people, to fall harder and hurt more. Their more painful experience, then, exerts a greater pressure on them to commit suicide.

Although the above three factors of suicide have been discussed separately, they are interrelated. This interrelationship is made possible by the concept of status. Thus it is the higher-status person who is more likely to get involved with a weak relational system, to experience weak external restraint, and therefore to commit suicide. It is also the higher-status person who is more likely to have a stronger superego and consequently a greater propensity to suicide. Finally, it is also the higher-status person who is more likely to experience greater frustration during an economic depression and thus is more prone to suicide. By tacitly integrating the sociological, psychological, and economic concepts into one theory, Henry and Short may be said to contribute a great deal to our knowledge about suicide. This is particularly the case because many sociologists have simply paid lip service to the necessity of integrating various perspectives on suicide, or are pessimistic about the prospect of such an integration, or both.[27]

Like Durkheim's theory, the Henry-Short theory is pregnant with meaningful concepts. But, also like Durkheim's theory, the Henry-Short theory has been subjected to criticisms. One major criticism is that the theory is not testable because its explanatory concepts (*strength of relational system* and *strength of external restraint*) cannot be measured. Another criticism is that, contrary to the theory's assertion, higher-status people do not always have higher suicide rates, as lower-status persons have also been known in some studies to have higher suicide rates.[28]

STATUS INTEGRATION THEORY   Like Henry and Short, Gibbs and Martin are inspired by Durkheim's theory.[29] But they find both the Durkheim and the Henry-Short theory to be scientifically inadequate. These two theories, in Gibbs and Martin's view, are not testable because their explanatory concepts are not empirically measurable. Therefore Gibbs and Martin attempt to reformulate Durkheim's theory so that it can be tested. They call their resulting reformulation *status integration theory*.

To make Durkheim's theory testable, Gibbs and Martin begin by reducing the rich and complex Durkheimian theory into a simple one. They discard Durkheim's ideas of altruistic, anomic, and fatalistic suicide, and retain only his concept of egoistic suicide. This is due to their feeling that Durkheim's theoretical statement concerning the causation of egoistic suicide is the least ambiguous one. Here is how Durkheim stated it: "[Egoistic] suicide varies inversely with the degree of *integration* of the social groups of which the individual forms a part."[30] (Emphasis added.)

Gibbs and Martin use this statement to initiate their reformulation of Durkheim's theory. They translate it into what they call their *Postulate No. 1*: "The suicide rate of a population varies inversely with the *stability and durability* of social relationships within that population."[31]

After translating Durkheim's *social integration* into *social stability and durability*, Gibbs and Martin find that they cannot measure their new concept. So they are compelled to relate it to another concept by stating their *Postulate No. 2*: "The stability and durability of social relationships within a population vary directly with the extent to which individuals in that population *conform* to the patterned and socially sanctioned demands and expectations placed upon them by others."

After introducing the new concept *social conformity*, Gibbs and Martin find that they cannot measure it either. So they are compelled once again to present another concept by offering *Postulate No. 3*: "The extent to which individuals in a population conform to patterned and socially sanctioned demands and expectations placed upon them by others varies inversely with the extent to which individuals in that population are confronted with *role conflicts*."

After stating this third postulate, Gibbs and Martin also cannot measure *role conflict*. So they try again and relate role conflicts to yet another concept in this *Postulate No. 4:* "The extent to which individuals in a population are confronted with role conflicts varies directly with the extent to which individuals occupy *incompatible statuses* in that population."

After stating the fourth postulate, Gibbs and Martin still find that it is not possible to measure its concept of *status incompatibility*. So they move on to introduce yet another concept in *Postulate No. 5*: "The extent to which individuals occupy incompatible statuses in a population varies inversely with the degree of *status integration* in that population."

Now, finally, Gibbs and Martin believe that, in this last postulate, they find the concept *status integration* to be measurable. Consequently, they state this testable theorem: "*The suicide rate of a population varies inversely with the degree of status integration in that population.*" (Emphases in all these quotes from Gibbs and Martin have been added.) According to this theorem, suicide rate and status integration are not directly connected but become connected through the above-mentioned four concepts in this manner: (1) High suicide rate → (2) lack of social stability and durability → (3) lack of social conformity → (4) role conflicts → (5) status incompatibility → (6) lack of status integration. Although Gibbs and Martin can only assume—without any supporting data—that all the five postulated relationships are credible, they are able to provide data to overwhelmingly confirm their theorem that the lesser the status integration of a group, the higher the suicide rate.

Now, for all the trouble Gibbs and Martin have taken to find a measurable concept, there arises the unsettling possibility that their theory is not as convincing as Durkheim's or Henry and Short's theory.

As their critics suggest, Gibbs and Martin's operational definition or measurement of status integration does not adequately reflect the conceptual meaning of that term.[32] Conceptually, *status integration* implies freedom from role conflict, from social tension, or from disrupted social relations in the individual's simultaneously occupying two or more statuses. But Gibbs and Martin operationally define *status integration* simply as: being a member of a relatively *large proportion* of people occupying the same set of two or more statuses, such as being male and a factory worker. In thus measuring status integration, Gibbs and Martin unwarrantedly assume that people who occupy a combination of two or more statuses that is shared by a *very small proportion* of the population, are very likely to experience role conflicts and to commit suicide. If this is true, we have to conclude, for example, that President Carter is almost certain to commit suicide because the combination of his sex status as a male and his occupational status as the president is shared by a nearly zero percent of the population.

Gibbs and Martin have to explain *why* so-called status integration has anything to do with suicide. The mere presentation of their impressive data to support the hypothesized relationship between the two variables can hardly explain it. This explanation requires the theorists to argue and reason that all their five postulates, from which they have derived the hypothesized relationship, make sense.

Their argument and reasoning may be convincing, but far less so than Durkheim's or Henry and Short's. Consider Gibbs and Martin's first postulate. If this postulate is true, we have to assume that white persons (who have been found to have higher suicide rates than black people) have *less* stable and *less* durable social relations with others than do black people. This is hardly convincing in view of whites' higher rates of employment, lower rates of divorce, and lower rates of arrest and imprisonment. But Durkheim and Henry and Short are more convincing when they argue that higher-status people (including whites) tend more to commit suicide because they are less socially regulated or less externally restrained than lower-status people (including blacks). Whites indeed enjoy greater freedom than blacks.

PHENOMENOLOGICAL THEORIES

Ultimately the validity of the above Durkheimian theories, both classical and modern, depends on the reliability of the official suicide statistics that have been used as the source of empirical support for the theories. The Durkheimian theorists assume that these statistics are reasonably reliable, and consequently consider their theories reasonably valid. But phenomenological sociologists believe that the official statistics are seriously unreliable. Therefore, they develop a different perspective on suicide.

There are two basic differences between Durkheimian and phenomenological theories. (1) Durkheimian theories are etiological, being primarily concerned with seeking out the *causes* of group differences in suicide rates.

In contrast, phenomenological theories are nonetiological, dealing instead with the social *meanings* of suicide or with how the suicidal person acts on these meanings. (2) Durkheimian theories look at suicide from a distance—through abstract official statistics. On the other hand, phenomenological theories look at suicide up close—through actual suicide notes, interviews with self-killers' survivors, and interviews with suicide attempters.

THEORY OF SUICIDAL MEANINGS   The proponent of this theory, Jack Douglas, seems to assume that, in the process leading up to suicide, individuals impute certain *specific* meanings to their prospective suicidal acts, these specific meanings being in turn influenced by the *general* meanings that their societies attach to suicide.[33]

Douglas presents three types of general meanings that our society attaches to suicide. (1) *"Suicidal actions are meaningful."* This meaning of suicide stems from members of our culture typically ascribing some motive to self-destruction. The motive can be depression, escape, or some other thing in the suicidal person. But the motive most frequently thought of is the *intention* to end one's own life. If this suicidal intention cannot be determined, the suicide involved is not seen as meaningful. So it can be said that society considers suicide as meaningful in that it results from the intention to kill oneself. (2) *"Something is fundamentally wrong with the suicidal person's social situation."* By imputing this meaning to suicide, members of our society often have in mind the deceased's significant others —his or her parents, spouse, lover, employer, and so on—who are to blame for the suicide. (3) *"Something is fundamentally wrong with the suicidal person himself."* Most people are jolted with shock, bewilderment, or disbelief upon hearing that someone they know has committed suicide. The reason is that the society has conditioned them to view suicide as a very unnatural act. People who kill themselves are consequently thought of as "crazy."

The above three general social meanings of suicide enable suicidally inclined individuals to construct more specific meanings for themselves. These specific meanings apparently make it easier for them to end their own lives. Douglas divides these meanings into four types. (1) *"Suicide is a way of transporting the soul from this world to the other world."* The suicidal action, then, is viewed as going to God. This meaning is most clearly represented in religious suicides. (2) *"Suicide is a way of changing the view of oneself held by others in this world or by God."* Atonement suicides are considered as achieving this objective. Nasty persons, for example, may through such suicides become lovable in the eyes of others. (3) *"Suicide is a way of achieving fellow-feeling."* In other words, suicide is defined as an action that deserves pity or sympathy from the surviving others. (4) *"Suicide is a way of getting revenge."* Suicide is viewed as a weapon for making others feel guilty of having caused the self-destruction.

It may be noted that the social meanings of suicide described above are mostly *positive* in nature. They serve to facilitate the suicidal process— encouraging the suicide prone to kill themselves. Therefore, Douglas does not spell out the various stages of becoming a suicide victim, as if to say that once people decide to kill themselves they are guided by these suicidal meanings to quickly end their lives. While Douglas focuses on largely positive types of suicidal meanings and thus makes little of the suicidal process, the next theory views suicidal meanings as *negative* in nature and consequently makes much of the suicidal process.

THEORY OF SUICIDAL PROCESS　Jerry Jacobs, the author of this theory, views the social meanings of suicide as basically social prohibitions against suicide, for suicide is defined by society as "a violation of the sacred, God-given trust of life." Thus Jacobs is interested in showing how a prospective suicide overcomes the social prohibitions so as to eventually take his or her own life. Jacobs presents a series of ten steps in the process of becoming a suicide: [34]

1. Individuals find themselves faced with unexpected, intolerable, and unsolvable problems.
2. They view these problems not as isolated incidents, but as part of a long-standing history of problems. At the same time, they expect more problems in the future.
3. They believe that death is the only way to solve these problems.
4. Their belief in the efficacy of death intensifies through increasing social isolation, because they cannot share their problems with others.
5. They now work hard to overcome the social prohibition against suicide, which they have so internalized that they view suicide as immoral.
6. They succeed in overcoming the social prohibition because they already feel isolated from others and therefore feel freer to act on their own.
7. They succeed in overcoming the social prohibition by rationalizing their intended suicide in such ways as, "Killing myself doesn't necessarily mean I don't hold life sacred. In fact, I still hold life sacred despite my suicide."
8. They are convinced by their rationalizations because they define the problem as not of their own making, as unsolvable despite their great personal effort to find a less painful solution, as solvable only through suicide.
9. Defining suicide as the necessary solution, they feel that they do not

have the choice not to kill themselves; they thereby free themselves from a sense of responsibility for their impending suicide and from the feeling of guilt.

10. Finally, just to make sure that they will not be punished in the after-life, they pray to God for forgiveness or leave a suicide note requesting the survivors to pray for their souls. Then, they decisively kill themselves.

POWER THEORY APPLIED

Applying power theory, we may divide suicide into two types: one is com-mitted more often by the relatively powerful, and the other by the less powerful. The former is *anomic suicide*, while the latter is *fatalistic suicide*. To further use Durkheim's concepts, we may say that powerful persons tend to commit anomic suicide because they are relatively unregulated by society. In contrast, powerless people tend to commit fatalistic suicide because they are more regulated. This suggests that there is an element of true *voluntariness* in the powerful person's act of committing anomic suicide, and that there is subtle *coerciveness* in the powerless person's fatalistic suicide.

Warren Breed, who correctly views blacks' suicide as fatalistic, discov-ered in his research in the South that black suicides were often forced to kill themselves by their fear of the police. He found that many blacks killed themselves if arrested, and that the police were often charged with beating and killing the black "suicide." In the following list of suicides by powerless minorities, as presented by Breed, we can detect the element of coerciveness in their suicides: "[Suicides by] Negroes in South Africa detained for six months as 'material witnesses'; Japanese who in feudal times took their lives when threatened by torture at the hands of the barons; suicides among indigenous peoples under colonial rule; the epidemics of Jewish suicide under severe oppression, as in medieval persecutions and in Berlin during 1938 through 1943; the hundreds of Russians who had left Russia during World War II and killed themselves rather than accepting repatriation after 1945; and Chinese women 'forced into suicide' by the rigid role requirements of the traditional Chinese family." [35] More subtly, many powerless workers are forced to slowly kill themselves, such as by developing black lung or cancer, because less hazardous occupations are closed to them.

In contrast, more powerful members of society are not forced by social oppression to commit anomic suicide. Their suicide seems to result from their being accustomed to the relative luxury of seeing and doing things their own way. Such accustomed luxury often leads them to have low tolerance for suffering; it encourages them to entertain high expectations for enjoyment from life, and inclines them to exaggerate and intensify their occasional disappointment with life. All this may generate their proneness to suicide. In addition, when they contemplate suicide, their being accustomed to the luxury of seeing and doing things their own way may make them feel too proud to turn to others for help. This may explain why higher-status suicide-prone persons (such as men as opposed to women) are not inclined to call the suicide prevention center for help. It may also explain why higher-status people tend less to merely attempt suicide (which often represents an implicit appeal for help) and tend more to actually kill themselves.

Further, we can envision that if euthanasia is legalized, society will subtly impose coerced euthanasia on the poor and guarantee voluntary euthanasia for the rich. Since the poor who are terminally ill cannot afford expensive medical care, physicians might be very inclined to recommend euthanasia. Euthanasia of powerless persons, then, would in effect be a coerced one. On the other hand, since the rich who are terminally ill can afford expensive medical care, physicians would less readily recommend euthanasia, and would allow their rich patients ample time to think it over before deciding to have their lives terminated. Euthanasia of powerful persons would genuinely be voluntary. But this distinction between coerced and voluntary euthanasia would be masked by higher-status people's "civilized" and "rational" talk about the right to die with dignity.

However, contrary to what power theory may suggest, the powerful are perhaps not more likely than the powerless to commit suicide. Instead, the powerless may be more pressured to commit coerced fatalistic suicide than are the powerful inclined to commit voluntary anomic suicide. The reason is that society does not even recognize the powerless suicide as suicide, much less exercising any control to prevent it. This may be related to the symbiotic relationship between the nature of powerful persons' suicide and that of powerless persons' suicide. As society defines suicide as a strictly voluntary act, the subtly coercive nature of many powerless persons' suicides is unrecognized. Thus the powerless' suicide continues to be coercive in nature and the powerful's suicide continues to be voluntary.

SUMMARY

Suicide is a relatively rare form of deviant behavior, but it has been studied by numerous sociologists and psychiatrists.

There are three types of suicidal people, each with a different kind of experience. (1) Suicide threateners are very explicit in communicating their suicidal intention to others. (2) Suicide attempters are less explicit with their suicidal messages and more likely to actually try to end their lives. (3) Successful suicides may have in the past threatened or attempted suicide or neither. Successful suicides may feel apologetic, vindictive, magnanimous, or surrealistic just before they die.

From official statistics it has been found that suicide rates are higher in modern than in nonliterate societies, in the present than in the past, in urban than in rural areas, among whites than among blacks, among Protestants than among Catholics and Jews, among men than among women, among the maritally unattached than among the attached, among older people than among younger, in higher-status occupations than in lower-status, and among college students than among nonstudents.

While societal response to suicide was punitive in the past, it is sympathetic today. Consequently, suicide tends to generate guilt feelings in the survivors, has sparked some interest in the right to die with dignity, and has helped establish hundreds of suicide prevention centers.

While psychiatric theories generally attribute suicide to mental disturbance of one type or another, sociological theories view the suicidal person as normal. There are two types of sociological theories. (1) Durkheimian theories are etiological, designed to explain the causes of the group differences in suicide rates. The classical Durkheimian theory suggests that high suicide rates result from either excessive or inadequate social integration and regulation. One modern Durkheimian theory includes sociological, psychological, and economic factors as causes of high suicide rates. Another modern Durkheimian theory links high suicide rates to the lack of status integration in the groups. (2) Phenomenological theories are nonetiological, focusing on the social meanings of suicide and on how individual suicides behave in accordance with those meanings. Two such theories were discussed. One of them deals with how society and the suicidal person define suicide; the other theory shows how individuals have to overcome the moral prohibition against suicide through rationalization before they can take their own lives. Finally, power theory enables us to see the coercive nature of the suicide committed by relatively powerless persons and the voluntary nature of the suicide committed by the more powerful.

SUGGESTED READINGS

Douglas, Jack D. *The Social Meanings of Suicide*. Princeton, N.J.: Princeton University Press, 1967.

Durkheim, Emile. *Suicide*. New York: Free Press, 1951.

Gibbs, Jack P., ed. *Suicide*. New York: Harper & Row, 1968.

Gibbs, Jack P. and Walter T. Martin. *Status Integration and Suicide*. Eugene: University of Oregon, 1964.

Henry, Andrew F. and James F. Short, Jr. *Suicide and Homicide*. New York: Free Press, 1954.

Henslin, James M. "Guilt and Guilt Neutralization: Response and Adjustment to Suicide," in Jack D. Douglas, ed. *Deviance and Respectability*. New York: Basic Books, 1970, pp. 192–228.

Jacobs, Jerry. "A Phenomenological Study of Suicide Notes." *Social Problems* 15 (Summer 1967): 60–73.

Lester, Gene and David Lester. *Suicide*. Englewood Cliffs, N.J.: Prentice-Hall, 1971.

Maris, Ronald W. *Social Forces in Urban Suicide*. Homewood, Ill.: Dorsey, 1969.

Stengel, Erwin. *Suicide and Attempted Suicide*. Baltimore, Md.: Pelican Books, 1969.

11 MENTAL DISORDER

Every year nearly 500,000 Americans are admitted to public mental institutions and approximately another 100,000 mental patients enter private hospitals. Today a total of about 1.7 million people are confined in mental institutions of various types all over the United States.[1] Almost half of all the hospital beds in this country are occupied by mental patients, and it has been estimated that one out of ten people will spend some time in a psychiatric hospital during their lives. But these statistics underestimate the actual number of mentally ill people in our society, because the great majority of them do not go to the hospital. One survey estimates that at least 20 percent of the entire U.S. population suffer from mental disorder serious enough to require hospitalization. The same survey also estimates that more than 80 percent show some degree of impaired mental health—in the form of psychosomatic disorders, feelings of nervousness, tension and restlessness, and difficulties in interpersonal relations.[2]

Mental disorder is indeed a very common phenomenon. It is even more common than the above statistics suggest. Although it is not exactly the same as physical illness, mental disorder can and does befall each one of us just as physical illness can and does. Of course, most of us do not have serious and prolonged physical illness. Similarly, most of us do not have serious and prolonged mental disorder. But it is no exaggeration to say that all of us occasionally come down with a cold or other minor physical ailments. Likewise, it is not farfetched to say that all of us occasionally come down with a depression—"the common cold of mental ailments"[3]—or other minor mental disorders. Yet, because of the horrifying stigma that society attaches to mental disorder, many people find it very difficult to accept the idea that all of us have been and shall be mentally ill in one way or another.

THE NATURE OF MENTAL DISORDER

At the outset, we may need to knock down some popular beliefs that stand in our way to understanding mental disorder.[4] First, the insane are popularly believed to be extremely weird. In actuality, most of the mentally ill, both within the mental hospital and without, are not extremely disturbed. Only a few inmates of mental institutions can be found spending their time cutting out paper dolls, screaming and yelling, posing as kings or queens, or masturbating and urinating in front of others.

Second, it is widely taken for granted that there is a sharp difference between "mentally ill' and "mentally healthy." This may be true, if we compare the very few mentally ill persons who are extremely disordered in their behavior with "normal" people. But most of the time even the psychiatrist or clinical psychologist cannot clearly differentiate the mentally ill from the mentally healthy. Nor can a group of experts unanimously distinguish a person as either mentally ill or healthy. The problem is not only that the behavior of different individuals ranges by imperceptible degrees from normal to abnormal, but an individual may shift at different times to different positions along that range.

Third, mental illness is popularly believed to be a hereditary defect. This may be true in a few cases, but in most cases—even in those where "insanity runs in the family"—the children seem to "inherit" the mental illness through learning or socialization rather than through the genes.

Fourth, mental illness is commonly felt to be hopeless, always incurable. Even after a person is discharged from a mental hospital as recovered, he or she is likely to be viewed with suspicion. In fact, some 70 to 80 percent of all hospitalized mental patients can recover and live relatively normal lives if their treatment has been adequate and received in time.

TYPES OF MENTAL DISORDER

As has been suggested, mental disorder may be quite similar to physical illness, in that it is extremely common with most of its symptoms (depression, anxiety, restlessness, and so on) relatively mild. Beyond this similarity, mental disorder is far more difficult to ·define. Nevertheless, psychiatrists have divided it into different types. First, there are two broad types: *organic* and *functional* disorders. These two disorders may show the same symptoms, such as hallucination, delusion, impaired judgment, and other behavior disturbances, but they can be differentiated on the basis of the underlying causes of those symptoms. Organic disorder is caused by damage to the brain, which in turn may have originated from a tumor, head injury, syphilis, lead poisoning, general deterioration from old age, or other acute physical damage. On the other hand, functional disorder is believed to result from psychological and sociological factors rather than those just mentioned. Functional disorder constitutes a much larger category of mental disorders than does organic disorder. Psychologists and sociologists are primarily interested in the study of functional disorder.

Functional disorder is further divided into three major categories: *psychotic*, *neurotic*, and *character disorder*. In general, psychotic disorder is typified by the loss of touch with reality, and neurotic disorder by a constant worry about trivial matters. A pyschotic can be likened to a person who thinks that 2 plus 2 is equal to 10 and strongly believes it, whereas a neurotic can be compared to a person who thinks that 2 plus 2 is equal to 4—but constantly worries about it. A third mentally disordered person, being antisocial, says "the hell with 2 plus 2" and neither believes nor worries about it; this person is not defined as psychotic or as neurotic. Psychiatrists put this person into a third category: character disorder. Let us examine the more specific symptoms of these three categories of functional disorder.[5]

PSYCHOTIC DISORDER   This disorder is considered more serious than neurotic and character disorder. There are different types of psychotic disorder; only two major ones are to be discussed here.

Schizophrenia is the most common type of psychosis. Schizophrenics have the following symptoms: they think and talk in unconventional, illogical, or ambiguous ways, such as "My body is a bottle." They express emotions inappropriately, such as laughing in response to sad news and crying in response to happy news. They withdraw from other humans into their inner selves, totally unresponsive to the surroundings. They engage in such infantile acts as thumb sucking and playing with feces. They have delusions of grandeur (for example, thinking they are Napoleon), and delusions of persecution (believing the whole world is plotting to assassinate them). They have hallucinations, hearing voices where there is only silence and seeing things that do not exist. Actually these experiences of distorted reality are not rare; all of us may have encountered them once in a while. But psychiatrists would not consider one schizophrenic unless these experiences occur so frequently that one's school, job, or family functions are severely disrupted. Because of the severe nature of their mental disorder, schizophrenics are thought to require hospitalization.

Another major type of psychosis is *manic-depressive behavior*. This involves a person's fluctuating between two opposite extremes of mood. One extreme is called *mania*, which is characterized by great exuberance, confidence, and excitement. Such individuals are constantly joking, laughing, and making speeches; however, they are far from happy or content. They are continually on the move, not because they enjoy it but because they are driven to it by powerful tension within them. In this hyperactivity, they are enveloped by grandiose delusions, thinking that they are superior or godlike, capable of achieving anything. After experiencing this manic stage, these people may suddenly find themselves in the opposite extreme, called *depression*. When brought down to this depressive state, individuals feel an overwhelming despair, experience the delusion of worthlessness, and think of committing suicide. Consequently they lose the desire to talk, move, eat, and sleep, and spend a lot of time crying.

NEUROTIC DISORDER   This disorder is considered to be less severe than psychosis. There is little distortion of reality, and most neurotics are still able to appear normal and do most of the things that normal people do, such as staying in school, keeping jobs, or maintaining family relations. The only problem is that their neurotic symptoms prevent them from being as happy as they otherwise would be. There are various types of neurosis, with each being characterized by a certain syndrome.

One is *anxiety reaction*. This represents a generalized, vague, freely floating apprehension; the object of apprehension cannot be identified. Although the normal person occasionally experiences such anxiety, the neurotic one characteristically exaggerates it to an extreme degree. If neurotics can identify a specific object of their anxiety, they are said to suffer from *phobia*. Phobic neurotics may have extreme, unreasonable fear of animals (*zoophobia*), fear of heights (*acrophobia*), fear of closed spaces (*claustrophobia*), fear of open spaces (*agoraphobia*), and so on.

The second type of neurosis is the combination of *obsession* and *compulsion*. Obsession involves some bothersome idea that keeps on interrupting the individual's train of thought. One college student describes his earlier obsession this way: "When I was about eight years of age . . . I thought I was going to cut my throat from ear to ear with a certain large butcher knife in my grandmother's kitchen. I couldn't throw off the idea. . . . I was afraid to go near the knife." [6] A compulsion involves some ritualistic action that neurotics feel they must perform. An example of this can be found in people whose extreme fear of germs and contamination by others drives them to wash their hands very frequently. Yet the more they wash them to get rid of their anxiety about germs, the more anxious they become.

The third type of neurosis is *depressive reaction.* Neurotic depression is distinguishable from psychotic depression, which is much more severe both in degree and in duration. The milder neurotic depression is characterized by the feeling of sadness, dejection, and self-deprecation. Although this depressive reaction may last for weeks or even months, it usually clears up eventually. In a few cases it may lead to suicide.

The fourth type of neurosis is *psychophysiologic disorder,* also called *psychosomatic illness, conversion reaction,* or *hysteria.* Its symptoms range from the relatively minor to the very severe, and include headaches, hypertension, skin rashes, ulcer, amnesia, paralysis, deafness, and blindness. These symptoms have no basis in physical injury or nerve damage; they are the physical expressions of some underlying psychological problems. Although they slow down their activity, these symptoms enable people to avoid threatening or anxiety-provoking situations.

CHARACTER DISORDER   This is a general category for all sorts of deviant behavior that the psychiatrist can think of but cannot diagnose as either psychotic or neurotic. This so-called mental disorder is sometimes referred to as *personality disorder* or *sociopathic* (psychopathic) *disorder.* Its most prominent feature is blatant disregard for society's rules. Its cause is thought to be a lack of moral development—failure to develop conscience, failure to acquire true compassion, or failure to learn how to form meaningful relationships. Examples of those suffering from character disorder have been identified as con men, dope pushers, drug addicts, pimps, prostitutes, alcoholics, homosexuals, rapists, sexual exhibitionists, voyeurs, masturbators, and other chronic criminals or delinquents. As a mixed-bag category, character disorder is also used to include such behaviors as stuttering, nail biting, muscle twitch, and bed wetting, as well as the behaviors of compulsive gamblers, unprincipled businessmen, shyster lawyers, quack doctors, high-pressure evangelists, and crooked politicians.[7]

The different types of mental disorder described above are schematically presented in Figure 11.1. They represent only a partial list of all the psychic disturbances that the American Psychiatric Association has classified in its *Diagnostic and Statistical Manual of Mental Disorders.* But often psychiatrists cannot accurately find the diagnostic category in which a given mental patient belongs, because the patient frequently displays symptoms from different categories. In consequence, various psychiatrists, each

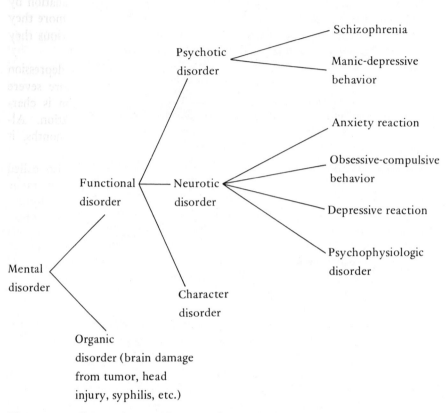

Figure 11.1 Schematic classification of mental disorders.

relying on his or her opinion, often cannot agree on what type of mental disorder the patient suffers from. In fact, they often cannot even agree on whether a person is mentally ill or not. As one psychiatrist says, "There is no single definition of mental health that comes anywhere near to encompassing a general professional consensus. . . . Mental disease turns out to be as ill defined as mental health. Its presence or absence is very hard to determine." [8] Critics have implied that the psychiatric classification system merely consists of fancy words expressing the lay person's, not the professional psychiatrist's, ideas about insanity. One critic, the leading psychiatrist Karl Menninger, dismisses the diagnostic system as "sheer verbal Mickey Mouse." [9] Despite these criticisms, many psychiatrists and other related professionals still use it. For it can be conveniently used for diagnosing, though not accurately, their patients. Without it, the professionals could hardly practice their profession.

SOCIAL FACTORS IN MENTAL DISORDER

Despite the difficulty of defining and classifying mental disorder, a number of traditional sociologists continue to assume that mental disorder is as real as physical disease. Thus they have attempted to study the epidemiology of mental disorder in the same way as scientists study the epidemiology of a physical disease. The epidemiology of mental disorder is supposed to show the occurrence and distribution of mental disorder in a population, from which the sociologists attempt to discover what social factors may have caused mental disorder.

There have been numerous epidemiological studies of mental disorder conducted in communities all over the world. But they differ greatly in their methods of finding the subjects as well as in their ways of defining mental illness. In some studies, the researcher finds the subjects among mental patients who are receiving treatment of one type or another. In other studies, the researcher seeks out the mentally disordered from the general normal population who do not receive any treatment. The treated cases are found in different places, such as in federal, state, county, other public and private hospitals and institutions. The untreated cases are found in different countries, cities, and towns. The psychiatrists at the various treatment centers define mental illness differently, so that a person diagnosed as mentally ill at one hospital may not be so diagnosed at another. Similarly, the epidemiological researchers at different places differ in their definitions of mental disorder—some would only define bizarre hallucination as indicative of mental disorder, while others would define mere nervousness as a symptom of mental disorder. "These contrasts in concepts and methods," says Bruce Dohrenwend, a veteran researcher in the field, "render any attempt to make substantive comparisons of absolute rates of various types of disorder across different studies frustrating and uninformative." [10] A part of the legacy from these epidemiological studies is that, due to the contrasts in concepts and methods and hence the conflicting findings, it is not possible to discover the exact social causes of mental disorder. But Dohrenwend observes:

There is, however, a second part of the legacy from these studies that gains in impressiveness precisely because it survives the methodological differences. This second part of the legacy is a set of highly consistent *relationships* between various types of psychiatric disorders and a number of important sociocultural factors. . . . Three sets of variables are involved in these consistent relationships with psychiatric disorder: Sex, rural versus urban location, and social class.[11]

Let us take a closer look at these three social factors as well as some other factors that have been less consistently shown to be related to mental disorder.

SEX There are conflicting findings as to which sex is more likely to become mentally disordered. Some studies show men to be more likely; other studies report women as more likely; and still others fail to find any difference between the sexes. It should be noted, though, that these conflicting findings concern mental disorder in general. When data on specific types of disorder are examined, sex differences can be discovered. Females have consistently higher rates of neurotic and psychotic depression, while males have consistently higher rates of antisocial behavior. How can we account for this sex difference?

It appears that it has to do with the different social roles played by women as opposed to men. Female roles are comparatively restrictive and oppressive, so constraining the woman to her inner self that she tends to express her frustration and anger to herself. In contrast, male roles are more liberative, encouraging the man to be bold and assertive in his attempt to achieve whatever he wants in the wide, open world. If he is frustrated and angry, he feels freer to take it out on other people.

RURAL VS. URBAN SETTINGS Psychotic disorder is more prevalent in rural areas, while neurotic and personality disorder are more common in urban areas. Why? Perhaps rural residents are more likely to feel that life in a small town is relatively restrictive. They may find it difficult to express frustration and anger in the company of people who are their relatives, friends, acquaintances, and others likely to know who they are if they cause trouble. By suppressing their frustration, they gradually build up seething caldrons of tension until they suddenly explode in the form of psychotic disorders. As psychotics, they behave in defiance of conventional reality by breaking the ties between them and other people. On the other side, urban dwellers can more easily escape family and friends, and are freer to express frustration in the midst of strangers, who tend more to tolerate unconventional behavior or antisocial outbursts. If they persist in doing so, however, they are neurotics or show the syndrome of character disorder, which, unlike psychosis, does not make them lose contact with conventional reality.

SOCIAL CLASS Of all the social factors assumed to be related to mental disorder, social class has been the most consistently and most clearly demonstrated to be associated with the disorder.

The first epidemiological study of mental disorder was conducted by Robert Faris and Warren Dunham in Chicago more than forty years ago.[12] In examining the records of all the patients admitted to public and private mental hospitals in the city between 1922 and 1934, Faris and Dunham discovered that the rates of hospital admission for mental illness (mostly psychosis) were not randomly distributed throughout the city. Instead, the highest percentage of mental patients came from the most disorganized areas—those areas marked by high rates of broken homes, crime, unemployment, and congested living conditions. Conversely, the lowest percentage of mental patients came from the stable suburban areas. Thus the social disorganization of the inner city was the biggest producer of mental illness. Since the social disorganization was assumed to characterize the condition of the lower classes, the data were considered as supporting the idea of social class being inversely related to mental disorder.

In 1950 August Hollingshead and Fredrick Redlich did a basically similar study in New Haven, Connecticut.[13] But there were some differences. Unlike their Chicago predecessors, who were not interested in measuring social class, Hollingshead and Redlich were interested in the social class standings of their subjects on the basis of their place of residence, nature of occupation, and length of education. Also, unlike the earlier Chicago researchers, who focused on hospitalized patients only, Hollingshead and Redlich did not only investigate all the patients in public and private mental hospitals but also those receiving outpatient treatment from private clinics and psychiatrists' offices.

The results from this New Haven study confirmed the Chicago findings, namely, that the lower the social classes, the higher the rates of psychosis. Hollingshead and Redlich also found that, while psychosis was more common in the lower classes, neurosis was more prevalent in the upper classes. In addition, they discovered that social class had a bearing on the type of psychiatric treatment received by the mental patient. There were three types of treatment: (1) psychotherapy, which involves individual and group therapy based on discussion and reeducation; (2) organic treatment, which includes the use of various types of sedative medication, electric shock therapy, and lobotomy (psychosurgery or brain surgery); and (3) custodial care, which simply involves keeping the patient institutionalized without any therapeutic treatment at all. Hollingshead and Redlich found that the overwhelming majority of neurotic patients—most of whom came from the upper classes—received the relatively beneficial and pleasant psychotherapy; whereas the great majority of psychotic patients—most of them from the lower classes—received the useless custodial care and harsh organic treatment.

Both the Chicago and the New Haven Study relied on information about *treated* cases—mental patients who were admitted to the hospital or treated by their private psychiatrists. Thus those two studies actually only indicated the inverse relationship between social class and *treatment* for mental illness, not social class and *mental illness*. This means that the huge number of mentally ill people who do not receive treatment have been ignored by the Chicago and the New Haven researchers. In order to get a more conclusive test of the inverse relationship between social class and mental illness, one has to go to the general population outside the mental hospitals and psychiatrists' offices.

This is what a team of researchers did in midtown Manhattan in 1954. This Manhattan study was such an ambitious project that its results were not published until eight years later.[14] The Manhattan researchers interviewed randomly selected samples of people from the area, and asked them, among other things, whether they had experienced nervousness, restlessness, nervous breakdown, difficulties in interpersonal relations, and other symptoms of emotional disturbance. Most of these symptoms do not indicate disabling mental illness but largely represent regular emotional "aches and pains." The information from the interviews was given to a group of psychiatrists who were asked to rate each case as to the degree of psychiatric impairment. The result gave added support to the Chicago and the New Haven Study: a higher proportion of lower-class than upper-class people were found to suffer from impaired mental health.

The above three major studies suggesting or showing social class as an important factor in the occurrence of mental illness have stimulated a great number of similar studies by other researchers. They all have more or less consistently produced data to support the key finding of the earlier three major studies, namely, that mental illness increases as one goes down to the lower stratum of the social class hierarchy. This finding, however, has prompted two conflicting explanations. One is that lower-class people are more prone to mental disorder because they are constantly subjected to social *stress* in their lives. The other explanation is that the heavy concentration of mental disorder in the lower-class neighborhood is the result of the downward *drift* of mentally ill people into, and the upward *drift* of mentally healthy people out of, the neighborhood. Both stress and drift have been found to play a role in the genesis of lower-class mental disorder, but it is still at issue which factor plays a stronger role.

OTHER SOCIAL FACTORS   Aside from the preceding three social factors, there are a number of less consistent and more tentative findings on other social factors.[15]

First, there appear to be some cultural and subcultural influences on the emergence of mental illness. Residents of Mexico City have been found to have higher scores on psychiatric impairment when compared with residents of midtown Manhattan. In each social class, Puerto Ricans have been found to show more psychopathological symptoms than have been found among black, Irish, and Jewish people. Of the lower classes, Puerto Ricans and blacks are more likely than Irish and Jews to have sociopathic inclinations ("I can easily make people afraid of me and sometimes do just that for the fun of it"), as well as paranoid tendencies ("Behind my back people say all kinds of things about me"). While blacks are more likely to show paranoid disorders (viewed by the researchers as anger expressed outwardly against others), Jews tend more to manifest depressive disorders (viewed as anger turned inward against oneself).

Second, old age seems to be an important factor in the causation of mental disorder. Many studies show that in our society older people are more likely to suffer from greater impairment of their mental health than are younger people. The psychiatric problems of the aged are often attributed to our society's neglect. The aged are not given meaningful and satisfying roles to play in society, as these roles are largely given to the young, on whom industrial production depends heavily. Deprived of respect by others, older people become isolated. As they begin to develop psychopathological symptoms, their families and other close relatives do not bother taking them to the hospital or psychiatrist. By the time their psychopathology becomes hopelessly severe, they are brought to a mental institution where they will be kept out of their families' sight for a long time.

Third, family condition has been found to underlie the occurrence of mental disorder. Extreme deprivation of parental love and affection as well as extreme lack of social interaction with parents has been observed to bring about heightened anxiety and thus a marked rise in mental illness in one's childhood and adult life. Further, divorced people have been found to show a higher degree of psychological impairment when compared with married persons.

SOCIETAL RESPONSE TO MENTAL DISORDER

More than any other form of deviant behavior, mental disorder has been studied implicitly or explicitly from the standpoint of labeling theory. Therefore, unlike the preceding discussion that focuses on the social causes of mental disorder, the following discussion will center on how society responds to the mentally disordered.[16] Let us begin by taking a look at how people in the past dealt with the mentally ill.

THE PAST ATTITUDE Throughout human history, the attitude toward the insane has for the most part been unfavorable. It is true that for hundreds of years in ancient Greece, madness was viewed with awe. Even the famous philosopher Socrates believed that madness was the greatest blessing, for which both states and individuals in Greece should be thankful. Epilepsy, which was then equated with madness, was considered sacred—a sign of divine favor. Later, in the Middle Ages, the mad person was portrayed by artists and writers as the only one in touch with ultimate reality.

However, throughout most of human existence, the insane have been badly treated. During the Stone Age, insanity was attributed to some evil spirit that had somehow entered the body. Archaeological evidence suggests that Stone Age people were the first to perform what is today called *lobotomy* on their mental patients. Their psychosurgcial technique, called *trephining*, involved boring a hole in the skull to allow the evil spirit to escape.

With the beginning of the Hebrew and early Greek civilizations, the evil spirit was still considered the cause of insanity. The fear surrounding the insane is reflected in this biblical statement: "A man also or woman that hath a familiar spirit, or that is a wizard, shall surely be put to death" (Leviticus 20:27). This pronouncement later provided the rationale for witch burning in medieval Europe, when the church defined the insane as witches who had invited the devil to reside in their bodies. Witch burning took several forms: some witches were burned alive; others were strangled or beheaded before being burned; and still others were mutilated before being thrown into the fire. For example, in 1636 a man in Königsberg, Germany, claimed that he was God, and the authority treated his "demon possession" by cutting out his tongue, cutting off his head, and burning his body. Some three hundred years later, though, this approach to treating mental illness was refined by Hitler, who felt that mental patients deserved "mercy killing." He built gas chambers in mental hospitals and managed to exterminate fifty thousand patients (who were non-Jewish Germans) within only two years.[17]

By the middle 1700s, demonology and witch burning began to disappear, but the mentally ill were still harshly treated. Those who were believed to be dangerous were kept in jails and poorhouses, while those considered less violent were allowed to beg for food in the streets. There were also a few institutions for treating the mentally ill. One such institution, Bethlehem Hospital in London, became widely known as "Bedlam," and it handcuffed and chained its patients to the walls. This hospital even put its patients on display for the amusement of the public. Tickets were sold for a lunatic sideshow featuring the wilder, more agitated patients. Similarly, the insane in France were not only treated like animals, but their asylums were much worse than zoos. One French physician of the period reported:

I have seen them naked, or covered with rags, and protected only by straw from the cold, damp pavement. I have seen them in squalid stinking little hovels, without air or light, chained in caves where wild beasts would not have been confined. There they remain to waste away in their own filth under the weight of chains which lacerate their bodies. Whips, chains, and dungeons are the only means of persuasion employed by keepers who are as barbarous as they are ignorant.[18]

In 1793 a revolutionary change in attitude toward the insane occurred when the physician Phillippe Pinel was placed in charge of a large asylum in Paris. Pinel removed the chains from the inmates. Then he administered to them what has become known as moral treatment—treating them like human beings and encouraging them to have hope and confidence in themselves. The result was that, instead of acting wild and destructive as they were popularly believed to be, the patients became thankful and docile, and some who had been chained for more than twenty years were able to leave the hospital a few months later. Soon after Pinel did this, his moral treatment was adopted in England and the United States. Many insane inmates in jails and poorhouses were moved to new asylums to receive the new humane treatment. But gradually the asylums became overcrowded and served largely as warehouses for the mentally disordered. The condition in many mental institutions became almost as dismal as before. By 1955, however, new alternatives to mental institutions began to emerge. Examples of these are general hospitals that opened outpatient clinics, private psychiatrists, private clinics, and community mental health centers, all of which have attempted to be more therapeutic than asylums were in the past. But this therapeutic objective is still far beyond fulfillment for many mental patients. We shall now turn to this problem in the following.

THE PUBLIC One major difficulty in trying to help the mentally ill lies in the public's negative attitude toward them. Although the public today does not believe in burning the insane as devils, basically the same attitude of the past still remains: the mentally ill are felt to be moral lepers. A study by Jim Nunnally shows that most people, whether they are old or young, highly educated or with little schooling, feel that the mentally ill are "dangerous, dirty, unpredictable, and worthless."[19] But unlike the barbaric ancients who openly showed their intolerance toward the mentally ill, the civilized moderns try to hide their intolerance by maintaining a front of tolerance. Thus the mentally ill are often *publicly* spoken of as unfortunate but dignified as human beings, while they are at the same time *privately* considered as dangerous subhumans. Nunnally also finds that, although the general medical practitioners ought to know better, their underlying attitude toward the mentally ill is as negative as the general public's. This attitude may partly explain why medically trained psychiatrists do not even want to touch their patients, especially if the latter are poor and confined at public mental institutions. As one psychiatrist observes:

The curious thing to note about psychiatrists as doctors is in the realm of what they do. They never touch their patients. . . . The exceptions to this are rare and are frowned upon by the profession. I can clearly remember one of my supervisors confiding to me during my training that he sometimes patted his patients on the back on their way out of the office. Horrors! If discovered, he may be branded as an infidel.[20]

Just as psychiatrists are unconsciously afraid to touch their patients as if they were lepers, people with ordinary emotional problems may be reluctant to go near psychiatrists for fear of being stigmatized as insane. This fear seems justified. As one study suggests, individuals exhibiting a given behavior—whether normal or abnormal—are increasingly rejected as they move from (1) seeking no help, to (2) seeing a member of the clergy, to (3) consulting a physician, to (4) going to a psychiatrist, to (5) being admitted to a mental hospital. Individuals are much more likely to be rejected when they utilize the last two sources of help.[21]

THE COURT Since the public does not appreciate having the insane around, the court obliges by putting them away. The court can do this in three ways: by using involuntary commitment proceedings, abrogating the right to trial, and accepting the defense of insanity.

To take the first way, the court can hospitalize mentally ill people against their will. This involuntary hospitalization is for an indefinite period; it may be just for a few days or for a lifetime. Individuals can be released only if they can convince the hospital authorities of their recovery from mental illness. This is difficult to do, and it is not uncommon that many have been confined for over twenty years. The number of involuntarily confined mental patients at any given time in the United States has been estimated to range from 170,000 to 350,000 (or 40 to 90 percent of the total inmate population of public mental hospitals). In order for individuals to receive involuntary commitment, they need not commit a crime, nor be convicted of a crime, nor be charged with a crime. They only have to be judged by a court-appointed psychiatrist as mentally ill or, more commonly, as dangerous to themselves or others.

Since involuntary hospitalization is a serious matter, elaborate safeguards have been set up to protect the rights of the mentally ill. But these safeguards are often sidestepped or ignored. Many studies have shown that the judge, the psychiatrist, and the attorney are relatively careless in handling the commitment proceedings. Usually they take only two or three minutes to decide whether to commit the individual to a mental institution for an indeterminate period.[22] This is hardly enough time for serious psychiatric investigation and for proper presentation by the attorney—only enough time for presentation by the patient's relatives, the ones who usually try to get the patient committed in the first place. In addition, court psychiatrists are relatively incompetent and, even if they were highly competent, the psychiatric diagnostic procedure is relatively unreliable. As a result, many mentally ill persons who are not dangerous at all are coercively committed. For example, in one study, a substantial majority (63 percent) of patients committed were discovered to be not dangerous.[23]

It may be pointed out that, according to a recent U.S. Supreme Court ruling, a state may not involuntarily confine any mentally ill person who is not dangerous. In addition, many public hospitals have already decided on their own to release nondangerous patients.[24] Despite all this, findings from relevant studies still lead us to expect that the poor, blacks, and those who cannot afford legal counsel are more likely than the better-off to continue getting psychiatrically incarcerated.[25]

Another way the court hospitalizes people is by saying that they do not have the right to be tried. It is our fundamental right to stand trial if we are charged with a crime. But this right is typically taken away from the mentally ill. Thus, when individuals are accused of a crime, the court will decide whether to try them or not. If a person is found to be mentally ill, the court will rule that he or she is not competent to stand trial.

Without benefit of a trial and thus without having been found guilty, the defendant in question is ordered committed to a mental hospital—usually a hospital for the criminally insane—for an indefinite period. In effect, this person who has not been convicted of a crime receives harsher punishment than does another person who has been convicted. The hospital rarely gives the nonconvicted defendant any therapy. Commitment to the hospital is not just similar to commitment to a prison. It is worse, because the nonconvicted defendant is incarcerated for a longer period than the convicted criminal. According to one estimate, over 50 percent of these nonconvicted defendants who have been found incompetent to stand trial (many of whom have been charged with trivial misdemeanors only) spend the rest of their lives in mental institutions.[26] Even many criminals who have been convicted of murder do not suffer such a severe penalty.

Finally, the court can imprison a criminally charged person in a mental institution by accepting a defense of insanity. There have been two major rules for playing the game of insanity defense. The first is the M'Naghten Rule, according to which the accused can successfully claim insanity if at the time of committing the crime the individual did not know "the nature and quality of the act he was doing or, if he did know it, that he did not know he was doing what was wrong." This is also known as the *right-or-wrong test*. This test has been in existence for over one hundred years and used in about two-thirds of the states in this country. But the M'Naghten Rule did not allow psychiatrists to judge whether the accused was indeed insane at the time of committing the crime. It only allowed them to offer an opinion on the accused's ability to tell right from wrong. Then in 1954 the U.S. Court of Appeals broadened the definition of the M'Naghten Rule by handing down the Durham Rule. This new rule states that the accused is not guilty if his or her crime "was the product of mental disease or mental defect." It is also called the *product test*. This has brought cheers from the psychiatrists as they are now able to play a bigger part in the game.

But the Durham Rule has created a great deal of confusion. The reason is that psychiatric diagnoses are often unreliable and, when presented by different psychiatrists, contradictory. Thus the Durham Rule is not often put in practice. It is used only in cases where there has been extremely erratic behavior on the part of the accused and everybody can easily agree that the accused is mentally ill. If the Durham Rule is used and the defendant is *acquitted* by reason of insanity, he or she does not actually get acquitted or gain freedom at all. Instead, the person is committed to a hospital for the criminally insane. This is worse than being sent to a prison. For many offenders spend more time in psychiatric confinement when "acquitted" than they would if they had been found guilty and served the maximum sentence in a prison.

In sum, the court's treatment of the mentally ill—whether by using the involuntary commitment proceedings, or by abrogating the defendant's right to trial, or by accepting the insanity defense—amounts to a form of cruel and unusual punishment. It is, in part, a legacy from the past, though it appears more civilized than burning or chaining the insane. Ironically, all this has been partly brought about by the worthy intention to humanize the penal system by replacing punishment of with treatment of criminals. In 1930 the renowned psychiatrist and humanitarian Karl Menninger wrote:

The declaration continues about travesties upon justice that result from the introduction of psychiatric methods into courts. But what science or scientist is interested in justice? Is pneumonia just? Or cancer? . . . *The scientist is seeking the amelioration of an unhappy situation.* This can be secured only if the scientific laws controlling the situation can be discovered and complied with, and not by talking of "justice." [27] [Emphasis added.]

THE MENTAL HOSPITAL The idea of hospitalizing the mentally ill can be traced to the Aesculapian temples of ancient Greece. These temples, named after the Greek god of healing, were essentially medical centers that admitted mental patients on the side. For these patients, the priest-physicians prescribed rest and potions as well as served as interpreters of their dreams. But these services were reserved for the elite only, and those who could not afford them were treated in the same dismal ways as in other societies, which we have already discussed. Then in the late eighteenth century, a group of English Quakers led by William Tuke established an asylum for the mentally ill. To avoid the bad connotation of the word *asylum*, it was named York Retreat. It offered its mental patients rest and a chance to recuperate. Word of its success spread to various countries. Yet most mental patients, particularly the poor ones, continued to be shabbily treated. In the midnineteenth century, a retired American school teacher named Dorothea Dix began to campaign for the humane treatment of the mentally ill, and within forty years she helped build over thirty state mental hospitals. These hospitals were relatively well staffed; they were indeed a far cry from the jails and poorhouses where patients had been locked up before. Gradually, however, those state hospitals became bogged down with such problems as lack of money, lack of staff, and overabundance of patients. As a consequence, custody replaced treatment as the hospitals' operating principle.

Today the essential characteristics of mental hospitals can be appreciated from sociologist Erving Goffman's portrayal of the hospitals as "total institutions." [28] A *total institution* is a place of residence and work where a large number of individuals are cut off from the larger society and lead an enclosed, regimented life. Prisons are the clearest example of this, and mental hospitals, especially when looked at from the patient's position, are no different from prisons. Thus the patients' needs and desires are subordinated to the smooth operation of the mental hospitals. More specifically, the hospital staff tend to treat the patients as if they were objects rather than humans. Various aspects of this dehumanizing treatment were recently observed by psychiatrist D. L. Rosenhan and his associates after they had got themselves admitted to twelve different mental hospitals by pretending to be psychotic. Rosenhan gives these revealing and telling examples of the dehumanizing attitude toward the patients:

A nurse unbuttoned her uniform to adjust her brassiere in the presence of an entire ward of viewing men. One did not have the sense that she was being seductive. Rather, she didn't notice us. A group of staff persons might point to a patient in the dayroom and discuss him animatedly, as if he were not there.[29]

By thus considering them as objects that can neither see nor feel, staff people tend to call their patients names, beat them, prevent them from talking to them unless they are talked to first, enter and examine their rooms and possessions at any time they wish, monitor their personal hygiene and waste evacuation in the toilet, and so on. Such dehumanization of the patient as a prisoner characterizes the inner workings of mental hospitals, though these hospitals may outwardly appear different from prisons.

There are a number of related consequences from the depersonalization of the patient. First, the patient tends to exhibit symptoms that are (incorrectly) taken by the staff as indicative of mental illness rather than (correctly) considered as resulting from the staff's own doing. For example, when the staff strip recalcitrant patients and put them in isolation, the patients may tear up mattresses or write with feces on the wall, which the staff will then interpret as befitting very sick people, rather than people who are attempting to express human individuality or to stand apart from the dehumanizing place forced upon them.[30]

Second, some patients develop what has been called "hospitalitis" or "institutionalism." This hospital-caused problem is characterized by a deep sense of hopelessness, pervasive loss of initiative, deterioration of social skills, and inability to function in larger society. Thus the patients are unwilling to leave the hospital, or are judged by the staff as so completely hopeless that they are institutionalized until they die.

Third, some mental patients become better diagnosticians of insanity than the professional staff. As Rosenhan found out, after he and his sane associates had themselves committed to insane hospitals, the mental patients could easily detect their sanity—while the staff could not. This need not be surprising. For the psychiatric staff, being aloof from the patients, cannot see the latter as whole, multidimensional persons, thereby failing to discern the numerous aspects of their behavior. In contrast, the patients, living intimately with one another, can develop deeper insight into one another's behavior and thus into insanity in general.

Perhaps as a result of their relative failure to cure their patients, mental hospitals have increasingly used tranquilizing and antidepressant drugs to alleviate the symptoms rather than eliminate the cause of mental disorder. In addition, legal groups and individuals have taken up the cause of mental patients, helping to change laws and policies so as to shorten the length of hospitalization. In consequence, the size of the mental hospital population has been decreasing since 1957. While the number of new admissions has been increasing, they are discharged in a much shorter time than before, so that this does not affect the decrease in the total hospitalized population at any given time.

COMMUNITY MENTAL HEALTH CENTER The notion of community mental health care was initiated in the 1950s, and then in 1963 Congress passed the Community Mental Health Centers Act to provide funds for helping states and communities to build and staff the centers. Today there are at least 450 such centers in various communities. The objective is to offer professional and paraprofessional help to the emotionally disturbed. Resources such as hospitals, courts, police departments, welfare agencies, schools, churches, employers, co-workers, neighbors, and other concerned citizens are integrated so as to provide support to anyone in time of stress. Patients can receive in-patient or out-patient care in their community. This fact is very important, for people do not have to suffer the inconvenience of leaving their usual surroundings; do not get put away in some distant, isolated, large, and dehumanizing institution; are free from the stigma usually attached to incarceration in a mental institution; and have a better chance of recovery because of the active participation of family members and others who are genuinely concerned and treat them with respect.

It may be necessary to discuss the last point. It appears that being highly professional as a psychiatrist but without relating to the patient on his or her social level, as has been observed in large mental hospitals, is relatively ineffective in treating the patient. Contrary to the belief of traditional or medically oriented psychiatrists, curing mental disorder is radically different from healing a broken leg, in that the latter may require only objective professionalism but the former requires mostly genuine compassion. This implies that nonpsychiatrists may do as good a job as, or even a better job than, psychiatrists in treating mental patients. As one psychiatrist observes:

Studies have been done with college students, housewives, medical corpsmen, hospital aides, and just indigenous neighborhood residents, showing that they obtained about the same results as the professionals using psychotherapy with patients. One such study, for example, compared college students with psychiatrists and psychiatric social workers doing group therapy with hospitalized psychiatric patients. The college students got the best results. . . . Psychiatrists, then, who turn out to be good psychotherapists, do so in spite of, not because of, their medical training.[31]

One therapeutic program involving the use of student volunteers has been very successful. The statement of one patient who was discharged after spending five years on the back ward of a mental hospital suggests the reason for the program's success. The ex-patient told one of the student volunteers: "What you did for me was to treat me like a human being, like someone you wanted for a friend and could like."[32] This is why compassionate student volunteers, along with other equally compassionate nonprofessionals and professionals, have been a great asset to community mental health centers.

However, the biggest problem plaguing the centers today is the psychiatrists who cannot shake off their traditional sense of omniscience—thinking that they know better than any nonpsychiatrist about how to treat the mentally ill.[33] It is this professional delusion of grandeur that has prevented psychiatrists from regarding their nonpsychiatrist colleagues as their professional equals—and from treating their patients as friends that they could like. Thus these psychiatrists may turn themselves into authority figures, but they are ineffectual therapists.

THEORIES OF MENTAL DISORDER

There are two conflicting ways of looking at mental disorder, similar to the two conflicting ways of looking at deviance in general, discussed in Chapter 1. The two views on mental disorder are often referred to as the *medical* (psychiatric) *model* and the *labeling model*.

THE MEDICAL MODEL

Two basic assumptions concerning the nature of mental disorder can be found in the medical model.

One assumption is that mental disorder is assumed to be an objectively real and thus clearly definable entity. This assumption underlies the fact that psychiatrists use the psychiatric diagnostic classification system to identify a mental illness in the same way as physicians use medical nosology to identify a bodily disease.

Mental disorder is also assumed to be the same as, or analogous to, physical disease. This assumption can be illustrated by the ways in which medically oriented psychiatrists and psychiatric researchers treat the subject. The following are some examples.

Psychiatrists have produced research evidence to support their belief that schizophrenia, the most common form of psychosis, has both genetic and biochemical causes. Although such evidence has been questioned by other scientists, medically oriented psychiatrists continue to conduct research along the same lines. Like medical researchers, they believe that more sophisticated instruments with more precise chemical tests and more accurate surgical techniques can be developed to produce more convincing evidence of the physical factors in mental illness. Moreover, psychiatrists use drugs and surgery in trying to cure mental illness, just as physicians use drugs and surgery to cure physical disease. If they use psychotherapy, these psychiatrists attempt to cure mental disorder as if it were a physical disease located within the patient's body. This is why they aim the treatment at mental patients *alone*—even though their fathers, mothers, spouses, or others may have made their lives so miserable that they developed the mental disorder. If they use the treatment of *involuntary commitment*, these psychiatrists have the mental patient, not the relatives or others who may have been responsible for the emotional disturbance, committed to mental hospitals—for the patient alone is assumed to have the disease just as a leper alone is assumed to have leprosy.

THE LABELING MODEL

The medical model has stirred criticism both from within the psychiatric profession and from without. These criticisms suggest, in one way or another, that mental disorder is not a sickness but rather a label imposed upon some disturbing behavior. We shall discuss three of these criticisms.

MENTAL ILLNESS AS A MYTH   Psychiatrist Thomas Szasz has sharply criticized the medical model for assuming that mental illness is just as real and objective as a bodily disease. Psychiatrists who embrace the medical model, according to Szasz, are actually spreading a kind of psychiatric propaganda: "Mental illness is a myth, whose function it is to disguise and thus render more palatable the bitter pill of moral conflicts in human relations." [34]

In saying that mental illness is a myth, Szasz does *not* imply that the behavior to which this label is attached does not exist. Szasz simply objects to the use of the label because it masks as well as distorts the true nature of the behavior labeled *mental illness* and implies that it is similar to physical disease.

The true nature of *mental illness*, in Szasz's view, can be more accurately referred to as "a problem in living," "moral conflict in human relations," or "a communication expressing some socially unacceptable idea." All these terms imply that so-called mental illness is not a medical problem, but a social and moral one. It stems not from within the individual—as physical illness does—but from without. More precisely, it is a conflict between the "mental patients" *and* those around them, such as family, neighbors, friends, or the whole society. But, in labeling them *mentally ill* as if they had a disease *within* them, psychiatrists are led to control them alone with such means as psychotherapy, electric shock treatment, lobotomy, psychiatric incarceration, or other forms of depriving the "patients'" civil rights. Such psychiatric "cures" are, in effect, not for the good of the "patient" but for the good of the others—who end up enjoying the double freedom from being "cured" and from being disturbed by the "patient."

MENTAL ILLNESS AS CONSEQUENCE OF LABELING   Sociologist Thomas Scheff also views mental illness as a myth. More precisely, he views it as an ambiguous label imposed on mental illness. He calls mental illness "residual rule-breaking" because it is such a residue of numerous diverse kinds of rule violations that the culture does not provide as clear-cut a label for it as it does for, say, criminal behavior. This is why the label *mental illness* does not clearly suggest the violation of a rule, while the label *crime* does. Thus it makes for a great deal of arbitrariness in defining mental illness, which in turn leads Scheff to emphasize the importance of *labeling* rather than the labeled *behavior* for the "mentally ill" person. Scheff's theory of mental illness, then, shows how labeling a person mentally ill may lead the person to develop stabilized or chronic mental disorder.[35]

First of all, Scheff assumes that psychiatric symptoms arise from diverse sources. These sources may include genetic, biochemical, physiological, and psychological factors, or whatever you can think of—such as fear of combat, combat fatigue, overwork, continuous lack of sleep, or ingestion of psychoactive drugs. Many people, after being influenced by one of these factors, show such psychiatric symptoms as hearing voices, seeing visions, or imagining fantastic events. Yet they are not labeled mentally ill. Why? The reason is that most psychiatric symptoms appear in apparently normal people who are prone to deny they are mentally ill, and the symptoms last only for a short while. Why do a small minority of these people eventually become chronically mentally disturbed?

The explanation, according to Scheff, is as follows: Members of the general public have absorbed the stereotyped imagery of mental disorder during their early childhood. In their first years of school, they already know what kind of person is "crazy," "a kook," "a nut," or "off his rocker." As adults, they continue to have the stereotypes of insanity reinforced by the mass media and by comments and jokes in ordinary social intercourse. These stereotypes of insanity enable about-to-be-labeled mentally ill people to "understand" the nature of insanity. Once labeled mentally ill, they are encouraged in one way or another to acknowledge their mental illness. If they ask to be admitted to mental hospitals, they may be complimented for "doing the right thing." If they refuse to see themselves as insane and thus are forced to enter the hospital, staff and patients may pressure them to admit their insanity. After release from the hospital, they may attempt to resume their normal life, but, as former mental patients, they are likely to be rejected by others. Consequently, they may become extremely confused, anxious, and ashamed. In such an emotional crisis, they accept their families', psychiatrists', and community's judgment that they are mentally ill.

In view of the foregoing, Scheff concludes that labeling a person mentally ill is the single most important factor in making the person with some psychiatric symptoms become a chronic mental patient.

INSANITY AS SUPERSANITY British psychiatrist R. D. Laing also considers mental illness a myth, but his way of attacking the myth differs from Szasz's.[36] Laing criticizes his fellow psychiatrists for believing in the myth that their mental patient's experience is somehow unreal, invalid, false, perverse, or otherwise inferior to their own and other normals' experience. How can insane people's experiences be inferior, while it is the normal people who have killed 100 million of their fellow human beings in the last fifty years? Psychiatrists are professionally and socially conditioned to say that the insane are *dis*oriented as to space and time, without consciously reflecting on the nature of space and time. Laing points out that there are two types of space and time, one being outer and the other inner. Thus when a psychiatrist prejudicially considers the mental patient as disoriented, the patient actually is oriented to *inner* space and time, while the psychiatrist is oriented to *outer* space and time. By *inner* orientation, Laing refers to the experience of seeing those realities that have no external or objective presence, such as imagination, dreams, fantasies, trances, and the realities of contemplation and meditation. For example, when you simply experience God's presence, you are having an inner experience; but if you rationally, objectively argue that God exists, you are demonstrating your orientation to the outer world.

Laing believes that insanity involves entering a state of more rather than less reality, of supersanity rather than subsanity, of mental breakthrough rather than breakdown. If insanity or supersanity is so wonderful, beautiful, and exciting, however, why do many mental patients appear so unhappy with their experience?

Their unhappiness can be traced to the society's extremely negative attitude toward madness. Due to our society's greater appreciation for outer consciousness than for inner, we are conditioned to *respect* individuals who explore a jungle, climb Mount Everest, fly a balloon across the Atlantic, rocket to the moon, or embark on other similar adventures. While we are conditioned to respect these travelers in the outer space and time of consciousness, we are conditioned to *dis*respect the other kind of travelers—travelers who journey into the inner space and time. This is why, when astronauts return from outer space, they are welcomed back as great heroes and are able to get the best jobs available, but when schizophrenics return from inner space, they are rejected as ex-mental patients and are lucky to get any job.

Because of our far more positive attitude toward outer than inner exploration, highly competent persons from favorable home environments would embark on the voyage into outer space willingly and with such advantages as moral support from others, prevoyage training and preparation, and all the information and apparatus necessary for making the voyage a successful one. In contrast, most mental patients have been forced into inner space and time by being placed in an untenable, unlivable position in the "normal" world. Therefore, being unknowledgeable about and unprepared for the voyage into inner consciousness, they do not know how to deal with the terrors, spirits, or demons to be encountered on the voyage. The result is that they get lost in the inner world, which is why they are unhappy.

CRITICISMS OF LABELING MODEL   Sociologists who adhere to the medical model have criticized the labeling model. They argue for one thing that mental illness is not a myth but real behavior that exists all over the world. For example, John Clausen and Carol Huffine write: "If mental illness is a myth, as Szasz and Scheff and others propose, it is remarkable that the manifestation of the myth should be found in antiquity and in preliterate societies as in modern industrial societies, in the People's Republic of China as in fascist states." [37] Apparently Clausen and Huffine misunderstand what Szasz means by calling mental illness a myth. By *myth*, Szasz refers to the use of the label *mental illness*, not the behavior so labeled. Further, Clausen and Huffine's criticism serves to divert attention from Szasz's reason for calling mental illness a myth, which is to show the reality of how the label *mentally ill* unjustly victimizes individuals so labeled.

Scheff also assumes that the label unjustly victimizes the individual. To Scheff, the victimization involves committing individuals to mental institutions, and thereby causing them to become chronic mental patients, even though they may have only mild, harmless psychiatric symptoms. This labeling argument has also been attacked by critics. One of them, Walter Gove, claims that many research studies have refuted Scheff's labeling argument:

The evidence shows that a substantial majority of the persons who are hospitalized have a serious psychiatric disturbance. . . . Once prospective patients come into contact with public officials, a substantial screening still occurs, presumably sorting out persons who are being railroaded or who are less disturbed. [In addition], the studies reviewed, while in no way denying the existence of the processes outlined by [Scheff], suggest that mental hospitalization does not necessarily or even typically lead to [chronic mental illness].[38]

Therefore, Gove concludes that the evidence supports his own medical model more than Scheff's labeling model. In response, Scheff claims that the studies that he analyzes give stronger support to his own labeling model than to Gove's medical model.[39] At this time, it is impossible to say which model is *more* valid. We can only say that *both* models are valid to *some*, as-yet-undetermined degree.

A third criticism from the scientific standpoint, is that Laing's concept of insanity as supersanity is worthless, as it is merely a value judgment that cannot be objectively validated. But scientifically oriented sociologists may still derive some useful propositions from Laing's analysis. They may derive, for example, this proposition: groups, societies, or cultures that appreciate inner consciousness have lower rates of mental disorder than those that do not. From this proposition, it may be hypothesized that religious groups have lower rates of mental illness than nonreligious groups; that American Indians have lower rates of mental illness than white Americans; that Eastern societies have lower rates of mental illness than Western societies, and so on.

POWER THEORY APPLIED

Power theory can be used to integrate the medical and the labeling models. With power theory, we may partially agree with the medical view that mental disorder can be clearly defined. Specifically, we can differentiate relatively severe types of mental illness from the far less severe—such as psychosis versus neurosis. At the same time, as power theory would suggest, the poor are more likely to develop the more severe psychoses while the rich the less severe neuroses. This fact has been amply supported by existing data, as we have seen.

On the other hand, we may partially agree with the labeling view that labeling people as mentally ill has undesirable consequences for them. At the same time, as power theory would suggest, relatively powerless people are more likely to be labeled mentally ill and suffer the consequences, when compared with more powerful people. Many studies have indicated this positive relationship between powerlessness and mental hospitalization. It has been illustrated by Szasz as follows:

The problem that sends the rich woman to Reno is likely to send the poor woman to the state hospital. When the butcher, baker, or candlestick maker thinks that the communists are after him he is easily dispatched to the mental hospital; when a Secretary of Defense thinks so, who will constrain him? These examples illustrate that to make a psychiatric diagnosis of a person is to constrain him. But how can the weak constrain the strong?[40]

In view of the lesser risk of social and legal oppression for their neuroses coupled with the privilege of channeling their neurotic energy into aggrandizing power and success, the powerful neurotics may be said to be under lesser social control than are the powerless psychotics. At the same time, powerful individuals are more likely to be very ambitious, which may make them fear the prospect of failure and thus drive them to work compulsively. Thus we may speculate that the powerful are more prone to neurosis than the powerless are prone to psychosis. But since powerful neurotics are very likely to enjoy the choice of seeing themselves as normal rather than neurotic, and since powerless psychotics are very likely to be coercively labeled by authorities as psychotic, we may expect research data to show a smaller proportion of higher-status neurotics than lower-status psychotics.

The symbiotic relationship between the powerful and the powerless in regard to mental disorder seems to operate in two ways. First, a neurotic obsession with power, which the powerful are more likely to have, may drive the powerful to work compulsively to achieve greater power.[41] In contrast, the psychotic symptom of withdrawal from the normal world, which the powerless are more likely to experience, may drive the powerless to a more powerless position in a mental institution or in the community. Thus, while powerful neurotics get more powerful and powerless psychotics get more powerless, the societal condition of inequality will be reinforced, which in turn keeps the vicious circle going by producing more neuroses among the powerful and more psychoses among the powerless.

A second way the symbiotic relationship operates is by the fact that the more the poor are labeled psychotic, the more the rich will be labeled neurotic. This is because the social and legal consequences for the psychotic (such as involuntary hospitalization) are so great that psychiatrists are usually more careful with diagnoses of the rich, and thus more likely to diagnose them as harmlessly neurotic. Since the highly skilled psychiatrists are usually induced to practice their profession lucratively with rich neurotic patients in their private offices, this leaves the court-related mental cases to the less skilled and less well-paid psychiatrists who are more likely to diagnose poor people as dangerously psychotic, and therefore have them committed to mental institutions.

SUMMARY

Mental disorder is an extremely common phenomenon. At least it is as common as physical illness. But just as there are different types of physical illness, so there are different types of mental disorder, which range from the very minor to the very severe. Only the more severe types have been discussed here.

There are two major categories of mental disorder: organic and functional. The former is strictly physical in nature, while the latter less so. Of these two, functional disorder is by far the more prevalent and has thus attracted much more attention from psychiatrists, psychologists, and sociologists. Functional disorder is further divided into three categories: psychotic, neurotic, and character disorder. Psychotic disorders are the most debilitating for the individual, neurotic disorder less, and character disorder least. Psychosis is characterized by being out of touch with reality, neurosis by being constantly worried about little things, and character disorder by any disturbing behavior that cannot be considered as either psychotic or neurotic. Each of these three types of functional psychosis is further divided into subtypes. This typology of mental disorder has been criticized for its relative unreliability in diagnosing mental disorder.

Sex, residence, and class have consistently been shown in many empirical studies to be related to mental disorder. Women are more likely than men to suffer from depression, while men from antisocial disorder. Psychosis is more common in rural areas, while neurosis and personality disorder are more prevalent in urban areas. Lower classes tend more to become psychotic and receive harsh or no therapy; upper classes tend more to become neurotic and receive mild and beneficial therapy. There are other social factors, such as cultural background, which have less consistently been found to be linked to mental disorder.

Mental disorder generates great emotion against, and thus maltreatment of, the individuals who suffer from it. In the past, the insane were believed to be possessed with the devil and so were burned alive. By the midseventeenth century, they were chained or otherwise treated like animals. Today the treatment of the insane is more refined than in the past. The public secretly considers the mentally ill as moral lepers; the court puts them away; and the mental hospital dehumanizes them. But the population of hospitalized mental patients has been on the decline, though the number of new admissions has increased. Shorter hospital stay, tranquilizers and antidepressants, community mental health centers, out-patient care, and other factors have helped reduce the hospitalized population.

Two models of mental disorder are in conflict. The medical model views mental disorder as objectively real and identifiable as physical disease. In contrast, the labeling model sees mental illness as a label that has undesirable consequences for individuals labeled mentally ill. Proponents of each model defend their model as well as attack the other model. Power theory can be used to integrate these two models and to show the symbiotic relationship between rich and poor mentally disordered.

SUGGESTED READINGS

Brandt, Anthony. *Reality Police: The Experience of Insanity in America*. New York: William Morrow & Co., 1975.

Friedrich, Otto. *Going Crazy: An Inquiry into Madness in Our Time*. New York: Simon & Schuster, 1976.

Goffman, Erving. *Asylums*. Garden City, N.Y.: Anchor Books, 1961.

Gove, Walter R. "Societal Reaction as an Explanation of Mental Illness: An Evaluation." *American Sociological Review* 35 (October 1970): 873–884.

Hollingshead, August B. and Fredrick C. Redlich. *Social Class and Mental Illness*. New York: Wiley, 1958.

Laing, R. D. *The Politics of Experience*. New York: Ballantine Books, 1967.

Nunnally, Jim C., Jr. *Public Conceptions of Mental Health*. New York: Holt, Rinehart & Winston, 1961.

Rosenhan, D. L. "On Being Sane in Insane Places," *Science*, January 19, 1973, pp. 250–258.

Scheff, Thomas J. *Being Mentally Ill*. Chicago: Aldine, 1966.

Spitzer, Stephan P. and Norman K. Denzin, eds. *The Mental Patient*. New York: McGraw-Hill, 1968.

Szasz, Thomas S. *Ideology and Insanity*. Garden City, New York: Anchor Books, 1970.

12 SWINGING

S*winging* may be defined as the temporary exchange of marital partners for sexual purposes. When this phenomenon was first discussed in several popular magazines in the mid-1950s, it was called *wife swapping*. In view of today's sensitivity to sexual equality, *wife swapping* has become a sexist and crude term. Instead of using it, sociologists coined the terms *mate swapping* or *comarital sex*. But the players of this sex game prefer to call themselves *swingers* and their game *swinging*. Thus sociologists also use these two words.

Swinging is a new form of adultery. While the traditional type of adultery involves having an extramarital affair behind the spouse's back, swinging is an open sexual event in which both husband and wife agree to participate. For this reason, swinging has been referred to as open, consensual, or faithful adultery.

Being open adultery, swinging provokes horror or outrage from conventional society. If a man proposes to his best friend that each have sexual intercourse with the other's wife, his best friend would be likely to consider him crazy and their friendship would probably immediately break up. The same result would happen to a married woman if she suggests to her closest girlfriend that they swap their husbands for sexual purposes. It appears that conventional couples are not so much horrified by adultery per se as by the openness of adultery in swinging. For the traditional, covert, or secret adultery is relatively common in our society. Even thirty years ago —according to the Kinsey Report—about 50 percent of American married men and 26 percent of American married women had committed adultery by the time they reached the age of 40. The report also indicated that over 70 percent of men wished at one time or another to have extramarital intercourse.[1] Compared with this traditional type of adultery, swinging is far less common. Swingers constitute probably no more than one percent of the married population.[2]

Although it is considered extremely deviant, swinging has clearly become more public. Back in the mid-1950s, the popular press only occasionally published sensational stories about some suburban swap clubs or sex orgies. Today, all the major cities in this country have a number of clubs and bars that openly cater to swingers. Swinging parties are regularly held and swinging magazines are regularly published, so that swingers can easily find sexual partners. Since 1970, movies about swinging, such as *All the Loving Couples* and *Bob & Carol & Ted & Alice* are no longer considered hardcore pornography as they were in the past.[3]

THE NATURE OF SWINGING

Almost all the sociologists and anthropologists who have studied swinging have used the participant-observation method of investigation. Some of them have merely observed the swinging scene—without actually participating in it. Others have actually participated in swinging, though to a lesser extent than the average swinger. Out of this social scientific research, there has emerged a rapidly growing literature on swinging. The aspects of swinging that have been frequently discussed are: how swingers get together; the variety of sexual experience in swinging; the subcultural values of swinging; the characteristics of swingers; and the consequences of swinging for the people involved. Let us turn to each of these five topics.

GETTING TOGETHER

Four ways of finding swinging couples have been identified. They are personal seduction, personal reference, swingers' bars or clubs, and through advertisement.

PERSONAL SEDUCTION This method involves seducing acquaintances or friends into the swinging scene. As has been implied above, this is an extremely difficult method to apply because of conventional society's powerful taboo against mate swapping. The seduction attempt may easily backfire and thus break up the friendship. Swingers rarely resort to this method of finding like-minded couples.

The few swingers who do succeed in soliciting new couples for mate swapping usually rely on a subtle method of seduction. They may bring up the subject of swinging during a casual conversation, and then assess their friends' reactions toward it. If they find that the other couple do not object to it, the swingers may proceed to ask the couple whether they themselves could ever get into swinging. From then on, the swingers would decide whether to seduce the couple or to back off. The trick is for the swingers to make the mate-sharing encounter appear to occur spontaneously. Some swingers, in fact, began their swinging careers in a spontaneous manner. Here is how a female swinger describes the spontaneous way in which she and her husband began to swing with their friends:

Tom and I had been friends with Johnny and Carol for several years. Actually, Tom and Johnny went to college together. We went many places together and usually got together at least two or three times a month. One evening someone brought up the subject of "wife-swapping" and we all started to talk about it, and no one actually was totally against it. The next time we got together, we talked about it again, and decided after several sessions that it might not be the worst thing that could happen. Carol and I told the men that we would not simply go to bed with a person cold, that is, jump into bed with someone whom you did not care emotionally about. Oh, I liked Johnny, but I never actually thought about going to bed with him. Well, to tell the truth, the thought had crossed my mind a few times. Well, to make a long story short, we played some party games, strip poker, and then when everyone started to get into the mood, we did it. After that, the swinging became more and more evident as a focal point of our relationship.[4]

PERSONAL REFERENCE   In order to meet new couples by personal reference from other swinging couples, you obviously have to know some swinging couples first. Thus the personal reference method can be used only if other ways of contacting swingers have been employed. Personal references can be obtained from veteran swingers. Veteran swingers usually keep albums or scrapbooks containing the pictures, body statistics, ages, names, and telephone numbers of the couples with whom they have swung. To introduce you to a given couple in the album, the swingers tell you that the couple is very nice. Such may be the case even if they do not like the couple at all. For example, when anthropologist Gilbert Bartell asked an attractive young female swinger why she kept the names and phone numbers of what she called "moldy" (old, ugly, or no good) couples, she replied, "Why, to give to other couples who are moldy, of course." [5]

THE SWINGERS' BAR   Particularly for those who live in a large city, visiting a swingers' bar is a productive way to find swinging couples. The bar owner may advertise in swingers' magazines or underground newspapers, may use mailing lists from swingers' clubs to invite the swingers to come to the bar for free drinks during certain hours on certain days, or may regularly contract with swingers' organizations to let them have exclusive use of the bar for a "swingers' night."

In some ways, the swingers' bar can be compared to the gay and the singles' bar. For one thing, like the other two, the swingers' bar is basically a sexual marketplace where sexual objects can be searched for and picked up. Another thing is that the sexual traders in the swingers' bar, like those in the gay and the singles' bar, place a high premium on youthfulness and physical attractiveness of their intended sexual partners. Also, in all three kinds of bars, once a sexual exchange is agreed upon, it will be carried out in a hotel room or private home rather than on the premises of the bar.

The scene in a swingers' bar, however, seems to differ from that in the other two types of bar. Swinging couples appear bolder than gays or singles in soliciting sexual partners. Upon entry into the bar, swingers scan the crowd, and once they have spotted an attractive couple, they walk over and strike up a conversation and then quickly determine whether the couple wants to swing with them. If the couple does not, they simply move on to another couple and start over again. The swinging husband and wife seem to have less fear of rejection, because they operate as a team and thus can easily derive moral support from each other. If they have not found an attractive couple willing to swing with them by the time the bar is about to close, they usually become less choosy and settle for a less attractive couple. Very often swingers find more than one willing couple, in which case they will exchange names, addresses, and phone numbers with these couples so that swinging dates can be made at some other time. This is why most couples bring pens and address books or paper to swingers' bars.

ADVERTISEMENT   The most common method of contacting swinging couples is to place an advertisement or to answer one in a swingers' magazine. Almost all swingers have at some time tried this method. There are about fifty nationally sold swingers' magazines. The main function of each of these magazines is to make money by publishing personal ads. The larger magazines, such as *Select* and *The Seeker*, carry thousands of ads from married and single swingers all over the United States. Each of the ads has a code number and shows the place where the advertising couple resides. Usually it is also accompanied by a picture showing the wife's naked body. Examples of these ads are as follows:

C-60,214 Detroit

Attractive, professional couple in early 30's, seek other happily married couples for swinging pleasures. He's 6', 178, dark blond hair and blue eyes. She's 5'4", 115, 37–25–37, blond hair and green eyes. Send photos of both and phone for early reply. Discretion assured and expected.

26,720-C Newark

Attractive, happily married, responsive couple, he's 28, 5'9", 150, she's 26, 5'2", 110, would love to meet you if you are sincere, discreet and into swinging for sheer enjoyment without hassles. All with photo and phone answered promptly.

In answering an ad, you have to put the letter in an envelope on which you write the code number, enclose it with a stamp and forwarding fee in another envelope, and send it to the publisher of the magazine, who will in turn send your letter to the advertiser. The letter is usually concise, giving the letter-writing couple's ages, heights, and weights, stating the kinds of sexual acts they enjoy, and containing the picture and phone number asked for by the advertiser.

If the two couples tentatively decide that they might want to swing with each other, they arrange for a meeting at a given time and place. Usually the first meeting takes place on "neutral ground," such as a bar or restaurant, where neither couple need feel committed to swing. If they find each other compatible, the couples will swing at the home of one of the couples. Sometimes they use a couple's home for their first meeting, but with the understanding that they would swing only if both couples want to—no pressure would be used if one couple does not want to swing.

VARIETIES OF SWINGING EXPERIENCE

After the two couples get together and are in the right mood to exchange partners, they may choose to *swing closed* or to *swing open*.[6] Closed swinging means that the two couples swap partners and then go off to separate bedrooms to make love. In open swinging, the two couples exchange partners and engage in sexual activity in the same room or on the same bed. These two patterns of sexual exchange also appear in any party scene involving three or more swinging couples. Another variation of open swinging involves a threesome—husband and wife swinging together with a third person who may be male or female. In sum, there are four specific forms of swinging experience: closed swinging; open swinging; swinging party; and threesome swinging.

CLOSED SWINGING   After an hour or so of drinking and talking in the living room, closed swinging may begin with one male asking another's wife to go into the bedroom. Sometimes some sexual preliminaries are carried out in the living room, but kissing is often avoided in the presence of one's own spouse. Yet once the two swinging partners are in the privacy of the bedroom—separated from their respective spouses—they do a great deal of kissing.

Since the situation is usually charged with excitement, tension, anxiety, and nervousness, the male may either fail to have an erection or prematurely ejaculate. In either case, he will feel embarrassed, as he is usually under the influence of the popular belief that a man is a sexual failure if his partner fails to achieve orgasm. Consequently, he is driven to perform cunnilingus on her. This oral activity usually relieves him of his anxiety, as his partner can be more easily brought to orgasm. Then he will penetrate her, even if by that moment she has already climaxed. After this first round of sexual activity is over, he and she may rest, drink, smoke, talk, or fondle each other. In so doing, they are actually getting ready for the second round.

When the second round is supposed to start, the woman is all ready to go but the man is usually not. She will perform fellatio on him until he can perform again, and then they will have intercourse and both may climax together. Otherwise, he will practice cunnilingus on her. In so doing, he may take a long time to achieve an erection, but this does not disturb his masculine ego as prolonged oral action can lead his partner to climax. When they have satisfied each other, they may rest again and wait for a third round. Most swingers would call it quits after the second or third round—mainly because the man cannot make it any more.

Some couples who prefer open swinging consider closed swinging as "no better than cheating." This is primarily because closed swinging may cause a great deal of anxiety and jealousy in some mate swappers. The anxiety is over the possibility that one's spouse may find his or her swinging partner sexually superior to oneself.

For other mate swappers, closed swinging may have a number of advantages. One, it eases the fear that one may not perform adequately in public—with three or more people watching. Closed swinging is particularly good for the rookie swinger, as he or she is usually very nervous. Even many veteran swingers begin the evening with closed swinging so that they may become more relaxed and able to participate in open swinging. Two, closed swinging enables the man to feel free to do many things with his swinging partner, which he is afraid to do if his wife is watching. He can tell his swinging partner how beautiful she is, kiss her all over, act out wild fantasies with her, and ask her to do whatever turns him on. Third, swinging separately may help to maintain marital harmony between the swinging couple. After the swinging is over, husband and wife can lie to each other that they have not really enjoyed the swinging experience or that their swinging partner is not as sexually competent as their own spouse is.

OPEN SWINGING The first round of open swinging is generally the same as that of closed swinging. Two or more couples exchange partners and then each pair of swinging partners engages in about the same sexual activity that closed swinging partners engage in. After the first round is completed, the men rest, smoke, drink, and talk. During this rest period, the men may encourage the women to play with each other. Most of the women oblige. It may be noted that such lesbian action rarely occurs *before* the men have enjoyed orgasm with the women. The purpose for the men encouraging their female partners into homosexual action is twofold: (1) The men will be able to relieve themselves from the task of sexually satisfying the women, thereby giving themselves the needed time for building up another erection. (2) They will also be able to enjoy the voyeuristic thrill of watching a lesbian show, which in turn will help them achieve the erection faster. It may also be noted that, although most of the female swingers enjoy the lesbian experience, almost all the male swingers refrain from homosexuality because they find it too threatening to their masculine self-image.

SWINGING PARTY A swinging party usually starts out as if it were a cocktail party. There is talking and drinking but no sexual action. Although they are eager to do as soon as possible what they have come to the party for, the swingers are usually thwarted by the problem of how to get started. Their behavior has been compared to that of adolescents at a high school prom, where no couple wants to be the first one on the dance floor. Thus, fearing that everyone will become too sleepy or too drunk to perform if there is too much talking and drinking, the host and hostess try to persuade their guests to play a game such as strip poker, Spin the Bottle, or Interaction, until everybody is naked. By then most of the partygoers will be aroused enough to start swinging.

The swinging party has become increasingly popular, particularly among the younger couples. Many of these couples have become tired of spending too much time and effort on running ads and writing letters for contacting individual couples only. They now find that there are a number of advantages to entering the party scene. One, large parties help to ensure the fearful husband and wife that each will not get emotionally involved with a swinging partner. This is because having brief sexual contacts with many different people at large parties makes it difficult for swingers to develop emotional attachment to one another. Two, there is a greater selection of available sexual partners at the party. This reduces the risk of being embroiled in the awkward couple-to-couple situation where the husband likes the other man's wife but his own wife does not want to swing with the other man. Three, since they are still afraid of being discovered as swingers by their relatives, friends, and fellow workers, some swingers appreciate the anonymity provided by large parties, where they need not reveal their real names, telephone numbers, and addresses. Four, although in the couple-to-couple context no one need feel pressured to swing, this is even more true at the swinging party, where a person may simply watch and not perform at all.

THREESOME SWINGING   In threesome swinging, most couples swing with a female rather than a male. The selection of the extra female may appear to be determined by the husband more than by the wife. But this does not necessarily mean that the wife will not be able to enjoy having the other woman as much as he will. In fact, both husband and wife can derive the same amount of sexual pleasure from the other woman. Also, both the husband and the other woman can work together to satisfy the wife, just as both the wife and the other woman can simultaneously work on the husband.

If the third person is a male, the husband, being repulsed by male homosexuality, cannot enjoy as much as his wife can, except that he may settle for the voyeuristic pleasure of watching his wife in sexual entanglement with another man. In such a threesome situation, the two males may simultaneously work on the female, one performing coitus with or cunnilingus on her and the other kissing or caressing her. Or the two men take turns having sexual intercourse with her. Consequently, the woman will have more orgasms than either of the men. Although most couples will swing in a threesome with a single woman, there are many fewer single women than men who run ads in search of swinging couples. This is why swingers' magazines always encourage single females to place ads—by not charging them.

SUBCULTURE OF SWINGING

Swingers have developed a special language for communicating with one another; it may be referred to as the swinging language. Most of the words in this language are euphemisms alluding to various sexual acts.

"Straight" refers to heterosexual sex or, more specifically, coitus.

"French culture" means oral sex; "Greek culture" is anal intercourse; and "Roman culture" is group sex or an orgy. "English culture" is a variation of "B and D," which refers to bondage (tying, handcuffing, or otherwise restraining an individual) and discipline (spanking, whipping, or beating in some other way) designed for achieving sexual stimulation. "Versatile" or "AC/DC" means bisexual. "Animal training" involves the use of dogs, horses, or pigs for sexual gratification; "TV" is transvestism (wearing clothes of the opposite sex); "water sports" requires individuals to urinate on one another; "colonic water sports" calls for the administration of enemas for sexual thrill; "way outs" or "weirdos" is usually applied to the practitioners of "B and D" or of any other acts that are considered bizarre. "Home movies" are pornographic films starring and produced by the swingers themselves; "indoor sports" is a catchall term for swinging activities; "parties" refers to group swinging of more than two couples; "social" is for swingers to meet one another without the obligation to swing; "virile" stresses the ability of a man to take a long time to climax or to repeat his performance four or more times in the course of the evening; and "sepia" is a black swinger.

Swingers use these euphemisms for several purposes: to avoid offending other swingers, to safely sound out potential swingers, and to conceal the swingers' identity from their children and straight friends. Their common language also fosters an in-group feeling among the swingers. But as swinging is a relatively new phenomenon, new terms frequently appear in swingers' ads. Even the publishers of swingers' magazines often fail to understand the meanings of the new terms. To minimize misunderstanding among swingers and thereby control more effectively their sociosexual interaction, swinging magazines usually publish in each issue a glossary of terms commonly used in the swinging world. In addition, a number of largely unspoken rules have emerged to govern swingers' behavior, which are to be discussed below.

Probably the most important rule is that married players should not get emotionally involved with their swinging partners. They should separate sex from love, treating swinging as a source of sexual pleasure, not an opportunity for developing emotional intimacy. This rule serves to prevent swinging from generating jealousy between husband and wife and also from threatening their marriage. This may explain why most couples swing with another couple only once or twice and then seek new swinging partners. In the few cases where a couple swings with another on a regular basis, a friendship may blossom between the two couples, but it is usually treated like the friendship between two nonswinging couples. The concern with their marital stability has often led swingers to claim that "the family that swings together, stays together."

Related to the preceding rule is the prohibition against expressing deep affection for the swinging partner. Thus it is not all right to say "I care for you" or "I love you." But it is all right to say, "You have a terrific body," or "You sure know how to make love." Such compliments are not viewed as threatening to marriage, presumably because they are directed to the swinging partner as a temporary sex object rather than as a potential lifelong mate. Also, kissing the swinging partner in the presence of one's own spouse is usually forbidden, probably because kissing is supposed to be reserved for loved ones only. This is similar to the attitude of many prostitutes who feel that it is too personal to kiss their customers.

Related to the above is the rule that prohibits the husband or the wife from swinging alone with a third person without the knowledge or consent of the spouse. This prohibited behavior is considered as marital infidelity, thus very threatening to marriage.

Although females are encouraged to play with other females, it is a taboo for men to engage in homosexual activity. Swingers may claim that they are so sexually liberated that they would not object to male homosexuality, but the fact remains that almost all male swingers abstain from it.

Swinging partners should be clean before each sexual contact. This reflects the swingers' preoccupation with personal hygiene and fear of venereal diseases. Thus some female swingers would rather engage in sexual activity with other women than with men. Almost all the women douche themselves after each act of sexual intercourse with a man. The men also wash themselves after each orgasm. At large parties the washing activity in the bathroom seems to compete with the sexual one in the bedroom.

Swingers are not supposed to freely give out the names, addresses, and telephone numbers of the couples with whom they have swung. This is what they mean when they assure a prospective swinging couple that they are very discreet. They may give you a swinging couple's name only if they have obtained the couple's approval.

Vulgar behavior is forbidden at swinging parties. But the swingers' notion of vulgarity is in some ways different from, and in other ways similar to, the nonswingers'. Here is how Bartell describes swingers' notion of vulgarity:

Vulgarity is a "don't." One is vulgar if one swears or uses crude language. This does not apply to certain terms for sex or for parts of the body. . . . One is vulgar if one insults someone else, or if one is loud and/or rude. One is vulgar if one gets very drunk. Almost everyone drinks, but the hostess will not forgive the swinging guest who gets drunk and then insults someone, burns a hole in the carpet or the coffee table, breaks glasses, spills things, or in any other way damages

the house. . . . Having sex in an inappropriate place is also vulgar.
. . . Sex is inappropriate in the living room or in whatever the central
gathering place may be.[7]

At a party, swinging couples should not violate the spirit of swinging—
by engaging in sexual activity with their own husband or wife. This is
the easiest rule for swingers to follow, and they do follow it religiously. If
they break it, they will become the laughingstock of the party:

If, in the middle of a group scene, a man finds accidentally that his
wife is fellating him, or he is performing cunnilingus on her, we have
heard someone laughingly say, "That's incest." Others have been
known to ask, "You mean you make it with your own wife at a party?"[8]

COLLECTIVE PROFILE OF SWINGERS

Most swingers are middle-class, suburban whites. The majority of them
are between twenty-five and thirty-five years of age. Politically they are
somewhat conservative, particularly if they live in Middle America. They
are also mildly prejudiced against such minorities as blacks, Puerto Ricans,
and Mexicans, and strongly antihippie. Most of them are Protestant. Although they themselves do not attend church regularly, they often send
their children to Sunday School or give them religious instruction. Both
the men and the women have very limited outside interests, hobbies, or
activities. The women's activities are largely restricted to making their
houses neat, bringing up their children, and watching television. The men
enjoy reading or looking at *Playboy* magazine. In general, swingers appear
to be bored, frustrated, and incapable of living a joyful and stimulating
life—very much like their nonswinging neighbors. Such is the broad picture of the swingers presented by Bartell.[9]

A closer look at swingers by comparing them with a control group of
nonswingers has more recently been taken by sociologist Brian Gilmartin.[10]
The two groups were closely similar as to their age, occupation, income,
number of children, and involvement in local clubs and organizations. He
found that swingers are no more unhappy, bored, neurotic, or perverted
than nonswingers are. These findings largely support Bartell's observation
mentioned above. "Other than their sexual deviance," Gilmartin concludes,
"the most remarkable thing about the swingers is how unremarkable they
are."[11]

But Gilmartin did discover significant differences between swingers and
nonswingers in some other areas of life. First, swingers have a much lower
rate of church attendance. Second, swingers tend more to have had unhappy childhoods—they seldom talked informally and often felt reluctant

to discuss their problems with their parents. Third, swinging husbands are far more likely than nonswinging husbands to have divorced parents or unhappily married parents, though there is not much difference for the wives. Fourth, swingers are more likely to be alienated from their parents, to have very little agreement with them on the important things in life. Fifth, swingers began dating earlier, dated more frequently, had their first sexual intercourse at a younger age, and married earlier. Sixth, swinging couples are more likely to have been divorced before. And seventh, although swingers (on the West Coast) are more likely to be liberal on social and political issues, they feel detached from, rather than committed to, their beliefs. In sum, compared to nonswingers, swingers have looser ties to the three traditional institutions of social control, namely, religion, family, and community.

Since they resort to swinging as a way of expressing their liberation from social control agencies, many swingers seem to think that they are the vanguard of a sexual revolution, replacing male-female inequality with equality. It is obviously true that both the swinging husband and wife have an equal share of sexual promiscuity. But this does not necessarily mean that they have abolished sexual inequality. In fact, as many researchers have found out, swinging is basically a male institution.[12] In almost all cases of mate swapping, it is the husband who initiates the idea of swinging, which is often objected to by his wife. Then the husband strong-arms, subtly coerces, or persuades his wife into swinging. Even after she has become enthusiastic about it, she is still playing the traditional role of pleasing the master. Her enjoyment of swinging results from the kind of social psychology that has helped her husband to lead her successfully into swinging in the first place. "Hence, like her nonswinging counterparts," as anthropologists Charles and Rebecca Palson conclude, "a woman in swinging will judge herself in terms of her desirability and her attractiveness to men much more than thinking about her own [sexual pleasure]."[13] As for the man's attitude toward swinging, psychologist Gordon Bermant observes:

The most likely truth about swinging men was put quite precisely by
one of Bartell's informants when he said, "People will tell you they
do all sorts of things, but when it comes right down to it they're only
interested in going off to another room and screwing your wife."
So there you have it: the more things change, the more they stay the
same.[14]

In other words, swinging is merely a new version of the old tradition of male domination over women.

CONSEQUENCES OF SWINGING

Contrary to what moralists may expect, swinging has been found to improve marital relations. Gilmartin's study, for example, shows that swinging couples consistently report a higher level of marital happiness than nonswinging couples. More specifically, there is a greater amount of intimacy, affection, and communication as well as a higher frequency of marital sex between swinging spouses than between nonswinging ones.[15]

Does this mean that swinging tends to improve marriage, thereby confirming the swingers' ideology that "the family that swings together, stays together"? The answer is yes, *if* one applies Davis's functional theory of prostitution to swinging. For just as sexual but nonemotional involvement with prostitutes contributes to marital stability by diverting the husband from the possibility of falling in love with another woman, so does sexual but nonemotional involvement with swinging partners. This similarity between the function of swinging and that of prostitution appears clearer in light of the fact that swinging, like prostitution, is basically a male institution designed to serve men's sexual needs more than women's, as has been suggested previously.

Nevertheless, one can hardly ignore the obvious difference between prostitution and swinging, namely, that the former is still more impersonal than the latter. Thus some swingers, particularly those who are more sensitive and intellectually inclined, may want to treat their sex games with other men's wives as something more than an experience with prostitutes. But if they go too far and get emotionally involved with their swinging partners, this may threaten or disrupt their emotional attachment—the basis of their marriages—to their own wives.[16]

Therefore, swinging may have both positive and negative consequences for the swingers. There are other ways in which the same aspects of swinging may create opposite effects on the swingers. Let us look at three of these ways.

One, for some swingers, mate swapping is extremely exciting because it entails an element of danger—mostly the danger of being discovered by relatives, friends, and workmates. But for other swingers, the same element of danger becomes so threatening that they eventually quit swinging. Two, some women report that they benefit a lot from swinging because it has enabled them to shed the sexual inhibitions that they have been raised with. Yet other women, who have discontinued swinging, feel that they have lost their self-esteem because swinging made them "see themselves as sleeping with anyone who comes along." Three, to some couples, one of the greatest advantages of swinging is that the participating couple feels closer because the husband and wife spend more time together searching for new swinging partners. However, other couples have dropped out of swinging because they complain that swinging took much of their time and energy and that "their continued search for new couples put them on a merry-go-round." [17]

One may conclude that swinging is like a two-edged sword—it may swing in the direction of creating positive consequences or in the opposite direction of generating negative consequences. The nature of the consequences depends more on the individual who uses the sword than on the sword itself.

THEORIES OF SWINGING

A number of sociologists and anthropologists have attempted to explain why swinging has emerged in American society. Perhaps because swinging is a relatively new form of deviant behavior, the attempted explanations are generally not clearly or systematically presented. But some causal factors of swinging can be identified. These factors may be divided into two categories. One deals with the etiology of swinging in a general way; the other, in a more specific way.

GENERAL THEORY

The increased sexual freedom of women is believed to be responsible for the emergence of swinging in our society. As sociologists Duane Denfeld and Michael Gordon state:

Mate-swapping is an outgrowth of the dramatic changes that have taken place in this century in the position of women in American society and, more crucially, changes that have taken place in the conceptions of female sexuality and female sexual rights. . . . The current conception of female sexuality as legitimate and gratifying coupled with enlarged opportunities for women to pursue sex without unwanted pregnancies is likely to have greatly increased the incentive for women to seek— as men have always done—sexual variety outside marriage.[18]

Anthropologists Charles and Rebecca Palson also believe that the experience of increased sexual freedom by women—especially their new awareness that sex is for recreation rather than for procreation—contributes to swinging activity. But the Palsons go one step further by suggesting that economic prosperity is the root cause of swinging—and that economic slump will bring about the decline of swinging. The Palsons argue that in times of prosperity, women experience increased economic independence, which enables them to gain "sexual privileges more equal to those of men." Swinging, then, results from the increased equality between men and women in sexual matters.[19]

However, one may mention two weaknesses in the preceding argument. For one thing, the assumption that there is sexual equality in swinging is more apparent than real, as has been suggested before. For another, even if it is true that women have recently enjoyed increasing sexual freedom, this still cannot explain why the women choose swinging over other forms of extramarital sex.

Other factors such as marital sexual monotony and feelings of loneliness are also believed to lead people into the swinging scene.[20] Again, these factors cannot tell us why those people choose swinging rather than other, equally exciting forms of sexual activity (such as falling in love with another man or woman).

A more systematic discussion on the emergence of swinging as a middle-class deviant subculture has been presented by sociologist Mary Walshok. She points out three factors as giving rise to the swinging subculture:

(1) The centrality of sexual deviation within the middle class is a consequence of the high personal and social *value placed on sexuality*.
(2) The emergence of this subculture in predominantly middle-class groups is suggested to be a consequence of the *marginal status* of individuals new to the middle class which makes them more responsive to intense forms of experience. (3) Finally, the highly formalized and routinized quality of the swinging subculture is interpreted as essential for the maintenance of conventional commitments along with the deviant ones. . . . [Swinging is particularly common] among groups whose conventional life style in general manifests elements of *corporateness, standardization, and formalization*.[21] [Emphasis added.]

In other words, the swinging subculture arises from among new middle-class people, because they (1) are obsessed with sex in a heavily sex-oriented society, (2) experience stress and anxiety as the result of their marginal status in the middle-class suburbs, and (3) have acquired a mechanistic, impersonal lifestyle from the highly technological society. However, the conception of these three factors is so general that it can explain all kinds of impersonal sexual activity. We may want a more specific theory that can indicate why swinging, and not other types of sexual activity, occurs among middle-class couples.

SPECIFIC THEORY

There are two factors that, when combined, may specifically determine why swinging rather than other types of sexual activity is chosen. These two factors are: the male's sexual fantasy, and the male's need for preserving the traditional male-dominated marriage.

According to Bartell as well as many other sex researchers, in our society men have been socialized to be far more preoccupied with sex than have women. But due to our restrictive norms, adolescent boys tend to express their sexual preoccupation in masturbation. This solitary sex usually encourages young boys to indulge in the fantasy of enjoying sexual thrills with many different women.[22] By the time they are married, men are likely to find that they still have not fulfilled their earlier sexual fantasies. Further, this sexual fantasy life becomes even more powerful when married men are bored by their marital sex life. Consequently, married men are motivated to search for extramarital sex that may help them realize their sexual fantasies.

There are several forms of extramarital sex available to married men. One is the traditional type of adultery, but this may be seen as too threatening to marriage. Another kind of extramarital sex involves using the service of prostitutes. Although this is impersonal and thus not threatening to marriage, the men want something more personal—the kind of sexual adventure that will help to actualize their fantasy of being a successful Don Juan, James Bond, or playboy. Therefore, they are most likely to choose swinging, which not only promises to turn their sexual fantasies into reality but also assures them of the preservation of their marriage.

POWER THEORY APPLIED

As swinging is comarital sex, we may put it in perspective by comparing it with premarital sex. It is self-evident that while premarital sex is engaged in by some members of the less powerful younger generation, comarital sex is engaged in by some members of the more powerful older generation. Although both forms of sex are similar in being relatively impersonal and recreational, the less powerful's sex is less discreet and more discoverable than the more powerful's comarital sex. This is why participants in premarital sex are better known as such by their nonparticipating friends and acquaintances than are participants in comarital sex by theirs.

Given the greater secrecy surrounding comarital sex and thus better protection against social stigma, we may expect from power theory that comarital sex should be more prevalent than premarital sex. But it is doubtful that this is the case, because comarital sex is still a very new form of deviant behavior. Power theory, however, may be used to suggest some symbiotic interaction between the powerful's comarital sex and the powerless' premarital sex. It appears that the more one form of sex is practiced, the more the other is practiced, and vice versa. The reason is that both forms of sex can help make sex more impersonal and recreational, which may cause sex to become in the future one of the popular leisure sports.

SUMMARY

Swinging involves the temporary exchange of marital partners for sexual purposes. It is a form of adultery, but both husband and wife jointly participate in it.

There are four ways to get together with swinging couples. The first way calls for seducing one's friends into the mate-swapping scene. The second method relies on one's association with experienced swingers, from whom new swinging couples can be contacted. The third way is to visit swingers' bars or clubs, where swinging couples can be approached and solicited. And the fourth method is to place or answer an ad in a swingers' magazine.

There are four types of swinging experience. (1) In closed swinging, the two exchanged partners go off to a bedroom and close the door before engaging in sex. (2) In open swinging, all the participants perform in the same room or on the same bed. (3) At a swinging party, three or more couples participate in closed or open swinging. (4) Threesome swinging involves a couple having sex together with a third person.

The subculture of swinging consists of a specialized language used by swingers as well as unspoken rules to govern their sociosexual interaction. Nonswingers may not be able to understand the swinging language, but swingers themselves may have difficulty in understanding some of its newly emergent words. The unspoken rules are generally designed to prevent jealousy between husband and wife and thereby protect their marital stability.

Swingers are largely from the middle class. They are very similar to other middle-class people who do not engage in swinging. The obvious difference is that swingers are by definition couples who engage in swinging as a form of deviant behavior. Less obvious differences between swinging and nonswinging couples are that the former are more likely than the latter to have looser ties to social control institutions.

Swinging may have positive consequences for some mate swappers but negative consequences for others. The major positive consequence is the improvement of marital relations. The major negative consequence involves disruption of marital stability.

There are two types of theories about swinging. General theory cites the following as the causes of swinging: women's increased sexual freedom, prosperity, marital sexual monotony, obsession with sex, middle-class anxiety, and impersonal society. But none of these can explain why people choose swinging over other forms of sexual activities. Specific theory pinpoints the combination of the male's sexual fantasy life and need for preserving male-dominated marriage as determinants of swinging. Power theory may be used to put swinging in perspective by comparing it to premarital sex.

SUGGESTED READINGS

Bartell, Gilbert D. *Group Sex.* New York: Signet, 1971.

Denfeld, Duane. "Dropouts from Swinging," *The Family Coordinator*, January 1974, pp. 45–49.

Denfeld, Duane and Michael Gordon. "The Sociology of Mate Swapping." *Journal of Sex Research* 6 (May 1970): 85–100.

Gilmartin, Brian G. "That Swinging Couple Down the Block." *Psychology Today* 8 (February 1975): 54–58.

Henshel, Anne-Marie. "Swinging: A Study of Decision Making in Marriage." *American Journal of Sociology* 78 (January 1973): 885–891.

Palson, Charles and Rebecca. "Swinging in Wedlock." *Society* 9 (February 1972): 28–37.

Symonds, Carolyn. "Sexual Mate-Swapping and the Swingers." *Marriage Counseling Quarterly* 6 (Spring 1971): 1–12.

Varni, Charles A. "An Exploratory Study of Spouse-Swapping." *Pacific Sociological Review* 15 (October 1972): 507–522.

Walshok, Mary Lindenstein. "The Emergence of Middle-Class Deviant Subcultures: The Case of Swingers." *Social Problems* 18 (Spring 1971): 488–495.

13 ILLEGAL DRUG USE

The general public, including many intellectuals, has often misled itself by using the term *drug abuse*. This term does not mean what it says. It does not mean the use of a dangerous drug. Neither does it mean the misuse of medically prescribed and over-the-counter drugs. Instead, it often refers to the mere use of an *illegal* drug, a drug that the public believes—often incorrectly—to be dangerous or simply does not like. More specifically *drug abuse* is not generally used to refer to the mere use (or misuse) of such legal drugs as alcohol, tobacco, Nytol, Compoz, No-Doz, and other popular sedatives, tranquilizers, and stimulants. Rather, *drug abuse* is popularly used to refer to the mere use of marihuana, LSD, heroin, cocaine, and other socially disapproved drugs.

It should be clear, then, that the term *drug abuse* is not a scientific or objective one, but a social or subjective one. It is society's code word for certain socially disapproved behaviors; it has very little or nothing to do with the real nature of the drugs used. As Erich Goode says:

In actuality, the term "drug" is a social fabrication. . . . This does not mean that drug effects are not "real." Drugs, of course, have chemical and pharmacological properties; they do act on human tissue. But the way they act has relatively little to do with how they are viewed and defined. Society's attitudes toward a given substance have very little to do with its laboratory-identified properties—and a great deal to do with sentiment and emotion. Society, or rather certain segments of society, define what a drug is, and the social definition, the linguistic device, largely determines our attitudes. The statement "He uses drugs" calls to mind only certain specific *kinds* of drugs [such as marihuana, LSD, and heroin]. If what is meant by that statement is "He smokes cigarettes and drinks beer," we are disappointed; cigarettes and beer are not part of our stereotype of what a drug is, even though we will find a description of the effects of nicotine and alcohol in any pharmacology textbook.[1]

We may therefore simply define *drug abuse* as, or equate it with, the use of *illegal* drugs. Further, illegal drug use should not be considered as a unitary phenomenon. It may appear in different forms, ranging from the slightest to the deepest involvement with a given illegal drug. The National Commission on Marihuana and Drug Abuse has identified five types of drug-using behavior, which are relevant to our present subject of illegal drug use.

First, *experimental use* is defined as the occasional, short-term trial of one or more drugs. The individual simply feels curious about drug effects or wants to experience new feeling states. After giving the drugs a few trials in the company of some drug-experimenting friends or acquaintances, the individual never uses the drugs again.

Second, *recreational use* involves the use of drugs for the purpose of having a good time at a party, with friends and acquaintances. Such drug users are like social drinkers. Compared to experimental users, recreational users are more knowledgeable about drug effects and use drugs more often, but they do not escalate their drug use to uncontrolled use.

Third, *situational use* refers to the use of a drug for coping with a specific situation. Students may utilize stimulants to keep alert for examinations; long-distance truckers may use similar drugs to stay awake; soldiers may rely on drugs to relieve stress in combat situations; athletes may resort to drugs as a means of improving their performance; and housewives may take tranquilizers or sedatives to deal with their boredom, tension, anxiety, or sleeplessness.

Fourth, *intensified use* is the outcome of drug-use escalation among a small minority of recreational or situational users. As intensified users, individuals ingest drugs every day in order to seek relief from persistent problems, but they are still capable of functioning normally in their social and economic lives.

Fifth, *compulsive use* represents the deepest involvement with a drug. Such users have developed a psychological dependence on the drug; drug use has become a dominant factor in their lives. Compulsive users may also have developed a physical dependence on the drug, so that they will experience withdrawal sickness if they stop taking the drug.[2]

THE NATURE OF ILLEGAL DRUG USE

The discussion on the use of illegal drugs should be first put in proper perspective by pointing out several facts about the use of *legal* drugs. One, the use of such legal drugs as alcoholic beverages and tobacco cigarettes are considerably more common than the use of such illegal drugs as marihuana, heroin, and LSD. Other legal drugs such as sedatives, tranquilizers, and stimulants, though less popular than alcohol and tobacco, are still more widely used than the illegal heroin and LSD. Two, the popular use of those legal drugs, particularly alcohol and tobacco, has caused far more deaths, sickness, violent crimes, economic loss, and other social problems. And third, societal reaction to various drugs changes with time and place. Opium is today an illegal drug and widely condemned as a panopathogen ("cause-all" of all ills), but in the last two centuries it was a legal drug and popularly praised as a panacea (cure-all of all ills). In contrast, cigarette smoking is legal in all countries today, but in the seventeenth century it was illegal in most countries and the smoker was harshly punished in some countries. For example, the penalty for cigarette smoking was having one's nose cut off in Russia, lips sliced off in Hindustan, and head chopped off in China.[3]

EFFECTS OF ILLEGAL DRUGS

Of all the illicit drugs, three—marihuana, LSD, and heroin—are at present most commonly associated with the problem of "drug abuse." We shall therefore discuss these three drugs and their effects.

MARIHUANA This drug is derived from the Indian hemp plant called *cannabis sativa*. The top of the plant produces a sticky resin that contains the psychoactive substance. A small portion of this psychoactive resin flows downward and coats the lower part of the plant. What is typically sold and bought as marihuana ("grass," "weed," "pot," or "dope") in this country comes from the entire plant. But when only the top of the plant is harvested, the product is *hashish*, which is far more psychoactively potent than marihuana. Both marihuana and hashish can be eaten or drunk, but are more commonly smoked in the form of cigarettes ("joints" or "reefers"). The cannabis plant can grow all over the world, but the better grades come from Mexico and the Orient.

When it was first used in ancient times, marihuana was considered a sacred and useful drug. This can be illustrated by the following passages from ancient Indian literature:

To the Hindu the hemp plant is holy. A guardian lives in bhang
[marihuana]. . . . Bhang is the joy giver, the sky flier, the heavenly
guide, the poor man's heaven, the soother of grief. . . . No god or man
is as good as the religious drinker of bhang. The students of the scrip-
tures of Benares are given bhang before they sit to study. At . . . holy
places, yogis take deep draughts of bhang, that they may enter their
thoughts on the Eternal. . . . By the help of bhang, ascetics pass days
without food or drink. The supporting power of bhang has brought
many a Hindu family safe through the miseries of famine.[4]

Yet there has been a great deal of sentiment against using marihuana in
our society. This has affected the judgment of both lay and scientific
people about the effects of marihuana. In the early 1950s, the former head
of the Bureau of Narcotics expressed the popular view of the effects of
marihuana this way: "In the earliest stages of intoxication the will power is
destroyed and inhibitions and restraints are released; moral barricades are
broken down and often debauchery and sexuality result. Where mental
instability is inherent, behavior is generally violent." [5] More recently, however, an extensive review of the relevant facts has led the National Commission on Marihuana and Drug Abuse to "conclude that marihuana use is not
ordinarily accompanied by or productive of aggressive behavior, thus con-
tradicting the theory that it induces acts of violence." [6]

In the early 1970s, a number of scientists claimed that there are serious
health hazards in smoking marihuana. Specifically, they found from their
studies in this country that marihuana damages the brain and the lung, causes
the user to age prematurely, lowers the body's resistance to infectious disease
and cancer, brings about precancerous changes in the lung cells, increases the
likelihood of sterility or impotence, and contributes to birth defects and
hereditary diseases in the user's children.[7]

But these findings have been contradicted by studies conducted in other
countries where marihuana has been smoked daily for generations, and
where the marihuana smoked is much more potent than that smoked in the
United States. In general, these studies have not shown any adverse effects
of marihuana use. Moreover, careful examination of the above-cited findings
in the United States has led the Consumers Union to conclude:

Out of all these many studies (and others not reviewed here), a general pattern is beginning to emerge. When a research finding can be
readily checked—either by repeating the experiment or by devising a
better one—an allegation of adverse marihuana effects is relatively
short-lived. No damage is found—and after a time the allegation is
dropped (often to be replaced by allegations of some other kind of
damage due to marihuana).[8]

Yet the Consumers Union did not conclude that marihuana was harmless. Instead, the Union indecisively and ambiguously said that "no drug is safe or harmless to all people at all dosage levels or under all conditions of use." Such an assessment of marihuana effects is not completely satisfactory as it does not answer the question: "Is marihuana harmless or dangerous?" The best answer to the question has been offered by Erich Goode:

> Of course, marihuana can be a "dangerous" drug. Of course, some damage will be associated with marihuana use. There is no drug or chemical agent of any kind, no activity known to humanity, no phenomenon whatever in fact that is completely harmless. One can die of an "overdose" of water—and in fact thousands do every year, from drowning. Humans have been known to choke to death while eating. Men have died of a heart attack while making love.[9]

In other words, smoking marihuana is as harmless *or* dangerous as drinking water, eating lunch, or making love.

Although it is not too dangerous, marihuana does have some immediate physical effects on its smoker. These effects are generally very mild. Soon after marihuana is smoked, the individual may feel his heart beat a little faster, his throat and mouth get slightly dry, and his eyes become somewhat irritated. In fact, these are similar to the effects of smoking ordinary cigarettes. You can also get "high" on marihuana, but only if you smoke it efficiently—to insure that an adequate dose of the psychoactive substance is absorbed into your body. This usually requires inhaling deep puffs of the marihuana smoke, along with a lot of air, holding the breath for a while, and then exhaling the smoke very slowly. Again, the resulting high is not unique to marihuana; you can experience the same result with an ordinary cigarette—if you smoke it in the same way that marihuana is typically smoked, as just described.[10]

Marihuana is not *physically* addictive. If marihuana use is discontinued, the user will not suffer withdrawal sickness, no matter how much has been smoked or how long it has been smoked. The drug, however, has often been claimed to be *psychologically* addictive, in the sense that users can become so dependent on it that they cannot stop using it. Yet the fact is that most marihuana smokers are experimental or recreational users—few are intensified or compulsive users. Further, it should be noted that the psychological addiction in the few users does not result from the drug itself but from the personal characteristics of the users.

Many surveys have shown that the marihuana user is more likely than the nonuser to try and use a wide range of hard, dangerous drugs such as heroin, cocaine, and LSD. This finding does not necessarily mean that marihuana use leads to dangerous drugs in the sense of marihuana itself being the cause of the drug escalation. Sociologists generally assume that the cause lies in the marihuana user's involvement with friends who use hard drugs. As Goode says after reviewing a number of studies, "It is obvious that *having heroin-using friends is far more potent in influencing heroin experimentation than is the level of marihuana use.* Even the regular use of marihuana does not 'lead to' the use of heroin in the absence of having heroin-using friends." [11]

It appears that the effects of marihuana have more to do with how the drug is used than with the inherent nature of the drug. Obviously, if too much of it is used, marihuana can become a dangerous drug—just like cigarettes, alcohol, or anything else. Most people use marihuana for enhancing the pleasure of their recreational activities, such as eating, engaging in sexual intercourse, listening to music, watching television or movies, attending a party, and the like. They generally succeed in intensifying their enjoyment of these leisure activities. At the same time, most users refrain from smoking marihuana when they engage in serious activities such as working, studying, or reading. Being high, they find, impairs serious activities rather than improves them.[12]   However, a small minority of users, particularly those who are inexperienced in the use of marihuana, have been observed to have a "bad trip." An extensive review of relevant data has led to this conclusion: "In most instances, the marihuana intoxication is pleasurable. In rare cases, the experience may lead to unpleasant anxiety and panic, and in a predisposed few, to psychosis." [13]

LSD   This drug was first synthesized by the Swiss chemist Albert Hoffman in 1938. Its psychoactive property was not discovered until Hoffman accidentally inhaled a minute dose of the drug in 1943. He described what happened to him:

I had to interrupt my laboratory work in the middle of the afternoon and go home, because I was seized with a feeling of great restlessness and mild dizziness. At home, I lay down and sank into a not unpleasant delirium, which was characterized by extremely excited fantasies. In a semiconscious state, with my eyes closed (I felt the daylight to be unpleasantly dazzling), fantastic visions of extraordinary realness and with an intense kaleidoscopic play of colors assailed me.[14]

Hoffman later considered this a psychotic experience, thereby paving the way for psychiatrists to view the effects of LSD in negative terms. Psychiatrists at first called LSD a *psychotomimetic* drug, implying that it had the quality of producing a psychic state that mimics madness. Then they named it a *hallucinogenic* drug, suggesting that it had the ability to create hallucinations that psychotics typically experience. As psychotomimetic or hallucinogenic drug, LSD was used primarily for experimental studies of psychosis and limited psychiatric therapy until the late 1950s. In the early 1960s, the Harvard psychologist Timothy Leary attempted to persuade average normal people to take LSD by glorifying its "mind-expanding" properties. This is why Leary's followers called LSD a *psychedelic*, suggesting that the drug can make the mind perceive differently—that the individual under its influence can think and see more clearly and more deeply. In actuality, LSD rarely produces a genuinely manifest consciousness or a true hallucination.[15] Thus when the effects of LSD are described below, we need not make the value judgment as to whether they are "mind-expanding" or "psychotic."

LSD is a colorless, odorless, and tasteless substance whose psychoactive potency is greater than that of other similar drugs. A very minute dose of LSD is usually packed into a capsule or tablet, so that it can be taken orally. (The usual dose of LSD in one capsule ranges from 200 to 500 micrograms, which is very minute when compared with an ordinary headache tablet containing over 300,000 micrograms of aspirin.) That minute dose is able to produce powerful effects on most people.

In general, LSD alters the user's ordinary way of seeing, hearing, and feeling. Under the influence of LSD, people may "see" objects with their eyes closed; "hear" color or "see" sound; see through things; see brick walls, buildings, and other solid structures flow like liquid; see small objects expand into gigantic sizes; feel the height of ecstasy at one moment to be immediately followed by the depth of despair; have the feeling of timelessness; or sense the futility of words for communicating thoughts. The following is a young man's description of his LSD experience:

When my girl friend was peeling an orange for me, it sounded like she
was ripping a small animal apart. I examined it carefully. It seemed
to be made up of tiny golden droplets stuck together. I'd never seen an
orange before. My girl friend was eating scrambled eggs, and it was
as if I was watching a pig with its face in a trough of garbage. A
few bits of egg clung to her teeth, and it seemed as if gobs of garbage
were oozing down her face and out of her mouth. But I knew I was
imagining it.[16]

LSD is physically and psychologically nonaddictive. But tolerance for it builds up rapidly so that increased dosages are required to experience the original effects. "Bad trips" with disastrous consequences may occur, particularly if the user has some emotional problems. Nearly all LSD users interviewed by Goode admitted that they had had uncomfortable moments while under the influence of the drug, but most of them claimed that they were able to handle the discomfort and some even asserted that a "bad trip" could be a rewarding experience. At any rate, the LSD experience takes different forms. As Goode reports, "The many LSD experiences described to me, and to all other investigators of the psychedelic drug scene, vary enormously—some intense (or 'extreme'), some mild and pleasant, some ecstatic, and some depressing or terrifying. Most trips are all of these, at different moments." [17]

HEROIN This drug was first produced in 1898 from morphine, which was in turn first derived in 1803 from opium. Both morphine and heroin are *analgesics* (painkillers) and have been used as such. But heroin use is now a major source of our society's concern with the problem of drug abuse.

Heroin can be sniffed through the nose, taken orally, or injected into the skin, a muscle, or a vein. Injection of the substance into a vein, otherwise called "mainlining," produces the quickest and most intense high. Taken in moderate doses, heroin can not only dull pain but also diminish anxiety and tension as well as induce mild euphoria. Actually heroin itself does not bring about the euphoric feeling; the user has to *learn* to achieve the sense of pleasure from heroin injection. The novice user typically encounters an unpleasant experience from the first shot. Yet the negative experience can easily be rationalized, thus opening the way for taking more heroin trips. One young woman described her first heroin experience with her boyfriend:

The rush [initial impact] was so powerful that he almost fell down. He turned white and began to sweat profusely. . . . I, too, began to sweat and tremble. If anyone had seen . . . us walking out of the house, he would have called an ambulance . . . we could barely walk. For some insane reason, we had decided to drive home immediately after shooting up. . . . I had to keep pulling over to throw up on the side of the road. . . . I was truly surprised that we both didn't die that very first night. I was more physically miserable than I had ever been before. The whole night was spent vomiting. The thing that surprises me is that we didn't forget about heroin right then and there. It was horrible! But we later decided that our dear friend had given us too much. So I decided to give it another chance.[18]

Once this woman as well as other people try heroin several times, they feel an extreme pleasure from the drug experience. Many heroin users, both male and female, claim that the heroin rush is more satisfying than orgasm and the heroin high far more glorious and pleasurable than anything the nonuser could possibly experience. This can easily lead to psychic dependence on the drug. Furthermore, heroin is highly addictive. It may take only a few weeks for a regular user to get physically addicted to the drug. If deprived of it for just one day, the addict may suffer withdrawal sickness, of which the symptoms include profuse sweating, running nose, watering eyes, chills, cramps, nausea, and diarrhea—resulting in the loss of five to fifteen pounds.

In order to relieve or avoid these withdrawal symptoms, the addict obviously has to keep on using heroin. This obvious fact has led many experts in the drug field to believe that once people become addicted, they can no longer experience the pleasurable effects of preaddiction drug use—addicts use heroin only for relieving or avoiding the withdrawal distress. As the influential drug expert Alfred Lindesmith states, "The critical experience in the fixation process is not the positive euphoria produced by the drug but rather the relief of the pain that invariably appears when a physically dependent person stops using the drug." [19] More recently, however, William McAuliffe and Robert Gordon presented data to show that, contrary to Lindesmith's belief, addicts do continue to experience euphoria following each injection of heroin. McAuliffe and Gordon argue that if it were not for the promise of euphoria, addicts would not persistently go to the trouble of stealing and robbing to get money for the next fix, or that if they only wanted to avoid withdrawal distress, they would quickly seek help at some drug treatment center. But this is not the case.

Once dependent [on heroin], the promise of euphoria holds the addict
to his habit, and the pursuit of it drives up his tolerance, increases the
high overhead cost of his addiction, and depletes his legitimate resources. If he remains determined to pursue euphoria at a maximum
level in the face of these developments, rather than contenting himself
merely with avoiding the abstinence syndrome, he must commit himself more completely to the life-style of the criminal addict. As such a
hardcore addict, he is less likely to seek relief voluntarily and to
respond to attempts at rehabilitation. [20]

This euphoria thesis has in turn been attacked by Lindesmith and then defended by McAuliffe and Gordon. [21] The difference between these two interpretations of heroin use may be more apparent than real. It appears that addicts' euphoric experiences are *subjectively* the same as their experience of relief from withdrawal distress, because for a person threatened with or experiencing acute pain, the avoidance or relief of that pain can be a highly pleasurable experience. If you were in a desert without a single drop of water for days, the immense relief of your thirst could well be the most pleasurable experience in your whole life. In other words, Lindesmith as well as McAuliffe and Gordon have been too objective and thereby made too much of the (subjectively false) distinction between the experience of distress relief and the experience of euphoria.

Aside from the highly addictive nature of heroin, it is almost impossible to cure addicts of their dependence on the drug. There is a lot of truth in the old saw, "Once a junkie, always a junkie." Despite this unpleasant truth, heroin is actually harmless, when compared with other psychoactive drugs. Unlike cigarette smoking and alcohol drinking, prolonged use of heroin does not damage the organs, tissues, or cells of the human body. As long as heroin addicts do not neglect other aspects of their life, they can remain as healthy as the nonuser. As Jerome Jaffe, the physician who once served as President Nixon's adviser on drug problems, has observed:

The addict who is able to obtain an adequate supply of the drug through legitimate channels and has adequate funds, usually dresses properly, maintains his nutrition, and is able to discharge his social and occupational obligations with reasonable efficiency. He usually remains in good health, suffers little inconvenience, and is, in general, difficult to distinguish from other persons.[22]

A good example is the physician addict. Although they use a much greater quantity of narcotics than do "street junkies," physician addicts still manage to maintain their health and practice their profession.

As for street junkies, they are far more likely to suffer the consequences of narcotic laws. Because of these laws, heroin's black market prices are so exorbitant that these addicts have to spend a great deal of their time frantically searching for money to buy the next fix. In their frantic search for money, they hardly have the time to eat nutritious food, with the result that they become physically weak. Their frantic search for money tends to involve committing burglary, shoplifting, and other acquisitive crimes, thereby exposing themselves to the risk of arrest and imprisonment and thus to psychic tension. By the time they get enough money to buy a packet of "junk," they are likely to be both physically drained and mentally distressed. In addition, there is no way for them to know how pure or potent the packet is—its heroin content may range from 0 to 80 percent. If they are used to no more than 10 percent heroin and happen to buy a packet of 50 percent, they may die of an overdose. If addicts do not die from overdoses, the unsterilized needles that they use may cause them to contract such diseases as hepatitis and tetanus.

Contrary to popular belief, then, heroin use does not cause crime, death, and disease, but it is rather the antinarcotics laws that do.

PROFILES OF ILLEGAL DRUG USERS

On the basis of several surveys, it can be roughly estimated that, of the American adult population, more than 30 percent have smoked marihuana, about 5 percent have used LSD, and only 1 percent have shot heroin. Research has shown that these three types of drug users are in some ways similar and in other ways not.[23]

SIMILAR CHARACTERISTICS These three types of drug users have been found to share the following seven characteristics:

1. Most of them live in large cities in the West and Northwest of the United States.

2. They are more likely to be males than females.

3. They are likely to have parents who use legal drugs such as cigarettes, alcohol, and prescription drugs for relieving tension and combating insomnia. From their parents, they first learned to use legal drugs—before turning to illegal ones.

4. Among.those who have gone to college, illegal drug users have largely majored in the social sciences, fine arts, and humanities rather than in the natural sciences.

5. Illegal drug users are likely to favor liberal politics, to be estranged from religion, and to have a generally permissive and anticonventional outlook. They are also likely to show their anticonventionality by living with women to whom they are not married. Such anticonventionality has been described as the "hang-loose ethic":

One of the fundamental characteristics of the hang-loose ethic is that it is *irreverent*. It repudiates, or at least questions, such cornerstones of conventional society as Christianity, "my country right or wrong," the sanctity of marriage and premarital chastity, civil obedience, the accumulation of wealth, the right and even competence of parents, the schools, and the government to head and make decisions for everyone— in sum, the Establishment.[24]

6. On the occasion of their first drug use, the drug was given to them by friends. It is little wonder that they, as current users, have at least a few friends who also use the same drugs.

7. The majority of illegal drug users find it relatively easy to obtain the drugs, while nonusers think that it is difficult.

DISSIMILAR CHARACTERISTICS   Research has shown some differences among these three types of drug users. Most of the differences are between marihuana users and LSD users on the one hand, and heroin users on the other:

1. Marihuana users and LSD users are younger than heroin users. The former are typically between eighteen and twenty-five years old, while the latter between thirty and forty.

2. Marihuana users and LSD users are more socioeconomically favored than heroin users. The former tend more to be whites and to come from the middle classes, the latter black and from the lower classes.

3. Marihuana users and LSD users tend more to utilize the drugs for positive purposes, while heroin users tend more to depend on the drug for negative purposes. More specifically, marihuana users and LSD users are more likely

to say that they use drugs in order to heighten their sense of taste, touch, and hearing; heroin users are more likely to say that they use drugs to help them forget their worries and troubles.

4. Marihuana users and LSD users appear to enjoy their drug use more than heroin users do theirs, but marihuana users seem more satisfied than LSD users with their drug experience. In 1974 and 1975, among those who said they might probably continue to use their favorite drugs in the future, were 87 percent of the marihuana users, 67 percent of the LSD users, and 50 percent of the heroin users.

5. Marihuana users and LSD users—particularly the former—are more likely than heroin users to perceive benefits such as sharpened consciousness from their drug use. Conversely, heroin users tend more to experience problems such as bad trips.

6. Marihuana users are more likely to think that "it's all right to use marihuana whenever you feel like it," and to advocate the abolition of the anti-marihuana laws. On the other hand, heroin users are more likely to believe that "heroin makes people lose their will to work" and that "people are likely to hurt themselves or take foolish risks while high on heroin."

7. Marihuana users are much more likely to have used LSD than heroin; LSD users are also much more likely to have used marihuana than heroin; and the overwhelming majority (over 92 percent) of heroin users have used both marihuana and LSD. This suggests that marihuana and LSD are far more popular than heroin.

BECOMING AN ILLEGAL DRUG USER

Isidor Chein and his associates have distinguished four stages in the process of becoming involved with heroin, comparable to the five types of illegal drug use discussed earlier. These stages are experimentation, occasional use (once a week or less), habitual or regular use (every day or more), and futile efforts to break the habit. Chein and his associates have further noted that a user may go through all these stages or may stop at any stage. Thus a person may experiment but does not repeat the experiment. Another person may use heroin occasionally but never become habituated. A third person may become a habitual user but manages to break the habit. And a fourth person may become firmly hooked on heroin, despite a strenuous effort to kick the habit.[25]

It appears that, of the users of the three types of illegal drugs, heroin users have the best chance of graduating into the third and fourth stage; marihuana users of remaining in the second stage, and LSD users of briefly staying in the first stage. According to Goode's observation, LSD has the highest drop-off rate after the first few experimental trials. The typical "user" of LSD is more an experimenter than user; LSD is "the experimental drug par excellence." Why? Goode explains:

> One explanation undoubtedly involves the truly monumental effort the typical LSD experience requires. To go through eight hours of an LSD high—sensory bombardment, psychic turmoil, emotional insecurity, alternations of despair and bliss, one exploding insight upon the heels of another, images hurtling through the mind as fast as the spinning fruit of a slot machine—is draining and exhausting in the extreme.[26]

As for marihuana users, the reason for their likelihood of remaining occasional users—smoking once a week or less—may be twofold. One reason may be that marihuana is typically a weekend party drug. Another reason may be that it is not a physically addictive drug that drives the user into habitual use. In contrast, heroin is addictive, so that the chance of becoming a habitual user or being unable to kick the habit is great.

How do users of each of the three types of drugs get into the stage characteristic of the particular drug? First, prospective users are ordinarily offered the drug by their friend(s) in a simple, casual way. This can be illustrated by the following accounts of how two young men had their first try with heroin:

> It was raining, and I was tired. I was standing in a doorway when this friend of mine came by. He said, "Want a pick-up [injection]?" I said "Sure," so we popped [took a shot].

> I was at a party. Everybody was having a good time. I wanted to be one of the crowd. I thought, if it didn't hurt them it wouldn't hurt me. That started the ball rolling. They were sniffling it that time. Two or three pulled out a few caps [heroin capsules]; said, "Here, if you want to, try." I accepted. They weren't trying to addict me; they just gave it to me.[27]

Contrary to popular belief, then, it is not the strange drug peddler, the so-called "merchant of death," who pushes drugs on the innocent young. Rather, it is their friends who introduce them to drug use.

Once having tried the drug, would-be users go through a learning process —with explicit or implicit instruction from their drug-introducing friends. Howard Becker has identified three steps in the process of learning to become a marihuana user.

First, learning the *technique* to get high. As beginners tend to smoke marihuana like an ordinary cigarette, they may fail to induce the desired drug effects. Thus they may watch their experienced friends smoke or they may receive direct coaching from them on the proper way of smoking grass. They essentially learn to inhale deeply and then hold the smoke in the lungs long enough for the bloodstream to absorb the psychoactive substance of marihuana.

Second, learning to *recognize* the drug effects. After learning the proper technique of smoking marihuana, new users may still not get high. So they have to learn from friends that having cold feet, rubbery legs, intense hunger, and unawareness of the passing of time are some of the signs of a marihuana high.

Third, learning to *enjoy* the drug effects. While being high, novices may have such feelings as dizziness, thirst, tingling of the scalp, misjudgment of time and distance, feeling themselves being simultaneously at two places, and hearing or otherwise sensing things in strange ways. These feelings may be unpleasant or even frightening to beginning drug users. But they must learn to redefine these sensations as pleasurable. Otherwise, they will not use the drug again. Usually they do learn to enjoy these experiences because of the encouragement and reassurance from experienced friends—who, for example, may tell them such things as, "You sure are lucky; I'd give anything to get that high myself. I haven't been that high in years." [28]

With the use of heroin or LSD, the beginner may also have to learn the first step described above—the technique of taking the drug. The second step—learning to recognize the drug effects—may be relevant to the LSD experience, but not to the heroin experience. For the mind-altering effects of LSD are more ambiguous than those of heroin. But the third step—learning to enjoy the drug effects—could be involved in the process of becoming an LSD or heroin user. As Goode says, "Just as the marihuana user *learns to enjoy* his drug, so the addict goes through a process of becoming sensitized to the nuances of a heroin high, and of discounting or underplaying those aspects that he regards as unpleasant." [29]

THE WAR ON ILLEGAL DRUG USE

For the last one hundred years, there have been many attempts to control the use of illegal drugs in our society. But these attempts have largely demonstrated the durable nature—the reality—of illegal drug use, as it obviously still survives today.

The first attempt to control the use of opiates in the United States appeared in the form of a city ordinance against the operation of opium dens in San Francisco in 1875. The custom of opium smoking had earlier been introduced in this country by Chinese coolies who were imported to work on railroad construction crews. At first their opium dens were tolerated. But then the Chinese presented a threat to the white labor market because they could be easily hired to work long hours for low wages. The white laborers started a campaign against the Chinese and their opium dens. This campaign was effectively led by Samuel Gompers, the president of the American Federation of Labor:

Gompers conjures up a terrible picture of how the Chinese entice little white boys and girls into becoming "opium fiends." Condemned to spend their days in the back of laundry rooms, these tiny lost souls would yield up their virgin bodies to their maniacal yellow captors. "What other crimes were committed in those dark fetid places," Gompers writes [in a widely distributed pamphlet], "when these little innocent victims of the Chinaman's wiles were under the influence of the drug, are almost too horrible to imagine. . . . There are hundreds, aye, thousands, of our American girls and boys who have acquired this deathly habit and are doomed, hopelessly doomed, beyond the shadow of redemption." [30]

In consequence, a number of cities followed San Francisco in passing ordinances against opium dens. The antiopium laws were, in practice, anti-Chinese laws, as they provided "a legal basis for unrestrained and arbitrary police raids and searches of Chinese premises" [31]—similar to the "no-knock" law passed in 1970 as a part of the Comprehensive Drug Abuse Act, which was, in practice, against the unconventional youth of today. In 1909 Congress enacted a law prohibiting the importation of opium for smoking. Then in 1914 Congress passed the Harrison Narcotic Act outlawing the sale or possession of opium and its derivatives. By this time, a socially undesirable class including prostitutes, thieves, and hoodlums had been known to use the forbidden drugs and therefore became "dope fiends" in the eye of the new law. In contrast, opiate users of higher social status were largely unaffected by the law, as they were legally able to obtain the drugs from their physicians—because the Harrison Act did not prohibit opiate use for "legitimate medical purposes." [32] It may be noted in passing that during most of the nineteenth century when opium derivatives were used—perhaps as commonly as alcohol and tobacco are used today—by many upper- and middle-class whites, no attempt was made to outlaw the drugs.

Around 1900 many state laws and municipal ordinances were also enacted against the use of another drug—cocaine. These anticocaine laws were, in effect, antiblack laws. In those days, cocaine was widely used by blacks, but whites fearfully believed that a cocaine high could spur blacks to violence against whites, stimulate blacks' sexual assault on white women, improve blacks' pistol marksmanship, make blacks unaffected by mere .32 caliber bullets, attain superhuman strength, and become cunning and efficient. The anticocaine laws, then, were useful for repressing blacks and keeping them in "their place."

In 1937 Congress passed the Marihuana Tax Act. This antimarihuana law was, in reality, an anti-Chicano law. The Mexican migrant workers in the

West and Southwest had been known to smoke marihuana, and Anglo-Americans, holding strong prejudice against them, had spread rumors that the weed often led the Mexicans to commit murder, rape, and other horrible crimes. In 1936, for example, a Colorado newspaper editor wrote the following letter to the Bureau of Narcotics:

I wish I could show you what a small marijuana cigarette can do to one of our degenerate Spanish-speaking residents. That's why our problem is so great: the greatest percentage of our population is composed of Spanish-speaking persons, most of whom are low mentally, because of social and racial conditions.
While marijuana has figured in the greatest number of crimes in the past few years, officials fear it, not for what it has done, but for what it is capable of doing. They want to check it before an outbreak does occur. Through representatives of civic leaders and law officers of the San Luis Valley, I have been asked to write you for help.[33]

In the 1950s, the social problem of heroin use was blamed on the Communists. They were believed to push heroin as part of their conspiracy against the United States. The Narcotic Drug Control Act, enacted in 1956, was indeed very tough on heroin peddlers. It provided the death penalty for the sale of heroin to a person under eighteen by one over eighteen.[34]

In the 1960s, many horror stories about the effects of marihuana and other psychedelics were widely publicized. One such story was announced in 1968 by Pennsylvania's Governor Shafer, who subsequently became chairman of President Nixon's Marihuana and Drug Abuse Commission. Governor Shafer told the press that six college students stared at the sun while under the influence of LSD and were consequently blinded. But the story was later exposed as a hoax.[35] In the same decade a series of new federal and state laws were enacted to increase the severity of punishment for illicit drug use. All these harsh laws served to oppress the youth who dared reject conventional values and scorn the establishment.

Today, however, there are attempts by some states to decriminalize drug abuse, such as legalizing marihuana use and creating methadone-maintenance programs for heroin addicts. This softening of the attitude toward illegal drug use is understandable in view of the increased number of conventional youth in the drug scene, who have helped to change the past status of users as a disliked minority or powerless group. This does not mean that illegal use of the same or other yet-to-be-discovered psychoactive drugs will totally disappear from our society. Rather, it means that public passion against the currently used illegal drugs will die down, but if the past history of drug control is allowed to repeat itself, public passion will be mobilized again in the future against some disliked minority that happens to use a certain drug.

The foregoing clearly suggests that drug laws are passed and enforced

for political reasons: drugs are used as scapegoats for larger societal problems, or for oppressing minority groups, or for both.[36] In other words, drug
laws have not reflected the reality of drug use. The reality is that drug use
is a fact of American life that cannot be eliminated—though the harmful,
excessive use of drugs can be minimized. In their attempts to eliminate illegal
drugs, harsh laws and their zealous enforcement have had a boomerang
effect: they have created a criminal class, increased the number of addicts,
and produced such social ills as an increase of criminal activity and a decrease
of civil liberty.[37]

THEORIES OF ILLEGAL DRUG USE

There are two major types of theories about illegal drug use: psychological
and sociological. In general, the psychological theories assume that the illegal
drug user is a defective person suffering from some personality disorder or
psychic trouble. According to such theories, then, the individual turns to
drugs as the result of a personality disorder or as the means of escaping from
psychic trouble. Most sociologists have rejected these psychological theories, mainly because the majority of illegal drug users are assumed to be no
different from ordinary normal people.

As for the sociological theories, not all sociologists themselves accept them.
Three major sociological theories are to be discussed: anomie theory,
cognitive association theory, and labeling theory.

ANOMIE THEORY

This theory, as you may recall from Chapter 2, was formulated by Robert
Merton to explain deviant behavior in general. Its concept of *retreatism* has
been used by Merton and his followers to explain illegal drug use. Like
the psychologists, Merton sees retreatism (such as drug use) as an escape
mechanism, but unlike them, he views the escape mechanism as one that
leads the drug user to escape from society's requirement that he or she work
hard to achieve success. Merton explains:

It is thus an expedient which arises from continued failure to near the
goal by legitimate measure and from an inability to use the illegitimate
route because of internalized prohibitions, this process occurring while
the supreme value of the success-goal has not yet been renounced. The
conflict is resolved by abandoning both precipitating elements, the goals
and the means. The escape is complete, the conflict is eliminated and
the individual is asocialized.[38]

In other words, individuals use drugs because they are unwilling to resort to criminal means of achieving these goals, even though they have repeatedly failed to achieve success goals by conventional means, and yet they still desire to achieve them.

Richard Cloward and Lloyd Ohlin modify this theory by first admitting that there are indeed some youthful drug users who are too morally inhibited to engage in criminal activities. But Cloward and Ohlin point out that the great majority of drug users had a history of delinquency before becoming involved with drugs. Thus the reason for their drug use is not that they are unwilling (morally inhibited) to commit crimes. Rather, the reason is that they are simply not capable of committing crimes—because they do not have the opportunity for criminal pursuit of success just as they do not have the opportunity for conventional pursuit of success. Drug addicts, then, fail to achieve success by *both* conventional and criminal means. This explanation of drug addiction is therefore known as the *double failure* theory.[39]

Many sociologists have criticized this theory. Their most damaging criticism is to the notion of lower-class drug addicts as "double failures." In actuality, they are "double successes." They are successful not only in making money illegally but also in obtaining illegal drugs.[40] This can be illustrated by the following account of what addicts do.

Their behavior is anything but an escape from life. They are actively engaged in meaningful activities and relationships seven days a week. The brief moments of euphoria after each administration of a small amount of heroin constitute a small fraction of their daily lives. The rest of the time they are actively, aggressively pursuing a career that is exacting, challenging, adventurous, and rewarding. They are always on the move and must be alert, flexible, and resourceful. The surest way to identify heroin users in a slum neighborhood is to observe the way people walk. The heroin user walks with a fast purposeful stride, as if he is late for an important appointment—indeed, he is. He is hustling (robbing or stealing), trying to sell stolen goods, avoiding the police, looking for a heroin dealer with a good bag . . . coming back from copping . . . looking for a safe place to take the drug, or looking for someone who had beaten him—among other things. He is, in short, *taking care of business.*[41]

COGNITIVE ASSOCIATION THEORY

While anomie theory is presumably intended for explaining the use of illegal drugs in general, what may be termed *cognitive association theory* is explicitly designed to explain opiate (morphine or heroin) addiction alone. Alfred Lindesmith presented the latter theory more than thirty years ago and it is still very influential today. Lindesmith describes his theory in this way:

The power of the opiate habit is derived basically from effects which follow when the drug is removed rather than from any positive effects which its presence in the body produces. Addiction occurs only when opiates are used to alleviate withdrawal distress, after this distress had been properly understood or interpreted, that is to say, after it has been represented to the individual in terms of the linguistic symbols and cultural patterns which have grown up around the opiate habit. If the individual fails to conceive of his distress as withdrawal distress brought about by the absence of opiates, he does not become addicted, but, if he does, addiction is quickly and permanently established through further use of the drug.[42]

Lindesmith has collected convincing data to support his theory. He observes that in many cases opiate addiction began only after addicts discovered by themselves or from their physicians that their withdrawal sickness was caused by suddenly discontinuing the use of opiates. In contrast, many patients who experienced the same withdrawal sickness without cognitively associating it with their prior use of opiates did not become addicted. Further, Lindesmith contends that the insane, idiots, young children, and animals are immune to addiction because they cannot understand the meaning of withdrawal symptoms even if it is explained to them.

Lindesmith's idea that addiction depends on the drug's elimination of withdrawal distress rather than on its production of euphoria, has recently been questioned by McAuliffe and Gordon. The latter believe that addicts do desire and experience euphoria from the drug. But we have previously suggested that the elimination of withdrawal distress and the production of euphoria may be subjectively the same experience. Here it may be noted that McAuliffe and Gordon have not offered any data or convincing argument against the heart of Lindesmith's theory, namely, the idea that addiction is brought about by the addict's *cognitive association* of withdrawal distress (or deprivation of euphoria) with discontinued use of the opiate.

LABELING THEORY

While the above two theories are meant to explain why people use drugs and become addicted, labeling theory is used to explain why drugs have certain effects on the user. According to this theory, as proposed by Howard Becker, the nature of drug effects depends largely on the way the user interprets, defines, or labels the effects rather than on the physiological action of the drugs themselves. The way the user labels the drug effects is, in turn, determined by the manner in which the drug-using culture or the antidrug society labels them.[43]

Becker divides drug effects into two types: positive and negative. Negative effects include psychotic episodes, "going crazy," "flipping out," "freaking out," jumping out of the window, and other similarly frightening experiences. Positive effects involve not only the absence of negative effects but also pleasurable, mind-expanding experiences. In an antidrug society or a society where there are not enough drug users to develop an influential drug-using culture, the drug-induced experience is defined in terms of negative effects. The general public and its doctors and psychiatrists believe in these negative effects, and the popular press helps to strengthen that belief by spreading horror stories about them. Drug users in such a society would become so influenced by the antidrug ideology that they would also expect negative effects in their drug experiences. In the manner of a self-fulfilling prophecy, drug users actually end up experiencing negative effects when they try the drugs. On the other hand, if the drug users are part of a drug-using culture, their drug-using friends would influence them to define drug effects as pleasurable and show the new users how to achieve these pleasurable effects—such as by using the proper dosage, anticipating certain effects, and coping with these effects. Consequently, drug users would enjoy positive experiences with the drugs.

Becker offers some historical evidence to bolster his theory. Medical reports of psychosis associated with marihuana use were very common in the 1930s and early 1940s when marihuana use was very rare and surrounded by strong antimarihuana propaganda about its horrible effects. These reports are much less common today as marihuana use is far more common and supported by a powerful marihuana-using culture. Becker also suggests, on the basis of his admittedly haphazard and informal observations of LSD use, that in the 1960s when LSD began to be used by college students, there were many reported cases of panic reactions to LSD, but these panic reactions can be expected to be less common today, because an LSD-using culture has started to develop. Finally, he cites the case of opiate addiction to show that, since opiates are widely known—by both opiate-using and anti-opiate cultures—to be highly addictive, the use of opiates can easily lead to the worst effect of drugs, namely, addiction.

In concluding his application of labeling theory to drug use, Becker cautions that it is "supported at only a few points by available research" and that "most of what has been said is speculative."

POWER THEORY APPLIED

The use of illegal drugs represents an unprofitable form of deviance because it carries some risk of arrest and imprisonment. Such risk, in turn, has resulted mainly from the fact that drug users are for the most part the young, who are relatively powerless members of society. These powerless people's illegal drug use contrasts sharply with the legal drug use of their parents, the more powerful members of society. The latter can enjoy the use of such legal drugs as alcohol, tobacco, and amphetamines without any hassle from the law. In view of this, the more powerful members' drug use may be considered a form of profitable deviance.

It may be assumed that the powerful adults are more involved in legal drug use than are the powerless youth in illegal drug use, because the use of legal drugs is not subjected to social control as is the use of illegal drugs. In fact, the powerful pharmaceutical industry has for many years been pushing its legal psychoactive drugs on the adult population. Each year that industry spends millions of dollars on advertising—coaxing and seducing people to use its drugs. Its detail men flood doctors' offices with free samples and talk them into pushing its drugs on patients. Consequently, it gains a profit of many hundreds of millions of dollars and creates a socially approved drug culture. This is further ensured by the support that the drug industry receives from the government. Such is the case with the lawful manufacturing and selling of amphetamine, "the drug of the white American with money to spend":

The lawmakers who have declared that possession of marihuana is a serious crime simultaneously defended and protected the profits of the amphetamine pill-makers. The Comprehensive Drug Abuse Prevention and Control Act of 1970 in its final form constitutes a victory for that alliance. . . . The victory could not have been secured without the firm support of the Nixon Administration. The end result is a national policy which declares an all-out war on drugs [such as marihuana and heroin] which are *not* a source of corporate income. Meanwhile, under the protection of the law, billions of amphetamines are overproduced without medical justification.[44]

There seems to be a symbiotic relationship between the powerful parents' legal drug use and their powerless children's illegal drug use. On the one side is the demonstration of a trickle effect—if parents use alcohol and prescription psychoactive drugs, their youngsters tend to use marihuana and other illicit drugs. This has been supported by research evidence, as previously mentioned. On the other side, the illegal drug use by the youngsters is likely to provoke their parents' condemnation, which in turn helps ensure the parents' continued use of legal drugs. This is possible because, in the words of Thomas Szasz:

As the war against heresy was in reality a war for "true" faith, so the war against drug abuse is in reality a war for "faithful" drug use: concealed behind the war against marihuana and heroin is the war for tobacco and alcohol; and, more generally, concealed behind the war against the use of politically and medically disapproved drugs, is the war for the use of politically and medically approved drugs.[45]

SUMMARY

Illegal drug use is often imprecisely referred to in the popular and scholarly literature as "drug abuse." It is not a unitary phenomenon; it may appear in any one of these five forms: (1) experimental drug use, (2) recreational use, (3) situational use, (4) intensified use, and (5) compulsive use.

Marihuana has been publicized by its opponents as dangerous. But *dangerous* is a relative term; if marihuana is used by a person with a terminal case of lung cancer, it can be as dangerous as it is for a person with severe heart disease to have sexual intercourse. Marihuana is not physically addictive, but its users are more likely than nonusers to use hard drugs also. LSD is more potent than, but just as nonaddictive as, marihuana. Its proponents like to exaggerate its mind-expanding effects; its opponents like to tell horror stories about its mind-destroying effects. Actually, LSD is simply a drug that alters the user's ordinary way of seeing, hearing, and feeling, which can be a wonderful or terrifying experience. Heroin is a more powerful drug than the other two. It is also physically addictive. Once addicted to heroin, the individual can experience relief of withdrawal sickness or the rush of euphoric sensation or both subsequent to the injection of the drug. Heroin addicts do not necessarily have their health damaged or their careers ruined by the drug, but they may do both if they are not socially privileged and financially endowed. Research has shown that the users of these three types of illegal drugs are similar in some ways and different in other ways to each other.

According to Chein and his colleagues, there are four stages in the process of becoming an illegal drug user: experimentation, occasional use, habitual use, and futile efforts to break the habit. Heroin users tend to advance into the third and fourth stages; marihuana users often remain in the second; and LSD users seldom go beyond the first. In Becker's view, a prospective marihuana user characteristically learns these three things in a sequential manner: how to get high on the drug; to recognize the nature of the high; and to enjoy the high.

The history of futile social control has proven the durable nature of illegal drug use. The laws and their enforcement against various psychoactive drugs have been largely for using drugs as scapegoats or for oppressing minority groups or for both. At the same time, as these laws and their enforcement have failed to reflect the reality of illegal drug experience, they have unintendedly caused much social harm.

There are three major sociological theories about illegal drug use. Anomie theory states that some people turn to illegal drugs because they use them as a means of quitting the rat race after they have been beaten so many times. Critics of this theory point out that drug addicts are no quitters but instead work very hard as hustlers. Cognitive association theory says that you can become addicted to heroin only if you associate your withdrawal distress with your previous use of the drug. Criticism has been leveled at this theory, but no serious damage has been done to it. Labeling theory tells us that when one takes a drug trip it will be a positive experience if one is from a drug-using culture, and a negative experience if one is from an antidrug society. But the author of this theory admits that it needs more research in the empirical world to prove it. Finally, power theory is used to put illegal drug use in larger perspective by comparing it to legal drug use.

SUGGESTED READINGS

Becker, Howard S. "History, Culture and Subcultural Experience: An Exploration of the Social Bases of Drug-Induced Experiences." *Journal of Health and Social Behavior* 7 (June 1967): 163–176.

Feldman, Harvey W. "Ideological Supports to Becoming and Remaining a Heroin Addict." *Journal of Health and Social Behavior* 9 (June 1968): 131–139.

Finestone, Harold. "Cats, Kicks, and Color." *Social Problems* 5 (Summer 1957): 3–13.

Goode, Erich. *Drugs in American Society.* New York: Knopf, 1972.

Helmer, John. *Drugs and Minority Oppression.* New York: Seabury, 1975.

Lindesmith, Alfred R. *Addiction and Opiates.* Chicago: Aldine, 1968.

McAuliffe, William E. and Robert A. Gordon. "A Test of Lindesmith's Theory of Addiction: The Frequency of Euphoria among Long-Term Addicts." *American Journal of Sociology* 79 (January 1974): 795–803.

Masters, R. E. L. and Jean Houston. *The Varieties of Psychedelic Experience.* New York: Holt, Rinehart and Winston, 1966.

Musto, David F. *The American Disease: Origins of Narcotic Control.* New Haven: Yale University Press, 1973.

Szasz, Thomas. *Ceremonial Chemistry.* Garden City, N.Y.: Anchor, 1974.

14 ALCOHOLISM

O f all drugs alcohol is the most widely used. Relatedly, alcoholism is the most widespread and most serious of all drug abuses. As indicated by a 1972–1974 survey of American adults, more than two-thirds (68 percent) drank alcohol. The same survey also showed that slightly under a third of the adult population did not drink at all, that another third drank infrequently or lightly, and that the last third drank in moderate or heavy amounts. It was estimated that one out of ten Americans who drink becomes an alcohol abuser. In other words, close to 10 million Americans are either full-fledged alcoholics (addicted to the drug) or at least problem drinkers (drinking enough to cause trouble for themselves and others). Alcoholism is indeed our country's biggest health problem, surpassed only by heart disease and cancer. The economic cost of alcohol problems is staggering. For alcohol abuse annually costs the United States about $25 billion—through reduced industrial production, illness, and traffic accidents.[1]

THE NATURE OF ALCOHOLISM

Though prevalent and serious, alcohol problems do not seem to impress the general public. According to the Second Report of the National Commission on Marihuana and Drug Abuse published in 1973, only 39 percent of the adult population and 34 percent of the youth regarded alcohol as a drug. The percentages of these people may have increased recently, but today most people still refuse to consider as dope pushers hosts and hostesses who encourage their guests to drink heavily. In addition, only 7 percent of the people questioned in the 1973 survey saw abuse of alcohol as a serious social problem, as compared with 53 percent who considered use of other drugs—marihuana and heroin—as a serious social problem. From this lack of public consciousness of the use of alcohol have emerged a number of misconceptions about alcohol and its abuse. Although some of the popular conceptions (for example, "Drinking on an empty stomach can get you drunk fast") are indeed correct, many of them are false.

The most common myth is that most alcoholics are skid row bums. The fact is that skid row drunks comprise only a very small minority—1 to 5 percent—of the alcoholic population in the United States. The overwhelming majority of alcoholics are employed, relatively successful in their careers, and living with their families. Second, it is widely believed that mixing different kinds of alcoholic drinks can make a person drunk faster. Actually, it is not the mixture of different drinks, but the total amount of alcohol consumed and the length of time taken to consume it, which determine the speed of getting drunk. A third belief held by many people is that drinking black coffee or dousing one's head with cold water can sober one up. In fact, there is no effective method for getting over intoxication, other than waiting for the alcohol to leave the body—the length of the waiting period depending on the percentage of alcohol in the bloodstream. A fourth popular misconception has it that drinking beer only is very unlikely to make one an alcoholic. The truth is that beer drinkers are more likely to become alcoholics as compared to drinkers of gin, Scotch, or any other kind of alcoholic beverage. According to a fifth seductive myth, sex becomes more exciting after several drinks. However, since alcohol is a depressant rather than a stimulant of the central nervous system, one may feel less inhibited but find it more difficult to perform sexually. As Shakespeare says in *Macbeth*, drinking "provokes the desire, but takes away the performance."

EFFECTS OF ALCOHOL

Ever since Stone Age people became intoxicated from drinking the liquid oozing from fruit left too long in a warm place, alcohol has been bringing both joy and grief to humankind. Today most American adults apparently get enjoyment from drinking, but at least ten percent of them end up getting misery from it. Alcohol plays a significant role in holy ceremonies, but it also does in most cases of murder and aggravated assault. These conflicting effects of alcohol have spawned conflicting ideas in the folk wisdom about alcohol. For example, one Chinese proverb states that "Three glasses of wine can set everything to the right," yet another Chinese proverb says that "Medicine may heal imaginary sickness but wine can never dispel real sorrow." In the Bible we are told that "Wine maketh glad the heart of man," but we are also warned that "Wine is a mocker, strong drink is raging." [2] All this suggests that the effects of alcohol do not depend on alcohol alone but on other factors as well.

PHYSIOLOGICAL EFFECTS Alcohol is a drug since it affects our mental and physical activity. Although it is not a stimulant, alcohol is popularly thought of as one. A stimulant increases the functional activity of the body and mind. But most experts believe that alcohol is a depressant drug, belonging to the same class of drugs as anesthetics, sedatives, and narcotics. As a depressant, alcohol reduces our mental and bodily functional activity:

At the sensorimotor level, we all know that alcohol is an incompetence producer. We all know, too, that at least certain of the adverse sensorimotor effects to which its ingestion gives rise often impinge on the drinker's comportment in ways that are clearly untoward. Its effects on the drinker's equilibrium, for instance, may result in his stumbling, bumping into things, knocking them over, falling down, etc. In addition, things may be dropped or otherwise broken, judgments of time and distance may be thrown askew, tasks may be poorly executed, etc., and when the comatose state is approached, the drinker may fail to meet even the most imperative of his obligations. What is more, we all know that when a person is drunk, these sorts of alcohol-produced failings are both unintentional and beyond the drinker's power to overcome by sheer volition.[3]

It should be noted, therefore, that alcohol largely reduces the drinker's sensorimotor skill or mental and physical functional activity, as described in the above quote. Alcohol by itself, however, does not decrease one's moral competence.[4] It does not, for example, cause one to insult one's friends. But the general public strongly believes alcohol produces moral failings. This popular belief, in the manner of a self-fulfilling prophecy, is so strong that many people in our society indeed show moral failings after a few drinks. When they are sober again, they claim that their offensive behavior while intoxicated was due to the alcohol, thereby excusing themselves. Blaming the drinker's moral failings on alcohol rather than on the person who drinks it, is not only very common among the general public, it is also very common among experts in the field, who are apparently influenced by the same general views of society, which have traditionally blamed immoral behavior on "demon rum." Two leading authorities on alcoholism, for example, make the following statement to suggest how alcohol comes to change good behavior to bad:

The apparent "stimulation" from alcohol is the result of the lower brain centers being released from higher brain controls. This reduces inhibitions, and behavior which is untoward when the individual is sober becomes acceptable. For example . . . an always proper, ladylike woman may become obscene and promiscuous when intoxicated.[5]

In thus believing falsely that alcohol can reduce their inhibitions and knowing correctly that they will not be condemned for their immoral behavior while drunk, many men in our society often try to get themselves and their women friends drunk. But not all of them achieve the goal in the same way. Some are able to get drunk enough to feel uninhibited; others may get too sick or too drowsy to do or feel anything. There are, then, different levels of intoxication brought on by different factors. These factors are largely the body size and weight of the drinker, the type and amount of alcoholic beverage consumed, the presence or absence of food in the stomach, and the level of tolerance for alcohol.

One, a small-sized person may become intoxicated after only a glass of beer, while a large-sized one stays relatively sober after three or four glasses. Because alcohol is diluted in the bloodstream, a 100-pound woman cannot tolerate as much liquor as a 200-pound man. Two, the higher the percentage of alcohol in a beverage, the quicker the intoxicating effect. Thus a 90-proof whiskey (containing 45 percent alcohol) is more powerful than a 6-proof beer (containing 3 percent alcohol). Obviously, the greater the amount consumed, the more potent the intoxicating effect. Three, alcohol is not digested as food; it goes through the walls of the stomach and small intestine and is absorbed directly into the bloodstream. So food in the stomach can retard absorption of alcohol and weaken its intoxicating impact. On the other hand, drinking on an empty stomach will result in relatively quick absorption and quicker intoxication. Four, an individual with a higher level of tolerance for alcohol—through more frequent, heavier drinking—will become less intoxicated than one with lower tolerance if both consume the same amount of alcohol.

As has been noted before, the more intoxicated a person is, the greater the loss of his sensorimotor skill. This positive relationship between the degree of intoxication (measured in terms of the percentage of alcohol in the bloodstream) and the amount of deterioration of sensorimotor skill is shown in Table 14.1.

PHYSICAL AND SOCIAL CONSEQUENCES Moderate intake of alcohol can be socially, psychologically, and even physically beneficial. For example, studies have shown that the aged residents of nursing homes who drink alcoholic beverages moderately are able to enjoy improved sleep, heightened morale, and general well-being. Moreover, according to some research findings,

Table 14.1 Alcohol concentration in bloodstream and its intoxicating effects (after drinks taken on a stomach by a 150-pound person)

AMOUNT OF DRINKING	ALCOHOL CONCEN-TRATION IN BLOODSTREAM	EFFECTS
1 cocktail or 1 highball or 2 cans of beer	.03%	Slight changes in feeling
2 cocktails or 2 highballs or 4 cans of beer	.06%	Feeling of warmth; mental relaxation; mild sedation; driving ability impaired
3 cocktails or 3 highballs or 6 cans of beer	.09%	Exaggerated emotion and behavior—talkative, noisy, or morose
4 cocktails or 4 highballs or 8 cans of beer	.12%	Clumsiness—unsteadiness in standing or walking; legally drunk if involved in a driving accident
5 cocktails or 5 highballs or 10 cans of beer	.15%	Gross intoxication
10 cocktails or 10 highballs or 20 cans of beer	.30%	Extreme intoxication; coma or death may occur
20 cocktails or 20 highballs or 40 cans of beer	.50%	Heart action and breathing slowed; death occurs

SOURCE: Adapted from Leon A. Greenberg, "Intoxication and Alcoholism: Psychological factors," *The Annals* 315 (January 1958): 28; Joel Fort, *Alcohol: Our Biggest Drug Problem* (New York: McGraw-Hill, 1973), p. 28.

moderate drinkers have somewhat lower death rates than complete abstainers.[6] It is largely heavy drinkers and moderate-but-constant drinkers who are most likely to harm their health.

The most common damage done to the body by heavy or sustained drinking involves the liver. The constant intake of alcohol, coupled with malnutrition common among problem drinkers, can destroy liver cells and thereby cause fat to accumulate in the liver. The resulting scarred and fatty liver, called *cirrhosis* of the liver, is a major cause of serious illness and premature death in heavy and sustained drinkers. In fact, cirrhosis is the fourth largest cause of death among people aged twenty-five to forty-five in the United States.[7] Cirrhosis can also lead to sexual impotence. But at least 60 percent of all cirrhotics who stop drinking would recover within five years —though their sexual impotence would persist.[8]

A possible link between alcohol consumption and heart disease has been suspected by recent researchers. But thus far the findings on this matter are contradictory. On the one hand, drinkers have been found to have coronary heart attacks *less* often than nondrinkers or ex-drinkers. On the other hand, a less common form of heart disease, *cardiomyopathy*, (a disease of the heart muscle rather than of the heart's blood vessels) has been found to be associated with alcoholism.[9]

A number of epidemiological and clinical studies have suggested that heavy drinking—especially when combined with heavy smoking—increases the risk of developing cancer of the mouth, throat, and other areas of the body that have frequently been assaulted by alcohol. The use of alcohol does not seem to cause these cancers directly. Instead, heavy drinking helps to raise the risk of these cancers indirectly. (1) Alcohol acts as an irritant to the tissues of mouth, throat, and other related organs, thereby making them more vulnerable to *carcinogens* (cancer-causing agents) that invade them. (2) Some alcoholic beverages may carry their own carcinogens. (3) Poor diet in the heavy drinker facilitates the work of these carcinogens. And (4) the use of alcohol enhances the cancer-causing impact of smoking.[10]

Prolonged use of alcohol may cause muscle weakness and a muscle disease called *alcoholic myopathy*. This disease shows such symptoms as swelling, severe muscle cramps, and eventually, fragmentation of muscle fibers. Prolonged use of alcohol may also cause the brain to deteriorate. Taking two or three drinks a night on an empty stomach may impair a person's memory and ability to learn, because alcohol prevents the brain cells from manufacturing proteins and RNA (ribonucleic acid) necessary for normal mental activity.[11]

In addition to causing the health problems presented above, excessive use of alcohol helps cause a number of negative social consequences.

One consequence is that at least half of each year's automobile deaths and injuries can be traced to excessive drinking. In summarizing the findings on the implication of alcohol in automobile accidents, the National Institute on Alcohol Abuse and Alcoholism states:

The highway is the scene of a substantial portion of the accidental deaths and injuries in the United States. A large part of these are associated with the gross misuse of alcohol. The risk of a driver or pedestrian being involved in a traffic accident increases precipitously with the increased amount of alcohol in the body. Most people killed in traffic accidents after drinking, as well as most who are convicted of driving while under the influence of alcohol, have very high blood alcohol concentrations, averaging twice the level considered legally impairing [more than .10 percent]. Many of the arrested drivers have a history of repeated alcohol-related offenses and show numerous indications of being problem drinkers.[12]

A second consequence is that alcohol use is directly or indirectly involved in a great number of crimes. Offenses directly related to drinking are public drunkenness, driving while intoxicated, disorderly conduct, vagrancy, and violation of liquor laws. These kinds of offenses result in so many arrests that it puts a severe strain on the operation of the criminal justice system. Since the police usually arrest the homeless and the poor, and not the better-off, for drunken behavior, such arrest practices are obviously discriminatory. And a large number of those who are arrested have a long history of previous drunkenness arrests. One man, for example, has been arrested 277 times for public drunkenness, which is not too unusual. All this clearly attests to the futility of treating drunkenness as a crime. Consequently, in 1967 the President's Commission on Law Enforcement and Administration of Justice recommended that drunkenness not be punishable as a crime and that comprehensive treatment programs be instituted to help problem drinkers.[13] Although these recommendations have caused the percentage of arrests for alcohol-related offenses to decline since 1970, drunkenness offenses still constitute the largest arrest category today.[14]

The use of alcohol also plays a significant part, albeit indirectly, in the commission of more serious crimes, such as homicide, aggravated assault, forcible rape, and other sex crimes. More specifically, it has been found that alcohol was associated with 64 percent of all murders, 41 percent of all assaults, 34 percent of all forcible rapes, and 29 percent of all other sex crimes.[15] Those who commit these crimes seem to use alcohol as an excuse for expressing their aggression. As one experimental study indicates, interpersonal aggression was very likely to occur after heavy drinking by subjects who had low scores on measures of socialization, self-control, and responsibility, as well as a history of arguments and other aggressive acts.[16]

Third, if all the above-mentioned physical and social consequences of alcohol abuse are translated into economic costs, they may not match the cost of alcoholism to industry—incurred through the reduced productivity of alcohol-troubled workers. In 1971 the economic cost of lost productivity was conservatively estimated to be $9.35 billion—which was more than the cost of any other category of alcohol problem, such as the cost of alcohol-related health problems ($8.29 billion), the cost of alcohol-involved automobile accidents ($6.44 billion), or the cost to the criminal justice system for alcohol-related offenses ($.51 billion).[17] As for the source of lost productivity resulting from alcohol abuse, it has been stated as follows:

The cost of alcoholism to industry is made up of several components, including loss of efficiency, absenteeism, lost time on the job, faulty decision making, accidents, impaired morale of co-workers, and the cost of rehabilitation programs. A large significant portion of the economic impact of alcoholism also includes premature disability and death, resulting in the loss of many employees in their prime who have skills that are difficult to replace.[18]

PROFILES OF DRINKERS

Drinkers as a group tend to differ from nondrinkers.[19] The difference lies in a number of sociocultural factors, such as sex and age, racial and ethnic background, religious affiliation, socioeconomic status, and region and residence.

SEX AND AGE   Drinking is a characteristically male activity. Compared with women, men are not only more likely to drink, but also consume more when they drink. Not surprisingly, men are far more likely to become alcoholic; it has been estimated that men are at least four times more likely than women to become alcoholic. But this sex difference has been narrowing over the years, as women have been achieving more equality in various aspects of life.

The fact that drinking is a characteristically male activity may suggest a positive relationship between concern with one's masculinity and alcohol use. As young men are apparently more concerned with their masculinity than are older men, which is further reinforced by the social pressure of being able to "drink like a man," they can be expected to be more likely than older men to drink. Indeed, this expectation has been borne out by many studies. One national survey taken in 1972, for example, showed that the largest proportion of drinkers were young men mostly between twenty-one and twenty-four years old. Women are obviously less concerned with masculinity, and so the age difference in drinking among women is not as great as that among men. But younger women are still significantly more prone to drinking than are older women. Thus the age factor may have its own influence on drinking.

RACIAL AND ETHNIC BACKGROUND   Whites and blacks are about equally likely to drink, but black drinkers are more likely to become alcoholics. The alcoholism rate for blacks has been estimated to range from two to four times that for whites. The blacks' higher alcoholism rate may be partly due to the fact that black men start drinking at a younger age than do white men.

One study found that a larger proportion of black than white men started drinking before they were fifteen years old. This may imply that the younger drinkers are, the less competent they are to handle liquor. But the same study also suggests that, regardless of their age, blacks are still more prone to alcoholism than are whites.[20] Thus the age factor alone cannot fully explain the racial difference in alcoholism; other factors have yet to be sought out.

Among the ethnic groups in our society, Irish-Americans have the highest rate of alcoholism. This has been attributed to the Irish culture that accepts heavy drinking as normal and treats the drunk as a lovable person:

[In Ireland] drunkenness . . . is laughable, pleasurable, somewhat exciting, a punctuation of dull routine to be watched and applauded, and drunken men are handled with care and affection. The drunkard is handled with maternal affection, often referred to as "the poor boy," with a special connotation of sympathy, love, pity, and sorrow. If married, the drunkard is compassionately classed by his wife with "the min, Gold help us!" The man who is drunk is sometimes regarded with envy by the man who is sober.[21]

In contrast, Italian-Americans have one of the lowest rates of alcoholism although they consume more alcohol than do Irish-Americans. This is mainly because Italian-Americans usually drink with meals, do not encourage solitary drinking as a means of drowning one's sorrows, and have strong sanctions against drunkenness. Similarly, Chinese-Americans drink a lot but are relatively free from alcoholism. Like the Italians, the Chinese usually drink at meals, particularly on such special occasions as family ceremonies (births, weddings, rites for the dead) and national and religious celebrations. In fact, in China there is no such thing as a bar—a place where drinks are available but meals are not. Also, the Chinese do not think of drunken behavior as funny or comical. They look at it with contempt, because they believe that drunkenness can seriously disrupt interpersonal relationships, and only controlled drinking is a social lubricant.

RELIGIOUS AFFILIATION   American Jews, particularly orthodox ones, start drinking at a very early age but have one of the lowest rates of alcohol problems. This has been attributed to the fact that the Jews use wine for religious rituals—and it is considered abominable to use it to get drunk.

Conservative (usually fundamentalist and Pentecostal) Protestants prohibit the use of alcohol by the faithful. Therefore, they have the largest proportion of nondrinkers and the lowest proportion of heavy drinkers, when compared with Catholics and liberal Protestants. But if they drink, conservative Protestants are more likely to end up being problem drinkers. Many sociologists believe that conservative Protestants, having been brought up on a religion that preaches total abstinence from liquor, have not learned how to drink with moderation. But it is possible that the religious prohibition against alcohol use may not be at fault. The drinking problem of drinking conservative Protestants may be only a part of their overall pattern of deviation from their religious training. Their problem drinking, like their other undesirable behaviors, can hardly be blamed on their religious training.

SOCIOECONOMIC STATUS Proportionately more people of the higher socioeconomic levels drink than do those of the lower levels. Yet there are more problem drinkers and alcoholics from the lower classes. There may be two explanations for this paradoxical finding. One is that higher- and lower-status drinkers use alcohol for different purposes. Higher-status drinkers may be more likely to use alcohol as a facilitator of social interaction, while lower-status drinkers tend more to drink as a way of trying to solve their personal problems. It is apparent that alcohol serves the first purpose better than the second. In consequence, lower-status drinkers may keep on drinking to attempt to achieve a goal that gets progressively harder to achieve the more they drink. Another explanation is that there may in fact be no real difference in alcoholism between the higher and lower stratas. Lower-status people may only *appear* more prone to alcoholism because they are not as successful as higher-status people in hiding problem drinking.

REGION AND RESIDENCE Alcohol consumption is the highest in the regions of the Northeast, the Middle Atlantic, and Pacific Coast states; the lowest in the South; and intermediate in the Midwest. The states that have higher rates of alcohol use are generally more urbanized. Thus cities and suburbs have proportionately more drinkers than rural areas and small towns. Sociologists generally attribute the need for drinking as well as the resulting alcoholism to the stresses and strains of urban life or to the drifting of alcoholism-prone people into the city.

In sum, it appears that, with the exception of the Italians, Jews, and Chinese, the groups that have higher proportions of drinkers also have higher rates of problem drinking. Mere use of alcohol, then, has a good chance of leading to problem drinking. The following two charts summarize most of the preceding discussion.[22]

CHART 1
PROFILE ANALYSIS OF PERSONS WITH
HIGH ALCOHOL-PROBLEM RATES

Highest rates of alcohol-related problems for respondents in a 1973 national survey were found among:

· Men

· Separated, single, and divorced persons (in that order)

• Persons with no religious affiliation

• Persons who are beer drinkers as compared with those who are mostly hard liquor or wine drinkers

• Persons who were more likely (compared to other persons in the survey) to say:

"Drunkenness is usually *not* a sign of social irresponsibility" and
"Drunkenness is usually a sign of just having fun"

CHART 2
PROFILE ANALYSIS OF PERSONS WITH
LOW ALCOHOL-PROBLEM RATES

Lowest rates of alcohol-related problems for respondents in the 1973 national survey were found among:

• Women
• Persons over 50
• Widowed and married persons
• Persons of Jewish religious affiliation
• Residents of rural areas
• Residents of the South
• Persons with postgraduate education
• Persons who are mostly "wine drinkers"

BECOMING AN ALCOHOLIC

Ordinarily, when people take a drink for the first time in their lives, they do not immediately, nor will inevitably, become alcoholics. They have to encounter a sequence of events that culminate in alcoholism. But first, what exactly is alcoholism?

There is no universally accepted definition of alcoholism. But most scholars in the field seem to agree on what alcoholism consists of or on the nature of the problem suffered by so-called alcoholics. For example, most scholars appear to accept the following definition of an *alcoholic* offered by the World Health Organization in 1952: "Alcoholics are those excessive drinkers whose dependence upon alcohol has attained such a degree that it shows . . . an interference with their bodily and mental health, their interpersonal relations, and their smooth social and economic functioning." [23]

Yet experts disagree on how to label the alcoholic's problem as described in the above quote. Some label it a *disease;* others call it *problem drinking;* and others simply refrain from calling it either. A leading expert in the field who prefers the disease label argues:

But is alcoholism a disease? I think it is (and well named alcoholism, and I wouldn't attach the label alcoholism to anything that isn't a disease). I think it is a disease because the alcoholic can't consistently choose whether or not he shall engage in a self-injurious behavior— that is, any of the alcoholismic drinking patterns.[24]

Mark Keller, the author of this quote, earlier elaborated on the nature of the disease called alcoholism:

Alcoholism is a *chronic illness*, psychic or somatic or psychosomatic, which manifests itself as a disorder of behavior. It is characterized by the repeated drinking of alcoholic beverages, to an extent that exceeds customary dietary use or compliance with the social customs of the community and that interferes with the drinker's health, or his social or economic functioning.[25] [Emphasis added.]

As they object to the identification of alcoholism as a disease, some scholars do not want to use the word *alcoholism*. Instead, they prefer to employ the term *problem drinking*. One of them defines it this way: "Problem drinking is a repetitive use of beverage alcohol causing physical, psychological, or social harm to the drinker or to others." [26]

As for those researchers who neither consider alcoholism a disease nor call it *problem drinking*, they still use the term *alcoholism*, and define it in essentially the same way as the World Health Organization did many years ago. "We considered an alcoholic as one whose repeated drinking of alcoholic beverages interfered with his interpersonal relations or his social or economic functioning." [27]

In short, experts may differ in labeling the phenomenon or person in question, but they describe the nature of the phenomenon or person in about the same way. Thus, for our purposes here, we shall conceive of an *alcoholic* as a person who has one or more of the problems mentioned in any of the definitions quoted above. We should also note that alcoholics differ from one another. Some alcoholics may have only one problem, while others many problems. Relatedly, some alcoholics are in the relatively early stage of problem drinking while others are in the later stage. E. M. Jellinek, an influential pioneer in the study of alcoholism, has identified three stages of alcoholism, in addition to the introductory stage that a would-be alcoholic has to go through.[28]

THE INTRODUCTORY STAGE   Jellinek calls this stage *prealcoholic symptomatic phase*. Here prospective alcoholics begin as social drinkers. Through drinking, they discover the ability to experience some relief from tensions. But the more they drink, the less their tolerance for tensions; the less the tolerance for tensions, the more they want to drink to seek relief. This results in a vicious circle of more and more episodes of drunkenness and hangover. At the same time, the more individuals drink, the greater their tolerance for alcohol, so that they have to consume more and more alcohol in order to get drunk. These facts increase the psychological and physiological impact of alcohol on the drinker. This stage may last from six months to two years before the individual graduates into the next stage as a rookie alcoholic.

THE EARLY STAGE   In this stage, which Jellinek calls the *prodromal phase*, the rookie alcoholic starts to experience blackouts. A *blackout* is an attack of amnesia or memory loss, but it is quite different from passing out. When people drink beyond their alcohol-tolerance level, they may pass out on the spot, totally incapable of interacting with others. On the other hand, individuals experiencing blackouts may be the life of the party, or at least talk with others, move about freely, but the next day they cannot remember what they did.

In the early stage, individuals become excessive drinkers. When drinking socially, they begin to sneak drinks although they try to maintain an impression that they are drinking no more than anyone else. Their craving for alcohol becomes so great that they will consume huge quantities of alcoholic beverages, drink alone, and drink in the morning. Such excessive drinking begins to hurt their relations with relatives, friends, and fellow workers, and they therefore start feeling guilty about drinking too much.

THE MIDDLE STAGE   This stage, which Jellinek terms the *crucial phase*, is characterized by a loss of control over drinking. Once these individuals start drinking, they keep on doing so until the supply is gone or until they are too drunk to continue. Although this shows that the individuals cannot control their drinking, they themselves typically insist that they can stop if they really want to. To prove that they can, they will go on the wagon for a while or change their drinking patterns—switching types of liquor, trying different ways of mixing it, and altering speeds of consuming it.

But the more these people think they can control and try to control their drinking, the more they lose control. Consequently, they begin to invent excuses and rationalizations for drinking. They may, for example, blame their spouses or bosses for causing so much tension that they need to drink for relief. The drinking can break up their relations to bosses, friends, and family. This makes them become even more attached to liquor. They show this strong attachment by protecting or hiding their alcohol supply from the disapproving eyes of others. At this stage, people often skip meals in favor of liquor.

THE FINAL STAGE   This is, in Jellinek's words, the *chronic phase*. Unlike the alcoholics in the early and middle stages, those in the final stage show spectacular and even bizarre behavior. The major characteristic of this final stage is the onset of "benders" or drinking sprees—drinking and being in-toxicated continuously for several days without doing anything else. These people are completely dependent on alcohol. They are haunted by the tre-mendous fear that alcohol may be taken away from them. They have to have a drink just to be able to get up in the morning. They may be so far gone that to get liquor into their mouths becomes an almost impossible task to perform. But they usually work very hard at it—spending hours stumbling, crawling, vomiting, trembling, and failing to achieve the goal three or four times before finally succeeding in keeping a drink down. Since they rarely eat, they often suffer from malnutrition. They also suffer from delirium tremens, which often produces terrifying hallucinations—such as seeing mil-lions of little flies chasing, suffocating, or eating them. In this stage, they finally hit bottom, and may at this point acknowledge their total defeat by alcohol.

THE WAR ON ALCOHOLISM

Like illegal drug use discussed in the preceding chapter, alcoholism has been subjected to various attempts to control it, but it has proved to be a persistent aspect of American life.

During colonial days, the Puritans enjoyed drinking beer and rum in mod-eration. They only condemned excessive drinking. But during the next three centuries they became increasingly opposed to drinking per se, just as they opposed other forms of sensual pleasure.[29] Their opposition to drink-ing was similar to present-day opposition to any use of marihuana and heroin. Thus the early Americans, as well as their modern descendants who are opposed to drinking, considered an alcoholic anyone who drank alcohol re-gardless of the amount drunk. Then in the early 19th century there arose a crusade for total abstinence. This abstinence crusade, often misleadingly called the temperance movement (after the Woman's Christian Temperance Union), culminated in the enactment of the Eighteenth Amendment in 1919. During the next fourteen years, drunkenness did not go away from the face of America. On the contrary, Prohibition—sometimes called the "noble experiment"—was such a disastrous failure that it was repealed by the Twenty-first Amendment in 1933.

The origin of Prohibition in some way parallels the past and present out-lawing of psychoactive drugs, discussed in the last chapter. Although it ap-peared as a reform movement for improving living conditions of the urban working class, Prohibition originated mostly from an attempt to control the powerless segments of society. In postcolonial America, the temperance movement first emerged as an attempt on the part of the aristocracy of wealth to control the new upsurge of democracy.[30] Later the emergent dominant middle classes used the temperance movement to increase the prejudice and discrimination against Irish and German immigrants, Catholics and Jews, and the urban lower classes. The middle classes felt that their puritanical values of hard work were threatened by the "ne'er-do-well, unambitious, and irreligious" immigrants and poor Americans who traditionally "drank." Thus the puritanical middle classes formed such anti-alcohol organizations as the Anti-Saloon League and the Woman's Christian Temperance Union, which eventually led to the outlawing of alcohol. But by the time Prohibition came into effect, a new group had begun to emerge from within the middle class. Unlike the old middle class, who advocated total abstinence from drinking, the new one was not opposed to moderate use of alcohol. This temperate drinking, as opposed to abstinence from drinking, has become the norm of many middle-class people today.

With the rise of a corporate economy of large-scale organizations, a new middle class of salaried white-collar workers, managerial employees, and professionals has developed. The styles of life of such groups contrast with those of the old middle class of small enterprisers, independent farmers, and free professionals. . . . The cosmopolitans of the new middle class support the norms of permissive drinking. Unlike earlier periods, the aspirant to middle class status may now find that abstinence has become a negative symbol. The advocacy of moderate drinking has become widely held among church-going, respectable members of the middle classes in America.[31]

It may be noted that Prohibition failed largely because of its unrealistic goal of total abstinence at a time when large numbers of middle-class people were already given to moderate drinking, just as the present prohibition against marihuana is on its road to failure because of the moderate use of the drug among increasing numbers of middle-class adults.

Today, after more than forty years since the end of Prohibition, legal repression of the poor appears in a new form. As has been mentioned earlier, public drunkenness accounts for a very large proportion (between 30 and 40 percent) of the arrests made every year. The huge majority of public drunks are apparently from the lower classes. Although some states have repealed the law against public drunkenness and instituted detoxification programs and halfway houses for helping drunks, there still remain some thirty-odd states that look upon powerless drunks "as human vermin who have to be swept off the streets and thrown into drunk tanks." [32] Just as the earlier Prohibition failed to achieve its purpose of eliminating drinking, so the present law fails to achieve its purpose of eliminating public drunkenness.

A number of alcoholic treatment centers have been operating under the guidance of psychiatrists and psychologists since the beginning of the 1960s. Most of them use aversion therapy or a combination of this with group therapy. Group therapy involves bringing together a number of alcoholics (and in many cases, their wives or husbands and children) and trying to bring them back into society through a series of sessions with lectures, educational films, and discussions about drinking problems. Aversion therapy calls for the use of electric shock or nausea-inducing drugs designed to condition the alcoholic to feel sick at the very odor of liquor. Generally, this aversion therapy is effective only for a short time—the urge to drink returns within six to twelve months. The combination of this therapy with group treatment is more effective. However, the most effective method does not involve any professional therapist, but simply the alcoholics and ex-alcoholics themselves. It is the AA (Alcoholics Anonymous) method.

Alcoholics Anonymous was started in 1935, and today it is the largest and most successful organization for helping alcoholics. The only requirement for joining AA is the desire to stop drinking. Once having joined the organization, new members are assigned sponsors who are recovered alcoholics ready to come to their aid whenever needed. The treatment involves attending a series of meetings where a dozen or so alcoholics share their drinking histories. A very important part of the treatment requires one to admit to oneself and other AA members that one is an alcoholic and is powerless over alcohol. AA members also discuss, interpret, and attempt to follow the so-called Twelve-Step Program:

Step One: We admitted we were powerless over alcohol—that our lives had become unmanageable.

Step Two: Came to believe that a Power greater than ourselves could restore us to sanity.

Step Three: Made a decision to turn our will and our lives over to the care of God "as we understand Him."

Step Four: Made a searching and fearless moral inventory of ourselves.

Step Five: Admitted to God, to ourselves and to another human being the exact nature of our wrongs.

Step Six: Were entirely ready to have God remove all these defects of character.

Step Seven: Humbly asked Him to remove our shortcomings.

Step Eight: Made a list of all persons we had harmed, and became willing to make amends to them all.

Step Nine: Made direct amends to such people wherever possible, except when to do so would injure them or others.

Step Ten: Continued to take personal inventory and when we were wrong promptly admitted it.

Step Eleven: Sought through prayer and meditation to improve our conscious contact with God "as we understood Him," praying only for knowledge of His will for us and the power to carry that out.

Step Twelve: Having had a spiritual awakening as the result of these

steps we tried to carry this message to alcoholics, and to practice
these principles in all our affairs.[33]

The major reason for the relative effectiveness of the AA method is
the group support provided to alcoholics by people who have deep, personal understanding of drinking problems. The group support is particularly
important for alcoholics because they are typically people who have often
drunk *alone* to solve personal problems rather than participated in drinking
with other people for dietary, religious, or social reasons as the Italians, Jews,
or Chinese do. Nevertheless, not all alcoholics who have tried AA have won
their battle against alcoholism. In addition, although the government and
many private organizations have joined the fight against alcoholism, the
drinking problem persists on a large scale in our society. As Senator Hughes,
an ex-alcoholic who has done much to change the government's attitude
toward alcoholism, says, "I'm not optimistic that we're gaining on the problem. Instead, it's gaining on us." [34]

THEORIES OF ALCOHOLISM

There are numerous theories about the causation of alcoholism. They have
been divided into three broad categories: biological, psychological, and sociological theories.[35]

BIOLOGICAL THEORIES

Biologists often attribute alcoholism to such physical factors as nutritional
deficiencies, glandular disorders, innate metabolic dysfunctions, malfunction
of the central nervous system, or an unfortunate inheritance. Any one of
these biological factors is thought to cause a strong craving for alcohol,
which then leads to alcoholism. Since physicians generally consider alcoholism a disease, they look for the causes of alcoholism in the human body.
Thus the American Medical Association has offered the following physical
theories of alcoholism:

1. Alcoholism is caused by a metabolic disturbance which results in a craving
for alcohol.

2. Alcoholism is caused by an abnormal sugar metabolism.

3. Alcoholism is caused by any of a variety of endocrine deficiencies, including hypothyroidism, hypopituitarism, hypoadrenalism, and hypogo-
nadism.

4. Alcoholism is caused by dietary or metabolic deficiency of vitamins or
minerals.

5. Alcoholism is caused by glandular dysfunction, that is, liver deficiency, hyperinsulinism, or asynchronism of all the endocrine glands.

6. Alcoholism is caused by sensitivity to food, the symptoms of which are specifically relieved by use of alcohol.

7. Alcoholism is caused by defective function of an "alcohol appestat" in the hypothalamus, causing a thirst for alcohol.

8. Alcoholism is caused by an imbalance of the acetylcholine and receptor sites in the ascending reticular formation of the brainstem.[36]

Biological scientists have tested the preceding and other related theories, but the results have largely been contradictory or inconclusive. Take the study of heredity as a cause of alcoholism. Some researchers have found that people whose fathers are alcoholics often become alcoholics themselves. But other investigators found that when those whose fathers are alcoholics have been raised away from their original homes, they are less likely to develop alcoholism.

Biological researchers have also been criticized for confusing effect with cause. When they discover that alcoholics are more likely than non-alcoholics to have dietary deficiencies or glandular dysfunction, the researchers assume that these physiological defects are the causes of alcoholism. Critics, however, point out that the physiological defects may well be the effects, rather than the causes, of alcoholism. For the frequent and heavy consumption of alcoholic beverages is bound to have a damaging effect on the physical constitution.

Despite the inadequacies of the biological theories of alcoholism, a number of social scientists remain open-minded. As one leading sociological researcher on alcoholism says, "Although no specific physiological or biochemical factors have yet been satisfactorily identified as causing alcoholism, the existence of some biological deficiencies or sensitivities as possible contributing factors cannot be ruled out." [37] But the biological deficiencies are often assumed to contribute very little to the causation of alcoholism, when compared with psychological and sociological factors. Consequently, an increasing number of scholars have turned away from biological theories, and are paying greater attention to the psychological and sociological theories.

PSYCHOLOGICAL THEORIES

Psychologists, psychoanalysts, and psychiatrists usually attribute alcoholism to one or more negative personality traits. A large number of these personality traits have been identified.[38] These traits are sometimes collectively referred to as *the alcoholic personality*.

Psychologists William McCord and Joan McCord have classified these personality traits into three categories; each category is believed by a certain type of psychologists to be the cause of alcoholism. The first category includes such unconscious tendencies as self-destructive urges, oral fixation, and latent homosexuality, which Freudian psychologists associate with alcoholism. The second type of personality traits has to do with the striving for power—a reaction to a pervasive feeling of inferiority—which Adlerian psychologists consider as the cause of alcoholism. And the third group of alcoholic personality traits have been suggested by interpersonal psychologists, who emphasize the importance of dependency drives and aggressive urges.[39] Of these three, the last one is the most widely accepted as the cause of alcoholism.

In tracing a sample of boys into their adulthood, McCord and McCord found that those who had the personality traits of the first and second categories did not grow up to become alcoholics. But the McCords claim to have found enough evidence to support the theory that alcoholics have dependency personalities, which belong to the third category. The McCords argue that alcoholics' dependency personalities largely stem from a stressful and erratic home environment where the mother often comforts the child with loving indulgence but also often terrifies him or her with outright rejection. These conflicting childhood experiences tend to intensify the individual's need for love—the need for dependence on others. But this heightened need is not easy to satisfy, so that individuals become overwhelmed with anxiety, which in turn leads them to alcohol in order to get rid of the anxiety.

It should be noted that the McCords' data did not *directly* demonstrate the existence of dependency need in alcoholics. Instead, the McCords simply infer the presence of dependency desire from the alcoholics' erratic childhood experiences. Furthermore, there is an element of self-contradiction in the McCord argument that alcoholics do not show their dependency desires by being dependent and weak. Rather, they are observed to demonstrate it by being just the opposite—independent and tough. As the McCords contend:

Alcohol would be a major outlet available to such a dependent person. When intoxicated, he could achieve feelings of warmth, comfort, and omnipotence. His strong desires to be dependent would be satisfied. At the same time, he could maintain his image of independence and self-reliance. The hard drinker in American society is pictured as tough, extroverted, and manly—exactly the masculine virtues the alcoholic strives to incorporate into his own self-image.[40]

Many psychologists, like the McCords, obviously do not see any contradiction between their assumption that the alcoholic has a dependency need and their observation that the same alcoholic acts tough and aggressive.

This is because these psychologists consider the dependency need as a repressed, unconscious one, which causes alcoholics to compensate by acting, and believing themselves to be, tough and aggressive. But more recently psychologist David McClelland disagrees. He contends that a tough and aggressive personality, rather than a weak and dependent one, is the driving force behind alcoholism. McClelland argues:

> The fact that heavy drinkers are commonly counter-dependent and aggressive need not be interpreted as meaning that they have a repressed need for dependence, as many have argued. It may be taken *at its face value as evidence for a personalized power drive.* . . . Our main conclusion is that the alcoholic experience has a common core for men everywhere and that they drink to get it. While individuals in different cultures embroider and interpret the experience in different ways, and while it is more marked for distilled liquors than for wine and beer, the experience centers everywhere in men on increased thoughts of power. . . . And societies and individuals with accentuated needs for personalized power are more likely to drink more heavily in order to get the feeling of strength they need so much more than others.[41] [Emphasis added.]

In short, McClelland recognizes the desire for power as the only cause of alcoholism, while the McCords and many other psychologists do not necessarily quarrel with McClelland, because they acknowledge the power desire as the other, *conscious* aspect of the same alcoholic personality that is characterized by the *unconscious* need for dependency. The most popular idea among psychologists, then, is that heavy drinking serves the function of providing an appearance of toughness so as to cover up the alcoholic's weakness and inadequacy as a dependent person. But such a psychological theory has a weakness of its own: although it purports to be a scientific theory, there is no way to empirically demonstrate its concept of dependency needs.

SOCIOLOGICAL THEORIES

In sociology there are many theories of alcoholism. Only two will be discussed here. One is a strictly sociological theory, useful for explaining why some *groups* have higher alcoholism rates than do others. The other theory is social-psychological in character, explaining why some *individuals* become alcoholics but others do not.

EXPLAINING INDIVIDUAL DIFFERENCE According to the social-psychological theory, which has been provided by sociologist Harrison Trice, the unique factor that turns individuals into alcoholics is the fit between vulnerable personality traits and some drinking-group values and activities.[42] If people who have alcoholic personality traits associate regularly with drinking groups, they are likely to become alcoholics. On the other hand, if they lack regular exposure to drinking groups, these latent tendencies cannot be turned into alcoholism. More specifically, individuals have to go through four stages before they become alcoholic.

First, the person must have the qualifications for being a candidate, namely, possessing the vulnerable personality features. These personality features are about the same as those that psychologists such as the McCords have identified in the alcoholic. As Trice says, "A potential alcoholic has intense dependency needs and sharp feelings of worthlessness, self-hate, and inadequacy, which produce an unusual need to be looked upon by others and by himself as a 'man'." Such dependent individuals have deep anxiety about their own adequacy, which makes them highly susceptible to the influence of drinking groups.

Second, once they join drinking groups, they find that they fit right in. Members of drinking groups characteristically believe that drinking is a sign of masculine prowess. They are fond of encouraging a new member to "drink like a man," and praising him for being able to "hold his liquor." This is what the prospective male alcoholic badly needs because of his "unusual need to be looked upon by others and by himself as a 'man'."

Third, after drinking and enjoying his status as "a man" for some time, the individual finds it necessary to consume more and more liquor to prove his manhood. He reaches the point where he becomes an excessive drinker who has lost self-control. It is at this point that his drinking groups stop rewarding him for his alcohol consumption and start rejecting him as a loser. This is because the same social value that encourages a person to drink like a man, also emphasizes the importance of self-control—presumably another aspect of the same masculine character. In effect, drinking groups, being under the influence of that social value, seem to urge their members to drink as much as they can but not so much as to lose control over alcohol. The trouble with such urging is that the more one drinks, the less capable one is of knowing how much is too much. The consequence is that by the time one has lost control over alcohol, one may claim that one still has complete self-control. When individuals make such claims, they are ready for the next stage.

Fourth, after being ostracized by the drinking groups that initially encouraged the use of alcohol, excessive, uncontrolled drinkers seek out more tolerant drinking companions, other excessive, uncontrolled drinkers. In such company, alcoholics typically feel that they are still "men," and that they are able to control themselves although they continue to drink excessively. At this stage, they are securely locked into alcoholism.

EXPLAINING GROUP DIFFERENCES   The best-known sociological theory about alcoholism was presented in 1946 by Robert Bales.[43] This theory was partially derived from Bales's finding that there were striking differences in alcoholism rates among ethnic groups in the United States, particularly between the Irish (who had a very high alcoholism rate) and Orthodox Jews (who had a very low rate). According to Bales, there are three factors working together to produce high rates of alcoholism: production of acute inner tensions in people by their culture; a culturally induced attitude toward drinking as a means of relieving the inner tensions; and the failure of the culture to provide suitable substitute means for resolving the inner tensions.

To take the first factor, culturally produced inner tensions include feelings of anxiety, guilt, conflict, suppressed hostility, and sexual frustration. To show the way in which a culture can bring about these inner tensions in its members, Bales presented the case of Irish peasants, noted for their drunkenness during the past several centuries. Irish parents instilled fear, insecurity, and anxiety in their children by disciplining them with the threat of "bogey men," "spooks," and "fairies," and by smothering them with affection at one moment and beating them in a fit of anger at the next moment. The boys often had to stay on the farm and continue to work for their fathers until they retired or died. "So long as they stayed on the farm," Bales observed, "they had to work for him as 'boys' and were treated as boys, even though they might be forty-five or fifty years old." This created a huge reservoir of suppressed hostility against their fathers. Being kept under the father's thumb as "boys," these physically mature men could neither marry nor dally in premarital sexual escapades. Such a situation generated powerful sexual tensions.

Second, acute inner tensions, as just described, are almost always found as a background for compulsive drinking. And the tensions can easily find their outlet in compulsive drinking, if the culture has induced in the people the attitude that liquor is excellent for relieving the tensions. This is a part of what Bales referred to as the "individualistic-utilitarian" attitude toward drinking.

The alcoholism-prone Irish have such an attitude. Thus they resort to drinking when engaged in economic transactions. When Irish farmers buy or sell livestock at fairs, they treat each other with a few drinks in order to "soften the other guy up," and typically come home from fairs in a heavy state of intoxication. But their wives usually treat them with care and affection; their mothers lovingly call them "my poor boy"; and their friends, acquaintances, and others regard their intoxication with envy rather than pity. The Irish also consider alcohol as an effective folk remedy for "keeping the cold out of the stomach," for producing a feeling of warmth after exposure, for restoring consciousness in the case of fainting, for curing stomach aches, for combating insomnia, for reducing fatigue, for whetting the appetite, for feeling stronger physically and sexually, and even for getting rid of hangovers. With this attitude, the Irish find it natural to resort to drinking as a means of drowning their personal problems as well. The result is their relatively high rate of alcoholism.

Third, in coping with culturally induced stress, people would not turn to alcohol if they were provided with some other methods of resolving the stress. For Jews and Italians, eating seems to be their method of dealing with tension. Many Moslems are said to turn to hashish as well as strong tea and coffee. The Brahmins and Japanese are believed to rely on opium. As a result of their having culturally approved alternatives to the use of alcohol for resolving tension, these groups have low rates of alcoholism. But the Irish, being without an alternative to drinking, end up having a higher rate of alcoholism.

Of the three types of theories, the sociological theories appear to be the most satisfactory. As psychologists McCord and McCord admit, "Sociologists have produced impressive evidence demonstrating that rates of alcoholism are significantly related to the social factors." [44]

POWER THEORY APPLIED

Since it is physically and socially damaging to the individual, alcoholism may be viewed as a very unprofitable form of deviance. As such, there are more lower-class alcoholics than higher-class ones. In contrast, higher-class people tend more to use alcohol profitably, for example, as a means of helping make a desired business deal. Due to social approval of profitable drinking (social drinking) and social stigmatization of unprofitable drinking (alcoholism), the rich are far more likely to engage in social drinking than are the poor to become alcoholic.

The symbiotic relationship between the powerless and the powerful in regard to alcohol use may work in two ways: (1) Lower-status alcoholics may serve to create and reinforce the stereotype of alcoholics as skid row bums, thereby helping higher-status drinkers to keep on drinking without seeing themselves as alcoholics—because they cannot possibly see themselves as skid row bums. Higher-status drinkers, in turn, tend to perpetuate the stereotyped image of the lower-status alcoholic as worthless, which further aggravates lower-status alcoholics' drinking problems. (2) Alcoholism may be viewed by the public as an individual problem rather than a societal one. Such a view, in effect, blames the alcoholic; it prevents society from appreciating the role of the powerful liquor industry in the causation, perpetuation, and multiplication of drinking problems. Without limiting the availability and advertisement of alcohol, the power elite also aids and abets the liquor industry to push the number-one drug on the public.[45] All this makes for a powerful drinking culture, in which alcohol is used by the rich to rise to greater heights of success while it is used by the poor to drown themselves in greater depths of failure.

SUMMARY

Alcohol is the most popular drug, and alcoholism the most prevalent form of drug abuse. Yet the general public does not consider alcohol as a drug, and a number of myths about alcohol can be found in the public consciousness.

Alcohol is a depressant drug. As such, it reduces the drinker's sensorimotor ability but not moral competence. How much the sensorimotor ability can be reduced depends on the level of intoxication—the percentage of alcohol in the bloodstream. The latter, in turn, depends on such factors as the body size and weight of the drinker, type and amount of alcoholic beverages consumed, the quantity of food in the stomach, and the drinker's level of tolerance for alcohol. Taken in moderate amounts, alcohol can have some benefits for our body and social interaction. But when consumed in large quantities or drunk on a continual basis, alcohol may damage the liver, cause sexual impotence, bring about heart attack and cancer, weaken muscles, and impair learning ability and memory. Excessive alcohol intake has also been linked to automobile injuries and deaths, unserious and serious crimes, and huge economic costs to society.

Compared to nondrinkers, drinkers are more likely to be males, young adults, whites, liberal Protestants, higher-status persons, and residing in the Northeast, Middle Atlantic, and Pacific Coast states. But black, lower-status, and Irish-American drinkers tend more to end up as alcoholics.

There are four stages in the process of becoming an alcoholic. In the introductory stage, individuals discover their ability to use alcohol for relieving tension. In the next, early stage, rookie alcoholics begin to drink excessively and experience blackouts. In the middle stage, they lose control over drinking. And in the final stage, they become chronic alcoholics, so completely dependent on alcohol that they may have trouble getting up in the morning without first taking a drink.

There are three types of theories about the causation of alcoholism. Biological theories attribute alcoholism to such physical factors as nutritional deficiencies, glandular disorders, innate metabolic dysfunctions, and the like. Psychological theories blame alcoholism on such personality traits as dependency drive and aggressive urge. Sociological theories show how drinking groups encourage individuals with alcoholic personalities to become alcoholic, and how cultural groups can produce high rates of alcoholism. Finally, with power theory, we may define higher-status social drinking as profitable and lower-status alcoholism as unprofitable drinking, observe the greater prevalence of profitable drinking, and speculate on the symbiosis between both types of drinking.

SUGGESTED READINGS

Bales, Robert Freed. "Cultural Differences in Rates of Alcoholism." *Quarterly Journal of Studies on Alcohol* 6 (March 1946): 480–499.

Cahalan, Don. *Problem Drinkers*. San Francisco: Jossey-Bass, 1970.

Fort, Joel. *Alcohol: Our Biggest Drug Problem*. New York: McGraw-Hill, 1973.

Jellinek, E. M. "Phases of Alcohol Addiction." *Quarterly Journal of Studies on Alcohol* 13 (1952): 673–684.

MacAndrew, Craig and Robert B. Edgerton. *Drunken Comportment*. London: Nelson, 1969.

McCord, William and Joan McCord. *Origins of Alcoholism*. Stanford, California: Stanford University Press, 1960.

Pittman, David J., ed. *Alcoholism*. New York: Harper & Row, 1967.

Spradley, James P. *You Owe Yourself a Drunk*. Boston: Little, Brown, 1970.

Trice, Harrison M. *Alcoholism in America*. New York: McGraw-Hill, 1966.

Wiseman, Jacqueline P. *Stations of the Lost: The Treatment of Skid Row Alcoholics*. Englewood Cliffs, New Jersey: Prentice-Hall, 1971.

15 PROFITABLE DEVIANCE

Organized crime, white-collar crime, and governmental crime may be said to represent profitable deviance. They are profitable in that the individuals involved can illegally acquire a lot of money, power, or influence with a relatively low risk of harmful consequences to themselves. These three types of crime are presumably more profitable than the other forms of deviant behavior discussed in the preceding chapters.

Organized crime would appear to be less profitable than white-collar crime and governmental crime, however. Organized crime carries a higher risk of arrest or imprisonment in the conventional upperworld, as well as some risk of resulting in mayhem or murder in the criminal underworld. Related to this different level of profitability from the perpetration of crime, is the perpetrator's different level of social status and respectability. Generally, organized criminals have emerged from the lower-class neighborhood and are thus not so respectable in the eye of conventional society. White-collar and governmental criminals have higher social status and are therefore more respectable. Thus, organized crime may be considered lower-level profitable deviance, while white-collar crime and governmental crime are higher-level.

Compared with other forms of deviance, the nature of profitable deviance is far more difficult to determine. This is because people engaged in this type of deviance, being relatively successful and powerful members of their society, are able to successfully carry out their crimes and divert public attention, including the law enforcement agencies, from their crimes. Consequently, in the existing literature, these three types of profitable deviance still remain "ineptly defined, inadequately investigated, and inexpertly assessed in regard to causality and consequences." [1]

THE NATURE AND THEORY OF
ORGANIZED CRIME

Organized crime suggests two things: a criminal organization and its activities. These are apparent in the following definition of organized crime presented by the President's Crime Commission:

[1] Organized crime is a society that seeks to operate outside the control
of the American people and their governments. It involves thousands
of criminals, working within structures as complex as those of any
large corporation, subject to laws more rigidly enforced than those of
legitimate governments.
[2] Its actions are not impulsive but rather the result of intricate
conspiracies, carried on over many years and aimed at gaining control
over whole fields of activity in order to amass huge profits.[2]

Let us examine more closely the nature of the structure of organized crime and its activities.

STRUCTURE OF ORGANIZED CRIME

There are two conflicting views on this subject. On the one side is the official view—embraced by the President's Commission and most governmental officials—that organized crime is a tightly knit national organization, variously called the *Mafia, Cosa Nostra, the syndicate,* or *the mob.* Challenging this view is the unofficial belief that the Mafia does not exist, and that organized crime is at best only a loose, informal confederation of diverse groups of professional criminals operating independently in the same or different cities.

According to sociologist Donald Cressey, who worked for the President's Commission, the organized crime syndicate called *Cosa Nostra (our affair)* is a nationwide alliance made up of at least twenty-four families in America's largest cities.[3] Members of these families are immigrants from Italy and Sicily as well as Americans of Italian and Sicilian descent. There are about five thousand of them. Each family consists of a hierarchical structure of positions ranging from the highest to the lowest as follows: "Don" or boss, underboss, lieutenants, counselor, and "soldiers" or "button men" (so called because they do the bidding of the higher-ranking members when the latter "push the button"). The boss of each family directs the criminal activities of the members of his family. The bosses of the most powerful families constitute the "Commission," which controls, directs, or influences the interconnection among the various families—the interconnection being based on understandings, agreements, and treaties among the families. The number of the commissioners usually varies from nine to twelve.

The Cosa Nostra works with a large number of people who are not its members and not necessarily of Italian descent. These people are considered beneath the lowest-ranking member—the soldier—of the crime syndicate. Most of them do their work on the street, such as taking bets, driving trucks, and carrying messages. The relationship between these workers and the crime corporation can be illustrated by the following:

In Chicago, for example, the workers in a major lottery business operated in a Negro neighborhood were Negroes; the bankers for the lottery were Japanese-Americans; but the game, including the banking operation, was licensed, for a fee, by a Chicago "family" member. The entire operation, including the bankers, was more or less a "customer" of the Chicago branch of Cosa Nostra, in the way any enterprise operating under a franchise is a "customer" of the parent corporation. In this area, as in many others, the "small fry" were Negroes and the "big sharks" were Cosa Nostra men.[4]

These Cosa Nostra men owe their dominance in organized crime to their Italian and Sicilian forefathers. The latter, having immigrated to this country's urban slums, first started engaging in organized crime during the 1890s and then expanded their power and influence during the Prohibition years of the 1920s. Today the Italians and Sicilians still dominate organized crime, though there are signs that some blacks and Puerto Ricans in the urban ghettos have begun to form their own Mafia.

The syndicate governs its members by a code of conduct. This code is supposed to protect all the syndicate members, but is, in effect, administered and enforced for the protection of each family boss. The code, according to Cressey, consists of these rules: (1) Be loyal to other members of the mob; do not interfere with each other's interests. (2) Be rational and cool-headed, such as conducting illegal businesses in a quiet, safe, profitable manner or settling disputes among members in a cool, calm, nonviolent way. (3) Always do right by respecting womanhood and the elders. (4) Be a stand-up guy; don't sell out, no matter how severe the punishment or the threat of it by the police. (5) Have class; don't be a sucker.[5] The Mafia has the power to effectively enforce these rules. Particularly in regard to the code of loyalty and silence—rules 1 and 4—the Mafia's enforcement power is so great that if members become informers, they are likely to be murdered. In fact, this mob power has been thought to rival the power of the mighty United States government. As the President's Commission writes:

Robert F. Kennedy, when he was Attorney General, illustrated [the mob's] power simply and vividly. He testified before a Senate subcommittee in 1963 that the physical protection of witnesses who had cooperated with the Federal Government in organized crime cases often required that those witnesses change their appearance, change their names, or even leave the country. When the government of a powerful country is unable to protect its friends from its enemies by means less extreme than obliterating their identities, surely it is being seriously challenged, if not threatened.[6]

This official view of organized crime as a powerful, well-integrated, nationwide conspiracy is not only popular with the lay public but also with many writers of criminology textbooks.[7] As for the opposite, unofficial view, Ramsey Clark—when he was no longer attorney general—expressed it this way: "As with all crime, we oversimplify our definition of organized crime. There is far more to it than La Cosa Nostra. Our society is much too complex to expect only a single syndicate or type of illegal activity. There is no one massive organization that manages all or even most planned and continuous criminal conduct throughout the country."[8]

We should, however, note that the issue is not whether organized crime exists or not—for the consensus is that it exists. Rather, the issue is how tightly or loosely organized it is. Thus the official view suggests that organized crime is a tightly knit organization, while the unofficial view implies that it is so loosely organized that it should not be considered an organization at all. Because there is a lack of reliable information on the structure of organized crime, the conflict between those two views cannot be settled. But we may settle for the unquestionable fact that organized crime does involve certain patterns of criminal activities, to which we now turn.

ACTIVITIES OF ORGANIZED CRIME

According to the official view, organized crime is a multibillion-dollar enterprise. Its annual income has been officially estimated to be higher than that of any single legitimate industry or about equal to the combined profits of the ten largest industrial corporations, such as General Motors, Standard Oil, and so on. This means that even the "soldier"—who occupies the lowest position in the crime syndicate—is a millionaire. But Clark considers this official estimate as a wild exaggeration, saying: "There is big money in organized crime for a few, but for most it is dangerous, hard, dirty work for uncertain middle-class incomes."[9] This, however, does not necessarily contradict the official estimate. The few who are considered by Clark to be making a lot of money seem to be, in the official view, the five thousand members of the syndicate, while the majority who are regarded by Clark as doing the dirty work might in the official view be the nonmembers working for the mob. In whatever way one cares to look at its structure, organized crime is indeed a highly lucrative enterprise for ambitious lower-class people. This enterprise is supported by the following types of criminal activities.[10]

SELLING ILLEGAL GOODS AND SERVICES Organized criminals sell to millions of Americans such greatly desired illegal goods and services as illicit gambling, loan sharking, and narcotics. Illicit gambling includes betting on horse races, lotteries, and sporting events. It is the organized criminals' largest source of income; it brings in at least $20 billion a year (as compared with only about $5 billion reaped by legal betting at racetracks). The second largest source of revenue for organized crime is *loan sharking*—the lending of money at exorbitantly high rates, typically around 30 percent a week. Since their customers can only put up their bodies as security for the loan (if they had valuable property they would have gone to a legitimate loan company), the loan sharks ensure repayment by using violence or the threat of it against their customers. They may, for example, break their noses, arms, or legs; hang them by their feet out of a window twenty stories high; or call up a man's wife and say such things as, "If your husband don't pay the loan we'll cut off your teats and send them to him in a box." [11] But the loan sharks have enough business sense to avoid killing the debtor, for they know that a dead body can hardly procure money to pay off the loan. Finally, organized criminals deal in narcotics for maximum profit at minimum risk of interference from law enforcers. Thus they restrict their activities to importing and wholesale distribution, letting independent drug pushers take over the risky business of selling narcotics on the street. Though it does not earn billions of dollars as do illegal gambling operations or loan sharking, the narcotics trade still brings in about $20 million a year.

RACKETEERING This may take the simple form of a "protection racket," which involves the extortion of money from legitimate business people. The latter are given an offer they cannot refuse: the sale of the mob's "insurance policy" against such "accidents" as the burning of their stores and the busting of their store windows or their heads—to be carried out by the mobsters themselves if the business people refuse to buy the "insurance." The more elaborate and more common form is *labor racketeering*. This involves the manipulation of workers' employers and unions. More specifically, racketeers forcibly offer business people a "sweetheart contract," whereby the employers pay them a fee for having their employees join the racketeers' nonexistent union; or the racketeers extort money from employers by threatening them with labor strife; demand that the employing company hire them as "labor consultants" or put their relatives on the company's payroll; use threats of labor discord to force the trucking, construction, and waterfront shipping companies to ignore gambling, loan sharking, and pilferage on company property; or infiltrate the leadership of a union so as to steal its pension fund.

LARGE-SCALE THIEVERY   This is a part of organized crime that includes the large-scale narcotics trade.   Organized criminals leave such small-scale thefts as holdups, pickpocketing, mugging, housebreaking, and burglarizing of small shops to independent amateur or professional criminals. Organized criminals turn to the wholesale operation instead. For example, they steal whole carloads of merchandise (sometimes with the car itself) from docks and railway stations; they steal multimillion dollars' worth of automobiles and furnish them with proper identification, such as engine numbers and registration papers, necessary for selling them; or they steal huge quantities of negotiable stocks and bonds as well as credit cards. To sell these "hot" materials, organized criminals have a fence who works like a big-time merchandising operator.[12]

INFILTRATING LEGITIMATE BUSINESSES   Organized criminals have been increasingly infiltrating such legitimate businesses as Las Vegas casinos, nightclubs and restaurants, hotels and motels, trucking companies, wholesale food distributors; and the industries of banking and investment, construction, real estate, electronics, health services, and so on. By acquiring any one of these legitimate businesses, members of organized crime aim to achieve certain objectives: gain respectability; establish a legitimate source of income for paying taxes and thus avoiding income tax prosecution; invest "bad" money (from gambling and other illegal activities) in a legitimate business for legitimate profit; and use the legitimate business as a front for carrying out illegitimate schemes. One of these schemes involves insurance fraud: taking over businesses and then hiring professional arsonists to burn buildings and their contents, so as to collect on the fire insurance. Another scheme has to do with bankruptcy fraud, such as illustrated by the following:

With the original owners remaining in nominal management positions, extensive product orders were placed through established lines of credit, and the goods were immediately sold at low prices *before* the suppliers were paid. The organized criminal group made a quick profit of three-quarters of a million dollars by pocketing the receipts from sale of the products ordered and placing the firm in bankruptcy *without* paying the suppliers.[13] [Emphasis added.]

CORRUPTING PUBLIC OFFICIALS   This is necessary for successfully engaging in all the above patterns of activities. The public officials involved are of two types: politicians and law enforcers. The manner of corruption may involve either outright bribery or contribution to a political campaign. It has been observed that extensive corruption of law enforcers has been found whenever an investigating body has been created to look for it. It has also been estimated by political analysts that organized crime contributes about 15 percent of the costs of local and state political campaigns. Organized criminals, then, are able to have their "political front person" pass laws favoring their interests and prevent the passing of laws damaging to their illegal activities. Organized criminals are also able to have their "cousin in city hall" or their "beard in the police department" (the mob's terms for corrupted officials) ignore their mob activities.

THEORY OF ORGANIZED CRIME

Sociologist Daniel Bell sees organized crime as "an American way of life" for the poor but ambitious, particularly those who are immigrants in urban slums.[14] The implication is that organized crime exists because it serves a positive function: it enables poor but ambitious Americans to achieve success. As Bell writes: "For crime, in the language of the sociologists, has a 'functional' role in the society, and the urban racket—the illicit activity organized for continuing profit, rather than individual illegal acts—is one of the queer ladders of social mobility in American life." [15]

Other experts on organized crime agree with Bell. They all observe that organized crime has given various poor ethnic groups the opportunity to realize the American Dream. There is, then, an ethnic succession in organized crime. First, in the last century, the Irish dominated organized crime, to be followed by the Jews, and then by the Italians. Today blacks and Puerto Ricans are in the process of developing their own Mafia; they will succeed the Italians when the latter achieve greater success in the conventional upperworld.[16]

Moreover, Bell observes that there is nothing new about Americans' use of violence to climb the ladder of social mobility. For there is a historical link between ambitious poor Americans of the present and those of the past in their reliance on criminal means to achieve success. As Bell says:

The pioneers of American capitalism were not graduated from
Harvard's School of Business Administration. The early settlers and
founding fathers, as well as those who "won the West" and built
up cattle, mining, and other fortunes, often did so by shady speculations
and a not inconsiderable amount of violence. . . . [More recently]' later
comers [namely, organized criminals] pursued equally ruthless tactics.[17]

Of course, when those early American settlers and their descendants became no longer poor, they sought respectability by rejecting violence as the means of doing business. Today successful organized criminals are attempting to do the same.

THE NATURE AND THEORY OF WHITE-COLLAR CRIME

The term *white-collar crime* was first introduced by sociologist Edwin Sutherland in 1939. Today it is widely used by sociologists as well as the lay public. In this section, we shall deal with the definition of white-collar crime, provide some examples of it, seek out its underlying elements, and discuss its costs to society.

DEFINITION

Unlike organized crime, which is typically committed by lower-class persons, white-collar crime is characteristically engaged in by middle- and upper-class people. These people, according to Sutherland, are those in the middle, "wage-earning class, which wears good clothes at work, such as clerks in stores" *and* those in the upper class such as "business managers and executives." [18] But when Sutherland first introduced the concept of white-collar crime, he had in mind only the upper-class people. He also linked these respectable people's crime to their occupation. As Sutherland wrote:

White-collar crime may be defined approximately as a crime committed by a person of respectability and high social status in the course of his occupation. Consequently, it excludes many crimes of the upper class, such as most of their cases of murder, adultery, and intoxication, since these are not customarily a part of their occupational procedures. Also, it excludes the confidence games of wealthy members of the underworld, since they are not persons of respectability and high social status.[19]

Thus, in this classic definition, two things characterize white-collar crime. One, it is *occupational* crime, carried out during the course of one's occupation. Two, such a crime is committed by a relatively *respectable* person, who is more likely a higher-status person than a lower-status one. When Sutherland initially proposed this definition, it was subjected to various criticisms. For example, critics argued that so-called white-collar crime, such as individual income tax evasion, need not be occupational in nature nor committed by a respectable person. Today, however, most sociologists seem to accept the reality of white-collar crime. They also seem to recognize Sutherland's caution that his concept of white-collar crime "is not intended to be definitive, but merely to call attention to crimes which are not ordinarily included within the scope of criminology." [20] Gilbert Geis, for instance, regards white-collar crime as "not a scientific criminological designation but rather a label designed to call attention to the violation of a variety of criminal statutes by persons who at the moment are generally not considered, in connection with such violations, to be the 'usual' kind of underworld and/or psychological aberrant offender." [21]

We may, therefore, generally define *white-collar crime* as a largely occupational crime committed mainly by respectable people. In so defining it, we consider it as merely a sensitizing concept, designed to sensitize us to "respectable" as opposed to "ordinary" crimes.

SOME EXAMPLES

Specifically, what is white-collar crime? It consists of two types: crimes against the public (committed by a business or company) and crimes against the company (committed by its employees). Examples of crimes against the public are tax frauds; antitrust violations; deceptive advertising; deceptive sales practices; securities frauds; land frauds; home improvement schemes; adulteration of foods; illegal sale of untested drugs, unsafe cars, and other dangerous products; and unlawful pollution of the environment. On the other hand, crimes against the company may include employee theft, embezzlement, and expense account frauds.

It may be noted that while crimes against the company affect the company's money only, the crimes against the public may affect both the public's money and body. Consider, for example, the following case of Hormel Company, which in 1969 took stale meat returned by its retail store customers, repackaged and resold it for a higher profit to other stores—without the legally required reinspection by the U.S. Department of Agriculture officer in charge:

When the original customers returned the meat to Hormel, they used the following terms to describe it: "moldy liverloaf, sour party hams, leaking bologna, discolored bacon, off-conditioned hams, and slick and slimy spareribs." Hormel renewed these products with cosmetic measures (reconditioning, trimming, and washing). Spareribs returned for sliminess, discoloration, and stickiness were rejuvenated through curing and smoking, renamed Windsor Loins, and sold in ghetto stores for more than fresh pork chops.[22]

The crimes against the public do not only affect the poor, as the preceding illustration indicates, they may also affect the less poor, average Americans as well. The most striking example of this involves air pollution. As Ralph Nader says, "The efflux from motor vehicles, plants, and incineration of sulfur oxides, hydrocarbons, carbon monoxide, oxides of nitrogen, particulates, and many more contaminants amounts to compulsory consumption of violence by most Americans. There is no full escape from such violent ingestions, for breathing is required." [23]

ELEMENTS OF THE CRIME

White-collar crime has certain elements that distinguish it from lower-class criminality. The most distinguishable ones are its rational execution and its resulting high profit. Equally distinguishable but less obvious are the following components of white-collar crime: (1) the victim's unwitting cooperation, (2) society's indifference toward the crime, and (3) the perpetrator's noncriminal self-image.

VICTIM'S UNWITTING COOPERATION In contrast to such lower-class crimes as murder, robbery, rape, and assault, white-collar crimes require their victims' unwitting cooperation. This cooperation is unwitting because it is based on the victim's carelessness or ignorance. In a home improvement scheme, the victims do not bother to check the work history of the fraudulent company that solicits them, and they sign a contract without examining its contents such as in regard to the true price and the credit terms. Some victims purchase goods through the mail without checking the reputation of the firm. Physicians prescribe untested drugs after having relied on only the drug company's sales people and advertising.[24] It may be difficult for the victims to know they are victimized, even if they want to find out the true nature of their victimization. Grocery shoppers, for example, are hard put to detect such unlawful substances as residues of hormones, antibiotics, pesticides, and nitrites in the meat they buy. Even bank executives or their supposedly competent managers and auditors are rarely able to detect embezzlement by their employees. A case in point is as follows:

By entering fraudulent data into the bank's computer from a remote terminal in his branch office, a chief teller of a major New York savings bank stole a million and a half dollars from hundreds of accounts. . . . The manual auditing and the computer controls failed to show any fraudulent manipulation. The teller was not detected until a police raid on a gambling operation revealed that he was betting up to $30,000 a day on professional sports. Even then the teller had to explain his manipulations to the bank executives for them to fully understand what he had done.[25]

SOCIETY'S INDIFFERENCE While ignorance or carelessness leads the victim to unwittingly cooperate with white-collar criminals, society's indifference to their crimes is a blessing wittingly bestowed on them. Generally, little effort is made to catch white-collar criminals, and if on rare occasions they are caught, they rarely go to jail. For example, industrialists who openly violate antipollution laws are allowed to do so because the government, though professing a dedication to law and order, does not follow through on it. Also, workers, being understandably more concerned with their jobs, tend to be indifferent toward air pollution and supportive of their employers' rationalization that air pollution is "the smell of the payroll" and "the price of progress." [26]

When forty-five executives of major electric companies were found guilty of antitrust violations in the early 1960s, most of them were either given suspended thirty-day sentences or ordered to pay relatively small fines. When thousands of lawsuits were brought against the companies, they were settled out of court for about $500 million. But the companies' top executives succeeded in persuading the Internal Revenue Service to let them write off all their legal expenses, fines, and out-of-court settlements as "ordinary and necessary business expenses"—though the IRS would not allow the average citizen to deduct a fine for a speeding ticket as an "ordinary and necessary business expense," nor permit a convicted bank robber to deduct legal expenses.[27] The public was not only indifferent to the crimes of these executives, it was even sympathetic to those few who were sentenced to thirty days in jail.

As one executive convicted and sentenced to jail in the electrical conspiracy said: "On the bright side for me personally have been the letters and calls from people all over the country, the community, the shops and offices here, expressing confidence in me and support. This demonstration has been a warm and humbling experience for me." It is unlikely that a convicted burglar would receive such letters and calls.[28]

The indifference toward white-collar crime is so great that the government does not restrain profit-hungry business people from adulterating certain foods. The U.S. Department of Agriculture (USDA), for example, does not exercise enough restraint over the food industry; many food products have been massively adulterated and fraudulently labeled. Consider the following report on the hot dog labeled by its producer as "all meat":

[Today] the consumer is still confronted by such *pièces de resistance* as the hot dog, which by law can contain 69 percent water, salt, spices, corn syrup and cereal, and 15 percent chicken; that still leaves a little room for goat meat, pigs' ears, eyes, stomachs, snouts, udders, bladders and esophagus—all legally okay. There is no more all-American way to take a break at the old ball game than to have water and pigs' snouts on bun, but you might prefer to go heavier on the mustard from now on.[29]

The mustard can make your *hot* dog true to its name all right. But it may be added that under USDA regulations the "all meat" hot dog may also contain up to 30 percent fat. So you may also call it "fat dog." Further, for many years the "all meat" hot dog should also have been called "bone dog," for it was legally permitted by the USDA to contain 20 percent bone bits. (This USDA regulation was only recently suspended, after a lawsuit was successfully brought against it by consumer groups.)

CRIMINAL'S NONCRIMINAL SELF-IMAGE With their victims' cooperation and their society's indifference, white-collar criminals are able to maintain their noncriminal self-image, seeing themselves as respectable persons rather than as common criminals. This self-image plays an important part in the perpetration of various white-collar crimes.

These criminals usually express their noncriminal self-image through certain rationalizations. Convicted executives of the electric companies rationalized that their unlawful price-fixing schemes were far from being criminal. Instead, they viewed themselves as having really served a worthwhile purpose for the nation's economy by "stabilizing prices," and they congratulated themselves for having effectively served their companies by "recovering costs." There was no such thing as price fixing in their book. Embezzlers have also been found to define their stealing as only "borrowing" money; they insist that they will pay it back soon.[30] Perpetrators of the more common employee theft feel that they actually do not steal anything from their companies, because the latter are believed to make up the losses by using them as tax deductions and by charging customers higher prices.

COSTS OF THE CRIME

Despite such rationalizations, the President's Crime Commission believes that white-collar crimes do impose certain costs on society. It divides these costs into three types: economic, physical, and social.

ECONOMIC COST In 1949 Sutherland estimated the economic cost of white-collar crime to be several times as great as the cost of all the crimes customarily lumped together as the "crime problem" in the United States. In

1967 the President's Crime Commission gave a considerably higher estimate: the nation's annual loss to white-collar crime (including tax fraud, securities fraud, fraudulent drugs and medical devices, home improvement frauds, and auto repair frauds) is from 27 to 42 times as great as the annual loss to ordinary property crime (comprising all robberies, burglaries, auto thefts, larceny cases, and forgeries).[31] Further, as Sutherland suggested, it is extremely rare for a burglar or robber to make off with a million dollars, but it is not rare for an embezzler to steal that much. In fact, the million-dollar embezzler is only a small fry among white-collar criminals.[32]

From the standpoint of its individual victims, white-collar crime inflicts a high financial cost. This is particularly the case with the elderly and the poor who are victimized by consumer fraud. Again, white-collar crime costs its victims far more than lower-class crime. As former Attorney General Ramsey Clark says:

To the victims the consequences of white-collar crime are often
more dire than those that follow theft, burglary or robbery. White-
collar crime can dig deeper than the wallet in the pocket to wipe
out the savings of a lifetime. The thief takes only what is in the purse
or the dresser at the moment of his crime. The embezzler may
reach beyond to destroy the equity of a family, ruin a whole firm or
render corporate stock valueless.[33]

PHYSICAL COST   According to the President's Crime Commission, "physical injury or even death can come from tainted foods and harmful drugs sold in violation of the Pure Food and Drug Act, foods sold in violation of local health laws, and various violations of safety laws and housing codes." [34] We may add that physical injury or death can also come from pollution of the air and degradation of lakes and rivers.

There are no official statistics nor scientific studies to indicate the number of injuries and deaths caused by white-collar crime. This is because, unlike the crude form of violence customarily linked to the lower-class crimes of murder and mugging, the violence of white-collar crimes is far more invisible, more complex, less comprehensible, and less traceable to the culprits. Moreover, our conventional framework of thinking, values, social action and concern—which has long been conditioned to the raw violence of lower-class crime—prevents us from appreciating the subtle but deadly violence of white-collar crime. Nevertheless, we could force ourselves to perceive the white-collar criminal violence. We can become aware of the correlation between the white-collar criminal violations mentioned above and the tremendous toll of injuries and deaths that result. It can be roughly estimated that the violence inflicted on the public by white-collar criminals in their pursuit of profit, far exceeds the violence of all lower-class criminals combined. Consider, for example, this comparison given by Nader: "If you take all the riots [between the years 1967 and 1969] and throughout the nation, you will see the total of 206 dead. That's less than two days' toll of violence on the highway—less than two days!" [35]

SOCIAL COST   The social cost of white-collar crimes, though immeasurable, is felt to be more far-reaching than the financial and physical costs discussed above. Various writers have described the social cost in different ways, each emphasizing a certain dimension of the cost.

A former United States attorney general, stressing the tendency of white-collar crime to tear apart our moral fiber, writes: "White-collar crime is the most corrosive of all crimes. The trusted prove untrustworthy; the advantaged, dishonest. It shows the capability of people with better opportunities for creating a decent life for themselves to take property belonging to others. As no other crime, it questions our moral fiber." [36]

A sociologist sees white-collar crime as wrecking our social institutions: "White collar crimes violate trust and therefore create distrust; this lowers social morale and produces social disorganization. Many of the white-collar crimes attack the fundamental principles of the American institutions. Ordinary crimes, on the other hand, produce little effect on social institutions or social organization." [37]

A legal scholar is more specific, focusing on the effect of white-collar crime on business morality: "Every stock market fraud lessens confidence in the securities market. Every commercial bribe or kickback debases the level of business competition, often forcing other suppliers to join in the practice if they are to survive. . . . The pharmaceutical company which markets a new drug based on fraudulent test results undercuts its competitors who are still marketing the properly tested drugs, and may cause them to adopt similar methods. Competitors who join in a conspiracy to freeze out their competition, or to fix prices, may gravely influence the course of our economy, in addition to harming their competitors and customers." [38]

The President's Crime Commission includes lower-class criminality and juvenile delinquency as the effects of white-collar crime: "It is reasonable to assume that prestigious companies that flout the law set an example for other businesses and influence individuals, particularly young people, to commit other kinds of crime on the ground that everyone is taking what he can get. If businessmen who are respected as leaders of the community can do such things as break the antitrust laws or rent dilapidated houses to the poor at high rents, it is hard to convince the young that they should be honest." [39] In a similar vein, one United States senator blames white-collar criminals for causing discontent and riots among the oppressed minorities: "It seems undeniable that the scandalous gouging of minority groups by dishonest merchants and salesmen contributes to a potentially explosive situation in every ghetto in America and is one of the discontents leading to riots." [40]

THEORY OF WHITE-COLLAR CRIME

In 1949 Sutherland used his general theory of differential association (see Chapter 2) to explain white-collar crime. Sutherland did this because he believed that white-collar crime and ordinary lower-class crime are basically the same in their causation. As he stated, "The data which are at hand suggest that white-collar crime has its genesis in the same general process as other criminal behavior, namely, differential association." [41] By this Sutherland meant that white-collar criminals have learned to become what they are by *associating* with other white-collar criminals (who define white-collar criminal behavior favorably) more than with honest business people (who define white-collar criminal behavior unfavorably). These white-collar criminals, Sutherland insisted, are similar to lower-class criminals, because the latter have *associated* with other lower-class criminals more than with law-abiding lower-class persons.

But Sutherland also introduced a new concept that implies that the cause of white-collar crime is radically different from the origin of lower-class crime. The new concept is *differential social organization.* Sutherland used this concept to explain why white-collar crime occurs: "Business has a rather tight organization for the violations of business regulations, while the political society [the combination of government and public] is not similarly organized against violations of business regulations." [42] The implication is that the government and the public do not strongly disapprove of white-collar criminals nor impose stringent law enforcement on them. Now, this is hardly the case with lower-class criminals; the government and the public disapprove of them far more strongly and exercise much more stringent law enforcement on them.

Therefore, Sutherland's theory about white-collar crime is actually not completely derived from his theory of differential association. His theory about white-collar crime can be briefly stated as follows: white-collar crime results from two related causes. One is the individual's greater involvement with dishonest business people than with honest ones. The other cause is the society's lack of effort to control dishonest business practices.

Given these two causes of white-collar crime, we may not know the social-psychological process that the individual has to go through in order to become a white-collar criminal. Sutherland's former student, Donald Cressey, later developed a theory about this process from his study of embezzlement.[43] He found that people go through three stages in becoming embezzlers. In the first stage, they encounter what they perceive to be a *nonshareable* financial problem. They cannot share this problem with their spouses or friends because they feel too ashamed to tell anyone or have too much pride to ask anyone for help. In the second stage, they become aware of an *opportunity* for secretly resolving their problem. Such an opportunity is already imbedded in the very position of trust that they hold as a result of their occupations. And in the third stage, they violate that trust—through embezzling money with which they are entrusted—by *rationalizing* that they are merely borrowing the money rather than stealing it. Although Cressey has derived this theory from his study of embezzlement, it is presumably applicable to other forms of white-collar crime.

THE NATURE AND THEORY OF GOVERNMENTAL CRIME

Even more far-reaching than the social cost of white-collar crime is that of governmental crime. As Supreme Court Justice Louis Brandeis wrote in 1928, "If the government becomes a lawbreaker, it breeds contempt for law; it invites every man to become a law unto himself; it invites anarchy." [44] It is within this context that we can appreciate what Senator Lowell Weicker meant when in 1973 he referred to the Watergate criminals as those "who almost stole America." Let us see how the government perpetrates crime and how it characteristically attempts to neutralize crime.

PERPETRATING THE CRIME

The government usually perpetrates a crime for one of three purposes. One is for the government to maintain its *power*. Another is for government officials to flaunt their *arrogance* toward common citizens. And the third purpose is for obtaining *money*. These three functions of governmental crime are usually distinguishable, but sometimes go together in a single act of criminality. The following discussion will deal with each of these three types of governmental crime.

MAINTAINING POWER The government's proneness to lawlessness as the means of maintaining its power is likely to increase when it is either challenged by an opposing political party from within or threatened by dissident groups from without.

The most common instances of governmental lawbreaking involve political campaigns between opposing members of the power elite. In 1925 the U.S. Congress passed the Federal Corrupt Practices Act, which prohibits business corporations from making financial contributions to a party or candidate in an election. A later amendment to the act makes it unlawful for individual contributors to donate more than five thousand dollars; it also requires a campaign committee to report all contributions to Congress used for financing campaigns in more than one state. This campaign law is frequently broken or infringed upon. As an attorney who has worked for two senators and one president states:

Among the boldest, most notorious, and most flagrant occasions of contempt for the law are American political campaigns. The spirit of the law—if not its literal content—is violated by incumbent Presidents, Congressmen, Senators, and candidates alike; and the law-breaking has been ratified by a forty-five year refusal of Attorneys General to prosecute obvious violations. This is an area transcending partisanship: from Eugene McCarthy to Gerald Ford the law is regularly ignored.[45]

Another prevalent form of governmental lawlessness involves robbing dissident groups from outside the power elite of their constitutional right to dissent. This has long been a part of the government's tendency to welcome dissent in the abstract and punish it in the concrete. In the past, the government openly or tacitly permitted vigilantes to harass nonconformists and to lynch blacks and members of other minorities. More recently, the government has directly or indirectly participated in illegalities by inducing or allowing its law enforcers to violate the civil liberty of dissident groups as well as citizens mistaken for dissidents. For example, in the late 1960s and early 1970s, the National Guard and the police were allowed to commit these crimes with impunity: to kill unarmed students at Kent State in Ohio and at Jackson State in Mississippi; slaughter Black Panther members in Chicago; unlawfully arrest twelve thousand antiwar demonstrators in Washington, D.C.; and indiscriminately beat peaceful demonstrators, onlookers, pedestrians, journalists, and news photographers alike during the 1968 National Democratic Convention in Chicago. An illustration of how the Chicago police went about their job during that convention is given by the Walker Commission on the Causes and Prevention of Violence:

A priest who was in the crowd says he saw a "boy, about fourteen or fifteen, white, standing on top of an automobile yelling something which was unidentifiable. Suddenly a policeman pulled him down from the car and beat him to the ground by striking him three or four times with a nightstick. Other police joined in . . . and they eventually shoved him into a police van. A well-dressed woman saw this incident and spoke angrily to a nearby police captain. As she spoke, another policeman came up from behind her and sprayed something in her face with an aerosol can. He then clubbed her to the ground. He and two other policemen then dragged her along the ground to the same paddy wagon and threw her in." [46]

All this governmental lawlessness was topped by the Watergate scandal. In the early 1970s, some presidential aides engaged in numerous illegal activities in order to preserve their political power against antiwar dissidents, opposition political leaders, and whomever they believed to be a threat to what they called "national security" (which actually meant the president's own political security). Thus they compiled an "enemies list"—including several hundred persons who were mostly radicals and members of left-wing organizations, but also such people as the presidents of Harvard, Yale, the Massachusetts Institute of Technology, and Barbara Streisand, Steve McQueen, and Joe Namath. They then tried to use various federal agencies, in the words of a White House aide, "to screw our political enemies." For example, they used the IRS to harass their enemies with income tax audits; ordered the Postal Service to open and read their enemies' mail; and pressured the FBI and the CIA to investigate and monitor their enemies.

Similarly, political spying and sabotage were employed to create dissension within the opposing Democratic party. The Republican president's aides hired spies to infiltrate Democratic campaigns. Attempts were also made to break into the Democratic presidential candidates' headquarters and to place monitoring devices on their telephones. Best known were the "dirty tricks" played on the Democratic presidential candidates. One trick involved sending letters on one candidate's stationery to supporters of another candidate. These letters said that the other candidate had fathered an illegitimate child, had been arrested on homosexual charges, or had been arrested for drunken driving while in the company of a call girl. Other tricks involved posing as representatives of a candidate and calling voters after midnight; printing up fake press releases from a candidate announcing free food and drink, balloons for the kids, and speeches by famous movie stars; using a candidate's name to order large quantities of flowers, pizzas, fried chicken, liquor, limousine service, and even magicians, and inviting numerous dignitaries from foreign embassies to attend the candidate's fund-raising dinner; sprinkling a bad-smelling liquid on the grounds where a picnic was scheduled for a candidate's political rally and tossing some of it into the candidate's campaign headquarters; and recruiting hostile pickets against various Democratic candidates.

The above-mentioned "dirty" or illegal practices began to become known to the public after the presidential aides' agents were arrested for breaking into the Democratic National Committee headquarters in the Watergate building in Washington, D.C. in June 1972. Within the next two years, some cabinet members and White House aides, along with the Committee for the Reelection of the President, obstructed justice by attempting to cover up their part in the Watergate caper and by paying hush money to the Watergate burglars. Finally in August 1974 the pressure on President Nixon and his assistants was so overwhelming that he resigned from the presidency. Many of the men involved were later tried, convicted, and given either suspended or light sentences. The president himself was not even put on trial because he was granted a "full, free, and absolute pardon" by his successor, President Ford.

FLAUNTING ARROGANCE   Arrogance is characteristically an occupational hazard of government officials. Though public servants, they usually behave more like masters than servants of the public. "Congressmen," for example, "no matter how lofty their motives, have been flattered into believing that they are different from the rest of us, as if the process of election has somehow lifted them above other Americans and made them more knowing, more worthy, and less subject to reproach than the people who elect them." [47] It is not technically illegal for the bigwigs to express their low regard for the public, such as by squandering taxpayers' money to build the nation's most expensive ($122 million) office building for themselves as members of the House of Representatives.[48] But they often do engage in technically unlawful acts that range from petty offenses to serious ones. For example, while Congress has made it legal for its members to go through red lights and commit other traffic violations while they are commuting to or from sessions of Congress, this legal privilege is often abused. More serious are the kinds of official arrogance that create extreme hardship for the victim. A few examples may serve to illustrate the nature of this official arrogance: [49]

A judge once discovered that one of the two codefendants before him was sleeping. The judge angrily found both guilty of contempt and gave them a thirty-day jail sentence. When the wide-awake defendant pleaded "Why me? I was not sleeping," the judge yelled back "You are guilty by association. Get them out of here!"

A 1970 study of the criminal courts in Boston by the Lawyers Committee for Civil Rights Under Law discovered pervasive judicial contempt for the law. Disregarding the universal rule about the burden of proof, one judge was frank enough to express what many other judges often do when they attempt to resolve a difficult case. He said to the defendant, "Well, I don't know who to believe. Just to be safe I'll find you guilty."

It has been widely documented that judges commonly flout the law by denying bail or requiring excessive bail despite the possibility of the suspect being innocent. One circuit court chief judge justified such unconstitutional actions by saying, "What do you want me to do— cry crocodile tears for people who take advantage of their city? Didn't I read . . . all about President Johnson's 'War on Crime'?"

POCKETING MONEY   Governmental crime often involves receiving money and other financial benefits. This takes various forms. The most simple involves taking bribes as payments for official favors. For example, it has been reported that in the early 1970s, President Nixon's aides managed to squeeze some $700,000 from large milk producers in return for a government-approved milk price increase, as well as $400,000 from International Telephone and Telegraph as the price for dropping the Justice Department's antitrust suit against the corporation.[50] Another form of money-making government crime involves violating the conflict of interest law. This has to do with making business deals or practicing law while in office. Thus some members of Congress simultaneously serve on the Senate Banking Committee and are officials in large national banks or hold stock in the banks or accept loans at specially low rates from the banks. Other members of Congress continue to practice law and represent wealthy clients who want to have their interests protected or advanced by the federal government.[51]

NEUTRALIZING THE CRIME

Government officials take great care to cover their crimes. Even after their crimes have been uncovered, the officials—more than most people—rarely admit their guilt. Instead they automatically attempt to neutralize their crimes. Such an attempt has been called "the ritual of wiggle." There are different ways for government officials to wiggle out of their criminal activities. Only the most common ways are to be discussed: [52]

DENY THE OBVIOUS   The government denies that any wrongdoing has occurred, no matter how strong the suspicion or how gross the reality. The denial is as frequently and honestly repeated as possible. Sometimes the government admits that it has engaged in the act but denies that the act constitutes an offense. A precedent is diligently sought to support this denial. For example, when Attorney General John Mitchell was accused of engaging in unlawful wiretapping, he told the press that Presidents Roosevelt and Truman had also used wiretapping to protect national security.

IGNORE IT   If the crime is a private one committed by individual officials, they ignore it by disconnecting their phones, going into hiding or on a trip away from the press, or simply saying "no comment." If the government is supposed to take action against its officials for some lawbreaking, it resorts to evasive responses by insisting that the facts do not conclusively and absolutely warrant governmental intervention. Thus the government has failed to address itself adequately to the Kent State shooting, to the Chicago slaughter of Black Panthers, to the slaying of students at Jackson State, and to the issue of the legality of the United States' involvement in the Vietnam war.

ACCUSE THE ACCUSER In the case of private crimes, the individual official threatens or actually files a libel suit against the journalist who publicizes the crime. Although it is almost impossible to prove libel, the official hopes that the suit will divert public attention from the crime. The government hopes for the same thing when it accuses its accuser. For example, the Nixon administration often attacked the news media for distorting facts when its illegal activities were publicized by the news media. Also, when CBS-TV News broadcast its critical documentary, "The Selling of the Pentagon," a House Committee launched an investigation into CBS-TV News rather than into the Defense Department.

PROMISE INVESTIGATION When it is under intense pressure to do something about a certain incident, the government will publicly promise a thorough investigation of the incident. Yet behind the scene the promised investigation is not seriously carried out. For example, New York City officials once promised to investigate some allegedly unjustified police attack on the Black Panthers, but nothing came out of the investigation. When the Watergate scandal broke, Attorney General John Mitchell promised that the Justice Department's investigation of the scandal would be "the most extensive, thorough and comprehensive investigation since the assassination of President Kennedy." President Nixon even surprised his White House aide John Dean by announcing on national TV that Dean "has conducted a complete investigation of all leads which might involve any present members of the White House staff or anybody in the Government." The fact, of course, was that the Nixon administration did just the opposite—secretly attempted to squash the investigation of the Watergate incident.

POINT OUT THE NECESSITY FOR THE ACT This method of neutralization usually becomes necessary when the government finds it impossible to do any of the above. Thus the government will implicitly admit its wrongdoing, but justify it by arguing that it was necessary for the government to do it. Many government officials have, for example, justified unlawful wiretapping on the grounds that the danger of not using it against suspected criminals was too great. State officials have also argued that it was necessary to (illegally) cut off welfare benefits because the state was facing a financial crisis. Prosecutors and police have long contended that it is sometimes necessary to (unlawfully) apply the "third degree" (whipping, beating, prolonged deprivation of sleep, starvation, and the like) in order to extract confessions from suspects.

THEORY OF GOVERNMENTAL CRIME

Since they have not studied governmental crime, sociologists have not produced a theory to explain it. Recently Attorney Jethro Lieberman, after investigating numerous cases of governmental lawbreaking, suggested twelve different causes of governmental crime: general lawlessness; superabundance of ambiguous laws; inability to admit mistake; corruption; political pressure; stupidity, insensitivity, and oversight; mistakes and ignorance; lack of professionalism; lack of resources; inability to practice what one preaches; national crisis; and absurdity of the laws.[53]

Most of these can hardly be considered the causes of governmental crime, because they are either tautological or incapable of distinguishing governmental crime from noncriminal activities inside and outside the government. For example, "general lawlessness" and "corruption" are tautological in that they are the same as governmental crime itself; "stupidity, mistakes, and so on" can be found not only in governmental crime but in practically all modes of human conduct.

Nevertheless, two of these factors seem capable of explaining governmental crime. One is *superabundance of ambiguous laws* or lack of clearcut laws for controlling governmental action. Lieberman aptly describes the collection of ambiguous laws "as a wall of lattice-work: the thin strips of wood represent all of our legal rules, but the pervasive holes are very prominent; indeed, but for the holes there would be no design at all." [54] The consequence is a "discretionary wilderness" where government officials are relatively free to rely on their own judgment or whim when they are supposedly carrying out their duties. Given this great discretionary power, they can easily break or bend or circumvent the law.

The other factor that seems closely related to governmental crime is the attitude and mentality reflected in the government's *inability to admit mistakes*. The government is uniquely inclined to appear infallible; its officials apparently do not believe in the dictum "To err is human." Such a godly attitude can easily make a government official, particularly the president, feel above the law. This feeling is in turn made possible by the lack of clearcut laws for controlling and thus humbling government officials. In short, both the lack of clearcut laws and an attitude of infallibility may generate governmental crime.

POWER THEORY APPLIED

From what has been discussed in this and some previous chapters, it is obvious that the more powerful individuals tend more to engage in profitable deviant activities (organized, white-collar, and governmental crime), while the less powerful ones are more likely to commit unprofitable crimes (murder, rape, robbery, and mugging). Since the powerful's profitable deviance is subjected to considerably lesser social control than is the powerless' unprofitable criminality, the former may pervade the society to a much greater extent than does the latter. The symbiotic relationship between these two opposite forms of deviance has been amply discussed in Chapter 4.

It may be added that, of the three types of powerful criminals discussed in this chapter, governmental criminals may have the most profound effect on rank-and-file citizens. This seems to be particularly so in a democratic society like the United States. Compared with citizens of a relatively authoritarian society, Americans may be more strongly influenced by their ideology of democracy to expect to be equal to their government leaders. Thus, while citizens in an authoritarian society are more likely to accept with fatalistic equanimity the authoritative dictum of "Do as I say, not as I do," Americans are more inclined to do as their authoritative figures do, not as they say. This may be why, despite their self-praising speeches ("We're dedicated to Law and Order") to the citizenry, government officials' criminal doings are a potent stimulant of lawlessness among the American masses. More than fifty years ago, Justice Louis Brandeis clearly perceived the powerful criminogenic influence of governmental crime:

In a government of laws, the existence of the government will be imperilled if it fails to observe the law scrupulously. Our government is the potent, the omnipresent, teacher. For good or ill, it teaches the whole people by its example. Crime is contagious. If the government becomes a lawbreaker, it breeds contempt for law; it invites every man to become a law unto himself; it invites anarchy.[55]

SUMMARY

Organized crime, white-collar crime, and governmental crime are collectively referred to as profitable deviance, because they all are generally more profitable to the perpetrators when compared with other types of deviant behavior.

Organized crime has been viewed in two conflicting ways—as a tight and as a loose organization. Due to the lack of reliable information, these two views cannot be reconciled. But as a highly lucrative enterprise, organized crime involves selling illegal goods and services, racketeering, large-scale thievery, infiltrating legitimate business, and corrupting public officials. Bell's theory attributes the rise of organized crime to its function as the open sesame for ambitious members of the lower classes.

White-collar crime is more entangled with higher-status people's legitimate businesses and professions. It may be perpetrated against the public or against the company. It has three characteristics: the victim's unwitting cooperation, society's indifference, and criminal's noncriminal self-image. Substantial economic, physical, and social costs of white-collar crime have been estimated to hurt society and individuals alike. Sutherland's theory explains white-collar crime as the result of overinvolvement with dishonest business people coupled with the society's lax control over dishonest business practices. Cressey supplements this theory by showing the step-by-step process of becoming an embezzler or, by implication, most any other type of white-collar criminal.

Governmental crime enables its perpetrators to maintain their power, to express their arrogance, and to make money. When their illegal activities are revealed to the public, governmental criminals characteristically attempt to neutralize them. This neutralization takes such forms as denying the obvious, ignoring it, accusing the accuser, promising investigation, and pointing out the necessity of the illegal act. Lieberman's theory lists many disparate causes of governmental crime, two of which seem quite capable of explaining the crime—one being the lack of clearcut laws and the other the attitude of infallibility held by governmental officials.

The application of power theory largely recapitulates what has been said in earlier portions of this book.

SUGGESTED READINGS

Albini, Joseph L. *The American Mafia: Genesis of a Legend*. New York: Appleton-Century-Crofts, 1971.

Becker, Theodore L. and Vernon G. Murray, eds. *Government Lawlessness in America*. New York: Oxford University Press, 1971.

Cressey, Donald R. *Other People's Money*. Glencoe, Ill.: Free Press, 1953.

Cressey, Donald R. *Theft of the Nation*. New York: Harper & Row, 1969.

Geis, Gilbert and Robert F. Meier, eds. *White-Collar Crime*. New York: Free Press, 1977.

Green, Mark J., James M. Fallows, and David R. Zwick. *Who Runs Congress?* New York: Bantam/Grossman, 1972.

Lieberman, Jethro K. *How the Government Breaks the Law*. Baltimore, Md.: Penguin Books, 1973.

Sutherland, Edwin H. *White-Collar Crime*. New York: Holt, Rinehart & Winston, 1949.

Tyler, Gus, ed. *Organized Crime in America*. Ann Arbor: University of Michigan Press, 1962.

EPILOGUE

Taking all the preceding chapters as a whole, we may see that deviance is a multidimensional phenomenon. This is not only true of deviance in general, but also true of each concrete form of deviant behavior. This is why there are many different ways of defining, interpreting, or explaining the general as well as the concrete forms of deviance. These definitions or theories may simply reflect the different aspects of the same phenomenon. At the same time, each definition or theory, in reflecting one aspect of the deviant reality, necessarily obscures other aspects of the same reality. We should, therefore, not expect any theory to account for all aspects of deviance. We could instead integrate the various limited theories so as to broaden our view of deviance.

The broadened view from this book enables us to see that deviance can be profitable or unprofitable. Profitable deviance is likely to be the prerogative of the more powerful, while unprofitable deviance the curse of the less powerful. But it is more difficult to define clearly and to acquire hard data on profitable deviance, when compared with the unprofitable kind. It is little wonder that most theoretical and empirical research has been focused on unprofitable deviance. It can only be hoped that sociologists will in the future pay more attention to the other, more profitable type of deviance.

Further, we may see that deviance is more pervasive in the higher strata of society than in the lower. The kind of deviance that is more pervasive is the more profitable type. Since the public generally considers profitable deviance as relatively harmless or unserious, such deviance may be expected to continue to be more pervasive than the unprofitable type—which the public views as more harmful or serious.

Finally, we may speculate that there is a symbiotic relationship between these two types of deviance. But this relationship is often difficult to demonstrate empirically, because it is very subtle, indirect, or distant rather than open, direct, or immediate.

Some practical implications may be derived from our view of deviance. If our objective is to preserve the existing social order, the more powerful should be allowed to continue enjoying the relative freedom to participate in their deviant activities and the less powerful should continue to be restrained from committing their deviant acts. But if our goal is to create a more equitable society, the following should be carried out: in the case of serious crimes, such as civilized or beastly killing and sophisticated or crude robbery, powerful criminals should be as severely punished as are powerless criminals. In the case of self-enjoying and self-abusing deviant acts, such as overt or covert homosexuality and illegal or legal abuse of drugs, powerless individuals should be granted the same freedom from official harassment or the same opportunity for high-quality professional help as are powerful individuals. In addition, the living conditions of the powerless should be improved until they equal that of the powerful.

It should, however, be noted that power theory, though it may give us a broader view of deviance, is itself very limited because it is far from being a complete integration of all the various theories. Let us hope that other sociologists may attempt to achieve a more integrated theory of deviance so as to represent more aspects of the phenomenon. They may then provide a better solution to the practical problem of deviance in society.

NOTES

CHAPTER 1 – WHAT IS DEVIANT BEHAVIOR?

1. J. L. Simmons, "Public Stereotypes of Deviants," *Social Problems* 13 (Fall 1965): 223–224.

2. Talcott Parsons, *The Social System* (New York: Free Press, 1951), p. 206.

3. *Ibid.*

4. Robert K. Merton, "Social Problems and Sociological Theory," in Merton and Robert Nisbet, eds., *Contemporary Social Problems*, 3rd ed. (New York: Harcourt Brace Jovanovich, 1971), p. 824.

5. Albert K. Cohen, *Deviance and Control* (Englewood Cliffs, N.J.: Prentice-Hall, 1966), p. 1.

6. John Lofland, *Deviance and Identity* (Englewood Cliffs, N.J.: Prentice-Hall, 1969), p. 1.

7. Edward Sagarin, *Deviants and Deviance* (New York: Praeger, 1975), p. 5. See also Fred Davis, "Deviance Disavowal: The Management of Strained Interaction by the Visibly Handicapped," *Social Problems* 9 (Fall 1961): 121.

8. Norman K. Denzin, "Rules of Conduct and the Study of Deviant Behavior: Some Notes on the Social Relationship," in Jack D. Douglas, ed., *Deviance and Respectability* (New York: Basic Books, 1970), p. 121.

9. Don C. Gibbons and Joseph F. Jones, *The Study of Deviance* (Englewood Cliffs, N.J.: Prentice-Hall, 1975), p. 48.

10. William A. Rushing, ed., *Deviant Behavior and Social Process* (Chicago: Rand McNally, 1975), p. 4.

11. Leslie T. Wilkins, *Social Deviance* (Englewood Cliffs, N.J.: Prentice-Hall, 1965), p. 45.

12. Frank R. Scarpitti and Paul T. McFarlane, eds., *Deviance: Action, Reaction, Interaction* (Reading, Mass.: Addison-Wesley, 1975), pp. 5–6.

13. Howard S. Becker, *Outsiders* (New York: Free Press, 1963), p. 9.

14. Kai T. Erikson, "Notes on the Sociology of Deviance," *Social Problems* 9 (Spring 1962): 308. See also similar definition in John I. Kitsuse, "Societal Reaction to Deviant Behavior: Problems of Theory and Method," *Social Problems* 9 (Winter 1962): 253.

15. Merton, "Social Problems and Sociological Theory": 827.

16. Ronald L. Akers, "Problems in the Sociology of Deviance: Social Definition and Behavior," *Social Forces* 46 (June 1968): 463.

17. Jack P. Gibbs, "Issues in Defining Deviant Behavior," in Robert A. Scott and Jack D. Douglas, eds., *Theoretical Perspectives on Deviance* (New York: Basic Books, 1972), pp. 43–44.

18. Jack P. Gibbs, "Conceptions of Deviant Behavior: The Old and the New," *Pacific Sociological Review* 9 (Spring 1966): 121; Sagarin, *Deviants and Deviance*, p. 8.

19. David Matza, *Becoming Deviant* (Englewood Cliffs, N.J.: Prentice-Hall, 1969), p. 11.

20. Alexander Liazos, "The Poverty of the Sociology of Deviance: Nuts, Sluts, and Preverts," *Social Problems* 20 (Summer 1972): 109. See also Alex Thio, "Class Bias in the Sociology of Deviance," *The American Sociologist* 8 (February 1973): 1.

21. Travis Hirschi, "Procedural Rules and the Study of Deviant Behavior," *Social Problems* 21 (Fall 1973): 166–171.

22. See, for example, Sagarin, *Deviants and Deviance*, p. 407; Gibbons and Jones, *The Study of Deviance*, p. 9; Marshall B. Clinard, *Sociology of Deviant Behavior*, 4th ed. (New York: Holt, Rinehart and Winston, 1974), p. 26.

23. See, for example, Gideon Sjoberg and Roger Nett, *A Methodology for Social Research* (New York: Harper & Row, 1968), pp. 4–10; Richard W. Coan, "Dimensions of Psychological Theory," *American Psychologist* 23 (October 1968): 715; Robert W. Friedrichs, *A Sociology of Sociology* (New York: Free Press, 1970).

24. Merton, "Social Problems and Sociological Theory," p. 827.

25. Hirschi, "Procedural Rules," p. 169.

26. Gwynn Nettler, "On Telling Who's Crazy," *American Sociological Review* 39 (December 1974): 894.

27. Gwynn Nettler, *Explanations* (New York: McGraw-Hill, 1970), pp. 93–94.

28. Lester F. Ward, "The Place of Sociology among the Sciences," *American Journal of Sociology* 1 (July 1895): 21.

29. Albion W. Small, "Fifty Years of Sociology in the United States (1868–1915)," *American Journal of Sociology* 21 (May 1916): 857.

30. Mabel A. Elliott and Francis E. Merrill, *Social Disorganization* (New York: Harper, 1934), pp. 44, 182.

31. For a discussion on this procedural rule, see Nettler, *Explanations,* pp. 99–101.

32. Albert K. Cohen and James F. Short, Jr., "Crime and Juvenile Delinquency," in Merton and Nisbet, eds., *Contemporary Social Problems,* pp. 102–104.

33. Stanley E. Grupp, ed., *The Positive School of Criminology: Three Lectures by Enrico Ferri* (Pittsburgh: University of Pittsburgh Press, 1968), p. 54.

34. Edwin H. Sutherland and Donald R. Cressey, *Criminology,* 9th ed. (Philadelphia: Lippincott, 1974), pp. 76–77.

35. Becker, *Outsiders,* p. 9.

36. See, for example, Akers, "Problems in the Sociology of Deviance," pp. 463–464; see also notes 21 and 26.

37. Becker, *Outsiders,* p. 4.

38. See, for example, Earl Rubington and Martin S. Weinberg, eds., *Deviance: The Interactionist Perspective,* 2nd ed. (New York: Macmillan, 1973), p. 2.

39. Becker, *Outsiders,* p. 15.

40. This does not necessarily mean that humanists do not study deviants. As we will see later on, they do study deviants, but only in relation to the process of labeling.

41. Becker, *Outsiders,* p. 166.

42. Matza, *Becoming Deviant,* p. 25.

43. Robert K. Merton, "Insiders and Outsiders: A Chapter in the Sociology of Knowledge," *American Journal of Sociology* 78 (July 1972): 17–18.

44. *Ibid.,* 31.

45. Matza, *Becoming Deviant,* pp. 15–16.

46. *Ibid.,* pp. 43–44.

47. I. E. Farber, "Personality and Behavioral Science," in May Brodbeck, ed., *Readings in the Philosophy of the Social Sciences* (New York: Macmillan, 1968), p. 149.

48. Matza, *Becoming Deviant,* pp. 7, 8.

49. David Matza, *Delinquency and Drift* (New York: Wiley, 1964), p. 12.

50. Matza, *Becoming Deviant,* p. 68.

51. Quoted by Matza, *ibid.,* p. 75, from Daniel Bell, "Crime as an American Way of Life," in *End of Ideology* (New York: Free Press, 1962), p. 128.

52. Quoted by Matza, *ibid.,* p. 83, from Edwin Lemert, *Social Pathology* (New York: McGraw-Hill, 1951), p. 246.

53. Edwin M. Lemert, *Human Deviance, Social Problems, and Social Control,* 2nd ed. (Englewood Cliffs, N.J.: Prentice-Hall, 1972), p. 16.

54. See, for example, Becker, *Outsiders*, pp. 41–58; Matza, *Becoming Deviant*, pp. 109–142; Judy Lorber, "Deviance as Performance: The Case of Illness," *Social Problems* 14 (Winter 1967): 302–310; Richard L. Henshel and Robert A. Silverman, eds., *Perception in Criminology* (New York: Columbia University Press, 1975).

55. *Selected Works of Mao Tse-tung* (Peking: Foreign Languages Press, 1967), I, 343.

56. Alvin W. Gouldner, "The Sociologist as Partisan: Sociology and the Welfare State," *The American Sociologist* 3 (May 1968): 104.

CHAPTER 2 – SCIENTIFIC THEORIES OF DEVIANCE

1. *Primary deviance* refers to behavior that is committed by a person for the first time and labeled deviant by others; *societal reaction* may include the making or enforcing of rules against deviance; and *secondary deviance* is repeated, confirmed, or full-fledged deviant behavior. These terms will be discussed further in Chapter 3.

2. Robert K. Merton, *Social Theory and Social Structure*, rev. & enl. ed. (New York: Free Press, 1957), p. 121.

3. *Ibid.*, pp. 131–160. It may be worth noting that some sociologists believe that Merton's theory was solely inspired by Durkheim, apparently unaware of Merton's reaction against Freud as documented here.

4. *Ibid.*, p. 146.

5. *Ibid.*, p. 139.

6. Albert K. Cohen, *Delinquent Boys: The Culture of the Gang* (Glencoe, Ill.: Free Press, 1955).

7. Albert K. Cohen, *Deviance and Control* (Englewood Cliffs, N.J.: Prentice-Hall, 1966), p. 65.

8. Cohen, *Delinquent Boys*, p. 121.

9. For Cohen's criticism of Merton's individualistic concept of deviance, see Albert K. Cohen, "The Sociology of the Deviant Act: Anomie Theory and Beyond," *American Sociological Review* 30 (February 1965): 5–14.

10. Richard C. Cloward and Lloyd E. Ohlin, *Delinquency and Opportunity: A Theory of Delinquent Gangs* (Glencoe, Ill.: Free Press, 1960).

11. For a more detailed discussion on this and some of the other following points, see Alex Thio, "A Critical Look at Merton's Anomie Theory," *Pacific Sociological Review* 18 (April 1975): 139–158.

12. Edwin M. Lemert, *Human Deviance, Social Problems, and Social Control* (Englewood Cliffs, N.J.: Prentice-Hall, 1967), p. 8.

13. Gwynn Nettler, *Explaining Crime* (New York: McGraw-Hill, 1974), p. 165.

14. Studies on these are cited in Merton, *Social Theory*, p. 181.

15. Findings on deviance in these areas are discussed by Cohen, *Deviance*, pp. 78–82.

16. Edwin H. Sutherland and Donald R. Cressey, *Criminology*, 9th ed. (Philadelphia: Lippincott, 1974), pp. 71–91.

17. *Ibid.*, p. 88.

18. The following numbered and quoted statements are from Sutherland and Cressey, *Criminology*, pp. 75–76.

19. The following discussion is based on Sutherland and Cressey, *ibid.*, pp. 78–81.

20. Daniel Glaser, "Criminality Theories and Behavioral Images," *American Journal of Sociology* 61 (March 1956): 433–444; Robert L. Burgess and Ronald L. Akers, "A Differential Association-Reinforcement Theory of Criminal Behavior," *Social Problems* 14 (Fall 1966): 128–147.

21. Glaser, *ibid.*, p. 438.

22. *Ibid.*, p. 440.

23. Robert L. Burgess and Ronald L. Akers, "Are Operant Principles Tautological?" *The Psychological Record* 16 (July 1966): 310.

24. Sutherland and Cressey, *Criminology*, p. 83.

25. *Ibid.*, pp. 85–86.

26. *Ibid.*, p. 86.

27. *Ibid.*, p. 88.

28. Sheldon Glueck, "Theory and Fact in Criminology," *British Journal of Delinquency* 7 (October 1956): 94.

29. Victor M. Matthews, "Differential Identification: An Empirical Note," *Social Problems* 14 (Winter 1968): 376–383.

30. Ronald L. Akers, *Deviant Behavior: A Social Learning Approach* (Belmont, Cal.: Wadsworth, 1973), p. 51.

31. James F. Short, Jr., "Differential Association as a Hypothesis: Problems of Empirical Testing," *Social Problems* 8 (Summer 1960): 24.

32. Sutherland would have considered this an error; see p. 39.

33. Harwin L. Voss, "Differential Association and Reported Delinquent Behavior: A Replication," *Social Problems* 12 (Summer 1964): 85. See also James F. Short, Jr., "Differential Association with Delinquent Friends and Delinquent Behavior," *Pacific Sociological Review* 1 (Spring 1958): 20–25; Daniel Glaser, "Differential Association and Criminological Research," *Social Problems* 8 (Summer 1960), 6–14; Albert J. Reiss, Jr. and Lewis A. Rhodes, "An Empirical Test of Differential Association Theory," *Journal of Research in Crime and Delinquency* 1 (January 1964): 5–18.

34. For the second group, see Arthur L. Beeley, "A Socio-Psychological Theory of Crime and Delinquency: A Contribution to Etiology," *Journal of Criminal Law, Criminology, and Police Science* 45 (December 1945): 394–396; Albert J. Reiss, Jr., "Delinquency as the Failure of Personal and Social Controls," *American Sociological Review* 16 (April 1951): 196–207; Scott Briar and Irving Piliavin, "Delinquency, Situational Inducements, and Commitment to Conformity," *Social Problems* 13 (Summer 1965): 35–45.

35. Walter C. Reckless, *The Crime Problem*, 5th ed. (New York: Appleton-Century-Crofts, 1973), p. 56.

36. *Ibid.*, p. 56.

37. *Ibid.*, p. 55.

38. *Ibid.*, p. 56.

39. Walter C. Reckless, Simon Dinitz, and Ellen Murray, "Self Concept as an Insulator against Delinquency," *American Sociological Review* 21 (December 1956): 744–746; Frank R. Scarpitti, Ellen Murray, Simon Dinitz, and Walter C. Reckless, "The 'Good' Boy in a High Delinquency Area: Four Years Later," *American Sociological Review* 25 (August 1960): 555–558; Simon Dinitz, Frank R. Scarpitti, and Walter C. Reckless, "Delinquency Vulnerability: A Cross Group and Longitudinal Analysis," *American Sociological Review* 27 (August 1962): 515–517.

40. But some sociologists have criticized this research for its lack of precision in operationalizing *self-concept*. See, for example, Sandra S. Tangri and Michael Schwartz, "Delinquency Research and the Self-Concept Variable," *Journal of Criminal Law, Criminology, and Police Science* 58 (June 1967): 182–190; James D. Orcutt, "Self-Concept and Insulation Against Delinquency: Some Critical Notes," *Sociological Quarterly* 11 (Summer 1970): 381–391.

41. F. Ivan Nye, *Family Relationships and Delinquency Behavior* (New York: Wiley, 1958).

42. Travis Hirschi, *Causes of Delinquency* (Berkeley and Los Angeles: University of California Press, 1969).

43. This is why it makes sense for control theorists to assume that "conformity, *not* deviation, must be learned" (Nye, *Family Relationships*, p. 5; emphasis added).

44. Hirschi, *Causes of Delinquency*, pp. 162–186.

45. See notes 14 and 15.

CHAPTER 3 – HUMANISTIC THEORIES OF DEVIANCE

1. Howard S. Becker, *Outsiders: Studies in the Sociology of Deviance* (New York: Free Press, 1963); Kai T. Erikson, "Notes on the Sociology of Deviance" *Social Problems* 9 (Spring 1962): 307–314; John I. Kitsuse, "Societal Reaction

to Deviant Behavior: Problems of Theory and Method," *Social Problems* 9 (Winter 1962): 247–256. See also Edwin M. Lemert, *Social Pathology* (New York: McGraw-Hill, 1951).

2. John I. Kitsuse, "Deviance, Deviant Behavior, and Deviants: Some Conceptual Problems," in William J. Filstead, ed., *An Introduction to Deviance* (Chicago: Markham, 1972), p. 233.

3. Nonetheless, Becker says: "I will indulge my dislike of the conventional label for the theory [namely, *labeling theory*] by referring to it from now on as an interactionist theory of deviance." See Howard S. Becker, Labelling Theory Reconsidered," in Paul Rock and Mary McIntosh, eds., *Deviance and Social Control* (London: Tavistock, 1974), p. 44.

4. Herbert Blumer, *Symbolic Interactionism: Perspective and Method* (Englewood Cliffs, N.J.: Prentice-Hall, 1969), p. 65.

5. Becker, "Labelling Theory Reconsidered," p. 44.

6. Howard S. Becker, ed., *The Other Side: Perspectives on Deviance* (New York: Free Press, 1964), p. 3.

7. Blumer, *Symbolic Interaction*, p. 66.

8. Kitsuse, "Societal Reaction," p. 253.

9. Becker, "Labeling Theory Reconsidered," p. 62.

10. Frank Tannenbaum, *Crime and the Community* (New York: Columbia University Press, 1938), p. 20.

11. Lemert, *Social Pathology*, pp. 75–76.

12. *Ibid.*, p. 77.

13. Erikson, "Notes on the Sociology of Deviance," p. 314.

14. Jack P. Gibbs, "Conceptions of Deviant Behavior: The Old and the New," *Pacific Sociological Review* 9 (Spring 1966): 12.

15. David J. Bordua, "Recent Trends: Deviant Behavior and Social Control," *Annals of American Academy of Political and Social Science* 369 (January 1967): 153.

16. See, for example, Leroy C. Gould, "Who Defines Delinquency: A Comparison of Self-Reported Indices of Delinquency for Three Racial Groups," *Social Problems* 16 (Winter 1969): 325–336. For a humanist's critique of the definitive concept *variable*, see Herbert Blumer, "Sociological Analysis and the 'Variable'," *American Sociological Review* 21 (December 1956): 683–690.

17. Don C. Gibbons and Joseph F. Jones, *The Study of Deviance: Perspectives and Problems* (Englewood Cliffs, N.J.: Prentice-Hall, 1975), pp. 144, 150.

18. Nanette J. Davis, "Labeling Theory in Deviance Research: A Critique and Reconsideration," *Sociological Quarterly* 13 (Autumn 1972): 459.

19. This kind of criticism may also aptly describe the basically humanistic works

of Marx, Freud, Weber, and Durkheim. See Robert Bierstedt, "Sociology and Humane Learning," *American Sociological Review* 25 (February 1960): 3–9.

20. *Ibid.*, p. 7.

21. Portions of the following discussion are derived from Alex Thio, "Class Bias in the Sociology of Deviance," *The American Sociologist* 8 (February 1973): 5–8.

22. William J. Chambliss, *Crime and the Legal Process* (New York: McGraw-Hill, 1969), pp. 360–378.

23. In a general way, this theory is akin to ethnomethodology and existentialism in sociology. See Harold Garfinkel, *Studies in Ethnomethodology* (Englewood Cliffs, N.J.: Prentice-Hall, 1967); Edward Tiryakian, "Existential Phenomenology and Sociology," *American Sociological Review* 30 (October 1965): 674–688.

24. Jack D. Douglas, ed., *Deviance and Respectability* (New York: Basic Books, 1970), pp. 8–9.

25. Jack D. Douglas, ed., *Understanding Everyday Life* (Chicago: Aldine, 1970), p. 26.

26. David Matza, *Becoming Deviant* (Englewood Cliffs, N.J.: Prentice-Hall, 1969), p. 7.

27. Jack D. Douglas, *The Social Meanings of Suicide* (Princeton, N.J.: Princeton University Press, 1967).

28. Labeling theorists allude to the problematic nature of deviant meanings with such terms as *value conflict, value pluralism,* or *lack of value consensus.*

29. Douglas, *Social Meanings,* p. 339.

30. Jack D. Douglas et al., *Introduction to Sociology: Situations and Structures* (New York: Free Press, 1973), p. 107.

31. One phenomenologist says: "The investigator goes into the situation to be studied with a totally open mind—open, in fact, in depth to all the stimuli that impinge upon his consciousness." See Severyn T. Bruyn, *The Human Perspective in Sociology* (Englewood Cliffs, N.J.: Prentice-Hall, 1966), p. 272.

32. See Douglas, *Social Meanings,* pp. 235–337.

33. See Matza, *Becoming Deviant,* pp. 90–197.

34. *Ibid.*, p. 196.

35. For an explanation of why this is the case, see Alan Watts, *The Book: On the Taboo Against Knowing Who You Are* (New York: Collier Books, 1966), p. 110.

36. Thomas Merton, *The Asian Journal of Thomas Merton* (New York: New Directions, 1973), p. 143.

37. The following is derived, with some revision, from Alex Thio, "The Phenomenological Perspective of Deviance: Another Case of Class Bias," *The American Sociologist* 9 (August 1974): 147–148.

38. See, for example, Thorsten Sellin, *Culture Conflict and Crime* (New York: Social Science Research Council, 1938); Richard C. Fuller and Richard R. Myers, "Some Aspects of a Theory of Social Problems," *American Sociological Review* 6 (February 1941): 27–32; Willard Waller, "Social Problems and the Mores," *American Sociological Review* 1 (December 1936): 922–933.

39. This idea of social conflict was later developed further by George B. Vold in his *Theoretical Criminology* (New York: Oxford University Press, 1958).

40. Sellin, *Culture Conflict*, p. 68.

41. Waller, "Social Problems," p. 925.

42. Austin T. Turk, "Conflict and Criminality," *American Sociological Review* 31 (June 1966): 338–352; *Criminality and Legal Order* (Chicago: Rand McNally, 1969).

43. William J. Chambliss, *Crime and the Legal Process* (New York: McGraw-Hill, 1969); Chambliss and Robert Seidman, *Law, Order, and Power* (Reading, Mass.: Addison-Wesley, 1971).

44. Chambliss and Seidman, *ibid.*, p. 504.

45. Richard Quinney, *Critique of Legal Order: Crime Control in Capitalist Society* (Boston: Little, Brown, 1974), p. 16. See also Steven Spitzer, "Toward a Marxian Theory of Deviance," *Social Problems* 22 (1975): 638–651.

46. Richard Quinney, *Criminology* (Boston: Little, Brown, 1975), pp. 37–41.

47. Quinney, *Critique of Legal Order*, pp. 165–198.

48. Ian Taylor, Paul Walton, and Jock Young, *The New Criminology: For a Social Theory of Deviance* (London: Routlege and Kegan Paul, 1973), p. 282. See also Clayton A. Hartjen, *Crime and Criminalization* (New York: Praeger, 1974); Barry Krisberg, *Crime and Privilege: Toward a New Criminology* (Englewood Cliffs, N.J.: Prentice-Hall, 1975).

49. Gibbons and Jones, *Study of Deviance*, p. 102.

50. Ronald L. Akers, *Deviant Behavior: A Social Learning Approach* (Belmont, Cal.: Wadsworth, 1973), p. 20.

51. *Ibid..*

CHAPTER 4 — TOWARD AN INTEGRATED THEORY OF DEVIANCE

1. Andrew Hacker, "Who Rules America?" *New York Review of Books*, May 1, 1975, p. 9.

2. Albert K. Cohen, *Deviance and Control* (Englewood Cliffs, N.J.: Prentice-Hall, 1966), p. 110.

3. See the discussion on anomie theory in Chapter 2.

4. For data supporting this and the following view, see the relevant studies

cited in Alex Thio, "A Critical Look at Merton's Anomie Theory," *Pacific Sociological Review* 18 (April 1975): 139–158.

5. Robert K. Merton, *Social Theory and Social Structure* (New York: Free Press, 1957), p. 136.

6. Emile Durkheim, *Suicide* (New York: Free Press, 1951), p. 254.

7. Alexander Cockburn, "Million Dollar Yeggs," *New York Review of Books,* March 20, 1975, p. 21.

8. Andrew Hacker, "Getting Used to Mugging," *New York Review of Books,* April 19, 1973, p. 14.

9. William J. Chambliss, "Vice, Corruption, Bureaucracy, and Power," *Wisconsin Law Review* 1971, no. 4, pp. 1150–1173.

10. Jorge A. Bustamante, "The 'Wetback' as Deviant: An Application of Labeling Theory," *American Journal of Sociology* 77 (January 1972): 706–718.

11. Sydney Harris, "Strictly Personal," *Chicago Daily News,* February 21, 1968.

12. *The Challenge of Crime in a Free Society: A Report by the President's Commission on Law Enforcement and Administration of Justice* (New York: Avon Books, 1968), p. 130.

13. Joseph Bensman and Arthur J. Vidich, *The New American Society* (Chicago: Quadrangle Books, 1971), p. 148.

14. Edward Alsworth Ross, "The Criminaloid," in Gilbert Geis, ed., *White-Collar Criminal* (New York: Atherton, 1968), pp. 30–31.

CHAPTER 5 – MURDER

1. National Commission on Causes and Prevention of Violence, *Violent Crime: Homicide, Assault, Rape, Robbery* (New York: George Braziller, 1969), p. 34.

2. See, for example, "U.S. Homicides and Suicides 1960–1969," *The Official Associated Press Almanac,* 1974, p. 249.

3. Richard Quinney, "Suicide, Homicide, and Economic Development," *Social Forces* 43 (March 1965): 402.

4. Marshall B. Clinard and Daniel J. Abbot, *Crime in Developing Countries* (New York: Wiley, 1973), p. 59.

5. *Crimes of Violence,* Staff Report to National Commission on Causes and Prevention of Violence, prepared by Donald J. Mulvihill and Melvin M. Tumin with Lynn A. Curtis (Washington, D.C.: Government Printing Office, 1969), Vol. 11, p. 95.

6. Marvin E. Wolfgang, *Patterns in Criminal Homicide* (Philadelphia: University of Pennsylvania, 1958), p. 37.

7. Mulvihill et al., *Crimes of Violence,* p. 210.

8. *Ibid.*

9. *Ibid.*

10. Wolfgang, *Patterns*, pp. 174–180.

11. *Ibid.*, p. 99.

12. *Ibid.*, pp. 106–113.

13. *Ibid.*, pp. 123–124.

14. *FBI Uniform Crime Reports*, 1973, p. 9.

15. George D. Newton, Jr. and Franklin E. Zimring, *Firearms and Violence in American Life* (Washington, D.C.: U.S. Government Printing Office, 1969), p. 42.

16. Mulvihill et al. *Crimes of Violence*, p. 217.

17. Musa T. Mushanga, "Criminal Homicide in Western Uganda," quoted in Clinard and Abbott, *Crime*, p. 61.

18. Wolfgang, *Patterns*, p. 254.

19. Adapted from *ibid.*, pp. 253–254.

20. Marvin E. Wolfgang, "A Sociological Analysis of Criminal Homicide," in Wolfgang, ed., *Studies in Homicide* (New York: Harper & Row, 1967), p. 24.

21. Wolfgang, *Patterns*, pp. 277–278; T. L. Dorpat, "Suicide in Murderers," in Wolfgang, *ibid.*, p. 197.

22. These cases are slightly adapted from Mulvihill et al., *Crimes of Violence*, p. 231.

23. For references to this and other similar data, see William C. Bailey, "Murder and the Death Penalty," *Journal of Criminal Law and Criminology* 65 (September 1974): 416–423. But for the pros and cons on the death penalty, see James A. McCafferty, ed., *Capital Punishment* (Chicago: Aldine-Atherton, 1972).

24. William F. Graves, "The Deterrent Effect of Capital Punishment in California," in Hugo Adam Bedau, ed., *The Death Penalty in America* (Garden City, N.Y.: Doubleday Anchor, 1964), pp. 322–332.

25. William J. Chambliss, *Crime and the Legal Process* (New York: McGraw-Hill, 1969), pp. 360–378.

26. Paul Bohannan, ed., *African Homicide and Suicide* (Princeton, N.J.: Princeton University Press, 1960).

27. *Ibid.*, p. 237.

28. Konrad Lorenz, *On Aggression* (New York: Harcourt, Brace & World, 1966).

29. Richard G. Fox, "The XYY Offender: A Modern Myth?" *Journal of Criminal Law, Criminology and Police Science* 62 (March 1971): pp. 59–73; Ashley Montagu, "Chromosomes and Crime," *Psychology Today*, October 1968, pp. 42–49.

30. Gerald E. McClearn, "Biological Bases of Social Behavior with Specific Reference to Violent Behavior," in Mulvihill et al., *Crimes of Violence*, Vol. 13, p. 1003.

31. Sigmund Freud, *Civilization and Its Discontent*, trans. and ed. by James Strachey (New York: Norton, 1961), p. 66.

32. Donald T. Lunde, "Our Murder Boom," *Psychology Today*, July 1975, pp. 40–42.

33. "The Pride of Olean," *Newsweek*, January 13, 1975, p. 27.

34. Joseph W. Lamberti, Nathan Blackman, and James M. A. Weiss, "The Sudden Murderer," in Wolfgang, ed., *Studies*, p. 191.

35. Wolfgang, *Patterns*, p. 314.

36. John Dollard, Neal E. Miller, Leonard W. Doob, O. H. Mowrer, and Robert R. Sears, *Frustration and Aggression* (New Haven: Yale University Press, 1939), p. 1.

37. See, for example, Edwin H. Sutherland and Donald R. Cressey, *Criminology*, 9th ed. (Philadelphia: Lippincott, 1974), pp. 162–163; Leonard Berkowitz, "The Frustration-Aggression Hypothesis Revisited," in Berkowitz, ed., *Roots of Aggression* (New York: Atherton, 1969), p. 2.

38. Berkowitz, *ibid.*, p. 2.

39. For a brief review of the evidence, see Berkowitz, *ibid.*, pp. 7–11.

40. Stuart Palmer, *A Study of Murder* (New York: Thomas Crowell, 1960), p. 8.

41. Andrew F. Henry and James F. Short, Jr., *Suicide and Homicide* (New York: Free Press, 1954).

42. *Ibid.*, p. 17.

43. Martin Gold, "Suicide, Homicide, and the Socialization of Aggression," *American Journal of Sociology* 43 (May 1958): 651–661.

44. Rodney Stark and James McEvoy III, "Middle-Class Violence," *Psychology Today*, November 1970, pp. 52–54, 110–112; Howard S. Erlanger, "Social Class and Corporal Punishment in Childrearing: A Reassessment," *American Sociological Review* 39 (February 1974): 68–85.

45. Wolfgang, *Patterns*, p. 329.

46. Marvin E. Wolfgang and Franco Ferracuti, *The Subculture of Violence* (London: Tavistock, 1967), pp. 158–161.

47. Sandra J. Ball-Rokeach, "Values and Violence: A Test of the Subculture of Violence Thesis," *American Sociological Review* 38 (December 1973): 739, 743.

48. Stark and McEvoy, "Middle-Class Violence," p. 53; see also Colin Loftin and Robert H. Hill, "Regional Subculture and Homicide: An Examination of the Gastil-Hackney Thesis," *American Sociological Review* 39 (October 1974): 714–724.

49. Ralph Nader, "Corporate Violence Against the Consumer," in William Osborne, ed., *The Rape of the Powerless* (New York: Gordon and Breach, 1971), p. 14.

CHAPTER 6 – RAPE

1. Camille E. LeGrand, "Rape and Rape Laws: Sexism in Society and Law," *California Law Review* 61 (May 1973): 921.

2. The President's Commission on Law Enforcement and Administration of Justice, *The Challenge of Crime in a Free Society* (New York: Avon Books, 1968), p. 97.

3. Menachem Amir, *Patterns in Forcible Rape* (Chicago: University of Chicago Press, 1971).

4. *Crimes of Violence*, Staff Report to National Commission on Causes and Prevention of Violence (Washington, D.C.: Government Printing Office, 1969), Vol. 11, p. 212.

5. Haywood Burns, "Can a Black Man Get a Fair Trial in This Country?" *New York Times Magazine*, July 12, 1970, p. 44.

6. Charles R. Hayman, Charlene Lanza, Roberto Fuentes, and Kathe Algor, "Rape in the District of Columbia," *American Journal of Obstetrics and Gynecology* 113 (May 1, 1972): 94.

7. Martha Weinman Lear, "What Can You Say About Laws That Tell a Man: If You Rob a Woman, You Might as Well Rape Her Too—The Rape Is Free," *Redbook*, September, 1972, p. 83.

8. James Selkin, "Rape," *Psychology Today* 8 (January 1975): 74.

9. *Ibid.*, p. 72.

10. John M. McDonald, *Rape* (Springfield, Ill.: Charles Thomas, 1971), p. 66.

11. *Ibid.*, pp. 78–79.

12. LeGrand, "Rape," pp. 929–930.

13. MacDonald, *Rape*, pp. 96–97.

14. Sandra Sutherland and Donald J. Scherl, "Patterns of Responses among Victims of Rape," *American Journal of Orthopsychiatry* 40 (April 1970): 503–511.

15. Ann Wolbert Burgess and Lynda Lytle Holmstrom, "Rape Trauma Syndrome," *American Journal of Psychiatry* 131 (September 1974): 984.

16. Martha Weinman Lear, "Q. If You Rape a Woman and Steal Her TV, What Can They Get You for in New York: A. Stealing Her TV," *New York Times Magazine*, January 30, 1972, pp. 62–63.

17. "The Rape Wave," *Newsweek*, January 29, 1973, p. 59.

18. Gail Sheehy, "Nice Girls Don't Get Into Trouble," *New York*, February 15, 1971, p. 30.

19. *Ibid.*

20. *Ibid.*, p. 28.

21. The following account is based on Susan Griffin, "Rape: The All-American Crime," *Ramparts* 10 (September 1971): 4–5. See also Sybil Landau, "Rape: The Victim as Defendant," *Trial* 10 (July/August 1974): 19–22.

22. Clifford Kirkpatrick and Eugene Kanin, "Male Sex Aggression on a University Campus," *American Sociological Review* 22 (February 1957): 52–58.

23. Eugene J. Kanin, "Male Aggression in Dating-Courtship Relations," *American Journal of Sociology* 63 (September 1957): 201.

24. *Ibid.*

25. Lear, "Q. If You Rape," p. 63

26. LeGrand, "Rape," p. 925.

27. Griffin, "Rape," pp. 6–7.

28. Andra Medea and Kathleen Thompson, *Against Rape* (New York: Farrar, Straus and Giroux, 1974), p. 32.

29. *Ibid.*, p. 43.

30. *Ibid.*, p. 31.

31. Selkin, "Rape," p. 76.

32. Nan Blitman and Robin Green, "Inez Garcia on Trial," *Ms.*, May 1975, p. 86.

33. Pamela Lakes Wood, "The Victim in a Forcible Rape Case: A Feminist View," *American Criminal Law Review*, 11 (1973): 335

34. Quoted in Medea and Thompson, *Against Rape*, p. 37.

35. Kurt Weis and Sandra S. Borges, "Victimology and Rape: The Case of the Legitimate Victim," *Issues in Criminology* 8 (Fall, 1973): 81–85.

36. Griffin, "Rape," p. 6.

37. Weis and Borges, "Victimology," p. 83.

38. The following is largely based on Alan J. Davis, "Sexual Assaults in the Philadelphia Prison System," in John Gagnon and William Simon, eds., *The Sexual Scene* (Chicago: Aldine, 1970), pp. 107–124.

39. Edward Sagarin, "Sexual Criminality," in Abraham S. Blumberg, ed., *Current Perspectives on Criminal Behavior* (New York: Knopf, 1974), p. 146.

40. Charles H. McCaghy, "Child Molesters: A Study of Their Career as Deviants," in Marshall Clinard and Richard Quinney, eds., *Criminal Behavior Systems* (New York: Holt, Rinehart and Winston, 1967), pp. 79–81.

41. James L. Mathis, *Clear Thinking about Sexual Deviations* (Chicago: Nelson-Hall, 1972), p. 61.

42. Manfred S. Guttmacher, *Sex Offenses* (New York: Norton, 1951), p. 118.

43. *Ibid.*, pp. 67, 96.

44. R. J. McCaldon, "Rape," *Canadian Journal of Corrections* 9 (1967): 45.

45. Charles H. McCaghy, "Drinking and Deviance Disavowal: The Case of Child Molesters," *Social Problems* 16 (Summer 1968): 45.

46. McCaghy, "Child Molesters," p. 881.

47. McCaghy, "Drinking," p. 48.

48. Mathis, *Clear Thinking*, p. 54.

49. Murray Cohen, Ralph Garofalo, Richard Boucher, and Theoharis Seghorn, "The Psychology of Rapists," *Seminar in Psychiatry* 3 (August 1971): 310.

50. Almost all of these ideas are derived from a review of the relevant literature by Norman S. Goldner, "Rape as a Heinous But Understudied Offense," *Journal of Criminal Law, Criminology and Police Science* 63 (September 1972): 405.

51. Selkin, "Rape," p. 76.

52. Amir, *Patterns*, pp. 327–331.

53. *Ibid.*, p. 330.

54. Duncan Chappell, Gilbert Geis, Stephen Schafer, and Larry Siegel, "Forcible Rape: A Comparative Study of Offenses Known to the Police in Boston and Los Angeles," in James M. Henslin, ed., *Studies in the Sociology of Sex* (New York: Appleton-Century-Crofts, 1971), pp. 175–177.

55. Charles R. Hayman et al., "Roundtable: Rape and Its Consequences," *Medical Aspects of Human Sexuality* 12 (February 1972): 17, 27.

56. Robert A. LeVine, "Gusii Sex Offenses: A Study in Social Control," *American Anthropologist* 61 (December 1959): 987.

57. Susan Brownmiller, *Against Our Will* (New York: Simon and Schuster, 1975), p. 400.

CHAPTER 7 – ROBBERY

1. Compare, for example, *Crimes of Violence*, Vol. 11 (Washington, D.C.: U.S. Government Printing Office, 1969), pp. 208–258, with André Normandeau, "Patterns in Robbery," *Criminology* 6 (November 1968): 12, 15.

2. *FBI Uniform Crime Reports*, 1974, p. 15. For similar observations, see John E. Conklin, *Robbery and the Criminal Justice System* (Philadelphia: Lippincott, 1972), p. 79.

3. Conklin, *ibid.*, p. 79.

4. "The Private Intelligence of Bank Robbers: Two Self-Accounts," *Journal of Individual Psychology* 18 (May 1962): 79, 83.

5. Floyd Feeney and Adrianne Weir, "The Prevention and Control of Robbery," *Criminology* 13 (May 1975): 104.

6. Conklin, *Robbery*, pp. 81–83.

7. The following are largely based on *ibid.*, pp. 87–92.

8. *Ibid.*, p. 97.

9. Feeney and Weir, "The Prevention," p. 105.

10. David Burnham, "Fear of Muggers Looms Large in Public Concern Over Crime," *New York Times*, May 20, 1968, p. 1.

11. Conklin, *Robbery*, p. 98.

12. Everett DeBaun, "The Heist: The Theory and Practice of Armed Robbery," *Harpers*, February 1950, p. 73.

13. *Ibid.*, p. 75.

14. Conklin, *Robbery*, p. 105.

15. See, for example, Conklin, *ibid.*, p. 113; Feeney and Weir, "The Prevention," p. 105; Normandeau, "Patterns," p. 12.

16. Feeney and Weir, *ibid.*, p. 104.

17. *Ibid.*, pp. 120–122.

18. *Ibid.*, p. 113.

19. Arnold Sagalyn, *The Crime of Robbery in the United States* (Washington, D.C.: Government Printing Office, 1971), p. 14.

20. "Private Intelligence," p. 86.

21. Conklin, *Robbery*, pp. 109–110.

22. *Ibid.*, pp. 110–112.

23. *Ibid.*, p. 107.

24. The following data are largely derived from the *FBI Uniform Crime Reports*, 1974, p. 17.

25. Julian B. Roebuck and Mervyn L. Cadwallader, "The Negro Armed Robber as a Criminal Type: The Construction and Application of a Typology," *Pacific Sociological Review* 4 (Spring 1961): 21–26.

26. F. H. McClintock and Evelyn Gibson, *Robbery in London* (London: Macmillan, 1961), pp. 14–15.

27. *Ibid.*, p. 16.

28. The following are based on Conklin, *Robbery*, pp. 59–78.

29. Bruce Jackson, *In the Life: Versions of the Criminal Experience* (New York: Holt, Rinehart and Winston, 1972), pp. 40–41.

30. John Irwin, *The Felon* (Englewood Cliffs, N.J.: Prentice-Hall, 1970), pp. 23–26.

31. Quoted by Irwin, *ibid.*, from William Burroughs, *Junkie* (New York: Ace Books, 1953), p. 20.

32. John Luce, "End of the Road: A Case Study," in David E. Smith and George R. Gay, eds., *"It's So Good, Don't Even Try It Once": Heroin in Perspective* (Englewood Cliffs, N.J.: Prentice-Hall, 1972), pp. 145–146.

33. Werner J. Einstadter, "The Social Organization of Armed Robbery," *Social Problems* 17 (Summer 1969): 64–83.

34. *Ibid.*, p. 73.

35. *Ibid.*, p. 81.

36. Irwin, *The Felon*, p. 11.

37. Conklin, *Robbery*, pp. 12–58.

38. Leroy C. Gould, "The Changing Structure of Property Crime in an Affluent Society," *Social Forces* 48 (September 1969): 51.

39. *Ibid.*, p. 58.

40. *Ibid.*, pp. 56–57.

41. André Normandeau, "Robbery in Philadelphia and London," *British Journal of Criminology* 9 (January 1969): 71–79.

CHAPTER 8 – PROSTITUTION

1. For a survey on the many definitions of prostitution in the relevant literature, see Harry Benjamin and R. E. L. Masters, *Prostitution and Morality* (New York: Julian Press, 1964), pp. 21–32.

2. Paul H. Gebhard, "Definitions," in Donald S. Marshall and Robert C. Suggs, eds., *Human Sexual Behavior* (New York: Basic Books, 1971), p. 258.

3. Gail Sheehy, *Hustling* (New York: Delacorte Press, 1971), p. 4; Otto Friedrich, "Reflections on the Sad Profession," *Time*, August 23, 1971, p. 34.

4. The following is largely based on Paul H. Gebhard, "Misconceptions About Female Prostitutes," *Medical Aspects of Human Sexuality* 3 (March 1969): 24–30.

5. "White Slavery, 1972," *Time*, June 5, 1972, p. 24.

6. Some laboratory experiments on mice, however, have indicated that promiscuous intercourse in itself may reduce fertility. See Sidney M. Greenfield, "The Bruce Effect and Malinowski's Hypothesis on Mating and Fertility," *American Anthropologist* 70 (August 1968): 759–761.

7. Fernando Henriques, *Prostitution and Society* (New York: Citadel Press, 1962), pp. 21–43.

8. Benjamin and Masters, *Prostitution*, pp. 119–191.

9. *Ibid.*, pp. 124–125.

10. Charles Winick and Paul M. Kinsie, *The Lively Commerce* (Chicago: Quadrangle Books, 1971), p. 164.

11. Sheehy, *Hustling*, p. 16.

12. *Ibid.*, p. 63.

13. This section is based on Benjamin and Masters, *Prostitution*, pp. 125–130.

14. *Ibid.*, p. 128.

15. Winick and Kinsie, *The Lively*, p. 159.

16. *Ibid.*, p. 158.

17. This section is based on Albert J. Velarde and Mark Warlick, "Massage Parlors: The Sensuality Business," *Society* 11 (November/December 1973): 63–74. The following direct quotes are from this article.

18. This section is based on Harold Greenwald, *The Elegant Prostitute* (New York: Walker, 1970), pp. 3, 10–30.

19. *Ibid.*, p. 14.

20. Travis Hirschi, "The Professional Prostitute," *Berkeley Journal of Sociology* 7 (Spring 1962): 34.

21. Sheehy, *Hustling*, pp. 83–85.

22. James H. Bryan, "Apprenticeships in Prostitution," *Social Problems* 12 (Winter 1965): 287–297.

23. James H. Bryan, "Occupational Ideologies and Individual Attitudes of Call Girls," *Social Problems* 13 (Spring 1966): 443.

24. *Ibid.*

25. *Ibid.*

26. Hirschi, "The Professional," p. 44.

27. *Ibid.*

28. Bryan, "Occupational," p. 443.

29. Hirschi, "The Professional," pp. 44–45.

30. Bryan, "Occupational," p. 449.

31. Norman R. Jackman, Richard O'Toole, and Gilbert Geis, "The Self-Image of the Prostitute," *Sociological Quarterly* 4 (April 1963): 150–161.

32. Though other feminists have, to the outrage of prostitutes, advocated the elimination of prostitution because they feel that it is too degrading for a female to sell her body. See Friedrich, "Reflections," p. 35.

33. "The Unhappy Hooker," *Newsweek*, February 12, 1973, p. 43.

34. "Filles Sans Joie," *Newsweek*, June 23, 1975, p. 42.

35. "Call Me Madam," *Newsweek*, July 8, 1974, p. 65.

36. Barbara Sherman Heyl, "The Female House of Prostitution," in Irving Louis Horowitz and Charles Nanry, eds., *Sociological Realities II* (New York: Harper & Row, 1975), pp. 339–344; Winick and Kinsie, *The Lively*, p. 98.

37. Winick and Kinsie, *ibid.*, p. 99.

38. Heyl, "The Female House," p. 340.

39. Christina and Richard Milner, *Black Players* (Boston: Little, Brown, 1972), pp. 11–12.

40. *Ibid.*, pp. 8–9.

41. *Ibid.*, pp. 51–52.

42. Kate Millett, *The Prostitution Papers* (New York: Avon Books, 1973), p. 134.

43. Winick and Kinsie, *The Lively*, p. 119.

44. Sheehy, *Hustling*, p. 106.

45. Milner and Milner, *Black Players*, pp. 274–275.

46. See, for example, Winick and Kinsie, *The Lively*, pp. 193–198; Benjamin and Masters, *Prostitution*, pp. 194–197.

47. The following is based on Greenwald, *The Elegant*, pp. 221–237.

48. Benjamin and Masters, *Prostitution*, pp. 90–91.

49. *Ibid.*, pp. 89, 91–92.

50. *Ibid.*, pp. 93–94.

51. Greenwald, *The Elegant*, pp. 199–200.

52. See, for example, Wayland Young, "Prostitution," in John H. Gagnon and William Simon, eds., *Sexual Deviance* (New York: Harper & Row, 1967), pp. 112–113; Sheehy, *Hustling*, p. 101.

53. Kingsley Davis, "Sexual Behavior," in Robert Merton and Robert Nisbet, eds., *Contemporary Social Problems*, 3rd ed. (New York: Harcourt Brace Jovanovich, 1971), p. 347.

54. *Ibid.*

55. *Ibid.*, p. 350.

56. *Ibid.*

CHAPTER 9 – HOMOSEXUALITY

1. Alfred C. Kinsey, Wardell B. Pomeroy, and Clyde E. Martin, *Sexual Behavior in the Human Male* (Philadelphia: Saunders, 1948), p. 639.

2. *Ibid.*, pp. 650–651; Alfred C. Kinsey, Wardell B. Pomeroy, Clyde E. Martin, and Paul H. Gebhard, *Sexual Behavior in the Human Female* (Philadelphia: Saunders, 1953), pp. 474–475.

3. Robert Athanasiou, Phillip Shaver, and Carol Tavris, "Sex," *Psychology Today* 4 (July 1970): 50.

4. Martin Hoffman, *The Gay World* (New York: Basic Books, 1968), p. 35.

5. Laud Humphreys, "Tearoom Trade: Impersonal Sex in Public Places," *Transaction* 7 (January 1970): 17–18.

6. Albert J. Reiss, Jr., "The Social Integration of Queers and Peers," *Social Problems* 9 (Fall 1961): 102–120.

7. *Ibid.*, pp. 19–22.

8. David J. Pittman, "The Male House of Prostitution," *Transaction* 8 (March/April 1971): 21–28.

9. *Ibid.*, pp. 23–25.

10. *Ibid.*, pp. 22–23.

11. Barry M. Dank, "Coming Out in the Gay World," *Psychiatry* 34 (May 1971): 182.

12. *Ibid.*, pp. 183–184.

13. Evelyn Hooker, "The Homosexual Community," in John H. Gagnon and William Simon, eds., *Sexual Deviance* (New York: Harper & Row, 1967), p. 179.

14. Dank, "Coming Out," p. 190.

15. Martin S. Weinberg and Colin J. Williams, *Male Homosexuals* (New York: Penguin Books, 1975), pp. 285–286.

16. Hoffman, *The Gay*, p. 57.

17. Hooker, "The Homosexual," pp. 175–176.

18. Humphreys, "Tearoom Trade," p. 13.

19. *Ibid.*, p. 14.

20. *Ibid.*

21. *Ibid.*, p. 16.

22. Hoffman, *The Gay*, pp. 176–179.

23. *Ibid.*, pp. 185–186, 190.

24. Carol A. B. Warren, *Identity and Community in the Gay World* (New York: Wiley, 1974), pp. 72–74.

25. Jack H. Hedblom, "The Female Homosexual: Social and Attitudinal Dimensions," in Joseph A. McCaffrey, ed., *The Homosexual Dialectic* (Englewood Cliffs, N.J.: Prentice-Hall, 1972), p. 55.

26. Jess Stearn, *The Grapevine* (New York: Doubleday, 1964), p. 13; quoted by Hedblom, *ibid.*, pp. 34–35.

27. William Simon and John H. Gagnon, "The Lesbians: A Preliminary Overview," in J. H. Gagnon and W. Simon, eds., *Sexual Deviance* (New York: Harper & Row, 1967), pp. 251–252.

28. The following is based on *ibid.*

29. *Ibid.*, p. 252.

30. *Ibid.*, pp. 271–272.

31. Charles H. McCaghy and James K. Skipper, Jr., "Lesbian Behavior as an Adaptation to the Occupation of Stripping," *Social Problems* 17 (Fall 1969): 262–272; the following quotations are from this article.

32. David A. Ward and Gene G. Kassebaum, "Homosexuality: A Mode of Adaptation in a Prison for Women," *Social Problems* 12 (Fall 1964): 159–177.

33. *Ibid.*, p. 170.

34. "Gays on the March," *Time*, September 8, 1975, p. 32.

35. Edward Sagarin, *Odd Man In* (Chicago: Quadrangle Books, 1969), pp. 78–87.

36. Laud Humphreys, *Out of the Closets* (Englewood Cliffs, N.J.: Prentice-Hall, 1972), pp. 3, 99–100.

37. "Gays on the March," pp. 32–43.

38. Edward Sagarin, "The Good Guys, the Bad Guys, and the Gay Guys," *Contemporary Sociology* 2 (January 1973): 11.

39. Franz J. Kallman, "Comparative Twin Study on the Genetic Aspects of Male Homosexuality," *Journal of Nervous and Mental Disease* 115 (1952): 283–298

40. Robert E. Gould, "What We Don't Know About Homosexuality," *New York Times Magazine*, February 24, 1974, pp. 56-57.

41. Irving Bieber et al., *Homosexuality* (New York: Basic Books, 1962), pp. 303–304.

42. Otto Fenichel, *The Psychoanalytic Theory of Neurosis* (New York: Norton, 1945), p. 330.

43. Gould, "What We Don't," p. 60.

44. "Gay Liberation at the APA," *Science News* 104 (December 22, 1973): 389.

45. Bieber et al., *Homosexuality*, pp. 310–311.

46. Evelyn Hooker, "Parental Relations and Male Homosexuality in Patient and Nonpatient Samples," *Journal of Consulting and Clinical Psychology* 33 (April 1969): 141.

47. Hoffman, *The Gay*, pp. 130–155; Wardell B. Pomeroy, "Homosexuality," in Ralph W. Weltge, ed. *The Same Sex* (Philadelphia: Pilgrim Press, 1969), pp. 12–13.

48. Weinberg and Williams, *Male Homosexuals*, pp. 18–22. See also John H. Gagnon and William Simon, "Homosexuality: The Formulation of a Sociological Perspective," *Journal of Health and Social Behavior* 8 (September 1967): 177–185.

49. C. A. Tripp, *The Homosexual Matrix* (New York: Signet, 1976), p. 69.

50. *Ibid.*, p. 135.

CHAPTER 10 — SUICIDE

1. Gene Lester and David Lester, *Suicide* (Englewood Cliffs, N.J.: Prentice-Hall, 1971), pp. 3–4.

2. James Wilkins, "Suicidal Behavior," *American Sociological Review* 32 (April 1967): 204.

3. Lewis J. Siegal and Jacob H. Friedman, "The Threat of Suicide," *Diseases of the Nervous System* 16 (1955): 45.

4. Wilkins, "Suicidal Behavior," p. 295.

5. "Wrist-Cutting—a Road to Life, Not Death," *Psychology Today* 9 (April 1976): 20.

6. Erwin Stengel, *Suicide and Attempted Suicide* (Baltimore, Md.: Pelican Books, 1969), pp. 91, 97.

7. Wilkins, "Suicidal Behavior," pp. 289–295.

8. Jerry Jacobs, "A Phenomenological Study of Suicide Notes," *Social Problems* 15 (Summer 1967): 67–68.

9. Edwin S. Shneidman, "Classification of Suicidal Phenomena," in Simon Dinitz, Russell R. Dynes, and Alfred C. Clarke, eds., *Deviance* (New York: Oxford University Press, 1975), p. 376.

10. Raymond Firth, "Suicide and Risk-Taking in Tikopia Society," *Psychiatry* 24 (February 1961): 4.

11. Shneidman, "Classification of Suicidal Phenomena," p. 376.

12. "Wrist-Cutting," p. 27.

13. Jack D. Douglas, *The Social Meanings of Suicide* (Princeton, N.J.: Princeton University Press, 1967), pp. 163–231; Sanford Labovitz, "Variation in Suicide Rates," in Jack P. Gibbs, ed., *Suicide* (New York: Harper & Row, 1968), pp. 58–59.

14. The following data are derived from Labovitz, *ibid.*, pp. 59–73; Jack P. Gibbs, "Suicide," in Robert K. Merton and Robert Nisbet, eds., *Contemporary Social Problems* (New York: Harcourt Brace Jovanovich, 1971), pp. 281–300.

15. Louis I. Dublin and Bessie Bunzel, *To Be or Not To Be* (New York: Harrison Smith & Robert Haas, 1933), p. 15.

16. Albert C. Cain and Irene Fast, "Children's Disturbed Reactions to Parent Suicide," *American Journal of Orthopsychiatry* 36 (October 1966): 873–880.

17. James M. Henslin, "Guilt and Guilt Neutralization: Response and Adjustment to Suicide," in Jack D. Douglas, ed., *Deviance and Respectability* (New York: Basic Books, 1970), pp. 200–204.

18. *Ibid.*, p. 222.

19. Elizabeth Hall with Paul Cameron, "Our Failing Reverence for Life," *Psychology Today* 9 (April 1976): 108.

20. Stengel, *Suicide*, pp. 147–148.

21. Norman L. Farberow, "Ten Years of Suicide Prevention—Past and Future," *Bulletin of Suicidology*, No. 6 (Spring 1970): 9; Carl I. Wold, "Characteristics of 26,000 Suicide Prevention Center Patients," *Bulletin of Suicidology*, No. 6 (Spring 1970): 24–28.

22. Emile Durkheim, *Suicide* (New York: Free Press, 1951). It was first published in 1897.

23. *Ibid.*, p. 276.

24. *Ibid.*, p. 258.

25. Barclay D. Johnson, "Durkheim's One Cause of Suicide," *American Sociological Review* 30 (December 1965): 875–886.

26. Andrew F. Henry and James F. Short, Jr., *Suicide and Homicide* (New York: Free Press, 1954).

27. See, for example, Gibbs, "Suicide," pp. 309–310; Walter T. Martin, "Theories of Variation in the Suicide Rate," in Gibbs, *Suicide*, pp. 94–95.

28. See, for example, Gibbs, "Suicide," p. 307.

29. Jack P. Gibbs and Walter T. Martin, *Status Integration and Suicide* (Eugene: University of Oregon, 1964).

30. Durkheim, *Suicide*, p. 209.

31. This and the following quotes are from Gibbs and Martin, *Status Integration*, p. 27.

32. William J. Chambliss and Marion F. Steele, "Status Integration and Suicide: An Assessment," *American Sociological Review* 31 (August 1966): 526; Robert Hagedon and Sanford Labovitz, "A Note on Status Integration and Suicide," *Social Problems* 14 (Summer 1966): 79–84. See also Gibbs and Martin's replies in *American Sociological Review* 31 (August 1966): 533–541, and in *Social Problems* 15 (Spring 1968): 510–512.

33. Douglas, *Social Meanings of Suicide*, pp. 235–340.

34. Jacobs, "Phenomenological Study of Suicide Notes," p. 67.

35. Warren Breed, "The Negro and Fatalistic Suicide," *Pacific Sociological Review* 13 (Summer 1970): 160.

CHAPTER 11 – MENTAL DISORDER

1. Otto Friedrich, *Going Crazy* (New York: Simon & Schuster, 1976), pp. 21–22.

2. Leo Srole, Thomas S. Langner, Stanley T. Michael, Marvin K. Opler, and Thomas A. C. Rennie, *Mental Health in the Metropolis* (New York: McGraw-Hill, 1962).

3. Rona Cherry and Laurence Cherry, "Depression: The Common Cold of Mental Ailments," *New York Times Magazine*, November 25, 1973, p. 38.

4. The following misconceptions and others are discussed in James C. Coleman, *Abnormal Psychology and Modern Life*, 3rd ed. (Glenview, Ill.: Scott, Foresman, 1964), pp. 10–14.

5. The following is largely based on Sheldon Cashdan, *Abnormal Psychology* (Englewood Cliffs, N.J.: Prentice-Hall, 1972), pp. 25–60.

6. *Ibid.*, p. 28.

7. Coleman, *Abnormal Psychology*, pp. 353–361.

8. Jack Zusman, "Primary Prevention," in Alfred M. Freedman, Harold I. Kaplan, Benjamin J. Sadock, eds., *Comprehensive Textbook in Psychiatry*, (Baltimore: William & Wilkins, 1975), II, 2327, 2328.

9. Quoted in E. Fuller Torrey, *The Death of Psychiatry* (Radnor, Penn.: Chilton, 1974), p. 42.

10. Bruce P. Dohrenwend, "Sociocultural and Social-Psychological Factors in the Genesis of Mental Disorders," *Journal of Health and Social Behavior* 16 (December 1975): 368.

11. *Ibid.* The following data on these three variables are from this source.

12. Robert E. L. Faris and H. Warren Dunham, *Mental Disorders in Urban Areas* (Chicago: University of Chicago Press, 1939).

13. August B. Hollingshead and Fredrick C. Redlich, *Social Class and Mental Illness* (New York: Wiley, 1958).

14. Srole et al., *Mental Health.*

15. The following is drawn from Howard B. Kaplan, *The Sociology of Mental Illness* (New Haven, Conn.: College & University Press, 1972), pp. 141–191.

16. Portions of the following are based on Cashdan, *Abnormal Psychology*, pp. 4–12; 94–115.

17. Thomas S. Szasz, *The Manufacture of Madness* (New York: Dell, 1970), p. 314.

18. Quoted in Cashdan, *Abnormal Psychology*, p. 11.

19. Jim C. Nunnally, Jr., *Public Conceptions of Mental Health* (New York: Holt, Rinehart & Winston, 1961).

20. Torrey, *Death of Psychiatry*, p. 58.

21. Derek L. Phillips, "Rejection: A Possible Consequence of Seeking Help for Mental Disorder," *American Sociological Review* 28 (December 1963): 963–972.

22. See, for example, L. Kutner, "The Illusion of Due Process in Commitment Proceedings," *Northwestern University Law Review* 57 (September 1962): 383–399; Thomas J. Scheff, "Social Condition for Rationality: How Urban and Rural Courts Deal with the Mentally Ill," *American Behavioral Scientist* 7 (March 1964): 21–27.

23. Thomas J. Scheff, *Being Mentally Ill* (Chicago: Aldine, 1966), p. 132.

24. "Freeing Mental Patients," *Newsweek*, July 7, 1975, p. 45.

25. See, for example, Thomas J. Scheff, "The Labeling Theory of Mental Illness," *American Sociological Review* 39 (June 1974): 448–449.

26. John H. Hess and Herbert E. Thomas, "Incompetency to Stand Trial: Procedures, Results, and Problems," *American Journal of Psychiatry* 119 (February 1963): 713–720.

27. Quoted by Thomas S. Szasz, "Crime, Punishment, and Psychiatry," in Abraham S. Blumberg, ed., *Current Perspectives on Criminal Behavior* (New York: Knopf, 1974).

28. Erving Goffman, *Asylums* (Garden City, New York: Anchor Books, 1961).

29. D. L. Rosenhan, "On Being Sane in Insane Places," *Science*, January 19, 1973, p. 256.

30. Goffman, *Asylums*, pp. 306–307.

31. Torrey, *Death of Psychiatry*, p. 65.

32. *Action for Mental Health* (New York: Wiley, 1961), pp. 92–93.

33. For a hint of this point, see David F. Musto, "What Ever Happened to Community Mental Health?" *Public Interest* 39 (Spring 1975): 53–79.

34. Thomas S. Szasz, *Ideology and Insanity* (Garden City, New York: Anchor Books, 1970), p. 24.

35. The following are based on Scheff, *Being Mentally Ill*, pp. 40–101.

36. R. D. Laing, *The Politics of Experience* (New York: Ballantine Books, 1967).

37. John A. Clausen and Carol L. Huffine, "Sociocultural and Social-Psychological Factors Affecting Social Responses to Mental Disorder," *Journal of Health and Social Behavior* 16 (December 1975): 415.

38. Walter R. Gove, "Societal Reaction as an Explanation of Mental Illness: An Evaluation," *American Sociological Review* 35 (October 1970): 882.

39. Scheff, "Labeling Theory."

40. Szasz, *Ideology and Insanity*, p. 213.

41. For some examples of this relationship between power and madness, see Friedrich, *Going Crazy*, p. 217.

CHAPTER 12 – SWINGING

1. Alfred C. Kinsey, Wardell B. Pomeroy, and Clyde E. Martin, *Sexual Behavior in the Human Male* (Philadelphia: Saunders, 1948), pp. 584–585; Kinsey, Pomeroy, Martin, and Paul H. Gebhard, *Sexual Behavior in the Human Female* (Philadelphia: Saunders, 1953), p. 416.

2. Gilbert D. Bartell, *Group Sex* (New York: Signet, 1971), p. 21.

3. Brian G. Gilmartin, "That Swinging Couple Down the Block," *Psychology Today* 8 (February 1975): 55.

4. Ronald M. Holmes, *Sexual Behavior* (Berkeley, Cal.: McCutchan, 1971), p. 202.

5. Bartell, *Group Sex*, p. 89.

6. This section relies heavily on *ibid.*, pp. 103–126.

7. Bartell, *Group Sex*, p. 151.

8. *Ibid.*, pp. 143–144.

9. *Ibid.*, pp. 23–49.

10. Gilmartin, "That Swinging Couple," pp. 55–56.

11. *Ibid.*, p. 58.

12. See, for example, Anne-Marie Henshel, "Swinging: A Study of Decision Making in Marriage," *American Journal of Sociology* 78 (January 1973): 885–891.

13. Charles and Rebecca Palson, "Swinging in Wedlock," *Society* 9 (February 1972): 35.

14. Gordon Bermant, "Group Sex," *Psychology Today* 5 (June 1971): 84.

15. Gilmartin, "That Swinging Couple," p. 58.

16. For data that seem to support this point, see Duane Denfeld, "Dropouts from Swinging," *The Family Coordinator*, January 1974, pp. 45–49.

17. Bartell, *Group Sex*, pp. 196, 206, 211–212, 215.

18. Duane Denfeld and Michael Gordon, "The Sociology of Mate Swapping," *Journal of Sex Research* 6 (May 1970): 89, 92. See also Robert R. Bell, *Social Deviance* (Homewood, Ill.: Dorsey, 1976), p. 82.

19. Palson and Palson, "Swinging," p. 37.

20. Denfeld and Gordon, "The Sociology of Mate Swapping," p. 92; Bartell, *Group Sex*, p. 42.

21. Mary Lindenstein Walshok, "The Emergence of Middle-Class Deviant Subcultures: The Case of Swingers," *Social Problems* 18 (Spring 1971): 494.

22. Bartell, *Group Sex*, pp. 44–47.

CHAPTER 13 – ILLEGAL DRUG USE

1. Erich Goode, "The Criminology of Drugs and Drug Use," in Abraham S. Blumberg, ed., *Current Perspectives on Criminal Behavior* (New York: Knopf, 1974), p. 165.

2. National Commission on Marihuana and Drug Abuse, *Drug Use in America* (Washington, D.C.: Government Printing Office, 1973), pp. 30–32, 94–98.

3. Erich Goode, *Drugs in American Society* (New York: Knopf, 1972), pp. 129–130.

4. Quoted in Thomas Szasz, *Ceremonial Chemistry* (Garden City, New York: Anchor, 1974), p. 43.

5. Harry J. Anslinger and W. S. Thompkins, *The Traffic in Narcotics* (New York: Funk & Wagnalls, 1953), p. 21.

6. National Commission, *Drug Use*, p. 159.

7. Edward M. Brecher and the Editors of Consumer Reports, "Marihuana: The Health Questions," *Consumer Reports* 40 (March 1975): 143–145.

8. *Ibid.*, p. 149.

9. Goode, *Drugs*, p. 64.

10. *Ibid.*, p. 130.

11. *Ibid.*, p. 245.

12. *Ibid.*, p. 53.

13. National Commission on Marihuana and Drug Abuse, *Marihuana: A Signal of Misunderstanding* (Washington, D.C.: Government Printing Office, 1972), p. 59.

14. Quoted in John Cashman, *The LSD Story* (Greenwich, Conn.: Fawcett, 1966), p. 31.

15. The following discussion is largely based on Goode, *Drugs*, pp. 97–120.

16. *Ibid.*, p. 104.

17. *Ibid.*, p. 115.

18. *Ibid.*, p. 170.

19. Alfred R. Lindesmith, *Addiction and Opiates* (Chicago: Aldine, 1968), p. 8.

20. William E. McAuliffe and Robert A. Gordon, "A Test of Lindesmith's Theory of Addiction: The Frequency of Euphoria among Long-Term Addicts," *American Journal of Sociology* 79 (January 1974): 831.

21. See their debate in *American Journal of Sociology* 81 (July 1975): 147–163.

22. Jerome H. Jaffe, "Drug Addiction and Drug Abuse," in Louis S. Goodman and Alfred Gilman, eds., *The Pharmacological Basis of Therapeutics* (New York: Macmillan, 1965), p. 292.

23. This and the following discussion are based on Ronald L. Akers, *Deviant Behavior: A Social Learning Approach* (Belmont, California: Wadsworth, 1973), pp. 77–80, 99–100; Goode, *Drugs*, pp. 33–42; National Commission, *Drug Use*, pp. 65–71; John A. O'Donnell, Harwin L. Voss, Richard R. Clayton, Gerald T. Slatin, and Robin G. W. Room, *Young Men and Drugs: A National Survey* (Rockville, Maryland: National Institute on Drug Abuse, 1976).

24. Jerry L. Simmons and Barry Winograd, *It's Happening* (Santa Barbara, California, McNally and Loftin, 1967), p. 12.

25. Isidor Chein, Donald L. Gerard, Robert S. Lee, and Eva Rosenfeld, *The Road to H* (New York: Basic Books, 1964), p. 149.

26. Goode, *Drugs*, p. 120.

27. Chein et al., *The Road to H*, p. 151.

28. Howard S. Becker, *Outsiders* (New York: Free Press, 1963), pp. 42–58.

29. Goode, *Drugs*, p. 169.

30. Herbert Hill, "Anti-Oriental Agitation and the Rise of Working-Class Racism," *Society* 10 (January-February 1973): 52.

31. John Helmer, *Drugs and Minority Oppression* (New York: Seabury, 1975), p. 32.

32. For a while, however, law enforcers interpreted "legitimate medical purposes" as inapplicable to a physician's administering opiates to addicted patients. But this interpretation was rejected by the Supreme Court in 1925.

33. David F. Musto, *The American Disease: Origins of Narcotic Control* (New Haven: Yale University Press, 1973), p. 223.

34. Szasz, *Ceremonial*, p. 203.

35. *Ibid.*, p. 132.

36. See Szasz, *Ceremonial*; Musto, *American Disease*; Helmer, *Drugs*.

37. See Goode, *Drugs*, pp. 181–236.

38. Robert K. Merton, *Social Theory and Social Structure* (New York: Free Press, 1968), pp. 207–208.

39. Richard A. Cloward and Lloyd E. Ohlin, *Delinquency and Opportunity* (Glencoe, Illinois: Free Press, 1960), pp. 178–184.

40. Alfred R. Lindesmith and John H. Gagnon, "Anomie and Drug Addiction," in Marshall B. Clinard, ed., *Anomie and Deviant Behavior* (New York: Free Press, 1964), pp. 158–188. Also see Harold Finestone, "Cats, Kicks, and Color," *Social Problems* 5 (Summer 1957) 3–13; Harvey W. Feldman, "Ideological Supports to Becoming and Remaining a Heroin Addict," *Journal of Health and Social Behavior* 9 (June 1968): 131–139.

41. Edward Preble and John J. Casey, Jr., "Taking Care of Business—The Heroin User's Life on the Street," *International Journal of the Addictions* 4 (1969): 2; quoted in Goode, *Drugs*, p. 179.

42. Lindesmith, *Addiction*, p. 191.

43. Howard S. Becker, "History, Culture and Subjective Experience: An Exploration of the Social Bases of Drug-Induced Experiences," *Journal of Health and Social Behavior* 7 (June 1967): 163–176.

44. James M. Graham, "Amphetamine Politics on Capitol Hill," *Society* 9 (January 1972): 14–15.

45. Szasz, *Ceremonial*, p. 179.

CHAPTER 14 – ALCOHOLISM

1. *Second Special Report to the U.S. Congress on Alcohol and Health* (Rockville, Maryland: National Institute on Alcohol Abuse and Alcoholism, 1974).

2. Joel Fort, *Alcohol: Our Biggest Drug Problem* (New York: McGraw-Hill, 1973), pp. 46–47.

3. Craig MacAndrew and Robert B. Edgerton, *Drunken Comportment* (London: Nelson, 1969), pp. 169–170.

4. For a persuasive argument and abundance of evidence supporting this point, see MacAndrew and Edgerton, *ibid*. See also Alan R. Lang et al., "Effects of Alcohol on Aggression in Male Social Drinkers," *Journal of Abnormal Psychology* 84 (October 1975): 508–518.

5. Morris E. Chafetz and Harold W. Demone, Jr., *Alcoholism and Society* (New York: Oxford University Press, 1962), p. 9; cited in MacAndrew and Edgerton, *ibid*., pp. 6–7.

6. *Alcohol and Health*, pp. 27–35.

7. *Ibid*., p. 73.

8. Richard Selzer, "The Drinking Man's Liver," *Esquire*, April 1974, p. 178.

9. *Alcohol and Health*, p. 68.

10. *Ibid*., pp. 53–65.

11. "The Effects of Alcohol," *Time*, April 22, 1974, p. 77.

12. *Alcohol and Health*, p. 108.

13. The President's Commission on Law Enforcement and Administration of Justice, *The Challenge of Crime in a Free Society* (New York: Avon, 1968), pp. 532–542.

14. See *FBI Uniform Crime Reports*, 1974 (Washington, D.C.: Government Printing Office, 1975), p. 179.

15. *Alcohol and Health*, p. 42.

16. Richard E. Boyatzis, "The Predisposition toward Alcohol-Related Interpersonal Aggression in Men," *Journal of Studies on Alcohol* 36 (September 1975): 1196–1207.

17. *Alcohol and Health*, pp. 37–38.

18. S. Pell and C. A. D'Alonzo, "A 5-year Mortality Study of Alcoholics," *Journal of Occupational Medicine* 15 (1973): 120–125; quoted in *Alcohol and Health*, p. 39.

19. This section is largely based on *Alcohol and Health*, pp. 1–26.

20. Lee N. Robins, G. E. Murphy, and M. B. Breckenridge, "Drinking Behavior of Young Urban Negro Men," *Quarterly Journal of Studies on Alcohol* 29 (September 1968): 657–684.

21. Robert F. Bales, "Attitudes toward Drinking in the Irish Culture," in David J. Pittman and Charles R. Snyder, eds. *Society, Culture, and Drinking Patterns* (New York: Wiley, 1962), p. 170.

22. The charts are reprinted from *Alcohol and Health*, p. 19.

23. Quoted by Don Cahalan, *Problem Drinkers* (San Francisco: Jossey-Bass, 1970), p. 3.

24. Mark Keller's letter to Robin Room, quoted by Cahalan, *ibid*., p. 5.

25. Mark Keller and Vera Efron, "Alcoholism," *Encyclopedia Americana I*, p. 348.

26. Thomas F. A. Plaut, *Alcohol Problems* (New York: Oxford University Press, 1967), pp. 37–38; quoted by Cahalan, *ibid.*, p. 12.

27. William McCord and Joan McCord, *Origins of Alcoholism* (Stanford, Calif.: Stanford University Press, 1960), p. 9.

28. E. M. Jellinek, "Phases of Alcohol Addiction," *Quarterly Journal of Studies on Alcohol* 13 (1952): 673–684.

29. Rupert Wilkinson, *The Prevention of Drinking Problems* (New York: Oxford University Press, 1970), p. 8.

30. The following is largely based on Joseph R. Gusfield, "Status Conflicts and the Changing Ideologies of the American Temperance Movement," in Pittman and Snyder, eds., pp. 101–120.

31. *Ibid.*, p. 114.

32. "Alcoholism: New Victims, New Treatment," *Time*, April 22, 1974, p. 78.

33. *Alcoholics Anonymous* (New York: Works, 1939), pp. 71–72.

34. "Alcoholism," *Time*, p. 81.

35. See, for example, McCord and McCord, *Origins of Alcoholism*, pp. 22–44; Julian B. Roebuck and Raymond G. Kessler, *The Etiology of Alcoholism* (Springfield, Illinois: Charles C. Thomas, 1972).

36. Paraphrased from the American Medical Association, *Manual on Alcoholism*, pp. 15, 16, by Don Martindale and Edith Martindale, in *The Social Dimensions of Mental Illness, Alcoholism, and Drug Dependence* (Westport, Conn.: Greenwood, 1971), p. 225.

37. Robert Straus, "Alcohol and Alcoholism," in Robert K. Merton and Robert Nisbet, eds., *Contemporary Social Problems*, 3rd edition (New York: Harcourt Brace Jovanovich, 1971), p. 251.

38. See, for example, Ronald J. Cantanzaro, "Psychiatric Aspects of Alcoholism," in David Pittman, ed., *Alcoholism* (New York: Harper & Row, 1967), pp. 27–41.

39. McCord and McCord, *Origins of Alcoholism*, p. 28.

40. *Ibid.*, p. 155.

41. David C. McClelland, William N. Davis, Rudolf Kalin, and Eric Wanner, *The Drinking Man* (New York: Free Press, 1972), pp. 33, 336.

42. Harrison M. Trice, *Alcoholism in America* (New York: McGraw-Hill, 1966), pp. 42–61.

43. Robert Freed Bales, "Cultural Differences in Rates of Alcoholism," *Quarterly Journal of Studies on Alcohol* 6 (March 1946): 480–499.

44. McCord and McCord, *Origins of Alcoholism*, p. 35.

45. For a similar view, see Dan E. Beauchamp, "The Alcohol Alibi: Blaming Alcoholics," *Society* 12 (September/October 1975): 12–17.

CHAPTER 15 – PROFITABLE DEVIANCE

1. Gilbert Geis, "Upperworld Crime," in Abraham S. Blumberg, ed., *Current Perspectives on Criminal Behavior* (New York: Knopf, 1974), p. 134.

2. President's Commission, *The Challenge of Crime in a Free Society* (New York: Avon Books, 1968), p. 437.

3. Donald R. Cressey, *Theft of the Nation* (New York: Harper & Row, 1969), pp. 109–140.

4. *Ibid.*, p. 119.

5. *Ibid.*, pp. 175–178.

6. *Challenge of Crime*, pp. 437–438.

7. John F. Galliher and James A. Cain, "Citation Support for the Mafia Myth in Criminology Textbooks," *The American Sociologist* 9 (May 1974): 68–74.

8. Ramsey Clark, *Crime in America* (New York: Pocket Books, 1971), p. 57.

9. *Ibid.*

10. The following discussion is largely based on *Challenge of Crime*, pp. 440–447.

11. Cressey, *Theft*, p. 83.

12. Gus Tyler, "The Crime Corporation," in Abraham S. Blumberg, ed., *Current Perspective on Criminal Behavior* (New Yorf: Knopf, 1974), p. 199.

13. *Challenge of Crime*, p. 444.

14. Daniel Bell, *The End of Ideology* (New York: Free Press, 1962), pp. 127–150.

15. *Ibid.*, p. 129.

16. See, for example, Gus Tyler, "Sociodynamics of Organized Crime" and Francis A. J. Ianni, "New Mafia: Black, Hispanic and Italian Styles," in Francis A. J. Ianni and Elizabeth Reuss-Ianni, eds., *The Crime Society* (New York: New American Library, 1976), pp. 118–148.

17. Bell, *The End*, p. 148.

18. These quotes from Sutherland are cited in Geis, "Upperworld Crime," p. 119.

19. Edwin H. Sutherland, *White-Collar Crime* (New York: Holt, Rinehart & Winston, 1949), p. 9.

20. *Ibid.*

21. But Geis prefers to use the term *upperworld crime*, which means the same as *white-collar crime*. See Geis, "Upperworld Crime," p. 120.

22. Harrison Wellford, *Sowing the Wind* (New York: Grossman, 1972), p. 69.

23. Ralph Nader, "Foreword" to John C. Esposito, *Vanishing Air* (New York: Grossman, 1970), p. viii.

24. Herbert Edelhertz, *The Nature, Impact and Prosecution of White-Collar Crime* (Washington, D.C.: Government Printing Office, 1970), pp. 15–16.

25. Brandt Allen, "Embezzler's Guide to the Computer," *Harvard Business Review* 52 (July-August 1975): 79–80.

26. Nader, "Foreword," p. VIII.

27. Ovid Demaris, *Dirty Business* (New York: Harper's Magazine, 1974), pp. 10–12.

28. *Challenge of Crime*, p. 158.

29. Robert Sherrill, *New York Times Book Review*, March 4, 1973, p. 3; see also Wellford, *Sowing the Wind*, pp. 87–96.

30. Donald R. Cressey, *Other People's Money* (Glencoe, Ill.: Free Press, 1953), pp. 93–138.

31. Sutherland, *White-Collar*, p. 12; President's Commission, *Crime and Its Impact* (Washington, D.C.: U.S. Government Printing Office, 1967), pp. 102–103.

32. Sutherland, *ibid.*, p. 13.

33. Clark, *Crime*, p. 23.

34. *Challenge of Crime*, p. 157.

35. Ralph Nader, "Corporate Violence against the Consumer," in William Osborne, ed., *The Rape of the Powerless* (New York: Gordon and Breach, 1971), p. 14.

36. Clark, *Crime*, p. 23.

37. Sutherland, *White-Collar*, p. 13.

38. Edelhertz, *The Nature, Impact and Prosecution of White-Collar Crime*, p. 9.

39. *Challenge of Crime*, p. 158.

40. Quoted in Geis, "Upperworld Crime," p. 127.

41. Sutherland, *White-Collar*, p. 234.

42. *Ibid.*, p. 255.

43. Cressey, *Other People's Money*.

44. Louis Brandeis, *Olmstead v. United States*, 277 U.S. 438 (1928); quoted in Jethro K. Lieberman, *How the Government Breaks the Law* (Baltimore, Md.: Penguin Books, 1973), p. 15.

45. Lieberman, *ibid.*, p. 177.

46. Walker Commission, *Rights in Conflict* (New York: Bantam Books, 1968), p. 10.

47. Jack Anderson and Carl Kalvelage, *American Government . . . Like It Is* (New York: Warner Paperback Library, 1972), p. 14.

48. *Ibid.*, p. 16.

49. These examples are derived from Lieberman, *How the Government*, pp. 60, 73, 111–112.

50. *New York Times*, January 11, 1973, p. 1; Lieberman, *How the Government*, p. 208.

51. Mark J. Green, James M. Fallows, and David R. Zwick, *Who Runs Congress?* (New York: Bantam/Grossman, 1972), p. 139.

52. Lieberman, *How the Government*, pp. 219–232; Green et al., *ibid.*, pp. 156–159.

53. Lieberman, *How the Government*, pp. 233–252.

54. *Ibid.*, p. 237.

55. Quoted in Lieberman, *ibid.*, p. 15.

AUTHOR INDEX

SUBJECT INDEX